KU-148-763

Contents

Colour section	1–16

Introduction 6
Reasons to go 11

Where to go	17–124

Argentina 19
Belize 25
Bolivia 30
Brazil 36
Chile 44
Colombia 50
Costa Rica 56
Ecuador 61
El Salvador 67
Guatemala 72
The Guianas 77
Honduras 82
Mexico 87
Nicaragua 94
Panama 98
Paraguay 103
Peru 107
Uruguay 114
Venezuela 118

The big adventure	125–358

❶ Planning your route 127
❷ Studying, volunteering and working in Latin America ... 159
❸ Documents and insurance ... 172
❹ When to go 186
❺ How much will it cost? 199
❻ Guidebooks and other resources 211
❼ What to take 225
❽ Your first night 239
❾ Culture shock 250
❿ Getting around 270
⓫ Accommodation 294
⓬ Staying healthy 308
⓭ Keeping in touch 327
⓮ Crime, safety and sleaze ... 336
⓯ Coming home 354

Directory	359–380

Discount travel and online booking agents 361
Specialist tour operators 364
Volunteer organizations 367
Health 369
Official advice on international trouble spots 371
Responsible tourism 372
Travel book and map stores ... 373
Online travel resources 374
Specialist Latin American resource centres 376
Travel equipment suppliers 377
Final checklist 379

Travel store	381–390

Small print & Index	391–400

◄◄ Colonial house, San Cristóbal de las Casas, Mexico, ◄ La Paz Waterfall, Costa Rica

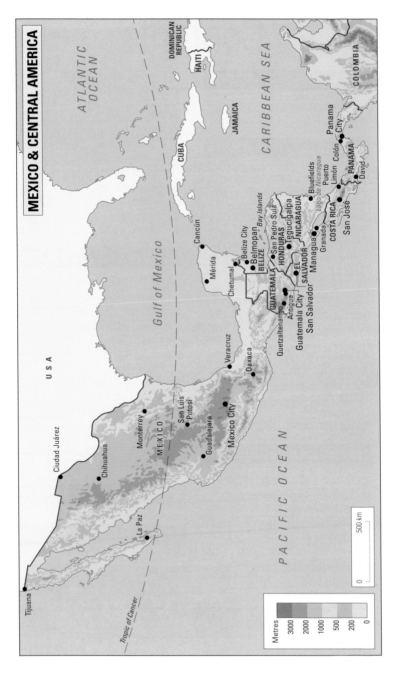

MEXICO & CENTRAL AMERICA

ATLANTIC
OCEAN

DOMINICAN
REPUBLIC

HAITI

JAMAICA

CUBA

CARIBBEAN SEA

COLOMBIA

Panama
City

Colón

PANAMA

David

Limón

Puerto

Bluefields

Lago de Nicaragua

San José

COSTA RICA

Granada

NICARAGUA

Managua

Tegucigalpa

San Pedro Sula

HONDURAS

Bay Islands

EL
SALVADOR

San Salvador

Guatemala City

Antigua

GUATEMALA

Quetzaltenango

Belmopan

Belize City

BELIZE

Chetumal

Cancún

Mérida

Gulf of Mexico

Veracruz

Oaxaca

USA

Ciudad Juárez

Chihuahua

Monterrey

MEXICO

San Luis
Potosí

Guadalajara

Mexico City

La Paz

PACIFIC OCEAN

Tijuana

Tropic of Cancer

Metres	
3000	
2000	
1000	
500	
200	
0	

0   500 km

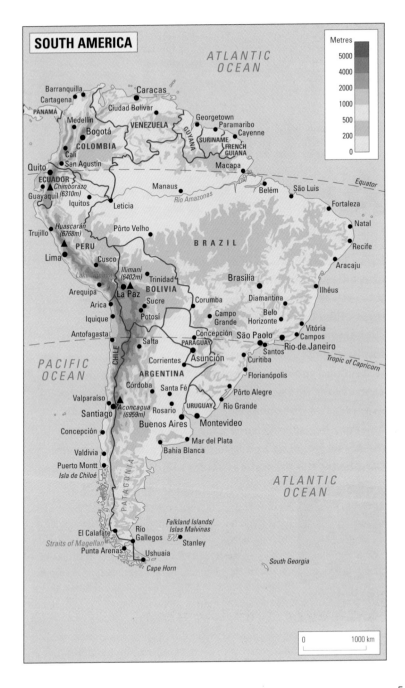

Introduction to

First-Time
Latin
America

Every year thousands of travellers set off on their own Latin American adventure. Some want to see for themselves the celebrated monuments left by the mysterious pre-Columbian civilizations, such as the spellbinding lost Inca city of Machu Picchu, or join the samba-dancing crowds at Carnaval in Rio de Janeiro, the largest and most spectacular of the region's countless extravagant fiestas. Others are drawn by the stunning scenery: the immense, wildlife-rich rainforests of the Amazon; the soaring snowcapped peaks of the Andes; the idyllic beaches and kaleidoscopic coral reefs of the Caribbean; the dramatic glaciers and fjords of Patagonia.

But perhaps the greatest attractions are the sheer vitality of daily life in Latin America and the rich and varied lifestyles of its inhabitants. For though from the outside the region may appear to have a relatively uniform culture, in fact each country is made up of a diverse and compelling blend of indigenous, European, African and (to a lesser extent) Asian influences, the product of Latin America's complex and extraordinary history. Even within individual countries, regional differences in human experience can be remarkable, ranging from bankers working in gleaming high-rises to semi-nomadic tribes hunting for their next meal with bows and arrows. During your travels you may find yourself sipping *caipirinhas* on Copacabana beach or salsa-dancing the night away in the steamy nightclubs of Cali; eating barbecue at a gaucho festival on the Argentine pampas or chewing coca leaves with llama herders in the high Andes; searching for leatherback turtles by moonlight on the shores of the Caribbean or watching the sun rise over ancient Maya pyramids in the jungles of Central America.

Isla Kuanidup, Panama

Nearly all these things are affordable even for travellers on a tight budget, because most of Latin America is inexpensive compared to Europe or the United States (though generally a more expensive place to travel than Africa or Asia). Managed carefully, your money will go much further than it does back home, allowing you to travel for longer and take in sights and experiences you might not be able to afford elsewhere. Unsurprisingly, a growing number of adventurers from all over the world are visiting the region, and there's now a well-established "Gringo Trail" linking the main attractions in each country, with many cities and towns home to a lively travellers' scene. This is nowhere near as intense as on the backpackers' trail in Asia, however, and one of the joys of travel in Latin America is that it's refreshingly easy to get off the beaten track and visit locales that as yet see few or no tourists. This becomes even easier if you learn a little Spanish – the one language that links the overwhelming majority of the region (pick up Portuguese if you're travelling in Brazil). You'll be able to speak to and understand almost everyone you meet, making it possible to engage the local culture and people in a way that (unless you are a brilliant linguist) you just can't do on a trip to other continents.

> One of the joys of travel in Latin America is that it's refreshingly easy to get off the beaten track

However, travel in Latin America can also be a disquieting experience. It's not unusual to be shocked by your first sight of a sprawling slum and upset by your first encounter with a malnourished child begging for

change. Many first-timers are distressed by the chaos and squalor of some Latin American cities and by the often appalling poverty and inequality. Some get frustrated by the sometimes labyrinthine bureaucracy that can complicate even the simplest transaction and by the locals' flagrant disregard for punctuality. Others feel unnerved by suddenly being a relatively wealthy person in a poor country and paranoid about the risks of rip-offs and violent crime that await the unwary. And then there are climatic factors like oppressive heat or extreme altitude to deal with, not to mention the unfamiliar food and strange local customs and attitudes. The truth is, every trip involves a

The Amazon

Of all the natural wonders of Latin America, none has captured the world's imagination more than the Amazon Basin. Covering an area almost as large as Australia and extending from its heart in Brazil across the border to cover great expanses of Colombia, Peru, Bolivia, Venezuela and the Guianas, the Amazon is the largest tropical rainforest and by far the most biologically diverse ecosystem on earth, home to a staggering variety of plant and animal life – rare birds and mammals, extraordinary insects and rep-

▲ Jaguar

tiles, and literally millions of plant species – all woven together into a rich and complex natural tapestry. Through this immense forest habitat, fed by innumerable tributaries, flows the mighty River Amazon itself, a vast river-sea that carries about a fifth of the world's running fresh water. Despite its immense size, however, the Amazon rainforest is disappearing at an alarming rate as a result of logging, mining, oil drilling, cattle ranching, and slash-and-burn agriculture. If current rates of deforestation continue, scientists fear the Amazon rainforest could be completely destroyed within the next few decades, fuelling global climate change and representing the loss of a vast, irreplaceable and largely unexplored repository of genetic resources. For the time being, though, you can still explore the astonishing natural beauty of the forest first hand by visiting one of the numerous national parks in the Amazon – by doing so you may even contribute to their conservation, as ecotourism can help local people earn a living without destroying the rainforest environment.

degree of hassle, and on reflection travel would be rather dull if everything always went as planned. Adventures are by definition unpredictable affairs, and it's often the dramas and surprises that make for the most memorable experiences.

Buenos Aires, Argentina

This book is intended to prepare you for your trip, whether it's a couple of weeks on the beach in Cancún or a twelve-month journey from Mexico down to Tierra del Fuego. It's a book to read before you go rather than an on-the-road guide, a planning handbook to help you decide on the kind of trip you'd like to make and prepare you for that journey.

The first thing you'll need to decide is which countries and regions in Latin America you want to visit and which places to skip. The opening section of the book, **Where to go**, outlines the possibilities with a profile on each country in Central and South America plus Mexico, including a roundup of the main highlights and suggested itineraries, as well as a selection of personal recommendations and more out-of-the-way attractions.

> It's often the dramas and surprises that make for the most memorable experiences

The middle section of the book, **The big adventure**, gives all the practical information you need to turn your dream of travel in Latin America into a reality. You'll find chapters on what to take, when to go and how to cope when you arrive, as well as detailed advice on how to choose the right ticket and sort out visas and insurance, and how to keep in touch with home. We also look at life on the road in Latin America, giving you an idea of what to expect in terms of transport and accommodation, advice on how to stay safe and healthy while you're away, and tips on how to avoid the potential hassles and hazards that await the unwary traveller. Finally, the **Directory** section is packed with useful addresses, websites and phone numbers for further information on everything from discount flight agents and specialist tour operators to jungle equipment suppliers and volunteer work opportunities.

▼ Flower market, Cuenca, Ecuador

The beautiful game

Everywhere you go in Latin America you'll find people watching, talking about and playing *futbol (futebol* in Portuguese). Latin Americans are so obsessed with the game that it's often compared to a religion, and across the region it is more of a common language than Spanish or Portuguese. Almost every village has a football pitch, even if it's just the verge of an airstrip carved out of the rainforest or the only flat piece of land in a mountain community, and it's not unusual to come across Latin Americans who are the proud owners of a pair of football boots but possess no other shoes.

First introduced to South America by British engineers and sailors in the nineteenth century, football was quickly adopted by the locals, who began playing with a style and verve that was all their own. The immense skill and flamboyant creativity of Latin American football went on to capture the imagination of the world, as Uruguay, Argentina and Brazil all produced a series of World Cup-winning teams. The region has also produced the two greatest footballers the world has ever seen, in the Argentine Diego Maradona and the Brazilian Edson Nascimiento da Silva,

▲ Football on the beach, Rio de Janeiro, Brazil

better known as Pelé. The intense carnival atmosphere of big matches in stadiums like the world-famous Maracanã in Rio de Janeiro is an experience not to be missed, even if you're not a football fan, while joining in a barefoot game on the beach or a kickabout on the streets is an excellent way of making contact with local people.

21

reasons to go

Latin America embraces such a range of cultures, climates and landscapes that the very diversity that makes it so appealing can also make it seem a daunting place to visit. The trick is to decide on what kinds of experiences you hope to have, rather than setting up a whirlwind tour of the major sights. What follows is a selective taste of things you could do on your adventure, from celebrating Carnaval to simply watching the sun rise; any one of them on its own is a compelling enough reason to go.

01 Shop in an indigenous market The unique cultural heritage of Latin America's many indigenous peoples is often on display at markets like this one in Guatemala, where farmers come into town to sell and trade crops, weavings and other handicrafts.

03 Get wet at a waterfall
Whether you take a dip at the foot of one of Central America's countless cascades or just feel the spray of mighty Iguazú Falls, Latin America's waterfalls are eminently refreshing after a long day in the sun.

02 Walk through the jungle canopy
High above the rainforest floor, treetop walkways provide close-up views of the denizens of the canopy, many of which never set foot on ground.

04 Explore a lost city
From Chichén Itzá in Mexico to Machu Picchu in Peru, the great stone cities built by civilizations like the Maya and Inca long before Europeans conquered Latin America are among the most beautiful and mysterious sites the region has to offer.

05 Take a slow boat down the Amazon
A boat trip down the world's mightiest river is a quintessential Latin American experience – even if at times you can't see either bank.

06 Go whale watching From the Pacific Ocean off Baja California in Mexico to Península Valdés in Argentina, excellent opportunities abound to spot majestic whales and other marine mammals.

07 Celebrate a fiesta The exuberance and vitality of Latin America shines through at the innumerable fiestas that mark the calendar throughout the year. The biggest of them all, Carnaval, is celebrated with wild abandon and most famously in Rio de Janeiro.

08 Explore the colonial past The legacy of Portugal and Spain is most evident in the elaborate colonial architecture that graces towns and cities throughout Latin America.

09 Learn to dance the tango Master the sensuous, melancholy moves of tango and you're halfway to being accepted as an Argentine. And if you don't fancy the tango, there's always salsa, cumbia or merengue.

11 Eat the world's best beef

The entire region is a carnivore's paradise, but the best cuts are to be found in Argentina, where succulent steaks and whole beasts are roasted over open fires.

10 Scuba dive in the Caribbean

The world's second largest barrier reef and a string of coral atolls make the Caribbean coast and islands of Mexico and Central America world-class scuba diving and snorkelling destinations.

13 Watch the sun rise

Sometimes, you have to get up early to see things at their most splendid.

12 Stay in an eco-lodge

Usually found in Latin America's most beautiful and pristine regions, eco-lodges are the perfect way to get close to the environment while helping to protect it.

15 Experience a football game

In most of Latin America football is closer to a religion than a game, and the atmosphere for big matches in stadiums like the Maracanã in Brazil is electrifying.

14 Enjoy a fruit juice

Latin America is home to a colourful array of tropical fruits, best enjoyed freshly squeezed at street and market stalls throughout the region.

16 Hike an Inca trail The high Andes of Ecuador, Bolivia and, above all, Peru are crisscrossed by a network of stone-paved pathways built by the Incas and other pre-Columbian civilizations, perfect for day hikes and extended treks.

17 Spot wildlife in the rainforest The tropical rainforests of Latin America are the most biodiverse environments on earth, home to an astonishing variety of wildlife including monkeys, toucans, dolphins and jaguars.

18 Hang loose in a hammock Arguably Latin America's greatest gift to the world, the hammock is both a perfect place to adjust to the local pace of life and a cool and comfortable alternative to a bed.

19 Listen to Andean music

With their panpipes, drums and twelve-stringed charangos, musicians in the Andes are liable to strike up a lively tune at any social gathering, with haunting tunes that seem inseparable from the mighty mountains they inhabit.

20 See icebergs up close

In the wild, austral region of Patagonia – a land much closer to Antarctica than the Amazon – some of the world's mightiest glaciers can be seen (and heard).

21 Ride a train

Latin America's few remaining railway lines allow you to travel in style through some of the most rugged and remote landscapes in the region.

First-Time
Latin America

Where to go

- Argentina   19
- Belize   25
- Bolivia   30
- Brazil   36
- Chile   44
- Colombia   50
- Costa Rica   56
- Ecuador   61
- El Salvador   67
- Guatemala   72
- The Guianas   77
- Honduras   82
- Mexico   87
- Nicaragua   94
- Panama   98
- Paraguay   103
- Peru   107
- Uruguay   114
- Venezuela   118

Argentina

Capital Buenos Aires
Population 37.3 million
Languages Spanish, Italian in Buenos Aires
Currency Argentine peso ($)
Climate Most of the country is temperate, though it varies from tropical in the northeast to sub-Arctic in southern Patagonia
When to go December to May
Minimum daily budget US$25

Argentina is an enormous country – the eighth largest in the world – containing within its ample borders attractions ranging from the elegant, European-style boulevards and cafés of Buenos Aires to the sub-Arctic glaciers and Andean mountains of Patagonia in the south. Despite its size, however, Argentina is culturally one of the most homogenous of all Latin American countries – the result of mass immigration from Europe during the late nineteenth century, as well as the almost complete extermination of the native populations. Most Argentines have Italian (or to a lesser extent, Spanish) ancestors – and in the cities, at least, the spirit of Europe is never far away.

Outside the major urban centres, however, a distinctively Argentine culture has developed. Known as *argentinidad* it is exemplified by the legendary gaucho, or Argentine cowboy, a legacy of the days in the early twentieth century when cattle ranching in the vast pampas of the interior made the country one of the wealthiest in the world. Even now, gaucho culture lives on in the Argentine obsession with meat-eating, while the famous gaucho drink, maté – an invigorating herbal infusion drunk through

△ Whale breaching, Península Valdés

ARGENTINA

PARAGUAY

La Quiaca

Salta

PUNA
CATAMARQUEÑA

Antofagasta
de la Sierra

Tucumán

Puerto Iguazú
Iguazú Falls

Corrientes

Posadas

RESERVA
NATURAL
DEL IBERA

BRAZIL

Laguna Mar
Chiquita

Córdoba

Santa Fe

Rio Paraná

Mendoza

Rosario

Rio Uruguay

URUGUAY

San Antonio de Areco

BUENOS AIRES

Santa Rosa

Bahía
Blanca

Rio Negro

LAKE
DISTRICT

Bariloche

Rio Chubut

Puerto
Madryn

Península Valdés

Trelew

ATLANTIC OCEAN

Perito Moreno

La Cueva de las
Manos Pintadas

Fitz Roy Massif

PARQUE NACIONAL
LOS GLACIARES

Glacier Perito Moreno

Rio Gallegos

Punta Arenas

TIERRA
DEL FUEGO

FALKLAND ISLANDS
(Islas Malvinas)

Straits of
Magellan

Ushuaia

Cape Horn

PACIFIC OCEAN

CHILE

CORDILLERA DE LOS ANDES

PATAGONIA

N

Argentine
Antarctic
Territory

0   200 km

a metal straw from a colourful gourd – remains the national drink.

For the visitor, Argentina's biggest draws, apart from its atmospheric capital, Buenos Aires, are largely outdoors. The southern third of the country, Patagonia, is the principal destination. Here, an extensive series of national parks protects some of the most extraordinary – and extreme – scenery the continent has to offer, including the majestic Andean peaks of the Fitz Roy Massif, site of some of the world's most challenging mountain-eering, the extraordinary glaciers of Perito Moreno, and the marine paradise of the Península Valdés – to name just three of the region's main highlights. Bariloche, in Patagonia's Lake District, is the region's busiest holiday resort, with wooden chalet-style buildings, an attrac-tive lakeside setting and fantastic skiing nearby at Cerro Catedral.

Patagonia by no means harbours the extent of Argentina's natural attractions, however. One of the world's great natural wonders, the Iguazú Falls, dominates the northeast of the country, whose flat swamplands are home to hundreds of bird species. The northwest is a beguiling mix of jungle-clad cloudforests to high Andean plateaus (known in Argentina as *puna*) and deserts roamed by flocks of llamas. Further south lie the rolling green hills of Argentina's wine region and its lively centre, Mendoza. Most of central Argentina is pampa or cowboy country.

Long considered among the safest, best organized but priciest countries to visit in Latin America, the economic crisis of 2001, during which the peso plummeted in value, has seen it become a much cheaper destination.

Main attractions

● **Buenos Aires** Argentina's capital city is one of the most atmospheric in Latin

America. Though its wide tree-lined avenues and architecture were inspired by those of Paris, Buenos Aires is very much its own place, with distinctive barrios – football-crazy La Boca with its colourfully painted streets, bohemian San Telmo, home to the best tango shows in town, and exclusive Recoleta, site of the magnificently grand cemetery where Eva Perón is buried.

● **Iguazú Falls** One of the world's most dramatic series of waterfalls, the majestic Iguazú Falls straddle the border between Argentina, Brazil and Paraguay. The statistics are staggering – 275 falls plunging over a precipice 80m high and 3km wide – you'll hear the deafening noise long before you can see anything. Although the best overall view of Iguazú is from Brazil, the falls' most extensive portion lies in the subtropical Argentine Parque Nacional Iguazú, a less touristy area with a well-organized system of trails and plenty of wildlife. The most spectacular spot is the Garganta del Diablo (Devil's Throat), where fourteen separate falls merge to form the world's most powerful single waterfall in terms of the volume of water flow per second.

● **Península Valdés** A treeless headland in northern Patagonia, Península Valdés is one of the world's most important marine reserves. As well as colonies of penguins, sea lions, elephant seals, dolphins and killer whales, the area's sheltered waters play host to over a thousand southern right whales between May and December – the giant mammal's breeding season. With visitors virtually guaranteed to get within a few metres of one of these gentle creatures, this is the time and place to go on a whale-watching trip.

● **The Lake District** Often billed as the "Switzerland of Argentina", the Lake District is characterized by vast lakes and densely wooded forests in a mountainous setting. Hugely popular among Argentines as a holiday destination, the area is known for its network of accessible national parks which are strung out along the western cordillera. Bariloche is the region's main holiday hub, with 700,000 visitors descending upon it annually, many of whom in winter come to hit the slopes at the nearby ski resort, Cerro Catedral. The city is also a starting point for the Ruta de los Siete Lagos, one of Latin America's most scenic drives, offering superb fishing en route.

● **Argentine wine** Argentina is one of the biggest wine producers in the world and is now beginning to match its output with a significant rise in the quality of its wine. Particularly famous as an Argentine varietal is malbec, which makes a gutsy red wine that goes very well with the local beef. The country's wine centre is Mendoza, where you can visit atmospheric bodegas and sample some of the best vintages in one of the city's many fine restaurants.

● **Parque Nacional Los Glaciares** Parque Nacional Los Glaciares in Patagonia is home to possibly the most impressive scenery in South America. Glaciar Perito Moreno in the south of the park is one of the few advancing glaciers in the world and offers an enthralling spectacle as it fragments into massive chunks of ice, some weighing hundreds of tons, which split off in spectacularly noisy fashion. The Fitz Roy Massif, a collection of mountain peaks centring on Monte Fitz Roy (3445m) on the park's northern boundary, is notably dramatic, its sheer needles of rock set in circles and rising up several kilometres into the Patagonian sky. If you're not an experienced mountaineer, the area still has plenty to offer, laced as it is with lakes, hiking trails and spectacular *miradors* (lookout points).

Also recommended

● **Reserva Natural del Iberá** A watery network of lakes, marshes and floating islands, the Reserva Natural del Iberá is a vast (13,000 square kilometres) protected area in the northeast of Argentina offering wonderful wildlife-spotting opportunities. Locals in the village of Colonia Carlos Pellegrini take visitors out in small motorboats to see birds, monkeys and caymans at close range.

● **Cueva de las Manos Pintadas (Cave of the Painted Hands)** Decorated with over 800 black, white and red handprints made by Paleolithic hunter-gatherers and dating as far back as 7300 BC, the *cueva* is really a series of overhangs in a cliff face. Probably the finest example of rock paintings in South America, the cave, in southern Patagonia, is best approached via a beautiful two-hour trek up the Cañon de Río Pintadas.

● **San Antonio de Areco** Just over a 100km west of Buenos Aires, the charming town of San Antonio de Areco, with its cobbled streets and colonial facades, is Argentina's centre of pampa culture. Every November the town hosts a popular gaucho festival, the Día de la Tradición (see p.198), when gauchos parade in their traditional outfits and display their cowboy skills, including *jineteadas* (bronco riding) and horse-breaking. A traditional *asado con cuero* when beef is cooked over an open fire rounds up the festivities.

● **Puna Catamarqueña** The altiplano of Catamarca province is an eerie and remote place, flanked to the west by the Andes and Chile and dotted with flocks of grazing vicuñas and flamingos on frozen lakes. The region's only settlement, Antofagasta de la Sierra, has a

2000-year-old mummified baby in its museum and a tranquil population of highland farmers and herdsmen. Bring some warm clothes, as temperatures drop at night to −30°C to 30°C/22°F.

● **Salta** Colonial capital of the beautiful northwest region, Salta is lively and youthful with well-preserved architectural gems (such as the Iglesia y Convento San Francisco) and a surprisingly vibrant nightlife. The town also makes an ideal base for visiting the nearby Quebrada del Toro, a dramatic gorge sliced into multicoloured rock.

● **Tierra del Fuego** A collection of islands at the southernmost tip of South America, Tierra del Fuego has long held a fascination for travellers. Its largest island, Isla Grande, is home to the region's capital, Ushuaia, which is beautifully situated between mountains and the sea. The city is also the starting point for boat trips along the Beagle Channel to the historic Estancia Harberton, a farmstead which became a refuge for Yámana, Selk'nam and Mannekenk Amerindian tribes, and today is home to the outstanding marine mammal museum, Museo Acatushún.

Routes in and out

Buenos Aires is easily reached by daily direct flights from Europe (London, Madrid, Rome), the US (New York, Miami and Chicago) and Australasia (Sydney and Auckland). There are principal border crossings to Brazil and Paraguay at Puerto Iguazú; from La Quiaca to Bolivia; and by ferry across the Río Plata to Uruguay. There are many border crossings with Chile – the scenic Paso Mamuil Malal in Patagonia connects with the popular Chilean backpackers' resort of Pucón, while the equally picturesque Cruce Internacional de los Lagos crossing links with Puerto Montt.

Itineraries

One week

In a country the size of Argentina you won't get very far in a week. The average bus ride from one tourist spot to another is ten hours; if you're pressed for time you should consider taking a domestic flight.

● You could easily spend seven days in Buenos Aires, exploring its elegant streets and barrios; or combine the city's attractions with a few days in the pampa town of San Antonio de Areco.

● If you're coming from southern Brazil or Paraguay, cross the border into Argentina via the Iguazú Falls, where you can explore the surrounding tropical forest as well as visit the falls themselves. Then move west to the vast wetlands of the Reserva Natural del Iberá and across the country to Bolivia or Chile.

● From Chile, cross the border in Tierra del Fuego and head north into Patagonia to explore the region's wealth of dramatic mountains, glaciers and lakes before flying to the capital and onwards to Uruguay or Brazil.

Two weeks

● After spending five or so days in Buenos Aires, travel westwards through the pampas, stopping off for a few days in San Antonio de Areco, and then up through the Argentinian altiplano to Antofagasta de la Sierra, before heading north to the attractive colonial city of Salta and on into Bolivia.

● Travel by bus south from Buenos Aires through the great expanses of Patagonia right to the world's most southerly region, Tierra del Fuego and the city of Ushuaia. On the way, spend some days hiking around Fitz Roy in Parque

Nacional Los Glaciares and admiring the spectacle of the Perito Moreno glacier.

• Cross the border from Chile into the Argentine Lake District and Bariloche. Tour the Seven Lakes Route before going north to the wine region of Mendoza. Move on to the highlands of the Puno Catamarqueña and then across the country to Buenos Aires before taking a ferry across the Río de la Plata to Uruguay and then Brazil.

One month

With a domestic airpass (see pp.179–180) you could visit three or four distinct regions of Argentina.

Travel south from Iguazú to the marshlands of the Reserva Natural del Iberá and head northwest towards Salta. From Salta travel south to the Puna Catamarqueña and on to San Antonio de Areco in the pampas, before arriving in Buenos Aires. After a week in Buenos Aires, continue south into Patagonia and Tierra del Fuego for ten days trekking in the mountains and national parks and visiting Ushuaia; from here you can cross into Chile.

Argentina online

Argentina Travel Net and **Argentina on View**
Ⓦ**www.argentinatravelnet.com** &
Ⓦ**www.argentinaonview.com** Bilingual tourism portals with several thousand links categorized by region or activity.
Buenos Aires Herald
Ⓦ**www.buenosairesherald.com**
Website of long-established English-language newspaper, with domestic and foreign news stories, travel features and trenchant opinions on current affairs.
El Sur del Sur
Ⓦ**www.surdelsur.com** Excellent set of essays on Argentina's history, geography and culture, with links to regional websites.

Belize

Capital Belmopan
Population 256,000
Languages English, Spanish, Maya languages, Garífuna
Currency Belize dollar (fixed to US$ at a rate of 2 to1; BZ$)

Climate Tropical with a rainy (May–Nov) season and a dry season (Jan–April)
When to go Late December to March
Minimum daily budget US$30

Belize is one of the smallest countries in Central America and the least densely populated, with a quarter of a million people occupying an area the size of Wales or Massachusetts. A British colony (known as British Honduras) until 1981, Belize has as much in common with the English-speaking islands of the Caribbean as with the Spanish-speaking Latin American mainland (although the presence of immigrants from other Central American countries is gradually eroding this distinction). This Anglo-Caribbean culture, known as creole, is evident in the country's biggest city, Belize City, with its balconied clapboard houses, reggae dancehalls and vibrant carnival, held in September.

Belize's biggest attraction is its offshore cayes, which sit on the largest coral reef in the Americas, stretching from Mexico to Honduras. The whole area is a protected marine park, teeming with hundreds of species of brightly coloured fish and other marine creatures. Crystal clear water means that the scuba diving and snorkelling around the cayes are superb. Of over four hundred islands only two have any kind of tourist infrastructure: Ambergris Caye, the largest, which attracts over half of all the visitors to Belize, and Caye Caulker, more popular with backpackers.

△ Caye Caulker

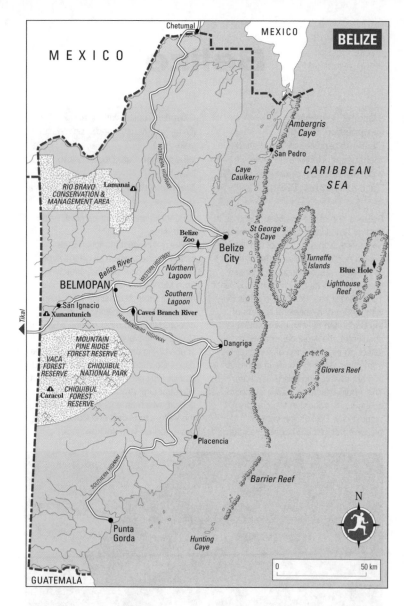

MAP. Belize

Chetumal · MEXICO

MEXICO

BELIZE

Ambergris Caye

San Pedro

Caye Caulker

CARIBBEAN SEA

RIO BRAVO CONSERVATION & MANAGEMENT AREA

Lamanai

NORTHERN HIGHWAY

St George's Caye

Belize Zoo

Belize City

Turneffe Islands

Blue Hole

Belize River

Northern Lagoon

Lighthouse Reef

WESTERN HIGHWAY

BELMOPAN

San Ignacio

Xunantunich

Southern Lagoon

Caves Branch River

HUMMINGBIRD HIGHWAY

Tikal

MOUNTAIN PINE RIDGE FOREST RESERVE

VACA FOREST RESERVE

CHIQUIBUL NATIONAL PARK

Dangriga

Glovers Reef

Caracol

CHIQUIBUL FOREST RESERVE

SOUTHERN HIGHWAY

Placencia

Barrier Reef

N

Punta Gorda

Hunting Caye

0   50 km

GUATEMALA

Away from the coast, Belize is a sleepy backwater country of dense forests and easy-going rural communities. The interior is home to the highest waterfall in Central America, myriad rivers and caves and a network of national parks and reserves – Belizeans are very conscious of their environment and over forty percent of the country is now protected by law. With eco-tourism seen by many Belizeans as the country's economic future, it's not surprising that there are some specta-cular eco-lodges in Belize. Also in the interior are Belize's ancient Maya ruins, principally Caracol, Xunantunich and Lamanai, which, though less impressive than those in Guatemala and Mexico, are well worth visiting – and Tikal in Guatemala is easily accessed from Belize. In the far south of the country, dotted through the foothills of the Maya mountains, traditional Maya live in small communities, similar to those in Guatemala, where you can stay and in some cases participate in village life.

Belize is one of the safest countries in Latin America – crime against tourists is minimal and its capital city, Belmopan, is one of the safest, though dullest, in Central America. You should exercise caution in the former capital, Belize City, which has a much larger population. Be warned that prices are fairly high for the region – if you arrive from Guatemala you could find your costs doubled overnight.

Main attractions

● **Caye Caulker** Laid-back Caye Caulker is much smaller – just over 7km long – and less touristy than neighbouring Ambergris Caye and has long been popular with independent travellers. Most visitors come to scuba dive or snorkel, and day-trips go to top diving spots, such as the Lighthouse Reef and the Blue Hole, a complex network of caves and crevices, made famous by Jacques Cousteau. On the island itself it's possible to birdwatch – there are many bird species and some, like the black catbird or white-crowned pigeon, are rarely glimpsed elsewhere; rent

kayaks or swim out to the reef, which lies just 1.5km offshore.

● **Ancient Maya sites at Lamanai, Caracol and Xunantunich** While historically not as significant as the Maya ruins in Mexico and Guatemala, the sites in Belize are far less crowded and consequently more atmospheric, with excellent English-language visitor centres and museums on site. Striking Lamanai, in the north of the country, is set in a 950-acre reserve and has wonderful views across the jungle from its temples. In western Belize, Caracol's largest structure, Canaa or the Sky Palace, is still one of the tallest buildings in the country at 42m. Conveniently located en route from Belize to Guatemala (and Tikal), Xunantunich's Maya ruins include a restored stucco frieze carved with abstract designs, human faces and jaguar heads.

● **Mountain Pine Ridge Forest Reserve** The range of rolling hills, peaks and gorges that comprise the Mountain Pine Ridge Forest Reserve in western Belize are perfect for hiking and mountain biking. Coursing through the area is the picturesque Río On, which forms a series of natural swimming pools before plunging into a gorge, and the Thousand-Foot Falls – actually 1600ft waterfalls.

● **Rio Bravo Conservation and Management Area** In the northwest of Belize, the Rio Bravo Conservation and Management Area protects 260,000 acres of diverse terrain ranging from forest-covered limestone escarpments through river valleys to palm- and pine-covered plains and swamp. The area has 240 endemic tree species, tapirs, monkeys, river turtles, crocodiles, all five of Belize's big cat species and 400 kinds of bird. If you're feeling flush, the nearby *Chan Chich Lodge* is one of the finest eco-lodges in the world.

Also recommended

● **Belize Zoo** The Belize Zoo, 40km west of Belize City, is widely recognized as the best in Central America and has achieved international acclaim in the fields of conservation education and captive breeding. Its collection of indigenous species includes tapirs, jaguars, toucans and crocodiles, all housed in spacious enclosures that replicate their natural habitat.

● **Placencia** One of the few places in mainland Belize with real beaches, Placencia is a laid-back fishing village with a range of inexpensive accommodation and funky live-music venues; it also makes a good base for day-trips to the nearby coral reef and cayes.

● **Toledo Environmental Association (TEA)** Based in Belize's southernmost town of Punta Gorda, the TEA has an excellent visitors programme that encourages tourists to stay in the Maya villages of the surrounding area. Visits are tailored to individual interests and may include storytelling, guided walks or boat trips and traditional harp music concerts. All fees go to the villagers to help them protect their environment.

● **Spelunking** Western Belize's (and particularly Cayo District's) limestone hills are home to a spectacular subterranean network, with the Chiquibil cave system in the south of the region ranking as the longest in Central America. Maya ceramics and carvings can be found inside, and some caves have underground rivers which you can float down on inner tubes or in canoes. A good starting point for a caving experience is *The Caves Branch Jungle Lodge*, 19km from Belmopan, which is run by the founders of the Belize Cave and Wilderness Rescue Team.

Routes in and out

There are daily flights to Belize City from Miami and Houston. Another convenient way to reach the country is to fly to Cancún in Mexico, served by regular flights from the US and Europe, from where it's a straightforward five-hour bus journey to Belize – from the border crossing at Chetumal there are frequent services to Belize City. The most popular border crossing with Guatemala (for Tikal) is at Benque Viejo. There are boat services from Punta Gordá in southern Belize to Puerto Barrios and Lívingston in Guatemala and, less frequently, from Dangriga and Placencia to Puerto Cortés in Honduras.

Itineraries

One week

● From Honduras or Guatemala take a boat to Punta Gorda in southern Belize. Spend a night in one of the Maya villages of Toledo before moving north to San Ignacio and then the Rio Bravo Conservation and Management Area. Head, via the Maya site of Lamanai, to Chetumal in Mexico and on to the Yucatán.

● From Belize City go to Caye Caulker and then loop back across the country to the Mountain Pine Ridge Forest Reserve, then the Maya site of Xunantunich, before crossing the border into Guatemala to visit Tikal.

● Take the boat from Puerto Cortés in Honduras to Placencia. Then head west to visit the caves of Cayo District and Caves Branch River, and the forests of Mountain Pine Ridge, before leaving Belize for Guatemala.

Two weeks

- In two weeks you can see all of Belize's highlights. Arrive in Placencia from Puerto Cortés in Honduras and then travel west to the Caves Branch River, the Mountain Pine Ridge Forest Reserve and the Maya ruins of Caracol and Xunantunich. Briefly cross the border into Guatemala to visit Tikal and then head east to Belize City, and out to Caye Caulker for a few days relaxing on the beach. Then go north from Belize City to the Rio Bravo Conservation and Management Area and on to Chetumal in Mexico.

Belize online

Belizean Journeys
ⓦ**www.belizeanjourneys.com** An online magazine with travel features which specialize in the more remote and unknown parts of Belize.

Belize Net
ⓦ**www.belizenet.com** Belize's best portal with hundreds of links as well as general information, destinations guides and travel planning.

Belize News Network
ⓦ**www.belizenews.net** Links to Belizean newspapers, magazines, TV and radio stations, with a changing selection of articles on Belize from international media.

Bolivia

Capital Sucre (official); La Paz (seat of government)
Population 9 million
Languages Spanish, Quechua, Aymara, Guaraní, plus thirty other minor indigenous languages
Currency Peso boliviano (B/.)
Climate Ranging from hot and humid in the tropical lowlands to extremely cold and dry in the highlands
Best time to go May–September (dry season); between November and March rains make many roads impassable, particularly in the Amazon lowlands
Minimum daily budget US$15

Landlocked and isolated in the centre of the continent, Bolivia is in many ways the forgotten heart of South America, home to some of its most dramatic landscapes, pristine ecology and deepest cultural traditions. From the glacial peaks and high-altitude deserts of the Andes to the exuberant rainforests and vast savannahs of the Amazon, Bolivia's geography is not just extremely varied, it's invariably extreme. This natural diversity is matched by the ethnic and cultural diversity of the population: the majority of Bolivians are of indigenous descent, and the strength of native cultures here is perhaps greater than anywhere else in Latin America.

Indeed, to think of Bolivia as part of *Latin* America at all is something of a misconception. Though three centuries of Spanish colonial rule have left their mark on the nation's language, religion and architecture, this European influence is essentially no more than a thin veneer. Most Bolivians are conscious inheritors of indigenous cultural traditions that stretch back long before the conquest, and which are rooted in an intimate relationship with the land itself. Though Spanish is the language of business and government, the streets of the de facto capital, La Paz, buzz with the very different cadences of Aymara, one of more than thirty indigenous languages spoken across the country. From the llama-herding settlements and mining camps of the high Andes to the fishing and farming villages of the tropical lowlands, these diverse and distinctive native cultures – alongside the breathtaking landscapes they inhabit – constitute Bolivia's most powerful attraction.

Geographically, Bolivia is dominated by the Andes, which march through the west of the country in two parallel chains, each rising to snowcapped peaks over 6000m, and between which lies the Altiplano, a virtually treeless high-altitude plateau often compared to Tibet. Boasting dramatic mountain scenery, populated by traditional Aymara and Quechua-speaking farming communities, and with a couple of the finest Spanish colonial cities in the Americas, this highland region encapsulates everything that outsiders think of as quintessentially Bolivian. However, the highlands occupy less than half of Bolivia's territory. The majority of

the country is covered by sparsely populated tropical lowlands, including some of the wildest, most pristine and most biodiverse protected areas in the Amazon basin.

Bolivia is about the poorest and least developed country in South America, and this combined with the harsh geography makes getting around a bit of a challenge: roads are poor, conditions tough and journey times unpredictable. It also suffers frequent bouts of political turmoil, during which radical peasants in the highlands block the main roads for days or weeks at an end. These difficulties together with its sheer remoteness mean Bolivia receives far fewer visitors than its obvious attractions merit. But for the travellers who do make it here, the fact that the country is not yet on the major tourist routes is an added advantage.

Whether hiking an Inca trail or exploring a national park, you're unlikely to find yourself sharing the experience with more than a handful of other foreign visitors, and the attitude of the locals towards you is as yet unlikely to be influenced by the impact of mass tourism. In addition, Bolivia is one of the least expensive countries in the region for travellers – if you're on a tight budget, you'll find costs here a welcome relief after countries like Brazil, Argentina and Chile – and despite its poverty and political instability, the country remains one of the safest in the region for the traveller, largely free of the violent crime that blights some of its neighbours.

Main attractions

● **La Paz** Spectacularly set in a deep canyon at an altitude of over 3500m, Bolivia's de facto capital is the highest in the world. With a largely indigenous Aymara population, it's also amongst the most fascinating: a postmodern crucible where modern banks and government offices coexist with vibrant street markets selling all manner of ritual paraphernalia for appeasing the spirits and mountain gods.

● **Inca trails** North of La Paz lies the Cordillera Real, a jagged ridge of soaring, glacial peaks that forms a barrier between the high Altiplano and the Amazon lowlands. The range offers some of the finest walking in the Andes, including several treks following pre-Columbian stone-paved roads – the so-called "Inca trails" – that plunge down into the humid subtropical valleys of the Yungas. The charming colonial town of Sorata, nestled in a deep valley at the northwestern end of the range, also makes an excellent base for trekking along the trails.

● **Isla del Sol** Reached by boat from the pilgrimage centre of Copacabana on the Bolivian shores of Lago Titicaca, the idyllic Isla del Sol is the spiritual centre of the Andean world, revered as the place where the Sun and Moon were created and the Inca dynasty was born. Scattered with Inca ruins, and populated by traditional Aymara communities, it's the best place to enjoy the scenic beauty of the vast, high-altitude lake that straddles the border with Peru.

● **The Salar de Uyuni and Reserva Eduardo Avaroa** The desolate landscapes of the far southern Altiplano are amongst the most extraordinary in all

△ Salar de Uyuni

Latin America. From the forlorn railway town of Uyuni jeep tours head across the Salar de Uyuni, the world's biggest salt lake, a vast, perfectly flat expanse of dazzling white surrounded by high mountain peaks. Further south lies the Reserva de Fauna Andina Eduardo Avaroa, a remote region of high-altitude deserts, surreal wind-blasted rock formations, icebound volcanic peaks and half-frozen mineral-stained lakes which is home to a surprising array of wildlife, including great flocks of pink flamingos and herds of vicuña, the highly endangered wild relative of the llama.

● **Potosí** Set at an altitude of over 4000m, the legendary silver-mining centre of Potosí is the highest city in the world, and at once one of the most interesting and tragic cities in Latin America. The city's magnificent colonial architecture reflects the fabulous wealth it once generated, but a visit to see the almost medieval working conditions endured by indigenous miners in the labyrinthine mineshafts that honeycomb the mountain overlooking Potosí reveals something of the horrific price in human lives paid for that wealth.

● **The Bolivian Amazon** The Bolivian Amazon is relatively undeveloped and boasts some of the most pristine and biodiverse protected areas in the region. The laid-back jungle town of Rurrenabaque is one of the cheapest and easiest places to organize trips by motorized canoe deep into the Amazonian wilderness. From here you can explore the rainforests of Parque Nacional Madidi (where you can also stay at the excellent Chalalán eco-lodge, operated by the local indigenous Tacana community) or along the Río Yacuma, which flows through savannah-like pampas and supports an astonishing density of wildlife including cayman, capybaras and pink river dolphins.

● **The World's Most Dangerous Road** Linking La Paz with the Yungas town of Coroico, this infamous road descends 3500m over a distance of just 64km, plunging down from the high peaks of the Andes through dense cloudforest. The road clings to steep mountainsides above hair-raising precipices, with views so spectacular that many travellers choose to go by mountain bike rather than by bus, an arduous and exhilarating downhill ride that's not for the faint-hearted. Bike trips are easy to organize with tour companies in La Paz.

Also recommended

● **Sucre** Known as the White City, Bolivia's official capital is a jewel of colonial architecture and a lively university city that combines serene dignity with an easy provincial charm. The beautiful highland region surrounding the city is populated by traditional Quechua-speaking communities famous for their exquisite weavings, which are best seen (and bought) at the Sunday market in the nearby town of Tarabuco.

● **The Jesuit missions of Chiquitos** Spread across a vast, sparsely populated region in the tropical lowlands of eastern Bolivia, the Jesuit mission churches of Chiquitos offer a splash of incongruous splendour in the midst of the wilderness, a reminder of the time in the eighteenth century when a handful of European missionaries organized the indigenous Chiquitanos into utopian agricultural communities where music, art and sculpture flourished.

● **Parque Nacional Noel Kempff Mercado** Occupying the far north-eastern corner of Bolivia on the border with Brazil, this is Bolivia's finest national park, with abundant wildlife, exuberant Amazonian rainforest and magnificent waterfalls tumbling down from the plateau that supposedly inspired Sir Arthur Conan Doyle's *The Lost World*.

● **Oruro Carnaval** Of all Bolivia's innumerable religious fiestas, the Carnaval celebrations (late Feb or early March) in the otherwise dour Altiplano mining city of Oruro are the country's most colourful and dramatic. Combining Catholic and indigenous religious beliefs, the festivities are marked by thousands of dancers in extravagant costumes parading through the streets accompanied by massed brass bands, while revellers indulge in heavy drinking and indiscriminate water fighting.

● **Samaipata** Set amid the lush eastern foothills of the Andes, the idyllic town of Samaipata is home to the mysterious ruined temple complex of El Fuerte, and is a perfect base for hiking and exploring the cloudforests of the Parque Nacional Amboró. It's also not far from Vallegrande, the town where the Argentine revolutionary hero Che Guevara was secretly buried after being killed in nearby La Higuera.

Routes in and out

La Paz and Santa Cruz are both served by direct flights from Miami in the US and major South American capitals, though flights to Bolivia are considerably more expensive than to neighbouring countries like Peru. Bolivia can be reached overland from Peru via Puno on the shores of Lago Titicaca, and is connected to northern Argentina and Chile by road and rail. The railway journey between Uyuni and Calama in Chile in particular passes through spectacular high Andean scenery, and you can also travel between Uyuni in southern Bolivia and San Pedro de Atacama in Chile via the remote border crossing at Laguna Verde as part of

an organized jeep tour of the Reserva de Fauna Andina Eduardo Avaroa. The main border crossing with Brazil is in the far east of Bolivia at Quijarro, opposite the city of Corumbá in the Brazilian Pantanal, from where there's a direct train link to Santa Cruz: this is the best route to take if you're travelling overland between Brazil and the Andean countries on the western side of South America. There are also several remote road border crossings between Bolivia and Brazil along the northern frontier in the Amazon. In the May to September dry season you can travel between Santa Cruz and Asunción in Paraguay by bus or lorry along a rough road that runs through the heart of the great thornbrush wilderness of the Chaco.

Itineraries

Remember that you'll need a few days to acclimatize to the altitude in highland Bolivia, especially if you want to do any trekking.

One week

● Spend a day or two in La Paz, visit the ruins at Tiwanaku then head to Copacabana and visit the Isla del Sol on Lago Titicaca. Return to La Paz to make the journey by bus or mountain bike down the spectacular Yungas road to Coroico.

Two weeks

● From La Paz head south by bus and train to Uyuni and take a four-day jeep tour of the Salar de Uyuni and the Reserva de Fauna Andina Eduardo Avaroa. From Uyuni, head across to Potosi and then Sucre for a couple of days in each city. When you get back to La Paz, you may still have time left to visit Lago Titicaca.

• Spend the first few days in and around La Paz and Lago Titicaca as described above, then either trek along one of the Inca trails across the Cordillera Real and spend some time on the Yungas; or fly north to Rurrenabaque in the Amazon and go on a wildlife tour by motorized dug-out canoe in the rainforests of Parque Nacional Madidi or the savannahs of the Rio Yacuma.

One month

• Spend a week in and around La Paz and Lago Titicaca, then either trek, mountain bike or take the bus down to Coroico in the Yungas. From there, continue overland by road to Rurrenabaque and take a three- or four-day organized tour looking for wildlife in the rainforest or the pampas along the Río Yacuma. If you return to La Paz by plane, you should then have a couple of weeks to explore the southern Altiplano, visiting the legendary mining city of Potosí and taking a jeep tour of the far southwest from Uyuni. If you've time, you can also visit Sucre for two or three days from Potosí.

• Spend the first five days or so exploring La Paz and visiting the Isla del Sol, then head south to Uyuni and take a jeep tour of the Salar de Uyuni and Reserva de Fauna Andina Eduardo Avaroa in the far southwest. From Uyuni, head northeast to Potosí and then on to Sucre, spending a couple of days

in each city. From Sucre, travel by bus to Santa Cruz, possibly stopping off in Samaipata for a day or two, then either visit Parque Nacional Noel Kempff Mercado by plane or do a circuit of the Jesuit mission towns of Chiquitos in the far east of Bolivia.

Bolivia online

Aymara Net
Ⓦ www.aymaranet.org Rambling Aymara website with links and information on all things indigenous, with particular emphasis on the political. Mostly in Spanish and Aymara, but some English too.

Bolivian Geographic
Ⓦ www.boliviangeographic.com A collection of thoughtful articles on Bolivian geography, environment and culture, with very good photos of some of the country's wildest places.

Boliviaweb
Ⓦ www.boliviaweb.com Good general Bolivian site with links to many other Bolivia-related web pages and general background information on subjects such as Bolivian art, history and food.

Coca Museum
Ⓦ www.cocamuseum.com Brilliant little English-language Bolivian website dedicated to the history of the controversial coca leaf, full of fascinating detail and astonishing photos of its many different uses and meanings.

Brazil

Capital Brasília
Population 172 million
Languages Portuguese, Spanish in border areas, plus around 180 indigenous languages
Currency Real (R$)
Climate Mostly tropical with distinct rainy seasons (south, southeast and north Nov–March; northeast April–Aug) and a temperate zone in the south with winter chills and occasional snow
Best time to go February (for Carnaval) to June or September to December
Minimum daily budget US$25

The fifth largest country in the world, Brazil occupies half the entire landmass of South America and encompasses all its diverse terrains – bar any mountains that can match the height of the Andes. Its enormous interior (which takes four days and nights to cross) consists of sparsely populated scrub, swampland and Amazon rainforest, with two-thirds of Brazilians living on or close to its 8000-kilometre coast and over half in cities.

It isn't just its size which sets Brazil apart from the rest of South America. The country was formerly part of the Portuguese empire, and consequently Portuguese is the dominant language rather than Spanish (although Spanish is widely understood). The Portuguese built attractive colonial towns much like those of the Spanish colonies – some of the prettiest are in the state of Minas Gerais. Virtually nothing is known of Brazil's indigenous culture before the Portuguese arrived in 1500 – there were no cities built in stone like those of the Inca, Aztecs and Maya, no metal or flint artefacts – although it is reckoned that 5 million pure-blooded Amerindians were scattered across the country in various tribes. Of these some 300,000 remain, most living deep within the Amazon where it's believed that some tribes remain undiscovered by the outside world.

The Amazon rainforest, the world's largest at six million square kilometres, covers over half of Brazil's landmass and extends into neighbouring Venezuela, Colombia, Peru and Bolivia. With 6000 known species of plant (and thousands more yet to be identified), one in five of all the earth's birds and one-fifth of the planet's fresh water, the Amazon is a vital part of the earth's biosphere. Increasingly, though, large tracts have been felled by loggers and cattle ranchers and deforestation is a real and continuing threat to the Amazon. The rainforest remains a highlight of many tourists' visit to Brazil and there are a growing number of eco-lodges close to the region's capital, Manaus.

Brazil's other natural attractions are impressive, too – the Pantanal swampland, which borders Bolivia to the west, is one of the best places to see wildlife in Latin America, with jaguars, rare blue macaws, armadillos and anacondas all commonly sighted. The Foz do Iguaçu waterfalls in the south of Brazil are another of Latin America's most visited attractions, a truly spectacular series of cascades surrounded by subtropical forest. Brazil's long Atlantic coastline has some lovely beaches, too, which remain mostly unspoilt with surprisingly little mass-market tourism.

Thanks to rapid postwar growth, Brazil is one of the most industrialized countries in Latin America, although most of the wealth is concentrated in the southeast region around Rio de Janeiro and São Paulo, the biggest city in Brazil – and South America – with over 17 million inhabitants. Though it lacks the spectacular setting of Rio de Janeiro, São Paulo has long surpassed it as the cultural powerhouse of the country and its international contemporary art exhibition or bienal, held every two years, is rivalled only by Venice's in prestige. The capital of Brazil is neither of these cities but Brasília, a planned city in the interior built in the 1950s, and interesting only on an architectural level – the Brazilian

△ Cable car to Sugar Loaf mountain, Rio de Janeiro

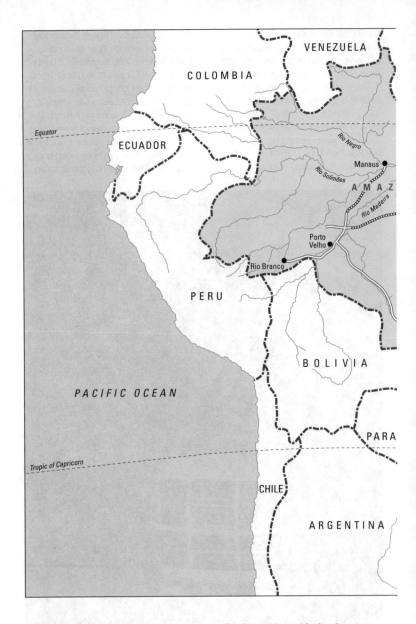

politicians and bureaucrats who work there arrive on Monday morning and leave on Thursday for the weekend.

Brazil is celebrated for its vibrant music and dance forms, the most diverse in South America – bossa nova

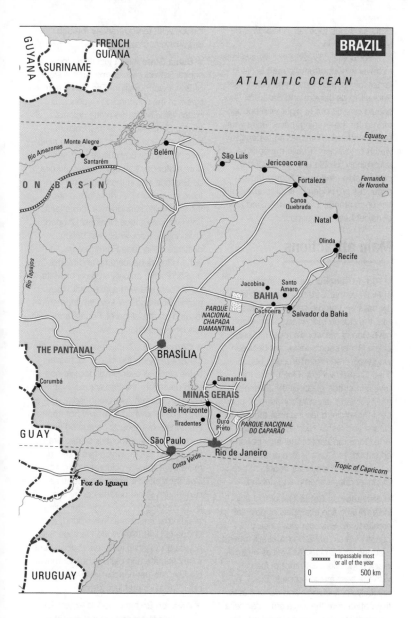

and samba are two of the best known, but there are dozens of others. Brazilians are famously hedonistic too, with tolerant attitudes to sexuality and a gregarious openness unsurpassed even in Latin America. The annual carnival brings all these things together in five days of relentless partying.

Unfortunately, Brazil is not always safe to travel in. Opportunistic theft is rife in larger towns and cities – particularly São Paulo, Rio de Janeiro and Salvador. You should only go out at night with enough money for the evening, never leave your bags unattended or wear an expensive watch or jewellery. Public transport is surprisingly reliable with a network of comfortable modern coaches, though distances are huge (24-hour journeys are not uncommon); if you have limited time, consider buying an airpass.

Main attractions

● **Rio de Janeiro** Cariocas (residents of Rio) say that God made the world in six days and on the seventh he created Rio, the *cidade marvilhosa* (marvellous city). One of the world's most exciting cities, Rio is spectacularly set between jungle-covered mountains and beach-lined Guanabara Bay. Don't miss the towering statue of Christ the Redeemer at Corcovado, a cable-car ride to Sugar Loaf mountain, a ferry across the bay to Niterói and Oscar Niemeyer's Museu de Arte Contemporanea, the leafy bohemian suburb of Santa Teresa and – most importantly – the vibrant beach culture at Copacabana, Ipanema and Leblon.

● **Salvador da Bahia** The oldest city in Brazil with fine examples of colonial architecture, Salvador was once the country's main slave port and still retains a strong African feel. As well as a largely black population, Salvador pulses with the best music scene in Brazil, a uniquely spicy cuisine and cultural activities dating from the slave era – *capoeira* (an elegant non-contact martial art) and *candomblé*, an Afro-Brazilian religion with a large cast of gods and goddesses (*orixas*) and ritual ceremonies which

induce wild, reeling trances through drumming and dancing.

● **Bahia State** It isn't just its regional capital Salvador which makes the state of Bahia worth visiting. The lush green plains of the surrounding Recôncavo countryside have two pretty colonial towns, Santo Amaro and Cachoeira. Inland, the arid plains of the *sertão* have an outback cowboy culture best seen during Monday's leather market in Feira de Santana and in the friendly mining town of Jacobina. Further inland are the waterfalls, strange rock formations and rivers of Parque Nacional Chapada Diamantina. Popular Bahian beach destinations include Porto Seguro, famous for its dancehalls, and Morro de São Paulo, actually a string of white sandy beaches with a laid-back hippy atmosphere and low-key development, located on the island of Tinharé and reached by boat.

● **Carnaval** Justifiably recognized as the biggest party on the planet, Carnaval takes place all over Brazil, for five non-stop days from the Friday (usually in February) before Ash Wednesday. There are three renowned Carnaval hot spots: Rio, where gorgeously costumed samba schools parade through a seated arena; Salvador in Bahia, which has a much more participatory celebration – many Brazilians claim it to be the country's best – with street parades dominated by electrifying *blocos*, large drumming bands that practise all year round; and Olinda (a UNESCO World Heritage Site adjacent to Recife in Pernambuco), host to an intimate and picturesque Carnaval packed into the narrow winding lanes of one of Brazil's prettiest towns.

● **Amazon** Both the world's largest tropical rainforest and longest river, the Amazon has 15,000 animal species, countless different plants and unique indigenous cultures. A boat ride along the vast river is a hypnotic and memorable adventure, although you'll have to venture down one of its tributaries – the rios Negro, Madeira, Solimões and Tapajós – to see Amazonian wildlife at close hand. Manaus, the region's capital, is the starting point for jungle expeditions; you shouldn't and won't really be able to head into the rainforest without a guide. Communities worth stopping off on the stretch of river between Belém and Manaus include Santarém, with a river beach at Alter do Chão, or Monte Alegre and its 10,000-year-old rock paintings.

● **The Pantanal** A vast swamp the size of France in the far west of the country, the Pantanal's flat open terrain makes it the best place in Brazil to see wildlife close-up. Over 250 bird species reside here, including jabiru storks, toucans and magnificent flocks of hyacinth macaws, while the area is also home to anacondas, anteaters and armadillos. There are very few roads into the Pantanal and its size makes it inaccessible and even dangerous to enter alone – you'll need to take an organized tour from Corumbá or Cuiabá.

● **Caipirinha** Quite possibly the world's most delicious – and most potent – cocktail, a *caipirinha* is made from crushed limes, sugar and *cachaça* (Brazilian rum). The finest *cachaça* is produced in the state of Minas Gerais, particularly around the city of Salinas, though the best place to find a first-class *caipirinha* are the fashionable beach communities of Rio – Copacabana, Ipanema and Leblon. Parati on the Costa Verde also boasts a number of bars serving excellent *caipirinhas* made from good local *cachaça*.

● **Iguaçu** One of the world's greatest natural sights, the Foz do Iguaçu or Iguaçu Falls is a series of 275 interlinking waterfalls stretching over three kilometres. Iguaçu is located on the far western Brazil–Argentina–Paraguay border and

surrounded by a vast subtropical nature reserve woven with hiking trails.

● **Costa Verde** One of Brazil's most beautiful stretches of coast which runs for 300km to the west of Rio de Janeiro, the aptly named "green coast" is a string of undeveloped beaches backed by verdant forest. Highlights on the route are the island and former penal colony of Ilha Grande, and Parati, a perfectly preserved colonial town.

Also recommended

● **Cidades historicas** Brazil's so-called "historic cities" are a string of colonial towns in Minas Gerais, the state directly north of Rio. Once bustling mining communities, created on the discovery at the end of the seventeenth century of a plenitude of gold and diamonds in the area, the towns are now tranquil and carefully preserved architectural gems. Ouro Preto, Diamantina and Tiradentes are three of the finest examples.

● **Fernando de Noronha** A pristine archipelago 350km off the coast of Pernambuco, Fernando de Noronha is a marine national park and prime ecotourism destination with a wide variety of birds and sea creatures to spot, including turtles, sharks and whales.

● **Football** Football is Brazil's passion and you shouldn't miss the opportunity to see a stadium match with all its attendant hysteria, live samba and fireworks. Rio's Maracaña Stadium is the world's largest, holding 200,000 people, and during November and December matches are held here three times a week. Otherwise fishermen and other locals play together, usually at dusk, on almost every beach in the country. Gringos are very welcome to join in, though the standard is always high and the game is played barefoot.

- **Parque Nacional do Caparão** In the east of Minais Gerais state, the Parque Nacional do Caparão has some of Brazil's most spectacular scenery, divided into two ecological zones: thickly forested valleys, hills and streams in its lower section which give way to craggy mountains and treeless alpine landscapes. Brazil's highest peak, Pico da Bandeira (2890m), is not difficult to climb and on a clear day those who reach the top will be rewarded with a panoramic view over Espírito Santo and Minas Gerais states.

- **Fruit juice** Freshly squeezed fruit juice or *sugo* is found everywhere in Brazil, particularly at dedicated juice stalls where drinks are made to order. As well as the common orange, mango and passionfruit (and dozens of others), juice is made from fruits only found in Brazil – graviola, bacuri and cupuaçu.

Routes in and out

Direct international flights usually land in Rio or São Paulo. These depart from New York, Los Angeles and Miami in the US; London, Paris, Amsterdam and Madrid in Europe; and Sydney via Auckland in Australasia. From Miami you can also fly straight to Brasília, Recife, Manaus and Belém. Brazil borders every country in South America apart from Chile and Ecuador, so there are myriad spots to arrive and leave the country. Overland border crossings are fairly straightforward, though the only direct access to Suriname is via plane from Belém (very expensive) or through its neighbours, Guyana or French Guiana.

Another option is to take a boat into and out of Brazil via the Amazon River. Standard routes link to Iquitos in Peru or, less popularly, Leticia in Colombia.

Itineraries

One week

The enormity of Brazil means that you won't be able to travel very far in one week. It's best to focus on one area, since bus rides between cities are often over 20 hours in length, and even a plane rides from one end of the country to the other takes five or six hours.

- Explore Rio de Janeiro and then spend the weekend relaxing on the Costa Verde south of the city.

- From Recife take a short bus ride to Olinda for a couple of days wandering through the steep cobbled streets, then fly to the Fernando de Noronha marine park for bird and shark spotting.

- Travel from Belém to Manaus (or vice versa) along the Amazon and stop off halfway for a day or two.

Two weeks

- Fly into São Paulo and spend a day or two enjoying the city's sophisticated cultural scene before travelling to Iguaçu, where you'll need at least three days to fully explore the waterfalls and national park. From there, head to the Pantanal for an organized trip into the swamplands. Depart from Rio after you've enjoyed all the city sights and spent a day or two on one of the beaches of the Costa Verde.

- Head north from Rio to the mining towns of Minas Gerais and then to the Parque Nacional do Caparão before looping back to Rio.

- Fly into Salvador and, after a few days in the city, explore the colonial towns, beaches and Afro-Brazilian culture of Bahia, one of Brazil's most fascinating states.

- Explore the river and rainforest in some depth with an initial trip down the Amazon and then take further boat trips along the river's tributaries, where you'll have a much greater opportunity to spot wildlife, learn about the complex Amazonian biosphere, and visit remote jungle towns.

One month

● From Rio and its environs, travel north to several of the colonial towns of Minas Gerais, and east to the Parque Nacional do Caparão. From Minas Gerais head to the city of Salvador and visit the various highlights of Bahia. Fly south to the Iguaçu Falls for a few days. Finish your trip on one of the beaches of the Costa Verde, between São Paulo and Rio de Janeiro.

● Travel from Salvador around the Atlantic coast to Belém, which sits at the mouth of the Amazon, spending several days each at a string of beach resorts and various other points of interest along the way: Chapada Diamantina in Bahia, Olinda and Recife, Fernando de Noronha marine park, the beaches of Natal (take a dune buggy ride), Canoa Quebrada and Jericoacoara and the faded charm of the Afro-Brazilian city São Luis.

Brazil online

BrazilMax

ⓦ**www.brazilmax.com** Billed as "The hip gringo's guide to Brazilian culture and society", this Internet magazine is written by American journalist Bill Hinchberger and has an excellent selection of articles – particularly on cultural activities – with an eclectic reading list, archived travel writings and further links.

Gringoes.com

ⓦ**www.gringoes.com** Brazil's first portal for its expat community, this website combines folksy articles on various aspects of Brazilian culture with hard facts on living and working in the country.

Maria-Brazil

ⓦ**www.maria-brazil.org** Written by an American smitten with the country, this site has entertaining features on such essentials as Brazilian bikinis and other light-hearted but important aspects of Brazilian culture.

Sonia-portuguese.com

ⓦ**www.sonia-portuguese.com** An excellent website, written in English by a Brazilian, for learning a little Portuguese before you arrive in Brazil.

Chile

Capital Santiago
Population 16 million
Languages Spanish, plus minority indigenous languages
Currency Peso Chileno (CH$)
Climate Temperate, with warm days and cool nights in the north and centre, colder in the south, particularly during the winter months from June to September
Best time to go November to March (summer) is the best time, though the north can be visited at any time; avoid June to September, which is winter in the centre and south
Minimum daily budget US$25

An implausibly narrow strip of land running down the west coast of South America, Chile measures over 4000km in length – the same distance as that from Britain to West Africa – though its width rarely exceeds 180km. Absurd as it may seem, however, this bizarre shape makes perfect sense geographically: hemmed in by the South Pacific to the west, separated from Argentina to the east by the Andes, and divided from Peru to the north by the arid expanse of the Atacama Desert, the country is a geographically self-contained unit.

The historic isolation brought by these natural barriers has helped create a nation very distinct from the rest of Latin America. Of all the countries in the region, Chile is the one where European cultural influence is strongest, a result both of the Spanish colonial period, subsequent waves of immigration from elsewhere in Europe, and major British commercial involvement in the nineteenth and twentieth centuries – until the arrest of the former Chilean dictator Augusto Pinochet in London in 1998, the Chilean upper classes liked to think of themselves as the English of South America, and would hold formal tea parties every afternoon. It's for Pinochet's brutal military regime, which ruled the country between 1973 and 1989, that Chile has become best known internationally, but in fact that dictatorship was an aberration from a long tradition of political stability, civilian government and the rule of law. Compared to the rest of the continent, Chile is a modern and relatively affluent society, and is without doubt one of the safest and easiest places to travel in South America. The police are generally helpful and efficient, the infrastructure is well developed and – most amazingly for Latin America – the buses run on time.

In terms of cultural interest, Chile can't really compete with other Andean countries like Peru and Bolivia, with their extremely diverse populations and deep-rooted indigenous traditions. (Chile's largest remaining indigenous group, the Mapuche, number a million but are largely confined to reservations in the Lake District.) What it lacks in culture, however, it more than makes up for with its astonishing variety of dramatic landscapes, which range from the Atacama Desert, the driest in the world, to the glaciers and ice fields of Patagonia. Between these extremes

are beautiful beaches; fertile valleys where vineyards and orchards flourish; huge temperate forests and dazzling emerald lakes; stunning fjords and bleak Patagonian steppes; and, towering above it all and running the length of the country, the jagged spine of the Andes, with its glacial peaks and smouldering volcanoes. Moreover, with a population of just sixteen million, largely confined to a few cities in a country three times the size of Britain, much of Chile's vast expanse is virtually uninhabited wilderness. Coupled with a well-organized tourism industry, this makes Chile an excellent country for the outdoor enthusiast, whether your preference is for skiing, birdwatching, sea kayaking, whitewater rafting, trekking, mountaineering, horse riding or fly fishing. As if all this wasn't enough, Chile also lays claim to far-flung Easter Island, almost 4000km out from the mainland in the Pacific Ocean, which was home to one of the world's most mysterious and remarkable prehistoric cultures, best known for the enormous stone idols that still dot the island's shores.

Chile's climate is much closer to that of Europe or the US than to most other Latin American countries, ranging from an almost Mediterranean climate in the centre of the country, to much colder conditions in the far south. Seasonal variations become more pronounced as you travel south, so while the southern hemisphere winter between June and September brings extremely cold weather in the far south, with heavy snow blocking access to many of the best national parks, the summer months from November to March enjoy good weather and long sunny evenings. This means you can fit much more into a day, and makes southern Chile the perfect place to escape from the winter back home.

Main attractions

● **Parque Nacional Torres del Paine** Situated in the far south of Chilean Patagonia, this remote park encompasses Chile's single most famous attraction, the stunning Torres del Paine, a small mountain range of magnificent near-vertical granite pinnacles that soar more

△ Parque Nacional Torres del Paine

than 2000m above the surrounding plains, amidst a pristine wilderness of glaciers, lakes and primeval forests – a paradise for walkers and mountaineers.

● **Lake District** Stretching some 340km between the towns of Temuco and Puerto Montt in the south of the country, the Chilean Lake District is a beautiful region of lush farmland, dense forest and deep, clear lakes which sit at the foot of a series of spectacular snowcapped volcanoes. Much of the stunning wilderness scenery of the region is protected by national parks such as Puyehue, which offer excellent hiking opportunities, with the added bonus of numerous volcanic hot springs where you can relax and soothe tired legs after a hard day's walking.

● **Chiloé** Just south of the Lake District and reached by boat from Puerto Montt, Chiloé is a peaceful and isolated archipelago famous for its traditional rural culture and rich folklore and mythology. The windswept west coast of the main island, Isla Grande de Chiloé, is covered with dense forest, much of it protected by the Parque National Chiloé, while the more sheltered east coast is dotted with quiet fishing and farming communities, with colourful wooden churches and traditional wooden houses built on stilts.

● **The Carretera Austral** Stretching over a thousand kilometres south from Puerto Montt to the remote settle- ment of Yungay, the Carretera Austral – the Southern Highway – is one of the most dramatic roads in Latin America, carving its way through great tracts of untouched wilderness between soaring, snowcapped mountains, ancient glaciers, narrow fjords, emerald rivers and swathes of temperate rainforest.

● **Parque Nacional Laguna San Rafael** Reached from the port of Chacabuco by a spectacular 200km boat journey through labyrinthine fjords, the iceberg-choked Laguna San Rafael,

at the foot of the glacier of the same name, is one of the most awe-inspiring sights in Chile. It's also a great place for observing penguins, sea lions, albatrosses and other marine wildlife, and is the centre of a vast national park that encompasses huge ice fields, high mountain peaks, primeval forests and hundreds of glacial lakes.

● **Valparaíso and the Litoral Central** The coastal city of Valparaíso, about 120km northwest of Santiago, is Chile's biggest port and a wonderfully atmospheric place, with labyrinthine cobbled streets lined with ramshackle, brightly painted houses that cover the steep hillside down to the seashore. Known as the Litoral Central (the Central Coast) or the Chilean Riviera, the stretch of coast either side of Valparaíso boasts bay after bay lined with beautiful white sand beaches and twenty or so resort towns, the largest and most famous of which is the upmarket Viña del Mar.

Also recommended

● **Atacama Desert** Stretching over 1200km south from the Peruvian border, the Atacama Desert is the driest desert in the world, a desolate plain of rock and gravel that contains areas where no rain has ever been recorded. The region also boasts a spectacular coastline, geysers, ancient petroglyphs and abandoned nitrate-mining ghost towns. The best way to explore the Atacama is on a jeep tour from the oasis village of San Pedro de Atacama, which is close to the otherworldly landscape of the Valle de la Luna.

● **Skiing** Chile boasts arguably the best skiing in South America: some skiers say that the very dry powder snow (known as "champagne snow") found on the country's high-altitude slopes is of a quality found nowhere else. The season runs from June to September and the best slopes and resorts – El Colorado, La Parva and Valle Nevado – are conveniently close to Santiago.

● **The Central Valley** Many travellers speed through Chile's Central Valley – the rich agricultural heartland stretching from Santiago 400km or so south to the Río Bío Bío – without stopping as they head to more spectacular attractions further south, but with its lush, pastoral landscape dotted with orchards and vineyards, its splendid colonial haciendas and tranquil villages, and its traditional rural culture, the region rewards those who stop off and explore away from the main road.

● **Easter Island (Rapa Nui)** Isolated in the vastness of the Pacific Ocean almost four thousand kilometres west of the Chilean mainland, tiny Easter Island – known to its indigenous Polynesian inhabitants as Rapa Nui – is one of the most remote places on earth, and home to the extraordinary monuments left by one of the world's most enigmatic prehistoric cultures. The coast of the island – which measures just over 20km across at its widest point – is dotted with huge, ancient monolithic stone statues of squat human torsos and heads, the origin and meaning of which remain a mystery.

Routes in and out

The Chilean capital Santiago is served by regular flights from major European capitals and cities in the US, and from Australia via New Zealand, Papeete and Easter Island in the Pacific; it also has regular flights to all the main South American capitals. By land, it's easy to enter and leave Chile across the northern border with Peru and at many points along the long eastern frontier with Argentina – if you visit Patagonia you

may well find yourself crossing the border between Chile and Argentina several times. There's a good road link between Arica in northern Chile and La Paz in western Bolivia, but you can also cross into Bolivia by train from Calama to Uyuni – a route that passes through spectacular high Andean scenery – or by jeep as part of an organized tour from San Pedro de Atacama, passing through the stunning Reserva de Fauna Andina Eduardo Avaroa in the far southwest of Bolivia.

Itineraries

The huge distances involved mean that if you've only got a short time to explore Chile but want to travel widely, you'll need to take one or more internal flights. The main airline, LAN Chile, frequently offers last minute discounts for internal flights; check their website, ⓦwww .lanchile.com, for details.

One week

● From Santiago head to Valparaíso or one of the nearby beach resorts for two or three days (or, if you're there in winter, spend a couple of days skiing near the capital), then either head north by road to San Pedro de Atacama and spend your remaining time exploring the Atacama Desert and the Altiplano, or head south overland and spend the time in the Lake District.

Two weeks

● Travel south by road from Santiago through the Central Valley and spend the first week or so exploring the Lake District and Chiloé, then take a four-day boat trip from Puerto Montt via Puerto Chacabuco to visit the San Rafael glacier, returning to Santiago by road from Puerto Chacabuco along the Carretera Austral. With any luck you'll have enough time at the end of the trip to spend a day or two in Valparaíso and one of the nearby beach resorts, or to ski near Santiago.

One month

● Spend ten days or so working your way south from Santiago, passing through the Central Valley and visiting the Lake District and Chiloé, then take a boat tour down from Puerto Montt to the Laguna San Rafael glacier. Next, head to Patagonia to visit Parque Nacional Torres del Paine, either by disembarking at Puerto Chacabuco as you return north from San Rafael and travelling by road down the Careterra Austral and through Argentina, or by returning to Puerto Montt and catching the weekly ferry to Puerto Natales. Return by plane to Santiago, then either fly out to Easter Island for a week, or spend the time visiting Valparaíso and some of the surrounding beaches and heading up into the Atacama Desert.

Chile online

Chilean Patagonia
Ⓦ**www.chileaustral.com** Tourist

information on Patagonia, full of practical detail with useful links and some inspiring picture galleries.
Chip Travel
Ⓦ**www.chiptravel.cl** Government-sponsored English language site offering a clear introduction to Chile's attractions, lots of useful practical information as well as online hotel booking and car rental.
Easter Island
Ⓦ**www.netaxs.com/~trance/rapanui .html** A good introduction to the history and culture of Easter Island, with plenty of good pictures, practical information and lots of useful links.
Sernatur
Ⓦ**www.sernatur.cl** High-quality National Tourist Board site with useful general information on the main attractions, plenty of pictures and maps, and links to online hotel bookings and other government websites.
Visit Chile
Ⓦ**www.visit-chile.org** Extensive general tourist information site with information on all the main attractions and activities from skiing to wine tours, as well as links to airlines, hotels and car rental companies and a wealth of other practical information.

Colombia

Capital Bogotá
Population 43 million
Languages Spanish, plus over a dozen indigenous languages and English Creole
Currency Colombian peso (Col$)
Climate Large variations in temperature: tropical along coast and eastern plains with wet (April–May & Sept–Nov) and dry (Nov–March) seasons; cooler in the Andean highlands
Best time to go November to March (dry season)
Minimum daily budget US$15

To most people, Colombia means only three things: coffee, cocaine and civil war. The country has been blighted by over fifty years of fighting between left-wing guerrillas and right-wing paramilitaries, with hundreds of thousands of Colombians losing their lives and many more being made homeless. As if this wasn't already enough, the country also reels under the influence of the billion-dollar cocaine trade – Colombia is both the world's largest grower of coca (the raw material of cocaine) and the world's leading processor of the drug – whose economic and social consequences permeate all levels of society, from peasant farmers coerced into growing coca to corrupt politicians in the pay of drugs cartels. Not for nothing is Colombia nicknamed Locombia, or "Mad Country".

Sadly, Colombia is as dangerous than ever to travel in. Several thousand kidnappings a year and high levels of guerrilla and paramilitary activity remain part of daily life for Colombians. If you decide to visit the country, make sure you check the latest political situation with the government travel advisories listed on p.371. At present, the entire country east of Bogotá is effectively out of bounds to tourists and the border areas with Venezuela and Panama should also be treated with caution. Additionally overland travel isn't currently safe at night or in remote areas – it's best to take internal flights between cities or travel with major bus companies on main routes during the daytime only.

These warnings aside, there are still parts of Colombia which are no more dangerous to visit than anywhere else in Latin America, and those travellers who do make it to Colombia often cite it as their favourite country in South America. Certainly, Colombia has a lot to offer, including one of the most geographically diverse landscapes of any Latin American country, with the Andes stretching right through its western side, unspoilt Caribbean and Pacific coastlines, and a large area of remote Amazon basin. Uniquely in South America, it's possible to see the ocean from the snowcapped Sierra Nevada de Santa Marta (rising to 5800m), while the lower Andes are dotted with a series of pretty colonial towns and traditional highland villages, along with several unique pre-Columbian sites: the Ciudad Perdida of the Tayrona people in northern Colombia and San Agustín and Tierradientro in the south of the

country. Additionally, you'll have most of Colombia's beauty spots to yourself – almost nowhere in the country is overrun by tourists.

But the country's greatest attraction is perhaps the Colombians themselves, a more homogenous people than that of most other South American countries, with over 75 percent of the population mixed (both mestizo and mulatto) race. Renowned for their exuberance and friendliness, they celebrate life in the midst of civil war with noisy parties whenever possible, and welcome the few tourists they see wholeheartedly. In spite of its continuing violence and criminality, Colombia remains a spontaneous, vibrant and remarkably open society.

Main attractions

● **Cartagena** Founded in 1533, the great walled city of Cartagena de Indias, on the Caribbean coast, was the main

Spanish port in northern South America for several hundred years. Cartagena's thick walls and ring of outer forts, built to protect the city from pirate attacks, are part of the unique character that makes it Colombia's main draw and one of the finest colonial cities in the Americas. You could easily spend days wandering through its maze of narrow streets, arcaded squares, grand buildings and ruined forts. Adjacent to the old city is a vibrant modern beach resort, and at night Cartagena comes alive with a mixture of live music, salsa and beachfront discos.

● **Parque Nacional Tayrona** The most popular national park in Colombia, Tayrona protects a 35-kilometre stretch of Caribbean coast, with glorious sandy beaches set in palm-fringed bays and backed by lush rainforest. A well-known hippy hangout, it's the perfect place

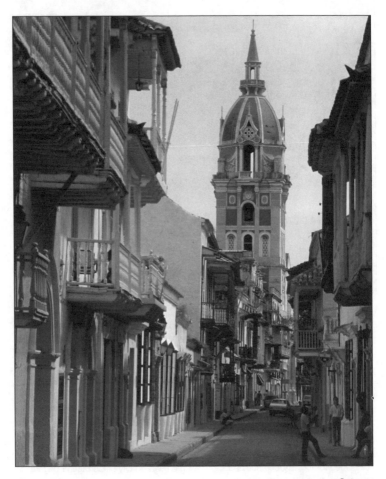

△ Cartagena

to take a break from travelling, though if you feel energetic you could make the five-day trek from the park to the Ciudad Perdida ("Lost City") or Teyuna – its indigenous name – of the Tayrona Indians, dating back to 500 AD, which occupies a spectacular location at 1100m on the northern slopes of the Sierra Nevada de Santa Marta. (Be aware that a group of trekkers were kidnapped at the Ciudad Perdida in 2003 though they were all released unharmed.)

● **Chocó region** This remote and unspoilt region encompasses the northern half of Colombia's Pacific coast, with virgin rainforest running down to miles of empty beach, a tropical backwater atmosphere and traditional communities of Chocó and Emberá Indians. The region's capital is the ramshackle riverside city of Quibdó – it's better to head straight for the remote and unspoilt coastal resorts of Nuquí, El Valle and Parque Nacional Ensenada de Utría. Highlights of the area include tiny Isla de Salomon, which has the prettiest white-sand beach around, and the small village of Tribugá, both stop-offs on the boat ride from Nuquí to El Valle.

● **San Agustín** Principally known for a number of mysterious carved statues in a series of nearby sites, San Agustín is a pretty market town in the rolling green foothills of the Andes, with locals on horseback and a thriving backpacker scene. The surrounding countryside is a scene of striking natural beauty, and there are several impressive waterfalls close to the town.

● **Salsa in Cali** Salsa is one of Colombia's most celebrated forms of music and dance and nowhere in the country is it more popular than in the salsatecas (salsa clubs) of Cali, an inland city with tropical temperatures and an atmosphere to match. Cali's citizens,

caleños, are among Colombia's friendliest locals – try and persuade them to take you to the authentic salsatecas in the barrio of Juanchito, which can be dangerous if you go alone. If not, there are salsa clubs dotted along Avenida Sexta, the city's main street for nightlife.

Also recommended

● **San Andrés y Providencia** A small archipelago in the Caribbean (it's actually closer to Nicaragua than Colombia), San Andrés y Providencia has a unique culture, a fusion of Jamaican and Colombian, marked by soca music and Creole-speaking inhabitants, while the islands' clear blue waters and coral reefs make them a great destination for snorkelling and scuba diving.

● **Popayán** Situated in the southwest of the country, Popayán is one of Colombia's most perfectly preserved colonial towns, boasting several noteworthy colonial churches and hosting spectacular Semana Santa (Easter) parades. It's a small, tranquil place with a mild climate, and there's little to do here other than wander through the pretty squares and cobbled streets, though it makes a good base from which to visit the Tuesday market at Silvia, where the local Guambiano Indians can be seen weaving textiles in their colourful blue and fuchsia costumes.

● **Mud volcanoes** Arboletes and El Totumo are the two most impressive of the series of natural mud lakes that stretch along the Caribbean coast of Colombia. Both have craters filled with the warm, thick stuff, in which you can bathe: the mud has beneficial healing properties and leaves your skin baby smooth – a weird and unforgettable sensation.

• **Bogotá** Colombia's noisy, gridlocked and exciting capital is well worth a visit, despite its (largely undeserved) reputation for danger. The city's lovely colonial quarter, La Candelaria, makes an atmospheric retreat from the city bustle, while other highlights include the world-famous Museo de Oro and the monastery of Montserrate, perched high above the city and boasting wonderful views – not to mention one of the best club scenes in Latin America.

• **Leticia** A small town in the south-eastern tip of Colombia, Leticia is the tourist centre of the country's remote Amazon region. The town itself is fairly ordinary but the surrounding area is dense rainforest dotted with Ticuna and Yagua settlements. Popular trips go to Parque Nacional Amacayucu, 75km upstream, where there are walking trails through the forest, and the Lago de Tarapoto, a beautiful lake featuring the famous *Victoria Amazonica* waterlily and occasional sightings of pink dolphins. From Leticia (which you'll have to fly to from within Colombia) it's possible to get a boat down the Amazon River to Brazil and Peru.

• **Coffee fincas** The *tierra paisa* or countryside around Medellin is known as the *zona cafetera*, where Colombia's coffee is grown. As well as enjoying the local stimulant it's possible to stay in one of 300 picturesque coffee farms. Hosts will organize horseback riding and guided walks and the surroundings are both pretty and very peaceful.

Routes in and out

There are direct daily flights to Bogotá from several cities in the US (principally Miami and New York), plus direct flights from Miami to Cartagena and Medellín. From Europe there are flights from London via Caracas to Bogotá thrice weekly, and direct flights from Madrid, Paris and Frankfurt to the capital. Overland border crossings from Venezuela to Colombia are at Cúcuta and the less popular Maicao, on the northern Guajira Peninsula. The border between Colombia and Ecuador is at Ipiales. Boats go irregularly from Colón in Panama to Puerto Obaldía (2–4 days), from where you can take an expreso or speedboat to the Colombian resorts of Capurganá and Acandi. The famous overland crossing of the Darién Gap (see p.153) is extremely dangerous and should on no account be attempted at present.

Itineraries

One week

• Spend four days in Colombia's capital and then fly to Leticia in the Amazon for some jungle exploration. From Leticia move on by boat to Brazil or Peru.

• Take an organized five-day trek from Santa Marta to the Ciudad Perdida, and then spend your last two days relaxing on the Caribbean beaches of Parque Nacional Tayrona.

• Fly from Medellín to Nuquí in the Chocó region. From Nuquí travel onward to El Valle by boat with an overnight stay on the Isla de Salomon and forays into Parque Nacional Ensenada de Utria.

Two weeks

• Cross the border from Ecuador to San Agustín. Spend several days relaxing in this small rural town before moving on to Bogotá for some big city life. Travel north to Cartagena for a few days and then go east to the Parque Nacional Tayrona for a long weekend or fly to the Caribbean island of San Andrés, from where you can fly on to Costa Rica or Panama.

• Head west from Bogotá to the seaside town of Nuquí in the Chocó region for several days on the Pacific coast. Head south from Chocó's regional centre, Quibdó, by bus to Cali and its salsa dance clubs. From there make your way to San Agustín and then on to one of Colombia's colonial highlights, Popayán, and the market town of Silvia.

Three weeks

● Fly into Cartagena from Panama and spend ten days on the coast exploring Cartagena, trekking to the Ciudad Perdida and relaxing in the Parque Nacional Tayrona. Travel south to Bogotá for four or five days and then on to Cali to check out its dance clubs. Visit San Agustín, Popayán and Silvia before crossing the border into Ecuador at Ipiales.

Colombia online

Colombia Journal
ⓦwww.colombiajournal.org
Campaigning American website with left-wing perspective which examines civil unrest and the drugs trade in Colombia in depth.

Colombia Support Network
ⓦwww.colombiasupport.net Website of the largest grassroots organization in the US working to improve human rights in Colombia, with articles and background information on the current political crisis.

El Tiempo
ⓦwww.eltiempo.com The well laid-out and comprehensive site (in Spanish only) of Colombia's best daily newspaper, *El Tiempo*.

Poor but happy and **Colombia Update**
ⓦwww.poorbuthappy.com/Colombia/ & ⓦwww.colombiaupdate.com Forum-based websites which provide useful and upbeat advice on travel in Colombia and articles by other travellers on their experiences.

Costa Rica

Capital San José
Population 3.8 million
Languages Spanish, Creole English
on the Caribbean
Currency Colón (¢)
Climate Tropical on the coast,
cooler in the mountains, with distinct
dry (Dec–April) and rainy (May–Nov)
seasons
When to go November, April and
May
Minimum daily budget US$30

In a region synonymous in many people's minds with civil war and natural disasters, Costa Rica stands out as a beacon of prosperity and stability – not for nothing is the country often described as the Switzerland of Central America. Today, as Costa Ricans will proudly tell you, the country has no army, more teachers than policemen, free and compulsory primary education, and a literacy rate of ninety percent. For the visitor, Costa Rica's overwhelming draw is its outstanding range of natural attractions, from stunning landscapes to rare and colourful birds and wildlife. Around a quarter of the country is now protected by a widely admired system of national parks and reserves which cover a fascinating diversity of terrains, from mysterious cloud- and rainforests to active volcanic peaks and stunning stretches of palm-fringed coast. And found within these parks is a remarkable array of biodiversity, some five percent of the world's total – an astonishing figure given the country's tiny dimensions – and including (to give just one example) some 850 species of bird, more than in the US and Canada combined.

All of which natural attractions have made Costa Rica one of the finest places in Latin America for ecotourists, birdwatchers and wildlife enthusiasts, with the result that Costa Rica is now Central America's most popular tourist destination, attracting around 1.5 million visitors annually – quite an achievement for a country whose entire population numbers less than four million. The large number of North Americans who come to visit (or, increasingly, to live in) the country means that many Costa Ricans now speak at least a little English and are used to dealing with foreigners. In sum, if you're nervous about culture shock, Costa Rica is the best place in Central America to ease into your Latin American adventure. Conversely, if you prefer to travel off the beaten track, Costa Rica isn't the place to go.

Away from the nation's national parks and reserves, there are outstanding beaches to be found on both coasts, some world-class surfing and white-water rafting. Man-made and cultural attractions are few, however, although the Jamaican-descended black population which lives around Puerto Limón on the Caribbean coast supplies a welcome splash of cultural diversity (and nightlife) in the country's overwhelmingly mestizo population.

As the visitor numbers would suggest, Costa Rica has a well-developed tourist infrastructure, including some of Latin America's most memorable eco-lodges and an efficient public transport network, even though some of the country's roads remain pretty appalling. This development comes at a price, however: Costa Rica is perhaps the most expensive country in Central America to travel in, with daily costs being twice those in neighbouring Nicaragua. On the plus side, it's still amongst the safest countries in the region, though levels of crime against tourists are unfortunately rising, and parts of San José should be avoided at night.

Main attractions

● **Parque Nacional Tortuguero** Most visitors come to Tortuguero to see hawksbill, green and leatherback turtles laying their eggs on the beach (March–May & July–Oct), but the park's network of inland waterways also teems with other forms of wildlife, particularly birds. The most popular way to experience Tortuguero is on an organized package tour with accommodation in comfortable though pricey lodges and all meals included. If you want to travel independently, the village itself has several cheap hotels and is extremely pretty, with pastel-coloured wooden houses and lots of rakish charm.

● **Puerto Viejo de Talamanca** Situated on the southern end of Costa Rica's Caribbean coast, the funky fishing village of Puerto Viejo de Talamanca has easily the liveliest nightlife in the whole country, with several buzzing beach-side discos. By day, there are miles of clean, sandy beaches to lounge about on, plus excellent surfing and snorkelling.

● **Volcán Arenal** One of the western hemisphere's most active volcanoes, Arenal spews out rivers of molten red lava on an almost nightly basis, although you'll need a clear night to see this amazing pyrotechnic display. The best views are from the north and west sides, however it's forbidden to enter the park at night unless you're on an organized tour. During the daytime be sure to hike one of several trails around the volcano and across its solidified lava fields.

● **Reserva Santa Elena** In northern Costa Rica, the Reserva Santa Elena comprises a small area of virgin cloud-forest with dense walls of dripping vegetation and brightly coloured birds and flowers. Though it's only a third the size of the famous Monteverde Cloudforest just down the road, it's also much less visited – and more tranquil – and profits go to local schools. The surrounding area was colonized by a group of US Quakers (a progressive and pacifist Christian movement) escaping the draft in the early 1950s, and now offers a rural idyll of small dairy farms and mountain scenery.

● **Osa Peninsula** Much less well known than other parts of Costa Rica, the Osa Peninsula is difficult to reach – getting to both the village of Aguijitas in Bahía Drake and Carate on the edge of the Parque Nacional Corcovado entails lengthy uncomfortable boat or bus rides – but rewards the few travellers who make it here with stunning scenery. Corcovado, with its series of rainforest-fringed beaches populated by flocks of scarlet macaws, is one of Costa Rica's most beautiful national parks, and there's wonderful marine life and snorkelling at Bahía Drake.

△ Parque Nacional Corcovado

Also recommended

● **Orosí** The peaceful Orosí river valley, 25km southeast of San José, is little visited by tourists but has much to offer, with a dramatic setting in a deep bowl of steep forested hills. There's a series of lovely walks and waterfalls in the area, and a very pretty village, Orosí, which has two outdoor swimming pools fed by hot springs and one of the oldest churches in Costa Rica, an evocative adobe and red-tiled structure built in 1735.

● **Rara Avis** A private rainforest reserve and research station 80km northeast of San José, Rara Avis offers one of the best ecotourism experiences in the country. Getting to the forest is half the adventure – its remoteness means that it's only accessible by tractor-drawn cart from the nearest village along a muddy track, with great views over the surrounding countryside and of toucans in the trees. Once there you can walk one of several excellent trails through the forest, check out the abundant flora (including rare palm species and orchids) or swim in a waterfall pool.

● **Liberia** In the northern province of Guanacaste, calm Liberia is Costa Rica's most attractive town, with wide streets of whitewashed houses lined with mango trees, while the town's main street, the Calle Real, has been restored to its original nineteenth-century glory and its buildings are the best example of colonial architecture in Costa Rica. The town is also a good jumping-off point for several national parks, the popular beaches of Guanacaste – tranquil Playa Sámara is the least developed of these while gringo-friendly Tamarindo is popular with surfers – and the Nicaraguan border.

● **Parque Nacional Rincón de la Vieja** Also in Guanacaste, Rincon de la Vieja is distinguished by its dramatically dry landscape with rock-strewn savannah, bubbling mud pots and sulphurous subterranean springs. The walking trail to the summit of the still-smoking volcano which gives the park its name is one of the most scenic in the country, passing through fields of purple orchids and deciduous forests. Animals include tapirs, peccaries, monkeys and all the country's big cats, while birders may spot oropendolas, trogons and spectacled owls.

● **Turrialba** In the Valle Central, Turrialba is a friendly agricultural town with few tourists. The pretty surrounding countryside, spreading over the eastern slopes of the Cordillera Central, is filled with a fresh mountain air that provides a welcome change from the stifling heat of the nearby Caribbean coast. Adrenalin junkies can sign up for a whitewater rafting or kayaking trip on the Reventazón or Pacuaré rivers, while the most important archeological site in Costa Rica – Monumento Nacional Guayabo – is 20km away. Several nearby alfresco restaurants serve delicious local fare – barbecued meat and *pozol*, a corn and pork soup – in attractive rustic settings.

Routes in and out

There are direct flights daily to San José from Miami, Chicago, Houston, Dallas and several other US cities as well as regularly scheduled flights from Madrid, Munich and Amsterdam. The border between Costa Rica and Nicaragua is at Peñas Blancas, close to the Pacific coast, and has direct bus routes on to Managua; it's also possible to cross the Río San Juan from Los Chiles to San Carlos. There are two main borders with Panama: Paso Canoas on the Panamerican Highway, and Sixaola on the Caribbean, convenient for the popular Panamanian resort of Bocas del Toro.

Itineraries

One week

● Take a bus or boat from San José to Tortuguero and then travel by boat down the Caribbean coast to the region's capital, Puerto Limón, and on to seaside party town Puerto Viejo de Talamanca.

● Head north from San José to Volcán Arenal and the Santa Elena cloudforest before stopping off in laid-back Liberia for a few days and visiting Rincón de la Vieja.

● Travel from San José to the Osa Peninsula, do the popular five-day trek in Corcovado National Park and then recover on the beaches of Bahía Drake.

Two weeks

● Travel from San José to Rara Avis and spend a few days bird-spotting, followed by a few days relaxing and exploring the tranquil Orosí valley, Turrialba and surrounds before heading east to Tortuguero.

● From Panama, cross the border into Sixaola and then head to Puerto Viejo de Talamanca. Head right across the country to the Orosí valley and then on to the Osa Peninsula, where you can hike through the Corcovado National Park or go snorkelling at Bahía Drake.

One month

● If you're travelling south through Central America, cross the border from Nicaragua to Peñas Blancas and head on to the cowboy city of Liberia – a pleasant introduction to Costa Rica. Continue on to the Santa Elena cloudforest and the Quaker communities of Monteverde, visit Volcán Arenal and then head south to the Osa Peninsula. Loop back to the centre of the country and Orosí, then cross over to the other coast and Puerto Viejo de Talamanca before moving on to Panama.

Costa Rica online

Cocori.com
Ⓦ www.cocori.com Excellent series of well-written articles on all aspects of life in Costa Rica including food, scuba diving and spelunking amongst others.

Costa Rica Net
Ⓦ www.costaricanet.net Links to thousands of Costa Rican websites and those set up by Costa Rica aficionados in the US.

Info Costa Rica
Ⓦ www.infocostarica.com Well-organized portal with hundreds of good links as well as in-house articles and a message board.

Tico Times
Ⓦ www.ticotimes.net Website of the award-winning weekly English-language newspaper, with a focus on national news as well as folksy columns on cooking, fishing and expat life in Costa Rica.

Ecuador

Capital Quito
Population 13 million
Languages Spanish, Quechua, plus minority indigenous languages
Currency US dollar ($)
Climate Hot and humid in the tropical lowlands of the coast and the Oriente, cooler in the highlands

Best time to go June to August in the highlands, December to April on the coast, and any time outside the June-to-August rainy season in the Amazon lowlands
Minimum daily budget US$15

Sitting on the equator between Peru and Colombia, Ecuador is the smallest of the Andean countries, covering an area only slightly larger than the United Kingdom. But despite its diminutive size, the country is packed with dramatic scenic contrasts, encompassing snow-capped volcanic peaks, palm-fringed beaches lapped by the warm Pacific, and the steaming tropical rainforests of the Amazon basin. Ecuador is also home to a diverse population, including a wide range of indigenous groups, while many of its towns and cities contain magnificent examples of colonial architecture. As if this wasn't enough, Ecuador's attractions are crowned by the Galápagos Islands, the famous archipelago whose unique and extraordinary wildlife played a key role

△ Volcán Cotopaxi

in shaping Charles Darwin's theories on evolution.

In many ways, Ecuador is a kind of pocket-sized South America, making it the ideal destination for travellers who want to experience a wide range of the continent's manifold attractions but only have limited time available. Unlike larger South American countries, where moving between different regions involves travelling vast distances, Ecuador's compact size means that getting around is straightforward and relatively quick, with few destinations more than a day's journey from the capital, Quito.

It also has a relatively well-developed tourist infrastructure, making it easy to arrange guided tours and treks, rainforest expeditions, or climbing, riding and mountain-biking trips.

Like the other Andean countries, Ecuador suffers from chronic political instability – in 1997 it went through three presidents in a year, including the infamous Abdalá Bucaram, known as "El Loco" ("The Mad"), who was removed from office on grounds of mental incompetence. Fortunately, these periodic political upheavals are rarely violent, but they do often involve mass protests and road blockades that paralyse the country and make travel virtually impossible, so it's important to check on the current political situation before you arrive. In recent years the economy – dependent largely on oil and banana exports – has also been in deep crisis, bringing increased poverty and unemployment and leading to the abandonment of the national currency in favour of the US dollar. Crime levels have also increased, ending Ecuador's reputation as one of the safest countries for travellers in South America. But for all that, the overwhelming majority of Ecuadorians remain remarkably cheerful, courteous and welcoming to foreign visitors.

Main attractions

● **Galápagos Islands** Lying almost 1000km east of the Ecuadorian mainland, the extraordinary Galápagos Islands – which inspired Charles Darwin's theory of evolution – are Ecuador's best-known attraction, home to a unique, abundant and virtually fearless range of wildlife including marine iguanas, giant tortoises, whales, dolphins, sea lions, penguins and boobies. Visiting the islands is relatively expensive – flights from the mainland, the national park entrance fee and the cost of a seven-night cruise around the archipelago will set you back well over $1000 – but few travellers who come here regret splashing out to experience one of the most astonishing nature-tourism destinations in the world.

● **Quito** Set at an altitude of 2800m in a valley at the foot of the soaring Pichincha volcano, the Ecuadorian capital has a beautiful old colonial quarter of narrow streets lined with exquisite churches, monasteries and mansions that warrants a day or two of exploration. The modern new town is packed with hotels, restaurants, tour companies and other useful facilities, and makes a convenient place to recuperate between trips around the country.

● **Avenue of the Volcanoes** South of Quito, the two parallel chains of the Andes that run the length of Ecuador rise to their most dramatic and spectacular, forming a double row of soaring, snowcapped peaks. The fertile basin between the two chains is the indigenous heartland of Ecuador, dotted with traditional farming villages and peaceful market towns, many of which can be visited in a 200-kilometre loop known as the Quilotoa Loop.

● **Reserva Faunística Cuyabeno** Though the ravages of oil development mean it's generally not as pristine as similar regions in Peru or Bolivia, Ecuador's Amazon lowland region – known as the Oriente – is fairly easily accessible from the highlands, making it an easy place to experience the Amazon rainforest. The best place to head for is the wildlife-rich Reserva Faunística Cuyabeno, in the northern Oriente, which you can visit on an organized tour from the oil town of Lago Agrio or by staying with one of several indigenous Amazonian communities that accept visitors.

● **Cuenca** Set amid the gentler mountain scenery of the southern Sierra, Cuenca is Ecuador's most captivating city, graced with elegant colonial architecture including glorious churches and monasteries. It's also within easy striking distance of the ruins of Ingapirca, Ecuador's only major Inca site, as well as the starkly beautiful wilderness of Parque Nacional El Cajas, which offers excellent hiking and trout fishing.

● **Parque Nacional Machalilla** Away from the unappealing industrial port cities of Guayaquil and Esmeraldas,

Ecuador's varied Pacific coastline is lined with some glorious beaches, dense mangrove swamps and peaceful Afro-Ecuadorian fishing villages, and several lively resort towns. One of the coastal highlights is Parque Nacional Machalilla, northeast of Guayaquil, which combines stunning unspoiled beaches, pristine tropical forests and, on the offshore Isla de la Plata, an inexpensive alternative to the Galápagos for viewing boobies, frigate birds and albatrosses.

Also recommended

● **Parque Nacional Cotopaxi**
Surrounding the perfectly symmetrical cone of Volcán Cotopaxi – at 5897m the highest active volcano in the world – the beautiful Parque Nacional Cotopaxi is Ecuador's most popular mainland park, with numerous hiking trails, campsites and mountain refuges that make it easy to explore the pristine ecology and stark landscape of the high Andean grassland or Paramo. Even if you've little or no technical mountain-climbing experience, if you're fit and acclimatized you can reach the summit with a guide.

● **Baños** With a warm, subtropical climate and a spectacular setting amid lush green hills streaked with waterfalls, the tranquil spa town of Baños is deservedly popular with Ecuadorian and foreign tourists alike. It's a good base for hiking, horse riding, mountain biking and whitewater rafting in the surrounding mountains, after which you can relax in the natural thermal baths that gave the town its name. Check the latest information before travelling here, however, as Volcán Tungurahua, which towers above the town, has been particularly active in recent years.

● **Otavalo's market** Every Saturday the Andean town of Otavalo, to the north of Quito, hosts one of South America's most famous and colourful indigenous markets, where locals from the surrounding mountains come to sell their beautiful textiles. With their proud indigenous heritage and highly distinctive costumes – the men in black ponchos and ponytails, the women in elaborately embroidered white blouses – the Otavalo Indians themselves are a major attraction. But it's their excellent marketing sense and skilled handiwork that make the market a real draw. Quite touristy, but still a great place to pick up a poncho, jumper or handmade musical instrument.

● **El Nariz del Diablo train ride** From the pleasant city of Riobamba in the Central Sierra, a dramatic train line runs down to the village of Sibambe, zigzagging down a near-vertical wall of rock known as El Nariz del Diablo – "The Devil's Nose".

● **Vilcabamba** Set in an idyllic valley surrounded by crumpled mountains, the village of Vilcabamba first came to international attention in the 1950s, when it was hailed as the "Valley of Eternal Youth" after researchers claimed its inhabitants enjoyed unusually long life spans, with many living well over a hundred years. These days, it's an archetypal gringo hangout popular for its beautiful scenery and laid-back atmosphere, as well as for the widely available – and highly illegal – hallucinogenic San Pedro cactus. It's also a good base for exploring the cloudforests of the nearby Parque Nacional Podocarpus.

Routes in and out

Quito and the coastal city of Guayaquil are served by regular flights from most major South American capitals, several cities in the US, and Amsterdam and Madrid in Europe. The main land crossing with Colombia is at Tulcán on the Pan-American Highway north of Quito. For Peru, the main border crossing is at Huaquillas on the southern coast; if you're heading to or from the highlands, it's much more convenient to cross the border at Macará in the Southern Sierra – you can travel on this route on direct buses between the southern Ecuadorian city of Loja and Piura in Peru. Following the resolution in 1998 of a long-standing border dispute with Peru it is – in theory at least – possible to cross the border at Nuevo Rocafuerte in the Oriente, travelling by irregular riverboat along the Río Napo – check with the immigration authorities and the Peruvian Embassy in Quito, however, before attempting this rarely travelled route.

Itineraries

One week

● Spend a couple of days in Quito, including if possible a day-trip to Otavalo for the Saturday market, then head south into the Central Sierra through the Avenue of the Volcanoes, stopping off in whichever town that has a market day coinciding with your trip and hiking for a day or two in the Parque Nacional Cotopaxi. Finally, continue south to take the Nariz del Diablo train ride from Riobamba.

Two weeks

● Spend the first week or so in Quito and the northern and central highlands, taking in Otavalo market if possible and visiting Cotopaxi and the Avenue of the Volcanoes. Then either head down to Lago Agrio in the Oriente by road and spend three or four days visiting the rainforests of the Cuyabeno Reserve on an organized tour or staying in a jungle

lodge, or stay in the highlands and continue south to visit Riobamba, Baños and Cuenca.

One month

● A month is long enough to take in all of Ecuador's main attractions. After a few days in and around Quito head across to the Oriente to visit the Amazon rainforests of Parque Nacional Cuyabeno. Return to the capital, and then wend your way south through the highlands to Cuenca, taking in the Avenue of the Volcanoes, Cotopaxi, Baños and the Nariz del Diablo train ride from Riobamba. From Cuenca, head down to the southern coast to visit Machalilla National Park, then north along the coast and back up to Quito. That should leave you time to fly to the Galápagos Islands and take a week-long cruise around the archipelago. If the Galápagos is outside your budget, take more time to explore the Southern Sierra, perhaps visiting Vilcabamba, or take in one or two of the beach resorts west of Esmeraldas as you head up the coast.

Ecuador online

Ecuador Explorer
Ⓦ www.ecuadorexplorer.com Excellent tourist information site with plenty of background on Ecuador's main attractions, practical advice for travellers, and details of an extensive range of tour operators and hotels.
Ecuaworld
Ⓦ www.ecuaworld.com Another general tourism site offering a fine introduction to the country and plenty of useful information including latest travel news and weather.
Galápagos Islands
Ⓦ www.darwinfoundation.org Website of the Charles Darwin Research Station

on Isla Santa Cruz, with masses of information on the ecology and biology of the Galápagos, the latest conservation and research news, details on volunteering opportunities, and good links to related sites.

Volcanoes
Ⓦ **vulcan.wr.usgs.gov/Volcanoes /Ecuador/framework.html**
Comprehensive links to sites with information and photos of Ecuador's major volcanoes.

El Salvador

Capital San Salvador
Population 6.2 million
Languages Spanish, Nahua
Currency US dollar ($)
Climate Tropical on the coast and temperate in the highlands with two distinct seasons, rainy (May–Oct) and dry (Nov–April)
When to go November to April
Minimum daily budget US$15

El Salvador is the smallest country in Central America, the most densely populated and one of the least visited, largely as a result of the violent civil war which raged from 1980 to 1992, and whose memory still colours outside perceptions of the country. Even now, a decade after the end of the conflict, the country is struggling to rebuild itself, a process which wasn't helped by the series of massive earthquakes which devastated the coastal and central regions of the country in 2001, during which a thousand people died and 145,000 homes were destroyed, leaving the country with a clean-up bill of US$2.8 billion – a sum which El Salvador can ill afford.

Nevertheless, El Salvador is a beautiful place, a land of mountain peaks and rolling green hills studded with no fewer than 25 volcanoes, not to mention a long swathe of palm-fringed beaches on the Pacific – one of the loveliest stretches of coastline in the region. Salvadorans, though sometimes initially wary of foreigners (particularly if you're North American), are known throughout

△ Cattle returning from grazing, Suchitoto

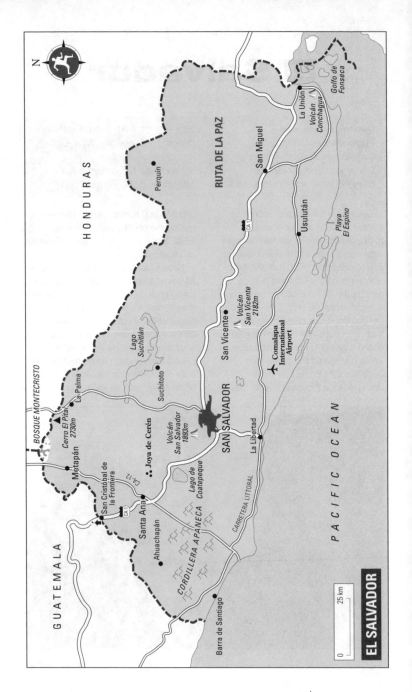

EL SALVADOR

N

GUATEMALA

HONDURAS

BOSQUE MONTECRISTO

Cerro El Pital
2730m

La Palma

Metapán

San Cristóbal de
la Frontera

Santa Ana

Ahuachapán

CA-12

Joya de Cerén

Volcán
San Salvador
1883m

Lago de
Coatepeque

CORDILLERA APANECA

Barra de Santiago

Lago
Suchitlán

Suchitoto

SAN SALVADOR

La Libertad

CARRETERA LITORAL

Perquín

San Vicente

Volcán
San Vicente
2182m

Comalapa
International
Airport

RUTA DE LA PAZ

San Miguel

Usulután

La Unión

Volcán
Conchagua

Golfo de
Fonseca

Playa
El Espino

CA 1

PACIFIC OCEAN

EL SALVADOR

0   25 km

Central America for their wry humour, vivacity and industriousness, and if you do venture into the country, you'll have the advantage of being one of the very few foreign tourists there: apart from a small surfing community at La Libertad, El Salvador remains almost unvisited.

Not surprisingly given its recent past, there's little tourist infrastructure, although a government-run network of *turicentros* – largely patronized by locals on holiday rather than by foreign visitors – at least provides basic eating and camping facilities in some places of particular natural beauty. And public transport, in the form of Bluebird buses, is incredibly cheap and well organized. Otherwise, there's a shortage of decent budget accommodation and almost no nightlife to speak of, while security is also a concern – extreme levels of poverty (a quarter of the population lives on less than US$1 a day) have led to rising levels of crime, particularly in the frenetic capital, San Salvador.

Main attractions

• **Suchitoto** Set amidst beautiful rolling countryside on the shores of Lago de Suchitlán, Suchitoto (the Nahuatl name means "city of birds and flowers") is the finest colonial town in the country, with low, red-tiled adobe houses, a tranquil and friendly atmosphere, and stunning views over the lake – an idyllic spot to swim and fish. Those interested in local culture should visit the decidedly eccentric Museo de Alejandro Cotto, which is housed in a restored colonial mansion with a beautiful garden overlooking the lake and displays collections of local paintings, indigenous artefacts and musical instruments.

• **Bosque Montecristo** The remote and pristine Bosque Montecristo "El Trifinio" straddles the borders between El Salvador, Honduras and Guatemala. The reserve rises through two climatic zones to its peak at Cerro Montecristo (2418m), surrounded by an expanse of virgin cloudforest home to orchids, huge oak and cypress trees, monkeys, jaguars and quetzals.

• **Pacific beaches** El Salvador has a long sweep of undeveloped Pacific coastline, with palm-fringed beaches, dramatic cliffs, mangrove swamps and unspoilt islands. Two of the prettiest beaches are Playa El Espino, towards the border with Honduras, and Playa Barra de Santiago, in the far west; both have a basic range of places to stay – Paradise in Central America in Barra de Santiago is the only upmarket choice – and eat. The coast's main settlement is the rather shabby fishing town of La Libertad, which has plenty of budget accommodation and café life catering to visiting surfers – beaches on both sides of the town have good, uncrowded waves.

• **Islas del Golfo de Fonseca** In the sheltered bay which straddles the coastal El Salvador–Honduras border, these four islands are secluded, peaceful and have calm seas for swimming and uncrowded hiking trails. The largest, Meanguera, has a small hotel and *comedores* (dining halls) in the local village serve fresh seafood.

• **Lago de Coatepeque** This stunning crater lake lies in the west of the country, shadowed by the volcanic peaks of Cerro Verde, Santa Ana and Izalco. The lake's deep blue waters are fed by hot springs and ringed by walking trails offering panoramic views over lush green slopes. Access to the water is easiest if you stay in one of a couple pleasant lakeside accommodation options – the best of these is a hostel, the *Amacuilco*, which has attractive dormitories and double rooms with an informal, party atmosphere.

Also recommended

- **Ahuachapán and the Cordillera Apaneca** Ahuachapán, close to the Guatemalan border, was one of the first Spanish settlements in El Salvador and is now a comfortably bourgeois city with quiet streets, a lively market and several attractive churches. The surrounding area, the Cordillera Apaneca, is studded with mountain peaks laced with pine forest and coffee plantations, which are at their most picturesque when their white flowers blossom in May.

- **Santa Ana** El Salvador's second city is a relaxing place with some lovely colonial architecture and a magnificent neo-Gothic cathedral. Set in the verdant Cihautehuacán valley, the city is close to three volcanoes, including the highest in the country, Volcán Santa Ana (2365m).

- **Ruta de la Paz** Part of a major project to develop tourism in the northeast of El Salvador, the so-called Ruta de la Paz ("Peace Route") encompasses a beautifully mountainous region dotted with small villages and a series of caves with pre-Columbian wall art.

- **La Palma** Known throughout El Salvador for its naif and brightly coloured *artesenia* (arts and crafts), La Palma is a sleepy mountain town with wooded outskirts and several excellent hiking trails – the most adventurous of these, to the summit of Cerro Pital, the country's highest peak, takes several days.

- **Mariscada** *Mariscada* is El Salvador's finest dish – a creamy seafood soup packed with lobster, crab and white fish – and is best eaten on the coast, in La Libertad. Oceanfront restaurants *Punta Roca* and *Sandra*'s fight it out for the best *mariscada* in the country and are consequently packed with Salvadoreño families, many on a day out from the city, at the weekend.

Routes in and out

There are flights daily to San Salvador from various cities in the US, including Los Angeles, Miami, Houston and New York, as well as daily flights from all the other Central American capitals and Mexico City. There are no direct connections from Europe or Australasia. You can cross overland into Guatemala at La Hachadura, near the Pacific (which is used by international buses heading to Mexico and is closest to Guatemala's Western Highlands); Las Chinamas, an hour from Ahuachapán, which has buses to Guatemala City; and, if you're visiting the Montecristo cloudforest, Anguiatú, which has connections to Esquipulas. The main crossings between El Salvador and Honduras are at El Amatillo, on the Panamerican Highway, and at El Poy in the north.

Itineraries

One week

- From Guatemala, cross the border to San Cristóbal and head south to the mellow city of Santa Ana for a few days, making day-trips to Lago de Coatepeque and its surrounding volcanoes before moving on to the Pacific coast.

- From Honduras, enter El Salvador and travel the pretty Ruta de la Paz. Then loop eastwards to San Salvador and make day-trips to the Maya ruins at Joya de Cerén and the colonial lakeside town of Suchitoto before finishing your week by the sea at La Libertad – the airport is close by.

- From El Salvador's airport go directly to the coast and, after a couple of days relaxing, head west to Guatemala via Santa Ana with a trip to the Lago de Coatepeque and its surrounding volcanoes and a stopover in Ahuachapán.

Two weeks

● Two weeks is long enough to visit all the country's main attractions. From Guatemala go first to the Bosque Montecristo and then on to the relaxing cities of Santa Ana and Ahuachapán and their volcanoes. Take the seaside road to La Libertad and then head inland to Suchitoto and La Palma before going east to the highlands of the Ruta de la Paz. Then head down to the coast and the islands of the Golfo de Fonseca and across the border into Honduras.

El Salvador online

Committee in Solidarity with the People of El Salvador (CISPES)
Ⓦ**www.cispes.org** Website of a left-wing organization which supports the FMLN or Frente Farabundo Martí de Liberación Nacional, campaigns against the introduction of CAFTA (Central American Free Trade Agreement) and has some volunteer projects.
El Diario de Hoy
Ⓦ**www.elsalvado.com** Spanish-only website of the national daily paper, with local and international news, features and listings of cultural and sports events.
El Salvador Trade
Ⓦ**www.elsalvadortrade.com.sv** Trade-based website with useful general information, history, politics and places of interest.
Julio Murra Saca
Ⓦ**www.murrasaca.com /elsalvadorpictures.htm** Extensive photo gallery of El Salvador's most beautiful places, taken by eminent gastro-enterologist Julio Murra Saca.

Guatemala

Capital Guatemala City
Population 13 million
Languages Spanish, although
40 percent speak one of twenty
indigenous languages (most widely
Quiché, Cakchique, Kekchi, Mam,
Garífina and Xinca)

Currency US dollar ($)
Climate Hot and humid in the
lowlands; cooler in the highlands
When to go February to May
Minimum daily budget US$15

After decades of civil war, Guatemala
has in recent years transformed itself
into one of Central America's most
popular tourist destinations, drawing
visitors with its memorable natural
landscapes, outstanding archeological
sites and, especially, by the strength of
its indigenous Maya culture. Compared
to the overwhelmingly mestizo populations of other Central American
countries, Guatemala remains quintessentially Amerindian: almost half the
country's population is pure-blooded
Maya, speaking their own languages and
living in small rural communities which
have barely changed in centuries. The
strength of this culture is everywhere
apparent, most obviously in the colourful traditional costumes worn across
the highlands and in the country's
absorbing markets and riotous fiestas,
less obviously in the society and beliefs
which continue to sustain Guatemala's
indigenous communities in the face of
constant change and challenges to their
traditional way of life.

The strength and longevity of Maya
culture is also witnessed by Guatemala's
outstanding Maya ruins, including not
only Tikal, perhaps the single most
impressive archeological site in the
whole of Latin America, but also in

dozens of less well-known but intriguing sites, many of them atmospherically
buried in the pristine rainforests which
cover much of the country's eastern
lowlands.

Maya culture apart, Guatemala also
boasts some of Central America's
most memorable landscapes, from the
towering volcanoes which surround
magical Lago de Atitlán in the highlands
to the vast expanses of rainforest which
blanket much of the eastern part of
the country, the Petén. In addition,
Guatemala is home to Antigua, Central
America's loveliest and liveliest colonial
city, which is also one of several
excellent places in the country in which
to study Spanish.

Thankfully, Guatemala has now
largely shaken off its turbulent past
and put its long and bloody civil war
behind it. The country is relatively safe
to visit, although incidents of armed
robbery and even rape are still reported,
especially around Lago de Atitlán
– don't walk alone, especially at night.
In common with other Central American
countries, Guatemala's climate varies
between the temperate highlands
and the hot and sticky regions along
the coast and in the Petén. The rainy
season runs from May to October,

when jungle trails in the remoter parts of the country get very muddy.

Main attractions

● **Antigua** Formerly the capital of Guatemala, and probably the most beautiful colonial city in Central America, Antigua retains its tranquil atmosphere despite a vibrant gringo scene, based around the city's dozens of language schools. Dating back to the Spanish conquest, the city's Semana Santa (Easter Week) celebrations are the most extravagant in the country.

● **Lago de Atitlán** In the highlands, a hundred kilometres north of Guatemala City, Lago de Atitlán is hemmed in by

△ Temple in Tikal

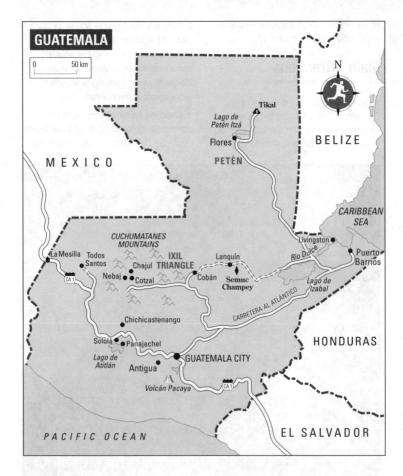

0 ____ 50 km

MEXICO

BELIZE

Tikal

Lago de Petén Itzá

Flores

PETÉN

CARIBBEAN SEA

Livingston

Río Dulce

Puerto Barrios

CUCHUMATANES MOUNTAINS

La Mesilla   Todos Santos   Chajul   **IXIL TRIANGLE**   Lanquín

Nebaj   Cotzal   Cobán   Semuc Champey

CA 1

Lago de Izabal

CARRETERA AL ATLÁNTICO

HONDURAS

Chichicastenango

Sololá   Panajachel

Lago de Atitlán   Antigua   ● GUATEMALA CITY

CA 1

Volcán Pacaya

PACIFIC OCEAN

EL SALVADOR

three soaring volcanoes and surrounded by a string of intriguing lakeside Maya villages, where traditional life continues more or less unchanged, despite the hordes of tourists who now descend on the lake. It's possible to walk round the lake in four or five days – the less energetic will also find plenty of day hikes, while boats regularly travel across the lake from village to village. Panajachel is the lake's principal community and the area's main base, with an abundance of cheap hotels and a long-established gringo scene.

● **Sololá market** Set high up on a hillside overlooking Lago de Atitlán, the village of Sololá is home every Friday to one of Central America's finest markets, with thousands of Maya traders in colourful woven clothes descending at dawn from the surrounding hills to sell their wares.

● **Tikal** Considered by many to be the finest of all Maya sites, the ruined city of

Tikal – which at its height around 500 AD was one of the most powerful and populous cities in the region – lies in the far east of the country, its ruined temples soaring majestically out of undisturbed rainforest which is home to monkeys, toucans and parakeets.

● **Volcán Pacaya** Just south of Guatemala City, Pacaya is one of Central America's most active and spectacular volcanoes, with dramatic night-time eruptions of molten orange lava. Pacaya is easily reached by public transport and has impressive views from its summit, which can be climbed in a day – but check on the volcano's current state of activity first.

● **Semuc Champey** Situated in the heart of Alta Verapaz, one of Guatemala's loveliest regions, Semuc Champey is a series of cool river pools with sparkling turquoise water hidden away in the forest. The nearby village of Lanquín has several cheap *pensiones* as well as the *El Retiro* lodge which has a picturesque river setting and a very popular bar.

Also recommended

● **Travelling along the Río Dulce** Starting in Lívingston on Guatemala's Caribbean coast, the spectacular journey along the Río Dulce passes through a steep, narrow gorge, hemmed in by sheer walls of tropical vegetation, before opening out into tranquil Lago de Izabal, which has some lovely beaches to swim from and boat trips around its shores.

● **Ixil triangle** Set in the verdant Cuchumatanes mountains at the northern edge of the Western Highlands, the remote Ixil region is one of the country's most traditional areas, whose Maya inhabitants speak a rare language and live much as their ancestors did centuries ago. The area has some

beautiful walking trails, while its three main towns – Nebaj, Chajul and Cotzal – are made of up picturesque white adobe houses and cobbled streets.

● **Celebrate the fiesta in Todos Santos** A famously traditional village in the Cuchumatanes mountains, isolated Todos Santos hosts a riotous annual fiesta on November 1 (All Saints or Todos Santos day) with all-day horse races, marimba music and relentless drinking.

● **Santo Tomás, Chichicastenango** The attractive small town of Chichicastenango is home both to a colourful indigenous (though touristy) market and also to one of Guatemala's most intriguing churches, Santo Tomás. Originally built in 1540 on the site of a Maya altar, the church offers a fascinating glimpse into the unique world of Maya religion, with its strange mix of indigenous and Catholic beliefs, incorporating in equal measure Christian saints and native shamans.

Routes in and out

There are direct daily flights to Guatemala City from cities in the US including Miami, Houston, Chicago and Los Angeles. Many travellers from Europe fly directly to Mexico City or Cancún and make their way overland. Travelling overland, Guatemala has frontiers with four countries – Mexico, Belize, Honduras and El Salvador. The border at Florido is conveniently close to the ruins of Copán in Honduras. A bus from Flores (near Tikal in the Petén) goes to Belize City and straight through Belize to the Mexican border town of Chetumal; there are numerous other border crossings between Guatemala and Mexico as well. The most popular crossing to El Salvador is at Asuncíon Mita on the Pan-American Highway.

Itineraries

One week

• Spend a few days in Antigua learning Spanish and then move on to Lago de Atitlán and climb one of the lakeside volcanoes or hike its periphery.

• From Honduras, cross into Guatemala on the Caribbean coast and travel upriver from Lívingston along the Río Dulce to Lago de Izabal. Continue from here by road to Tikal before moving on to Belize.

• From Guatemala City, head west to the Ixil triangle via the market towns of Sololá and Chichicastenango. Spend a few days hiking in the Cuchumatanes mountains, and then cross into Mexico at La Mesilla.

Two weeks

• From Antigua, go to Lago de Atitlán and spend five days walking round the lake. Then travel north to Tikal through Alta Verapaz and the stunning forest pools of Semuc Champey. After visiting Tikal explore the rainforests of the Petén and some of the lesser-known Maya sites nearby.

• Cross the border from Honduras at Corinto and go by boat to Lívingston. Take a trip down the Río Dulce and then travel by road to Tikal. From Tikal head south to Antigua and Lago de Atitlán and spend several days in each place. Visit the Ixil trangle for some trekking and then head west into Mexico.

One month

• From El Salvador, travel west to Antigua (you could stop for a week of Spanish study in one of the town's language schools), Lago de Atitlán and the market towns of Sololá and Chichicastenango. Loop back to Guatemala City for the main cross-country route to Río Dulce. Take a boat trip down the river to Livingston and back. Travel by road to Tikal and the Petén via Semuc Champay in Alta Verapaz before moving on to Belize.

Guatemala online

Guatemala Daily
Ⓦ www.guatemaladaily.com An English-language site providing all the latest news from Guatemala.

Guatemala Web
Ⓦ www.guatemalaweb.com Excellent website created by the owner of the *Posada Belén* hotel in Guatemala City, with articles and links on everything from visa requirements, the locations of cash machines, and the current government, to Guatemalan charities, festivals and cuisine.

Revue Magazine
Ⓦ www.revuemag.com English magazine based in Antigua with travel features mainly on Guatemala.

Siglo Veintiuno
Ⓦ www.sigloxxi.com The website of the daily newspaper, with crisp articles on domestic and foreign news and features on sport, culture and lifestyle.

The Guianas

Guyana
Capital Georgetown
Population 697,000
Languages Creole English, Hindi, Urdu
Currency Guyanese dollar (G$)
Climate Tropical – hot all year round, with two rainy seasons (Dec–Jan and April–July)
Best time to go February and March and August to November
Minimum daily budget US$20

Suriname
Capital Paramaribo
Population 405,000
Languages Dutch, Hindi, Javanese, Chinese
Currency Surinamese Guilder (Sf)
Climate As Guyana, above
Best time to go As Guyana, above
Minimum daily budget US$25

French Guiana
Capital Cayenne
Population 177,500
Languages French, Hindi, Chinese, some indigenous languages
Currency Euro (E)
Climate As Guyana, above
Best time to go As Guyana, above
Minimum daily budget US$45

Perched on the northern coast of South America, the three small countries known collectively as the Guianas (Guyana, Suriname and French Guiana) are the least visited in Latin America, with a complex blend of races and cultures unique to the region.

The three countries share an early history, all originally inhabited by Arawak and Carib peoples. In the sixteenth century, they were settled by the Dutch, English and French, rather than by the Spanish and Portuguese. Slaves were brought in from West Africa until slavery was abolished, after which indentured labourers were imported from other colonies, especially India and Indonesia. Today, Guyana and Suriname reflect this racial history with Creole, Hindi and Javanese spoken alongside the official languages, and temples and mosques almost as common as churches.

This is not the case in French Guiana, however, which is still a department of France – and the only remaining colony in mainland South America – with European living standards and prices to match. That said, it's only the urban areas that have the infrastructure, as well as what little French culture exists (notably restaurant cuisine).

Away from the coast – home to capital cities Georgetown, Paramaribo and Cayenne – all three countries comprise a largely unsettled wilderness, with vast tracts of unspoilt rainforest. (Suriname alone is said to contain more virgin jungle than almost all of Central America put together, and 85 percent of the country is classified as inaccessible.) Not surprisingly, ecotourism is beginning to take off in all three Guianas, and there are wonderful opportunities for wildlife spotting, trekking off the beaten track and bush camping – either in a spartan tent or at one of many swanky eco-lodges.

Infrastructure in the Guianas is still very basic and exploring these countries is not for the faint-hearted. Travelling might mean taking a horrendously bumpy truck journey on one of the few roads in existence or, more likely, an uncomfortable boat ride down one of many rivers. For the most part, the Guianas are relatively crime-free, with the exception of Georgetown, Guyana's capital – even during the day, some areas of the city are best avoided.

Main attractions

● **Kaieteur Falls (Guyana)** The Kaieteur waterfalls, situated on the upper Potaro River and surrounded by unspoilt forest, are one of the world's most spectacular, plunging down a sheer drop of 228m. Most people fly in on a day-trip from Georgetown – January, June and July are the best months to see the falls at their fullest.

● **Iwokrama Rainforest Programme (Guyana)** This 3880-square-kilometre conservation project is home to an exceptionally wide range of wildlife and is one of the best places in Latin America for spotting jaguars. You can also take guided treks through the forest to Mount Iwokrama and boat trips along the Burro-burro and Essequibo rivers.

● **Paramaribo (Suriname)** Suriname's lively capital is a melting pot of the country's diverse cultures – a wooden cathedral rubs shoulders with one of the biggest mosques in the Caribbean, with several Hindu temples nearby. There's some fine Dutch colonial architecture to boot, while on Sundays you can witness the unusual spectacle of the locals taking their pet birds to Independence

Square for the weekly birdsong competition.

● **Central Suriname Nature Reserve (Suriname)** This 1.6 million hectare rainforest park was formed in 1998 and is one of the most remote parts of the Amazon rainforest accessible – just about - to tourists. The area includes the Coppename River and the Voltzberg peak, which is usually climbed at sunrise for spectacular views. It's best to take an organized tour – these usually include a visit to indigenous villages and rapids in the area – since the park is hard to reach otherwise.

● **Plage les Hattes (French Guiana)** A few kilometres from the Suriname border, at the mouth of the Maroni River, is arguably the best of the Guianas' turtle-nesting spots, Plage les Hattes. The beach is home to an abundance of the most impressive species of turtle, the leatherback. Affordable accommodation is plentiful, and reaching the beach – four kilometres from the nearest town – is relatively easy.

● **Îles de Salut (French Guiana)** These tiny islands were the location of the notorious penal colonies which Henri Charrière made famous in *Papillon*. Popular with visitors because of their atmospheric ruins, they also have abundant wildlife and wild, palm-fringed beaches.

Also recommended

● **Bartica (Guyana)** The most enjoyable of Guyana's towns as well as its oldest settlement, Bartica is situated on the confluence of the Essequibo, Mazuruni and Cuyuni rivers. Its rowdy atmosphere – with a preponderance of bars and nightclubs – is in no small part due to the miners and lumberjacks who populate the town

but they are an extremely friendly and engaging bunch.

● **Lethem (Guyana)** In the far southwest of Guyana, Lethem is the gateway to a number of wildlife adventures and several of the country's best eco-lodges. Here, the Rupununi savannah, a large area of flat grassland, has great bird-spotting; there are waterfalls at Moco-Moco; and the Amerindian villages of Annai and Surama have set up ecotourism projects that take visitors on night trekking, boating and Land Rover trips. The town itself is friendly and hosts a rodeo at Easter which attracts cowboys from all over the savannah.

● **Surinamese food** Suriname's food is richly varied, showing a range of culinary influences that mirrors the country's history, with Indonesian dishes such as *bami goreng* (fried noodles) served up alongside Indian rotis and samosas and West Indian-inspired *pinda soep* (peanut soup with plantain dumplings).

● **Centre Spatial Guyanais (French Guiana)** Kourou is the location for a large space station that houses the European Space Agency's Ariane programme. With advance reservations, it's possible to tour the site which is as impressive as NASA's site in Florida and a surreal sight with rocket launch towers and state-of-the-art technology rising out of the dense jungle. If you write for an invitation it's also possible to watch one of the bi-monthly rocket launches which are best seem from one of Kourou's official observation points.

● **Carnival (French Guiana)** Carnival in French Guiana is Afro-Caribbean in style, with four days of unique and colourful parades, including Lundi Gras, which mocks the institution of marriage with men dressed as brides and women as grooms, and Mardi Gras, the next day, which sees locals dressed as devils in red outfits with horns and pitchforks.

Routes in and out

There are daily flights to Guyana from both New York and Miami; from Europe you'll have to go via Antigua, Port of Spain or Barbados in the Caribbean. To Suriname, there are direct flights from Amsterdam several times a week, as well as from Miami, Port of Spain and Curaçao in the Dutch Antilles. There are daily flights to French Guiana from Paris, Guadeloupe and Martinique, plus four times weekly from Miami.

It's not possible to travel by land between Guyana and Venezuela. Border crossings between the Guianas are complicated and because smuggling is rife, you may be checked several times – many tourists prefer to fly from one capital to another. Between Guyana and Brazil there's just one remote border crossing by ferry near Lethem in the Rupununi savannah (not always accessible in the rainy season). Between Guyana and Suriname, a ferry runs from Corriverton to Niew Nickerie, both coastal towns. Suriname and French Guiana are connected by frequent ferries from Albina to St Laurent-du-Maroni and a good connecting road to Cayenne. To reach Brazil from French Guiana, you'll need to hire a motorized canoe to take you across the Oiapoque river (15min) from St-Georges de L' Oiapoque (which is only accessible by plane from Cayenne) to Oiapoque and onto Macapá – it's much easier to fly all the way.

Itineraries

One week

● **Guyana** (dry season only) Take a truck from Georgetown to Lethem in the Rupununi savann ah and then on to the Iwokrama Rainforest Programme, returning to Georgetown by air. Alternatively, use the capital as a base for day-trips to the Kaieteur Falls or an overnight stay at Bartica.

△ Café, Cayenne, French Guiana

- **Suriname** Soak up the atmosphere of *Carnaval* in Paramaribo and then recover at the Central Suriname Nature Reserve.

- **French Guiana** From Cayenne, go west to Kourou, tour the space station and then take a boat to the Îles de Salut or a bus to Plage les Hattes.

Two weeks

- After a week in Guyana (see above) cross into Suriname and go from Paramaribo to the Central Suriname Nature Reserve.

- Another two-week option worth considering is to start your fortnight in Paramaribo, explore the interior of Suriname and then go south to Cayenne in French Guiana and follow the itinerary above.

One month

- In a month it's possible to visit the main attractions of all three Guianas and then either fly north to Venezuela from Georgetown or head down into the Brazilian Amazon overland.

The Guianas online

French Guiana
Ⓦ**www.terresdeguyane.fr/guyane** & Ⓦ**www.outremer.com/gf/guyindex .htm** Both websites, in French only, have useful tourist information as well as news, history, politics and culture.

Guyana: Land of Six Peoples
Ⓦ**www.landofsixpeoples.com** Comprehensive and informative, with articles on Guyanese history, society, politics, economics and ethnography.

Guyana News and Information
Ⓦ**www.guyana.org** Large US-based website with an emphasis on politics and diplomatic issues, and good links to business, sport and tourism websites.

Guyana Outpost
Ⓦ**www.guyanaoutpost.com** Lovingly maintained website of Guyanan Wayne Moses, with a comprehensive list of features, news items, recipes, folkloric stories, bookshop and useful information for tourists.

Suriname: Parbo
Ⓦ**www.parbo.com** Based in Suriname's capital, Paramaribo, the website also has useful tourist information on other areas of the country. Mostly in English with some Dutch.

Honduras

Capital Tegucigalpa
Population 5.6 million
Languages Spanish, Creole
English, Garífuna
Currency Lempira (L)
Climate Subtropical in the lowlands
and temperate in the mountains;
the rainy season runs from May to
November, while hurricane season is
in October and November
When to go March to May
Minimum daily budget US$15

Honduras is the original Banana Republic. From the late 1800s until the 1950s it was largely run by powerful US fruit companies who controlled not only the national banana trade (which accounted for no less than seventy percent of the country's foreign exports), but also its railways, banks and factories. The US influence lasted well into the twentieth century – while neighbouring El Salvador and Nicaragua suffered years of civil war, Honduras infamously served as the training ground for CIA-funded counter-revolutionaries, and was consequently kept stable by US investment and support throughout the 1980s. Nevertheless, it remains one of Latin America's poorest nations, one of its least developed and least visited.

In October 1998, Hurricane Mitch ripped through Central America, causing most of its destruction in Honduras, where it killed seven thousand people. Large parts of the capital, Tegucigalpa, were flattened and the river valleys of the western highlands turned into rivers of mud. Although international aid and experts helped to repair much of the damage, Honduras spent years reeling from the aftershock, with widespread poverty and soaring levels of street crime. However in recent years, the government of Ricardo Maduro has made strenuous efforts to bring order to the country, with some small success.

Geographically, Honduras boasts similar terrain – a cool, mountainous interior fringed by a humid Caribbean coastline – to neighbouring Guatemala and Nicaragua. Much of the country is protected by an extensive network of national parks and reserves, including the eastern cloudforest of Sierra de Agalta and the Río Plátano Biosphere Reserve in the remote wetlands of Mosquitia, which protect two of the largest stretches of pristine forest in Central America. The country is also sparsely populated, with fewer inhabitants than El Salvador despite being five times as large, while foreign tourists are also pretty thin on the ground – if you go to Honduras you'll have the place pretty much to yourself, apart from at the backpacker hot spots of Copán and the Bay Islands.

The bad news is that Honduras isn't the safest country in Central America – you'll need to be particularly careful in the Caribbean towns – Tela, La Ceiba, Trujillo – after dark, while the country's second city, San Pedro Sula, is now very dangerous, with rife crack cocaine usage and gang warfare. You should also avoid walking on deserted beaches. Honduras

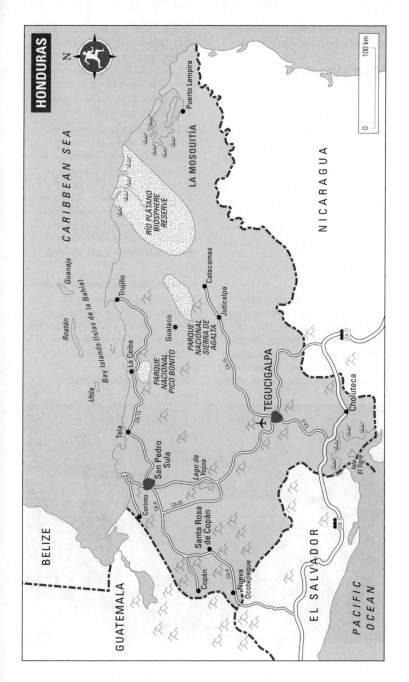

is, however, very cheap, with daily costs among the lowest in Latin America.

Main attractions

- **Copán** Copán is one of the most impressive of all Maya sites. Although not large – it's dwarfed in scale by Tikal and Chichén Itzá – the site boasts some of the Maya region's most magnificently carved sculptures, as well as the remarkable Hieroglyphic Stairway. There's also the outstanding on-site Museum of Maya Sculpture, featuring a full-scale replica of the stunning Rosalia Temple, along with many original sculptures from the Copán valley. The nearby town, Copán Ruinas, is an attractive and relaxing place to spend a few days.

- **Bay Islands** Honduras's biggest draw comprises three small Caribbean islands set on a coral reef. The scuba diving is superb and the Bay Islands' calm turquoise waters have become a mecca for divers, with some of the world's cheapest scuba courses on offer.

Utila is the most popular of the islands with backpackers and has a firmly entrenched gringo party scene with the occasional rave and regular full-moon parties. The largest island, Roatán, is much quieter, with good hiking trails and more upmarket accommodation.

- **Río Plátano Biosphere Reserve, La Mosquitía** Northeast Honduras is covered with remote and marshy wetlands, known as La Mosquitia after the Miskito Indians who still inhabit it. La Mosquitia is rarely visited – you'll have to fly in – but is home to the most significant nature reserve in Honduras, the Río Plátano Biosphere Reserve, which hosts eighty percent of the country's animal species.

- **Parque Nacional Sierra de Agalta** In the eastern Olancho region of Honduras, the Parque Nacional Sierra de Agalta protects a vast area of pristine and rarely visited cloudforest home to many rare animals including tapirs, jaguars and ocelots, as well as over 400 species of birds, including no

△ The Hieroglyphic Stairway, Copán

fewer than 33 different kinds of hummingbird alone.

● **Garífuna villages** Surrounding Tela on the Caribbean coast is a string of sleepy villages with palm-thatched huts which are populated by friendly Garífuna people – the descendants of African slaves brought to the Caribbean to work on banana plantations. Weekends are the best time to visit, when you'll have the chance to hear the seductive drum rhythms of Garífuna music performed by local musicians.

Also recommended

● **Nightlife in Tela and La Ceiba** These two Caribbean towns are home to the country's wildest nightlife, with vibrant dancehalls, patronized both by locals and foreign tourists, which churn out Garífuna punta rock music, reggae and Latin sounds. The best time to visit is during La Ceiba's carnival in May, during which 200,000 revellers descend on the town and dance until dawn.

● **Lago de Yojoa** Set among the mountains and coffee plantations of Honduras's western highlands, the expansive Lago de Yojoa boasts sparkling blue water and hundreds of bird species. Busy at weekends with wealthy Hondureños, during the week the lake is calm and peaceful.

● **Parque Nacional Pico Bonito** South of La Ceiba, the Parque Nacional Pico Bonito protects a remote expanse of broadleaf, cloud- and pine forests that's crisscrossed by twenty rivers and dominated by the dramatic peak of Pico Bonito (2435m). There is an abundance of wildlife – including armadillos, monkeys and pumas, while the Río Cangrejal has some of the best Class

III and IV rapids for whitewater rafting in Central America.

Routes in and out

There are direct international flights daily from the US (Miami and Houston) to Tegucigalpa, as well as to Honduras's second city, San Pedro Sula, and Roatán. There are no direct flights from Europe or Australasia. The most popular and useful overland border crossing into Guatemala is at El Florido (close to Copán), though there are several others; you can also cross overland from Honduras into El Salvador and Nicaragua. A weekly boat goes from the Caribbean town of Puerto Cortés to Belize; you may also be able to find a boat leaving from one of Honduras's Caribbean towns to Puerto Cabezas in Nicaragua. Large groups might be able to charter a boat from Omoa to Lívingston in Guatemala.

Itineraries

One week

● Travel from the capital Tegucigalpa to tranquil Lago de Yojoa. From here, continue towards Guatemala via Copán and its pretty village, Copán Ruinas.

● Cross the border from Guatemala to Corinto and then down the Caribbean coast to the lively coastal towns of Tela and La Ceiba. Make a day-trip to Parque Nacional Pico Bonito and then take a boat to the Bay Islands.

Two weeks

● From Copán and Copán Ruinas travel to Lago de Yojoa. Go eastwards via the capital, Tegucigalpa, to the Parque Nacional Sierra de Agalta and then north to La Mosquitia and the Río Plátano Biosphere Reserve.

- Cross the border from Nicaragua and travel on to Tegucigalpa. From here, fly to Mosquitia and then on to La Ceiba and the Caribbean coast before heading out to the Bay Islands for a week's scuba diving.

Three weeks

- In three weeks you can visit all the highlights of Honduras. Travelling from Guatemala, cross the border at El Florido for Copán and then head on to Lago de Yojoa. From Tegucigalpa, head north to La Mosquitia. Fly from here to La Ceiba, visit Telą and the Garífuna villages before taking a boat to the Bay Islands.

Honduras online

Country of Honduras
Ⓦ**www.honduras.com** Extensive website with general and travel information and essays on culture and history.

Honduras This Week
Ⓦ**www.marrder.com/htw** Award-winning website of the English-language newspaper, with national news coverage, tourist information and listings.

Honduras Tips
Ⓦ**www.hondurastips.honduras.com** Website of the free magazine, which has useful tourist information divided into regions and includes town maps marked with hotels and restaurants.

In-Honduras.com
Ⓦ**www.in-honduras.com** Comprehensive portal with hundreds of links to media, arts and entertainment, political and tourist websites – and also to personal websites featuring the travel journals of people who have visited Honduras.

Mexico

Capital Mexico City
Population 100 million
Languages Spanish and various indigenous languages, including Maya languages and Nahuatl
Currency Peso ($)
Climate Varies widely, from tropical to desert, with most of the country having two distinct seasons, wet (June–Sept) and dry (Oct–April)
Best time to go November to February
Minimum daily budget US$20–30 (depending on whether you visit major tourist resorts or not)

Mexico is overwhelmingly the most visited country in Latin America and has been for many years. Yet in spite of the steady influx of tourists and the large modern resorts and sophisticated facilities erected to cater to them, much of this large country remains steadfastly traditional, with daily life continuing as it has done over hundreds of years. The resulting culture is one that has had a powerful effect in shaping outside perceptions of what Latin America is like. Even those who don't know anything about the region probably will have seen poncho-clad Mexican cowboys at the movies, will have tasted the country's spicy, chilli-based cuisine, and perhaps will have heard the unmistakeable strains of mariachi music – all clichés, but all still very much part of Mexican life.

Even so, while to the rest of the Western world Mexico seems to embody all that's most Latin in Latin America, the country does have an identity all its own. Geographically, it's the only Latin American country in North America, and it has strong ties with that region, both historic – Texas and California were both once part of Mexico – and modern, through the North American Free Trade Agreement and the fact that so many Mexicans go to the US to work, often illegally. It's partly this dichotomy – between the desire for US-style consumerism and material prosperity on the one hand, and traditional Latin American values on the other – which lends the country so much of its particular character.

For visitors, however, it's the longevity and diversity of Mexican culture that's likely to make the strongest impression. It is home to two of the greatest of Latin America's pre-conquest civilizations, the Aztec and Maya, as well as countless others, and the country's indigenous populations – among them Maya, Mixtec, Zapotec – live much as they have done for hundreds of years, speaking their own languages and cultivating their land in the same way as their forebears did. The monuments of these ancient cultures can be seen everywhere – at the great Maya sites of Chichén Itzá, Uxmal and Palenque (to mention only the most famous) in the Yucatán; at the Zapotec sites of Monte Albán, Yagul and Mitla in Oaxaca state; and at the majestic Aztec sites of Tenochtitlán and Teotihuacán, in and close to present-day Mexico City. The country also boasts one of Latin

America's richest legacies of colonial architecture, including florid churches and perfectly preserved cities, ranging from the Zócalo (main plaza) in Mexico City to the picturesque silver-mining towns to the north. All of which offers the visitor a heady mix of cultures – Mexico City, for instance, boasts Aztec ruins, atmospheric Spanish-colonial architecture and ultra-modern architecture within the space of a few miles.

Geographically, too, Mexico offers an embarassment of riches, from the arid canyons and cactus-strewn badlands of the north to the tropical rainforests of the south – not to mention the thousands of kilometres of Pacific and Caribbean coastline, dotted with beach resorts ranging from brash Cancún on the Gulf of Mexico (from where it's a short trip out to the world's second longest barrier reef) to the somnolent

△ Tortilla vendor, Puebla

Bahía Concepción on the wild peninsula of Baja California.

Mexico's comparatively well-developed economy means that the country has a good infrastructure, with decent roads and public transport. There are many holiday resorts on both coasts, and accommodation is widespread and of every conceivable type. Costs vary enormously between established tourist resorts where they are relatively high and traditional inland regions where they remain low. Most of Mexico is safe to travel in, with the inevitable exception of Mexico City – take care at night.

Main attractions

● **Mexico City** The country's capital and the world's second largest city (with a staggering 19 million inhabitants), Mexico City sits at the spiritual and geographical heart of Mexico and is a fascinating blend of pre-Columbian, colonial and modern architecture and culture. Its long list of attractions includes the impressive colonial Zócalo, the world-famous Museo Nacional de Antropología, and Diego Rivera's celebrated murals of historic events, not to mention fascinating markets and frenetic street life.

● **Oaxaca** Some 500km southeast of Mexico City, Oaxaca is a colonial town of enduring charm in one of the country's most traditional regions. The city's main square is famously atmospheric, with live music in the evenings and local Zapotec and Mixtec Indians in indigenous costumes selling textiles, accessories and brightly coloured *faldas* (skirts made of striped woven cloth) and *huipiles* (embroidered blouses). Don't miss the lavish gilded interior of the Santo Domingo church or the Saturday market for locally made shawls, leatherwork, pottery and (most notoriously) fried grasshoppers.

● **Guanajuato** To the north of Mexico City, in the fertile hills and valleys of the Bajío, are the country's finest colonial remnants, cities founded by the Spanish on the wealth brought by silver- and gold-mining. The most beautiful of these is Guanajuato, for centuries the wealthiest city in Mexico and declared a UNESCO World Heritage Site in 1988. A maze of steep narrow streets and leafy squares surrounded by the grand colonial mansions of the mine-owners, Guanajuato also has a unique network of subterranean streets running under the city. The city's most distinctive – though rather macabre – draw is the grotesque Museo de las Momías (mummy museum), which displays over a hundred mummified bodies, some, buried alive with "silent screaming" features and others with their burial clothes still intact. On a lighter note, visitors to Guanajuato enjoy the *callejoneadas*, walking tours led by student minstrel groups, and the city's superb café life.

● **Maya sites in the Yucatán** Much of Latin America's spectacular pre-Hispanic ruins can be found in Mexico. The best known of these are the Maya cities situated on the plains of the Yucatán Peninsula in the country's southeast along an easily travelled circuit known as the Ruta Maya. Chichén Itzá is the most impressive site with its vertiginous temple, snail-shaped observatory and distinctive reclining statues or Chaac-Mools. Calakmul, though only partly restored, is the largest ruined city in Mesoamerica with the base of its great pyramid covering five acres and the view from the highest temple extending, on a clear day, as far as Guatemala. The smaller site of Uxmal is celebrated for its decorative geometric style and stone mosaic friezes. Palenque, while not strictly in the Yucatán but rather in neighbour-

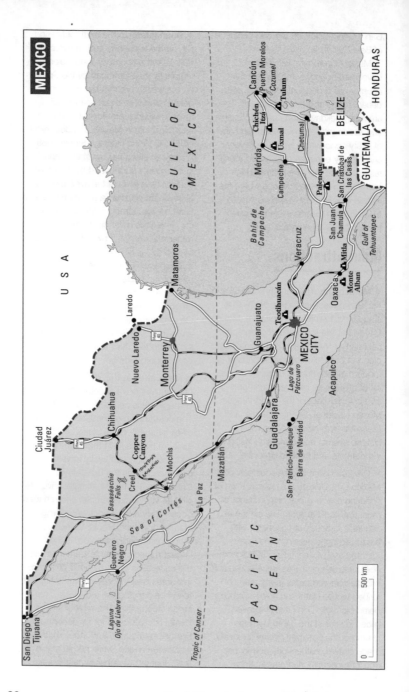

MEXICO

GULF OF MEXICO

USA

PACIFIC OCEAN

Sea of Cortés

Bahía de Campeche

Gulf of Tehuantepec

HONDURAS

BELIZE

GUATEMALA

San Diego
Tijuana

Ciudad Juárez

Guerrero Negro

Laguna Ojo de Liebre

La Paz

Chihuahua

Basaséachic Falls

Creel

Copper Canyon

Los Mochis

Mazatlán

Nuevo Laredo

Monterrey

Laredo

Matamoros

Guanajuato

Guadalajara

Lago de Pátzcuaro

San Patricio-Melaque
Barra de Navidad

Acapulco

MEXICO CITY

Teotihuacán

Veracruz

Oaxaca

Monte Albán

Mitla

San Juan Chamula

San Cristóbal de las Casas

Palenque

Campeche

Mérida

Uxmal

Chichén Itzá

Cancún
Puerto Morelos
Cozumel

Tulum

Chetumal

Tropic of Cancer

Hwy 45

Hwy 40

Hwy 40

500 km

0

ing Chiapas, has the loveliest setting, surrounded by jungle-clad hills.

● **Day of the Dead (Día de los Muertos)** Taking place annually on All Souls Day and its eve (November 1 & 2), this is the occasion for Mexicans to honour their dead family members and friends. Although a deeply religious ceremony, with all-night vigils held in cemeteries and shrines built in every home, it's also an incredibly picturesque event – papier-mâché skeletons, sweets shaped like skulls and banks of chrysanthemums abound. The place to aim for is the island of Janítzio in Lago de Pátzcuaro, 200km west of Mexico City. The night vigil here is particularly intense, with locals converging on the island by canoe as dusk falls, their boats each lit by a single candle.

● **The Yucatán's Caribbean coast** In the far southeast of the country, the Yucatán Peninsula's Caribbean coast offers long beaches of white sand and azure sea. Although much of the coast south of Cancún is being developed by large resorts, there are still pockets of relative tranquillity, like Puerto Morelos, Xpu-ha and Tulum. The "Riviera Maya", as this stretch of coast has been named by the Mexican Tourist Board, also fronts the world's second largest coral reef, which extends as far as Honduras and makes for breathtaking scuba diving and snorkelling. The otherwise nondescript island of Cozumel is a mecca for scuba diving, with a world-class series of drop-offs, walls and coral gardens.

● **Food and drink** Mexican food is celebrated worldwide for its fieriness and flavour. It is, naturally, much better in Mexico than the thousands of Mexican restaurants abroad which tend to serve an adulterated version, more Tex-Mex than the real thing. The country's imaginative cuisine ranges from street snacks of tacos (corn pancakes or

tortillas rolled around strips of meat or fish, and served with avocado dip and tomato salsa) to more refined dishes like *mole*, a classic sauce made from chilli and chocolate, all the way through to more outlandish offerings like *chapulines* or fried grasshoppers and maggots. The last two are not as unappetizing as you'd imagine – though they're still far from tasty – and Mexicans claim they're an excellent source of virility-enhancing protein. The country's drinks are no less irresistible, including the famous spirit, tequila. Mexican beer is excellent, too, with several brands of bottled lager (*cerveza clara*) and dark beer.

Also recommended

● **Whale watching in Baja California** During January and February, California gray whales arrive from Alaska to give birth in the relatively warm waters of the Laguna Ojo de Liebre, off the coast of Baja California. The scruffy town of Guerrero Negro serves as a base for Mexico's most memorable whale-watching excursions, which afford the chance to see up-close the newly born calves swimming calmly alongside their parents.

● **The train ride from Los Mochis to Chihuahua** The thirteen-hour train journey from the Pacific town of Los Mochis to Chihuahua is one of the most scenic in the Americas, crossing the Sierra Madre and offering breathtaking views over the 2000-metre deep Copper Canyon. The best stopping point for tourists keen to explore the area on foot is Creel, with its nearby canyons, pine forests and the Basaséachic Falls, claimed as North America's highest single cascade at 254m.

● **San Cristóbal de las Casas** San Cristóbal, at the centre of Chiapas state, is an attractive and relaxing mountain town with ample provincial and bohemian charm. There are a number of small museums and colonial churches to visit, an atmospheric local market and an abundance of attractive restaurants and places to stay in all price ranges. San Cristóbal also makes a perfect base for exploring the indigenous Maya communities which dot the surrounding hills, notably the nearby village of San Juan Chamula, whose famous church offers a rare insight into the unique forms of indigenous Christianity, with rituals and imagery drawn freely from both Catholicism and pre-conquest indigenous beliefs.

● **A tram ride through Campeche**
The capital of Campeche state, on the Yucatán Peninsula, is a lovely walled city with immaculately kept narrow streets and pastel-coloured houses. One of the best ways to see the city is on a picturesque tram ride – trams run along the seafront to the city's archeological museum, housed in an old fort, which includes jade death masks from the Calakmul Maya site among its treasures.

● **Bahía de Navidad** Directly west of Mexico City, Bahía de Navidad is one of the most beguiling stretches of Pacific coast in Mexico. Neither deserted nor overdeveloped, the entire length of the large bay is edged by fine sand and has two small communities, Barra de Navidad and San Patricio-Melaque, which are wholly Mexican in feel and great places to chill out.

Routes in and out

Mexico is one of the easiest countries in Latin America to reach, with daily flights from the US to a range of cities and resorts, including Mexico City, Cancún, Acapulco, Monterrey and Veracruz. There are also daily flights from Madrid to Mexico City

and Cancún, and thrice-weekly flights from London to Mexico City. By land there are dozens of border crossings between the US and Mexico, the most popular being between San Diego in California and Tijuana; El Paso in Texas and Ciudad Juárez; and Brownsville on the Gulf of Mexico and Matamóros. The most popular land frontiers between Mexico and Guatemala are from Tapachula to either Talismán or Tecun Umán on the Pacific coast of Guatemala. Hourly buses leave from Chetumal in southern Quintana Roo state to Corozal in Belize and on to Belize City. There are also several river crossings in northern Chiapas to the Petén region of Guatemala: Frontera Corozal–Bethel (30min by boat) and La Palma–El Naranjo (4hr) are the least complicated.

Suggested itineraries

One week
● Explore Mexico City, with a day-trip to the enormous pyramids of Teotihuacán, and then spend the weekend relaxing in laid-back Barra de Navidad on the central Pacific coast.

● From Cancún, visit the inland Maya ruins at Chichén Itzá and then head east to the island of Cozumel for the region's best scuba diving and snorkelling before moving on to Belize or returning to Cancún.

● Travel overland from Guatemala to San Cristóbal and then on to the Maya sites at Palenque, Uxmal and Chichén Itzá, before looping south again into Belize and to its offshore cayes.

Two weeks
● Travel south from the US border at San Diego to Baja California and take a ferry across the Sea of Cortez to

the mainland to connect with the train through the Copper Canyon. Head south for a few days relaxing on the Pacific coast, before moving on to Mexico City.

● Spend some time in Mexico City, then head north to Guanajuato before making your way across to the Pacific coast and Barra de Navidad for a few days' relaxation.

● Spend a fortnight on the Yucatán Peninsula visiting the attractive state capital, Campeche, and the Maya ruins at Chichén Itzá and Uxmal. End your trip relaxing on the Caribbean coast south of Cancún, from where you can easily head into Central America through Belize.

One month

● After a week in Mexico City take a bus to the Pacific coast and relax for several days in one of the smaller beach towns. Then travel on to Oaxaca and spend five days exploring the attractive market town and its surrounds. Travel south to Chiapas and visit the mountain town of San Cristóbal and the Maya ruins at Palenque. Spend a final week in the Yucatán Peninsula sunbathing on the Caribbean beaches and visiting the Maya sites of Uxmal and Chichén Itzá.

Then you can either fly out of Cancún or cross into Belize.

Mexico online

Exploring Colonial Mexico
ⓦ**www.colonial-mexico.com** A site run by Espadaña Press on colonial art and architecture with an excellent archive of photos and information on sites throughout Mexico.

Mexico Connect
ⓦ**www.mexconnect.com** Monthly e-zine providing information on all aspects of Mexico.

Mexico Travel Guide
ⓦ**www.go2mexico.com** Online travel guide with features and articles on culture, the environment and living in Mexico.

Mexicanwave
ⓦ**www.mexicanwave.com** Excellent English-language website with book reviews, articles on Mexican culture and life, shopping and links.

The News
ⓦ**www.thenews.com** Online version of the English-language daily, with news plus features on Mexican food, culture and travel.

Nicaragua

Capital Managua **Population** 4.9 million **Languages** Spanish, Creole English on the Caribbean coast, plus indigenous languages including Sumo, Rama and Miskito	**Currency** Córdoba (¢) **Climate** Tropical in the lowlands, cooler in the highlands; rainy season June to October **When to go** December to March **Minimum daily budget** US$15

Despite over a decade of peace, Nicaragua is still associated in many people's minds with the long civil war between the left-wing Sandinistas and the US-backed Contras which devastated the country from 1979 to 1990 and in which some 30,000 died. Indeed, whatever has changed in the last ten years, Nicaragua is still paying the price for that war – as well as for the 45 years of brutal dictatorship which preceded it – and currently has the lowest per capita income in Latin America, along with eighty percent unemployment.

Despite the lack of basic infrastructure (some of the roads are memorably appalling, while there's a real paucity of decent hotels, hostels and restaurants), the country is finally starting to realize its potential as a tourist destination – one of the last countries in Latin America to do so. It's in the beautiful colonial city of Granada which sits on the shores of Lago de Nicaragua that a foreign presence is most noted – cheap property prices and labour costs have encouraged a wave of expat Americans to invest in second homes and even to start planning large seafront resorts. Nicaragua may not remain unspoilt for long.

For the moment at least, other compelling attractions in the country include two long coastlines, picturesque highland scenery and a landscape dotted with lakes and volcanoes, including the vast Lago de Nicaragua (the largest in Central America).

Nicaraguans are famously friendly and have yet to become blasé or cynical about tourists in the way that the inhabitants of more visited countries can be. With so much unemployment, some families (particularly in touristy areas) are happy to take in visitors as paying guests for as little as US$10 a day, with all meals included. This is a great way to gain an insight into daily life, to contribute directly to the local economy and to practise your Spanish.

Nicaragua doesn't have the most temperate of climates – it's very hot and very dry some of the year and very hot and wet the rest – nor does it offer luxurious or even comfortable travel. It is, however, among the cheapest countries in Latin America to visit, as well as being one of the safest and – currently – most undeveloped.

Main attractions

● **Granada** A long-standing tourist favourite, Granada is one of the oldest and most attractive colonial cities in

NICARAGUA

HONDURAS

Puerto
Cabezas

CA 1

Estelí   Jinotega

Matagalpa

CARIBBEAN
SEA

León

Little
Corn Island

MANAGUA

Masaya   Lago de
Granada   Nicaragua

Bluefields   Corn Island

Isla de
Ometepe

PACIFIC
OCEAN

CA 1

Solentiname
Archipelago   San Carlos

San Juan del Sur

El Castillo

0   100 km   COSTA   Los Chiles   Río San Juan
                         RICA

Latin America. Founded in 1524, the city's position on the shores of Lago de Nicaragua led it to being an important commercial centre, though it now exists in a peaceful somnolence, with wide streets of imposing mansions and a leafy Parque Central. The city is changing fast, though – due to an influx of second-homers from the States, Granada is rapidly becoming cosmopolitan, with Western-style eateries and a more active nightlife than other towns in Nicaragua.

● **The Corn Islands** Two tiny islands in the Caribbean, Big Corn and Little Corn are a world apart from the rest of Nicaragua, with a largely black population of Jamaican descent. The islands make a perfect place to kick back for a few days, with sandy, unspoilt beaches, a laid-back pace and locally caught (and fantastically cheap) lobster on every menu; there's also superlative snorkelling around Little Corn.

● **Northern highlands** The cool green hills around Matagalpa and Jinotega in the north of the country offer the perfect escape from the searing heat of the Nicaraguan lowlands, a pine-studded landscape dotted with attractive coffee plantations and ranches. There are also several patches of cloudforest in the area, the most accessible being in the grounds of the *Hotel de la Montaña Selva Negra*, a popular eco-lodge with over a dozen walking trails into the forest and great birdwatching.

△ Cathedral, Granada

● **El Castillo** Situated on the Río San Juan roughly halfway between Lago de Nicaragua and the Atlantic, the village of El Castillo sits like a mirage in the midst of the remote and scarcely inhabited wetlands that line the river. It's a pretty little place, with wooden houses on stilts over the water and a ruined Spanish fort on a grassy knoll. There's little to do in the village except sit and watch boats sail down the river, though you could try persuading a local fisherman to take you out on a trip or rent a horse to trek into the forest.

Also recommended

● **San Juan del Sur** Set on a bay surrounded by towering cliffs, with a string of smaller, undeveloped beaches stretching down the coast nearby, San Juan del Sur is a laid-back seaside town with a growing gringo scene, largely thanks to the surfers who come here in search of uncrowded Pacific waves.

● **Masaya** The market town of Masaya is home to several beautiful churches and an enduring tradition of skilled craftsmanship; the locally produced hammocks are particularly impressive – you can watch them being woven and even have one custom-made. The best time to visit is during October and November when the town stages a two-month festival to celebrate its patron saint, San Jerónimo. This kicks off with two colourful processions (Sept 30 & Oct 7), when the saint's image is borne on a gaily decorated plinth round the town. Every Sunday throughout the festival is marked by fireworks, dancing and live marimba music.

● **Solentiname** Situated in the southern corner of Lago de Nicaragua, the tiny islands of the Solentiname Archipelago represent one of the country's most remote, peaceful and picturesque destinations. Home to an artistic community established by Nicaraguan poet Ernesto Cardenal, Solentiname has three inhabited islands where you can stay and watch the locals paint in their distinctive primitive style, or simply swim in the calm waters of the lake.

- **Isla de Ometepe** The island of Ometepe, in the middle of vast Lago de Nicaragua, takes its name (originally Ome Tepetl, or "the place of two hills") from the two striking volcanoes, Volcán Concepción and Volcán Maderas, which tower over it. Most visitors come to climb the volcanoes – it takes eight strenuous hours to ascend and descend Maderas, the smaller of the two, but the view from the top over the lake is stunning.

Routes in and out

There are several direct flights daily from Miami to Nicaragua's capital, Managua, as well as a once-daily service from Houston. If you're travelling from Europe, there's a well-priced Martinair flight four times a week from Amsterdam to San José in Costa Rica, from where you can make your way overland (around 9hr by bus). There's one land crossing between Nicaragua and Costa Rica at Peñas Blancas; you can also cross by river from San Carlos to Los Chiles. There are several land borders between Nicaragua and Honduras – the most popular is El Guasaule in the north of Chinandega province.

Itineraries

One week

- From Managua head north to the highlands of Matagalpa and the Selva Negra cloudforest before moving on into Honduras.

- Spend a few days in Granada, visit the market in Masaya and then head south to San Juan del Sur on the Pacific coast.

- Cross Lago de Nicaragua by ferry from Granada to the town of San Carlos

(16hr), and then visit the islands of Solentiname and El Castillo on the Río San Juan, both accessible by motor boat from San Carlos.

Two weeks

- Coming south from Honduras, spend several days in the northern highlands, then visit Masaya and Granada. Fly to the town of Bluefields, on the Caribbean coast, from where you can catch a boat to the Corn Islands to relax for a few days before flying back to Managua and moving on to Costa Rica via the border at Peñas Blancas.

- Take the boat from Los Chiles in Costa Rica to San Carlos in Nicaragua, then head down the Río San Juan to El Castillo. Return to San Carlos and visit the Solentiname archipelago for a few days, then take the ferry from San Carlos to Granada across Lago de Nicaragua, with a few days' stopover on the Isla de Ometepe. Spend your last few days exploring Granada.

Nicaragua online

Nicanet
ⓦ**www.nicanet.org** Website of a US organization committed to social and economic justice for the people of Nicaragua, with information on current campaigns and issues.
Nicaragua.com
ⓦ**www.nicaragua.com** Extensive portal with dozens of links to Nicaraguan general information, news, sport, travel and culture.
Nicaragua Guide
ⓦ**www.guideofnicaragua.com** Glossy online tourist magazine, with decent features on where to go and things to do, plus background on Nicaraguan culture.

Panama

Capital Panama City
Population 3 million
Languages Spanish, English and
minority indigenous languages
Currency US dollar ($), also referred
to as Balboa (B)

Climate Tropical
Best time to go December–April
(dry season)
Minimum daily budget US$25

Occupying the narrow, S-shaped
isthmus that forms the only land bridge
between Central and South America,
Panama is one the most underrated and
overlooked countries amongst travellers
to Latin America. In part, this is because
the land border between Colombia and
Panama across the Darién Gap (see
p.153) is virtually impassable, making
Panama a dead end for those heading
south from Central America, but mainly
it seems that Panama suffers something
of an image problem: known only for
its inter-oceanic canal and for its long-
standing dominance by the US, it's still
seen by many outsiders as a virtual
North American colony, even though the
last US troops left in 1999.

In fact North American cultural
influence, though strong, is only
one among many to affect this vital
thoroughfare of international trade:
Spanish, African, West Indian, Chinese,
Indian, European – all have contributed

△ The Panama Canal

to a compelling cultural mix, creating a society which is surprisingly cosmopolitan, open-minded and outward-looking. At the same time, Panama is also home to some of the most fascinating and unassimilated indigenous cultures in Central America, such as the Kuna who govern themselves on a remote and idyllic Caribbean archipelago.

The mighty canal joining the Pacific and Atlantic oceans remains Panama's defining feature and is still a truly monumental sight, but it has rather over-shadowed the country's many other attractions. Most travellers who make it to Panama are surprised by its outstanding natural beauty. With 1600km of Pacific and 1280km of Caribbean coast, the country boasts innumerable unspoiled beaches and coral reefs, making it a great place for snorkelling, diving, surfing or just lying out in the sun. And although it is neighbouring Costa Rica that has achieved world renown as an ecotourism destination, in terms of pristine wilderness and ecological diversity, Panama has little reason to envy its neighbour. Over half the country is covered by dense tropical forest, and large areas are protected by a system of nature reserves and national parks. With little tourist development, the infrastructure for visiting these protected areas is as yet limited, but while this may put some people off, to others it just adds to the attraction: whether watching turtles laying their eggs by night on pristine stretches of sand or searching for resplendent quetzals in the high cloudforest, visitors to Panama's national parks are unlikely to share the experience with more than a handful of other people. Though Panamanians have not yet become jaded with foreign visitors, the fact that it's now often described as "like Costa Rica twenty years ago" suggests Panama is finally catching on with travellers to Central America keen to escape the crowds.

Main attractions

● **Panama City** Panama City is one of Latin America's most cosmopolitan capitals, combining the intrigue and energy of its modern high-rise banking district with the laid-back street life and Spanish colonial architecture of its historic city centre and the antiseptic order of the former US-controlled canal-zone suburbs. With a spectacular setting on the Pacific coast, it's close to some beautiful beaches and surrounded by some of the best-preserved and most accessible tropical rainforest in the Americas. It's also the best base from which to explore the rest of Panama, including the canal.

● **Panama Canal** Almost a century after its construction, Panama's most famous landmark is still an astounding feat of engineering, impressive both for its sheer magnitude and its unexpectedly rugged beauty. Linking the Pacific and Atlantic oceans, the canal cleaves a narrow path through pristine rainforest and can easily be visited on a day-trip from Panama City, either by taking a cruise through the canal, riding the train that runs alongside it, or visiting the locks where massive ships are raised and lowered.

● **Kuna Yala** Stretching almost 400km along the northeastern Caribbean coast, Kuna Yala – also known as the San Blas Archipelago – is the self-governing homeland of the indigenous Kuna, who live in splendid isolation on a series of tiny palm-fringed coral atolls strung out along the densely forested mainland. Best known for the distinctive costumes worn by the women, the Kuna enjoy almost total autonomy, a status that has helped them maintain their unique and compelling traditional culture and way of life. This wildly beautiful region can easily be reached by light aircraft from

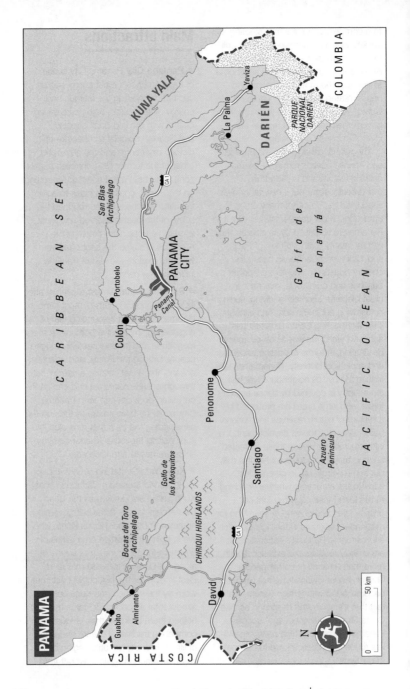

Panama City, and basic accommodation and other services – run by the Kuna themselves – are available on several islands.

● **Bocas del Toro** Long one of the best-kept travellers' secrets in Central America, the remote and beautiful Bocas del Toro archipelago on Panama's northwestern Caribbean coast is now the scene of growing tourist development. However, this has yet to change the laid-back approach to life adopted by the region's indigenous, English-speaking Afro-Antillano population, and the archipelago's richly varied ecosystems – tropical forests, deserted beaches, coral reefs, crystalline waters teeming with marine life – are still largely unspoilt.

● **Chiriqui Highlands** In the far west of Panama on the Costa Rican border, the Chiriqui Highlands are a beautiful region of cloudforest-covered peaks, fertile valleys dotted with orange groves and coffee plantations, and peaceful mountain villages. From the town of Boquete you can walk or drive up to the peak of the 3475-metre Volcán Barú, from where (on a clear day at least) you can see both the Pacific and Atlantic oceans, while the pristine cloudforests of nearby Parque Nacional La Amistad are perhaps the best place in all Central America to see the rare resplendent quetzal.

Also recommended

● **Portobelo and the Costa Arriba** Though the infamously poor and danger-ous Caribbean port of Colón should be avoided at all costs, the nearby Costa Arriba, which stretches northeast of the city, covers an isolated and enticing region of palm-fringed beaches, coral reefs and laid-back fishing villages, while the historic town of Portobelo preserves its formidable colonial fortifications, built to protect Spanish treasure fleets from pirate attack.

● **Azuero Peninsula** Jutting out into the Pacific southwest of Panama City, the dry and scrubby Azuero Peninsula is considered the cradle of Panamanian rural traditions and folklore and is home to many vibrant religious fiestas. It's also fringed with huge, deserted white-sand beaches and boasts two offshore nature reserves: Isla Iguana, which is excellent for diving and snorkelling, and the rarely visited Isla Cañas, where sea turtles nest in large numbers.

● **Parque Nacional Darién** Though guerrillas, drug traffickers and bandits mean that the adventurous journey overland across the Darién Gap to Colombia (see p.153) is now strictly off-limits, the splendid wildlife-rich rainforests of Parque Nacional Darién – one of the most biodiverse regions on earth – remain largely safe to visit, either independently or on an organized tour from Panama City.

Routes in and out

Panama City is a major transportation hub and is well connected by plane to other Latin American capitals, the US and Europe. Travelling overland, there are road crossings between Panama and Costa Rica on both the Pacific and Caribbean coasts – as a consequence, western Panama sees more backpack-ers than the rest of the country combined. Overland travel between Panama and Colombia is virtually impossible, however. Drug trafficking and guerrilla and bandit activity have made the famous crossing of the Darién Gap extremely dangerous – several travellers have been kidnapped and killed in recent years. The ferry service between Colón and Cartagena in Colombia no longer operates, but private yachts often carry travellers on this route, passing through the beautiful San Blas archipelago, for about the same price as a flight – ask around at the yacht clubs in Balboa (Panama City) or Cristobal (Colón), or at the *Voyager International Hostel* in Panama City.

Itineraries

One week

● Spend a couple of days exploring Panama City, another day or two visiting the Panama Canal and the surrounding rainforest, then either fly to one of the islands of Kuna Yala for a few days or head up to Portobelo on the Caribbean coast – at a push you could just about manage to do both.

Two weeks

● Spend the first week taking in Panama City, the Canal, and a few days in Kuna Yala, then travel west by road and divide the second week between the Chiriqui highlands and Bocas del Toro.

One month

● A month will give you enough time to visit all Panama's main attractions. Spend ten days or so taking in Panama City, the Canal and the Caribbean coast around Portobelo, before heading east to spend a few days exploring Parque Nacional Darién. Return to Panama City and head west by road to the Chiriqui Highlands, stopping off on the way for a few days in the Azuero Peninsula. From Chiriqui, continue across the continental divide to spend your last few days in Bocas del Toro.

Panama online

ANCON

Ⓦwww.ancon.org Website of the National Conservation Association, Panama's biggest and most influential environmental group, with general information on Panama's national parks, ecology and endangered species and voluntary work opportunities.

ANCON Expeditions

Ⓦwww.anconexpeditions.com Website of Panama's foremost ecotourism operator, with information and booking details for guided tours throughout the country and of their exclusive lodges in Darién.

IPAT

Ⓦwww.ipat.gob.pa The site of the Panamanian Tourist Institute, IPAT, with plenty of basic information on Panama's many attractions and good links to hotels, airlines and tour agencies.

Panama Canal Authority

Ⓦwww.pancanal.com Official site with plenty of information and news, a history of the canal in English and Spanish, plus pictures of the canal and a live webcam.

Panama Tours

Ⓦwww.panamatours.com One-stop resource for travel to Panama, with plenty of general information on the country's highlights and links to a range of related sites.

Paraguay

Capital Asunción
Population 5.5 million
Languages Spanish and Guaraní
Currency Guaraní (G/)
Climate Subtropical to temperate;
hot and humid in the east, hotter
and semi-arid in the west
Best time to go May to September
Minimum daily budget US$20

A remote backwater hemmed in by
giant neighbours, Paraguay is one of the
least-visited countries in South America.
Very few travellers come to Paraguay,
and those that do tend to pass through
only briefly as part of a multi-country
trip. The reason for this is simple: in
terms of conventional tourist attractions,
Paraguay has little to offer, especially
when compared to neighbouring
countries like Brazil and Argentina. There
are no soaring mountain ranges, beautiful beaches or lost cities here, and the
lack of infrastructure and limited tourist
development make the more interesting
wilderness areas difficult to reach. That
said, Paraguay is not without appeal,
and just coming here takes you firmly
off the beaten track, offering a far more
authentic (if less dramatic) experience of
Latin America than many more popular
destinations.

Paraguay's geographical isolation has
combined with a history of traumatic
wars (in 1865–70 almost half the population died when Paraguay took on the
combined might of Brazil, Argentina
and Uruguay in the disastrous War of

△ Jesuit mission, Trinidad

PARAGUAY

the Triple Alliance) and long-running military dictatorships (the last military ruler, General Stroessner, ruled for 34 years until he was deposed in 1988) to create an inward-looking society with a strong sense of national identity that can feel totally cut off from the outside world. Although few Paraguayans would describe themselves as indigenous, almost all speak the indigenous language Guaraní as well as Spanish, making Paraguay the most bilingual country in the region. Both are official languages, but outside the cities Guaraní is far more widely used, and even in the capital, Asunción, you'll hear its musical lilt every time you pass Paraguayans gathered to

share a chat and sip the ubiquitous yerba maté, a stimulating herbal tea drunk from gourds through metal straws that is both the country's favourite pleasure and one of its main exports.

Paraguay is one of the poorest countries in South America, its economy based largely on agriculture and smuggling (or "re-exporting") goods to neighbouring Brazil and Argentina – contraband flourished under Stroessner's corrupt military regime and the black economy is still thought to account for up to half Paraguay's gross domestic product.

Geographically, Paraguay is divided into two distinct regions by the river that gives it its name. East of the Río Paraguay is the country's traditional rural heartland, a rich agricultural region of rolling hills covered by well-watered grasslands and patches of subtropical forest. North and west of the river stretches the Gran Chaco, a harsh wilderness region of low plains covered by swamp, scrub and impenetrable thorn scrub stretching north to the Bolivian border, an area rich in wildlife and home only to scattered indigenous groups and remote settlements of German-speaking Mennonite farmers. In neither region is the scenery particularly spectacular, but travelling across the Chaco is still one of the great wilderness journeys in South America, particularly if you're heading to or from Bolivia, while the more populous agricultural region east of the Río Paraguay, with its deep-rooted cultural traditions and sleepy towns and villages, has an understated but timeless rural charm.

Main attractions

● **Asunción** Though it's the political and commercial heart of Paraguay, Paraguay's riverside capital retains the sedate atmosphere of a provincial backwater and an old-fashioned feel, with elegant nineteenth-century public buildings and some interesting – though rather militaristic – monuments and museums, dedicated above all to former dictators and war heroes. The pretty countryside and traditional farming towns of the surrounding rural heartland – including the lace-making centre of Itaugúa – can be visited on day-trips from the city, following a route known as the Circuito de Oro, but none are essential stops.

● **Parque Nacional Ybicuy** About 150km southeast of Asunción, this easily accessible region of rainforest-covered hills dissected by tumbling streams with numerous waterfalls has plenty of good hiking trails.

● **Gran Chaco** Covering more than half of Paraguay, the Gran Chaco is one of the last great wilderness regions of South America, a vast stretch of thorn scrub, savannah and swamp inhabited only by indigenous tribes and hardy colonies of Mennonites, a German-speaking religious sect. Comparable to the Amazon in plant and animal biodiversity and largely pristine, the Chaco is extremely rich in wildlife, and a paradise for birdwatchers. The inexpensive way to visit is by making the arduous journey by bus or truck through the heart of the region and on into Bolivia. However, to get a closer look at the wildlife you're better off taking a tour from Asunción – a number of companies there offer jeep trips into the remote Parque Nacional Defensores del Chaco.

● **Jesuit missions** In Trinidad and Jesús, close to the southern city of Encarnación on the Argentine border, stand the ruined churches and other buildings of the utopian Jesuit mission settlements established here in the eighteenth century, their well-preserved stone structures a vivid testimony to the artistic heights reached by the indigenous Guaraní under the tutelage of a handful of European priests.

Also recommended

● **A boat ride down the Río Paraguay** Travelling on one of the irregular passenger boats that ply the mighty Río Paraguay between Asunción and Concepción is one of the best ways of seeing the tranquil rural heartland of Paraguay.

● **Itaipú Dam** Close to the unattractive smuggler's paradise of Ciudad del Este on the Brazilian border lies the massive

Itaipú Dam, one of the world's biggest hydroelectric projects. Completed in 1984, it's a monumental sight – though apparently nowhere near as spectacular as the dramatic waterfalls drowned by the reservoir after it was built.

● **Working on an estancia** A number of farms and estancias or ranches accept paying guests, rather like "dude ranches" in the US, allowing you to experience at first hand the traditional way of life in Paraguay's rural heartland.

Routes in and out

The international airport at Asunción has frequent direct flights to most other South American capitals, a number of other cities in Brazil, and to Miami in the US. By land, you can cross the border from Brazil between Foz de Iguaçu and Ciudad del Este in the east and between Ponta Porã and Pedro Juan Caballero in the northeast. From Argentina there are road crossings between Asunción and Clorinda and between Encarnación and Posadas in the south, and you can also enter Paraguay from Puerto Iguazú via Foz de Iguaçu in Brazil. The overland route to and from Bolivia is along the Trans-Chaco Highway, an adventurous journey through the heart of the great Chaco wilderness. Alternatively, you can also enter and leave Paraguay on one of the irregular riverboats that travel the Río Paraguay between Asunción and Corumbá in Brazil.

Itineraries

One week

● Spend a couple of days in Asunción, explore some of the surrounding countryside, and then either visit the Jesuit missions of Jesús and Trinidad or head out to the Parque Nacional Ybicuy for a couple of days' hiking.

Two weeks

● Follow the one-week itinerary, then head north to Concepción, travelling by boat up the Río Paraguay if erratic schedules allow. Continue into the Chaco, either by taking a bus to the Mennonite centre of Filadelfia (and, if you're heading that way, on to Bolivia), or by joining an organized tour from Asunción into the Parque Nacional Defensores del Chaco.

Paraguay online

Senatur
Ⓦ www.senatur.gov.py Official Paraguayan tourist office site with good general information on the country's attractions and links to relevant sites.
Yagua.com
Ⓦ www.yagua.com Comprehensive Paraguayan Internet directory with links to all manner of Paraguay-related sites, including tourist information and the media.

Peru

Capital Lima
Population 28 million
Languages Spanish, Quechua, plus more than thirty other indigenous languages
Currency Nuevo Sol (S/)
Climate Tropically hot and humid in the Amazon lowlands, drier along the desert coast and much cooler with altitude in the Andes
Best time to go May to September (dry season for the highlands and Amazon), December to March for the coast
Minimum daily budget US$15

Peru is arguably the most varied and fascinating country in Latin America, a place to which even seasoned travellers return again and again, drawn back by the promise of endless new experiences. It's best known as home of the Incas, the rulers of the largest and most powerful of Latin America's pre-Columbian empires, and as the location of Machu Picchu, the original lost city in the jungle that encapsulates much of what outsiders find so mysterious and intriguing about South America. But though Machu Picchu and the Inca heartland around the unforgettable city of Cusco are rightly the main draws for visitors, their fame sometimes obscures the manifold attractions of the rest of the country. The Incas were just the last and best known of many civilizations that rose and fell in Peru before the Spanish conquest, and the whole country is dotted with magnificent archeological sites, with major new finds – from lost cities in the Andes to golden tombs in desert pyramids – being regularly discovered.

The country's astonishing archeological heritage is set amidst fabulously varied scenery, ranging from the deserts of the Pacific coastal strip through the high peaks of the Andes to the seemingly endless expanse of the Peruvian Amazon rainforest. This astounding range of different ecosystems and climates makes Peru one of the most biodiverse countries on earth, home to 84 of the 104 different life zones on the planet and to an incredible variety of plant and animal life. It also makes it an ideal setting for all kinds of adventure sports, including trekking, mountaineering, whitewater rafting and mountain biking.

This huge range of landscapes is more than matched by the diversity of the population, an intriguing blend of indigenous, Spanish, African and Asian peoples. The most distinctive of these cultures is found in the Andes, where most people are of indigenous descent and speak Quechua, the language of the Inca empire, as their first language. Their Inca heritage is also evident in deep-seated cultural traditions and beliefs, which are manifested most vibrantly in their music and dance and in the many colourful fiestas that combine Catholic and traditional indigenous beliefs and customs.

Peru's complex ethnic make-up, along with the legacy of conquest and underdevelopment, has produced a volatile political mix, but thankfully the violence of the 1980s and 1990s – when a bloody war between the state and the Maoist rebel group Sendero Luminoso (Shining Path) made large areas of the country too dangerous to visit – is largely a thing of the past. The political situation is now fairly stable (by Peruvian standards, at least), though some remote has an unfortunate reputation for theft and other scams. But though not entirely undeserved, this is exaggerated and shouldn't put you off this fascinating country. Most Peruvians are extremely open and welcoming to foreigners – indeed for some travellers the warmth and humour of the people far outweigh

Main attractions

• **Cusco** The ancient heart of the Inca Empire, Cusco is Peru's most famous attraction and one of the most compelling destinations in all Latin America. A beautiful colonial city built amidst the magnificent ruined temples and palaces of the Incas (and still largely inhabited by their Quechua-speaking descendants), Cusco is surrounded by spectacular mountain scenery and remarkable Inca archeological sites, including the monumental fortress of Sacsayhuaman, which towers above the city, and the numerous temples and palaces of the nearby Sacred Valley of the Incas. Cusco is also a great base for trekking, climbing, mountain biking and whitewater rafting trips, and for expeditions into the rainforests of the southern Peruvian Amazon. With all this plus good tourist infrastructure, a lively nightlife scene and some of the most colourful fiestas in the Andes, it's no wonder many travellers end up staying here much longer than they originally planned.

• **Machu Picchu and the Inca Trail** Of all Peru's archeological attractions, the most famous and dramatic is the lost city of Machu Picchu, set amid the dense forests north of the Inca capital, Cusco. You can reach the ruins either by taking a stunning train journey from Cusco or by hiking the Inca Trail, a well-preserved though usually overcrowded stone-paved Inca road that passes through spectacular high mountain scenery and numerous Inca sites before plunging down through the cloudforest to Machu Picchu. If the crowds sound too much for you, consider hiking one of the many other Inca trails that crisscross the Andes around Cusco, many of them linking archeological sites. One of the best of these is the newly opened route to Choquequirao, a complex Inca

citadel set high in the Apurimac that's an arduous ten-day return hike from the nearest road through remote and pristine mountain scenery.

• **Huaraz and the Cordillera Blanca** Nestled in the deep valley of the Callejon de Huayllas, Huaraz is the perfect base for trekking and climbing in the spectacular Cordillera Blanca, the highest tropical mountain range in the world, much of which is protected by the Parque Nacional Huascaran. It's also close to Chavín de Huantar, an ancient complex of ruined temples and underground labyrinths decorated with stylized stone carvings that was a major Chavín religious centre more than 2500 years ago.

• **Nazca Lines** Set in the arid coastal strip south of Lima, the Nazca Lines are one of the most mysterious and dramatic ancient sites in South America, a series of massive geometric shapes and animal figures drawn into the ground over some five hundred square kilometres of stony desert – their origins and meaning remain unknown, despite endless speculation. The Lines are best viewed from the air, and it's easy to arrange an overflight in a light aircraft from the town of Nazca. For those on a tight budget, there are also viewing towers where you can get a good look of some of the best sections.

• **Peruvian Amazon** Covering over half the country, the rainforests of the Peruvian Amazon are amongst the best preserved and least explored in South America. They're also amongst the least accessible, so you may want to save time by flying to one of the Amazon towns from where you can organize a rainforest expedition rather than make the arduous journey by land down the eastern slopes of the Andes. The best place to visit in the region is undoubtedly the stunning Parque Nacional

△ Sacsayhuaman

Manu in the southern Peruvian Amazon (accessible on organized tours from Cusco), arguably the most pristine, biodiverse and wildlife-rich national park in all South America. A cheaper alternative in the south is the more accessible Tambopata-Candamo Reserve, reached by boat from Puerto Maldonado, while in the northern Amazon the city of Iquitos, on the banks of the mighty Amazon itself, is the best-organized and established tourism centre, with plenty of companies offering everything from luxury cruises and eco-lodges to rugged survival expeditions and trips into the vast and virtually untouched Parque Nacional Pacaya-Samiria.

● **Arequipa** Set at the foot of the snowcapped El Misti volcano, the city of Arequipa boasts a lovely climate and some of the finest colonial architecture in

Peru, including the beautiful Monastery of Santa Catalina. From the city it's easy to organize trips into the surrounding mountains and the spectacular Colca Canyon, the world's deepest, which is an excellent place for trekking, white-water rafting and condor-spotting.

• **Ceviche** Served at restaurants and street stalls the length of the Pacific coast, *ceviche* is Peru's unmissable national dish, a cool and spicy combination of fresh fish and seafood marinated in chilli, onions and lime juice, best washed down with an ice-cold Cusqueña beer.

Also recommended

• **Lima** With its sprawling shantytowns, chaotic traffic, high crime rate and dismal, fog-bound climate, Lima can seem a pretty daunting and unattractive place. But beyond these first impressions the capital has much to offer, including excellent museums, such as the Museo de Oro, and an elegant colonial city centre that's gradually being restored. It also boasts perhaps the finest cuisine in Latin America and a vibrant nightlife scene, and if you stay out in the wealthy seaside suburb of Miraflores you can avoid the worst aspects of the city centre.

• **Lago Titicaca** Though the lakeside city of Puno is a drab, unexciting place, its location makes it the perfect base for exploring the magical scenery of the Altiplano, the high Andean plateau, and above all for making boat trips out across Lago Titicaca to the idyllic islands of Taquile and Amantani, where you can get a real taste of traditional rural Andean culture by staying with an indigenous family.

• **Chachapoyas** Set in the northern highlands, which are usually overlooked

in favour of the more famous attractions of the Cusco region, the remote town of Chachapoyas is the centre of a beautiful region of cloudforest-covered mountains dotted with scarcely explored pre-Inca ruins, including the spectacular walled city of Kuelap.

• **Ayacucho** Once the centre of Sendero Luminoso guerrilla activity in the 1980s and 1990s and long off-limits to travellers, the highland city of Ayacucho is once again safe to visit. And, with its fine colonial architecture and strong indigenous cultural traditions, you really should make the effort to see it, particularly if you're making the tough overland journey between Cusco and Lima, and especially during Easter, when it stages fabulous Semana Santa celebrations.

• **Cajamarca** A friendly market town in the northern Andes, Cajamarca is second only to Cusco in the grace of its architecture, the drama of its mountain setting and the resonance of its Inca past. It's also largely free of tourists most of the time, and a perfect spot to relax for a day or two as you journey through northern Peru.

• **Trujillo** The handsome colonial city of Trujillo on the north coast is surrounded by beautiful deserted Pacific beaches, peaceful fishing villages, and an amazing collection of ancient archeological sites, including the massive earthen pyramids of the Huaca del Sol and Huaca de la Luna, and the monumental ruined adobe city of Chan-Chan. It also boasts Peru's finest regional cuisine, based above all on the excellent local seafood. Favourites include *Chupe de Camarones* – an exquisite shrimp soup; *Picante de Mariscos* – a spicy shellfish stew; *Conchitas a la Parmesana* – scallops baked in their shells with Parmesan cheese; and of course *ceviche* in all its many forms.

Islas Ballestas The best way to experience the abundant marine wildlife that thrives on the nutrient-rich cold water current that runs along the coast of Peru is to visit the Islas Ballestas. Known as the "Poor Man's Galapagos", this group of rocky islands teems with sea lions, penguins and other marine birds, and can be easily reached on boat trips from the pleasant southern fishing town of Pisco.

Routes in and out

Lima is connected by frequent international flights to Europe, the US and most major Latin American capitals. Entering or leaving Peru overland by road across the Bolivian, Chilean and Ecuadorian borders is easy. You can travel to and from Colombia and Brazil by boat along the Amazon River from Iquitos, and there are also several more remote Amazon border crossings with Brazil and Bolivia.

Itineraries

Taking a local flight – particularly from Lima to Cusco or to Iquitos or Puerto Maldonado in the Amazon – is a good and relatively inexpensive way of maximizing your time. If you're flying into Lima and don't have much time, it can be worth booking a connecting onward internal flight in advance, so you can head on to Cusco without having to leave the airport and go into the city. On longer trips, you're likely to have a day or two in Lima at the beginning and end of your visit – more than enough to get a feel for the capital and take in some of the sights. Remember that you'll need several days to acclimatize to the altitude in the highlands, especially if you're planning to do some trekking.

One week

● Fly straight up to Cusco and spend the week exploring the city and the surrounding region, including a visit to Machu Picchu and the Sacred Valley of the Incas.

● Travel south along the coast from Lima, visiting the Islas Ballestas and the Nazca Lines before heading inland to Arequipa, from where you can return directly to Lima. From Nazca you could also continue along the Pan-American Highway into northern Chile.

Two weeks

● Fly to Cusco and spend at least a week in and around the city, or longer if you to walk the Inca Trail or one of the many other trekking routes in the region, then fly down to Puerto Maldonado in the southern Amazon and spend a few days in a rainforest lodge on Río Tambopata.

● Spend a week in the Cusco region, then take a train down to Puno on the shores of Lago Titicaca and visit one of the islands on the lake. From Puno, take another train to Arequipa and spend a few days exploring the city and visiting the Colca Canyon before taking a bus or plane back to Lima. Another option from Puno is to travel across Lago Titicaca into Bolivia, reaching La Paz in a day.

● From Lima, head up to Huaraz for a week or so trekking in the Cordillera Blanca, taking in the ruins at Chavín de Huantar while you acclimatize. Then head to Trujillo to sample the seafood and archeology of the north coast before heading across the northern Andes via Cajamarca to Chachapoyas, where you can visit the ruins of Kuelap before returning the way you came. From Trujillo you could also move on by road across the northern border to Ecuador.

One month

● Starting in Lima, travel to Cusco overland via Ayacucho. Spend a week or so in the Cusco region, including time to trek the Inca Trail and visit the major Inca sites, then either go on an organized tour down into the rainforests of the Parque Nacional Manu or fly to Puerto Maldonado for a shorter stay at a rainforest lodge. Return to Cusco, then head by train to Puno for a day or two on the islands of Lago Titicaca. Continue by train to Arequipa and spend a few days taking in the city and exploring Colca Canyon. If you take the shorter rainforest trip, you should then have a few days left to return to Lima overland from Arequipa along the south coast, visiting the Nazca Lines and the Islas Ballestas along the way.

● From Lima head up to Huaraz for a week or so's trekking in the Cordillera Blanca, allowing time to visit the ruins at Chavin while you acclimatize. Then head down to Trujillo for a few days on the North Coast before travelling by bus across the northern Andes via Cajamarca to Chachapoyas. Spend a few days exploring Kuelap and other ruins before heading by bus down to the town of Yurimaguas in the upper Amazon. From there, you can take a three- to five-day boat trip down the mighty river Amazon to Iquitos. Once there, you can either visit a rainforest lodge or – if you've enough time – take a trip to Pacaya-Samiria national park.

From Iquitos you can continue by boat along to Leticia in Colombia and on into Brazil.

Peru online

Andean Travel Web
ⓦ**www.andeantravelweb.com/peru**
Comprehensive English-language Peruvian travel site, with good information on all the main attractions, and links to all manner of useful sites including hotels and tour companies.

Machu Picchu
ⓦ**www.machupicchu.org** Links to all kinds of websites related to Machu Picchu, the Incas and Andean culture in general.

Peru Traveller Guide
ⓦ**www.geocities.com/perutraveller/**
Good independent travel guide to Peru, full of useful information and links.

PromPeru
ⓦ**www.peru.info/peru.asp** Official tourist promotion site with comprehensive information on everything from history and archeology to food and fiestas, as well as details on all the major attractions, practical advice on travel in Peru, and links to all manner of related sites.

Rumbos
ⓦ**www.rumbosperu.com** Peruvian environmental and travel magazine with good photos, travel articles, background information and practical tips on visiting a huge range of different sites.

Uruguay

Capital Montevideo	**Climate** Temperate, with long warm
Population 3.2 million	summers and mild winters
Language Spanish	**When to go** September to April
Currency Peso Uruguayo (U$)	**Minimum daily budget** US$25

Squeezed in between the vast expanses of Argentina and Brazil, diminutive Uruguay is usually overlooked by travellers to South America. It is, however, an oasis of stability in the fluctuating fortunes of the region, with moderate politics, an educated and tolerant population and a beguiling atmosphere of old-fashioned elegance reminiscent of neighbouring Argentina, whose neo-European culture Uruguay shares. There is no mass tourism in Uruguay and the country remains unspoilt and hospitable.

Given Uruguay's modest dimensions, its characterful capital, Montevideo, looms large in the national psyche – almost half the country's three million-plus inhabitants live here, and the capital is very much the economic, cultural and political heart of the country. Not that Montevideo is Uruguay's only attraction. Close to hand is the country's alluring Atlantic coastline, centred on the ritzy resort of Punta del Este, but also boasting more low-key seaside villages in which to loll on the beach and enjoy Uruguay's pleasantly Mediterranean climate. What really defines Uruguay, however, is its gaucho culture, which is even more ubiquitous and traditional than neighbouring Argentina's – you're still more likely to see farmhands wearing *bombachas* (loose trousers), bandanas and felt hats than jeans. The colourful three-day "Fiesta de la Patria Gaucha",

held in the town of Tacuarembó in late March, is a good place to see fine displays of gaucho horsemanship and other skills like horse-breaking and cattle herding.

Although parts of Montevideo aren't entirely safe at night, Uruguay is an otherwise safe place to travel, with reasonably priced accommodation and an efficient network of public transport.

Main attractions

● **Montevideo** Like nearby Buenos Aires, Montevideo's passions are tango, football and *mate*, although the city is more laid-back and relaxing than its brasher Argentine cousin. Along with elegant European-style coffeehouses and boulevards, the city also boasts a small colonial centre, the Ciudad Vieja, and one of the most atmospheric markets in South America, the Mercado del Puerto, housed in a large, nineteenth-century wrought-iron building and known for its delicious *parilla* (barbecues) – come here especially on Saturday afternoons to enjoy the grilled meat and mix with the locals for whom it's a long-standing weekend tradition.

● **Punta del Este** On the Atlantic coast, 85km east of Montevideo, the glitzy seaside resort of Punta del Este is popular with wealthy and trendy

URUGUAY

ARGENTINA

BRAZIL

R30

Rivera

Salto

LAS TERMAS

Tacuarembo

R26

Paysandú

Lago Ricon del Bonete

Mercedes

Durazno

R2

R8

Carmelo

R23

Chuy

Colonia del Sacremento

PARQUE FORESTAL CABO POLONIA

Aguas Dulces

R1

R11

La Paloma

MONTEVIDEO

Punta del Este

0   100 km

Brazilians, Argentinians and, from December to February, European clubbers in search of winter sun. While Punta's beaches are broad and sandy, most visitors come for the best nightlife south of Rio de Janeiro, with world-class DJs flown in from Europe and the US. Punta is far from cheap, though – costs are equivalent to those in the south of France.

● **Colonia del Sacramento** Founded by Portuguese settlers from Brazil in 1680, Colonia sits directly opposite Buenos Aires on the Río de la Plata. It's a charming town, Uruguay's prettiest, with whitewashed buildings, narrow cobbled streets and squares lined by plane trees, as well as the ruins of the seventeenth-century Convento de San Francisco and a nineteenth-century lighthouse, from where there are lovely views over the town.

● **Gaucho culture** Many Uruguayan estancias (ranches) offer comfortable home stays during which you can ride, rope steers and learn about farm life. You might also be encouraged to join in with daily tasks performed by ranch hands like branding cattle, shearing sheep or milking cows, or be taken out for a ride in a traditional horse-drawn carriage.

Also recommended

● **Dunes of Cabo Polonio** On the Atlantic coast 200km east of Montevideo, the Cabo Polonio offers one of Uruguay's wildest and most dramatic vistas, with a ten-kilometre stretch of shifting sand dunes, some of them reaching 30m in height, making for an invigorating coastal hike.

△ Punta del Este

● **Candombe** Montevideo's Barrio Sur is home to the country's colourful Afro-Uruguayan population, whose unique ceremonial form of music and dance, known as *candombe*, can be seen most weekends in the city's cabaret venues or, more authentically, outside on the barrio's Calle Carlos Gardel. As well as drumming and dancing, *candombe* events involve a fixed cast of characters including a matriarch, a medicine man and El Bastonero – a man with a magic wooden stick.

● **Aguas Dulces** If you fancy a quiet beach holiday, head for the quaint fishing village of Aguas Dulces, 120km east of Punta del Este, which has several good seafood restaurants and few tourists. The surrounding area has undeveloped sandy beaches, while 30km further north is the Parque Nacional Santa Teresa, which incorporates an eighteenth-century hilltop castle, pine and eucalyptus forests and marshes with abundant bird life.

● **Las Termas** Located in the geothermically active eastern part of Uruguay, Las Termas is a series of natural hot spring resorts where you can relax in naturally heated pools or enjoy a hydromassage. Particularly recommended is Termas del Daymán, 8km south of Salto and home to the first thermal aquapark in South America.

Routes in and out

There are no nonstop flights from the US, Europe or Australasia to Uruguay, although there are flights from Miami via Bolivia and Argentina to Montevideo four times weekly. The easiest way to reach the country is to fly directly to Buenos Aires from the US or Europe (London, Madrid and Amsterdam) and take the ferry across the Río de la Plata to Montevideo or Colonia. Alternatively, fly to São Paulo in Brazil and get one of several daily flights to Montevideo. There are a number of land crossings into Brazil – the most popular goes between Chuy at the northern end of Uruguay's Atlantic coast and twin city Chui in Brazil. There is also a land crossing to Argentina at Gualeguaychú, though this is less convenient than crossing the Río de la Plata.

Itineraries

One week

- Visit two of Uruguay's most interesting cities, Montevideo and Colonia.

- Explore the country's coast, varying the pace from the party town of Punta del Este to the tranquil fishing village of Aguas Dulces.

- Stay on an inland ranch and learn how to become a gaucho.

Two weeks

- Take the ferry from Argentina to Colonia and then move down the coast to Montevideo and the Atlantic beaches before crossing the border into Brazil at Chuy.

- Head inland from Colonia to the rolling hills and lowlands of the country's interior, stay on a ranch, and then end your trip with a few days relaxing in the hot springs of Las Termas.

Uruguay online

Discover Uruguay
Ⓦ **www.discoveruruguay.com** Online travel agency set up by expat Uruguayan with useful tourist information and essays on all things Uruguayan.

Uruguay Info
Ⓦ **www.uruguayInfo.com** The enthusiastic website of two Germans living in Montevideo. Available in German and English with information on living in Uruguay, and features on culture, history and tourism among others and hundreds of photographs.

Uruguay Total
Ⓦ **www.uruguaytotal.com** Uruguay's main internet portal, with hundreds of links on business, politics, the media and much more.

Venezuela

Capital Caracas	**Climate** Hot and humid in the
Population 25 million	lowlands, cooler in the Andes
Languages Spanish, plus minority	**Best time to go** November to June
indigenous languages	(dry season)
Currency Bolívar (B)	**Minimum daily budget** US$25–35

Venezuela is the fifth biggest country in South America and, like the continent's other Andean nations, encompasses a great variety of dramatic landscapes, from Andean peaks to the immense, wildlife-rich plains, swamps and rainforests of the Amazon and Orinoco basins. With almost three thousand kilometres of Caribbean coastline, Venezuela also boasts some glorious beaches, as well as numerous idyllic offshore islands surrounded by coral reefs. In addition, the wilderness hinterland is home to two of South America's most outstanding natural wonders: Angel Falls, the world's highest waterfall, with a drop of almost a kilometre; and the stunning, flat-topped sandstone mountains known as *tepuis* that rise almost vertically from the plains of the remote Gran Sabana – the biggest of these, Mount Roraima, is said to have provided the inspiration for Sir Arthur Conan Doyle's epic adventure novel, *The Lost World* (though a similar claim is made for the Parque Nacional Noel Kempff Mercado in Bolivia).

Given these attractions, Venezuela receives surprisingly few travellers, other than the package tourists who fly in to enjoy the beautiful beaches and duty-free shopping of the resort island of Margarita, and the smaller numbers who come specifically to see Angel Falls or visit less developed parts of the Caribbean coast. Many budget travellers are put off by the country's relatively high costs, by the fact that you have to pass through Colombia to get here from Ecuador or Peru, and by the visa requirement for travellers entering the country overland. The bottom line, though, is that for all its natural wonders, Venezuela can't quite match the romantic allure of other South American countries. Heavily westernized, it lacks the cultural vibrancy and exotic appeal of places like Peru and Brazil.

Economically, Venezuela depends overwhelmingly on its massive oil industry. It's one of the world's largest exporters, and oil revenues have funded a good road network and relatively modern infrastructure that make travel fairly easy. But the oil industry has acted as a disincentive to the development of tourism, and has also had a profound cultural impact. Uniquely in South America, Venezuelans prefer baseball to football – the legacy of US oil workers – and a brash commercial outlook predominates in the cities.

The capital, Caracas, has a dramatic enough setting amid rugged mountains near the coast, but otherwise it's a rather unattractive place, with a modern high-rise city centre ringed by depressingly poor shantytowns in a juxtaposition that encapsulates the deep inequalities created by the oil boom, and levels of violent crime which are high even by Latin American standards. You shouldn't let this put you off, though, as however unappealing the urban centres may be, the enormous and diverse natural beauty of the country's immense coastline and interior – much of it still sparsely inhabited wilderness – make Venezuela a fantastic travel destination. Moreover, the fact that it attracts relatively few visitors means that it's easy to mix with the locals, and even in the more popular destinations you'll rarely find yourself surrounded by crowds of other tourists.

Venezuela's massive oil exports mean it ought to be one of the richest countries in Latin America, but in fact the oil revenues have largely been squandered through decades of inefficient and corrupt government, leaving most of the population in poverty. Frustration with this led to the election in 1999 of

△ Angel Falls

VENEZUELA

CARIBBEAN SEA

Archipelago Los Roques

Grenada

Coro

Isla de Margarita

PARQUE NACIONAL MORROCOY

CARACAS

TRINIDAD & TOBAGO

Maracaibo

Colonia Tovar

9

Maturín

1

Orinoco Delta

5

CP

15

Mérida

Ciudad Bolívar

Ciudad Guayana

San Fernando de Apure

19

CP

Puerto Páez

Angel Falls

GUYANA

LA GRAN SABANA

COLOMBIA

N

BRAZIL

0   300 km

President Hugo Chavez, a former military coup leader and self-proclaimed revolutionary who's emerged as the most exciting – and controversial – radical political leader in Latin America for decades.

Benefiting from rising oil prices, Chavez has introduced a far-reaching programme to transform Venezuela, building schools, redistributing land, and sending Cuban doctors into the slums. In the process he's alienated the traditional political elites, leading to growing political tension and clashes on the streets. He's also alienated the United States, which imports huge quantities of Venezuelan oil. In 2002, Chavez was briefly overthrown in a military coup, allegedly supported by the CIA, before mass protests by his supporters forced his reinstatement.

Overwhelming victory in a referendum on his rule in 2004 has calmed the situation, but Venezuela remains politically polarized between those who love Chavez and those who hate him. The political situation is unlikely to affect your travel plans, but it's worth checking the media for the latest developments and steering clear of political demonstrations; presidential elections are due in 2006.

Main attractions

● **Angel Falls** Set amid pristine rain-forest inside the remote Parque Nacional Canaima in the southwest of the country, the Angel Falls (Salto Angel, named after Jimmy Angel, the US bush pilot who stumbled across them in the 1930s) are Venezuela's most famous attraction. Plummeting almost 1km – around fifteen times the height of Niagara Falls – this is by far the highest waterfall in the world, an amazing spectacle made all the more alluring by its remote wilderness location. Getting to the falls is no easy matter: you have to fly into the village of Canaima, from where you can either fly over the falls in a light aircraft or travel to their foot by motorized canoe. This latter option is only possible during the June to December rainy season, which is in any case the best time to visit, since the high water levels mean that the falls are at their most spectacular.

• **Archipelago Los Roques** Situated some 160km off the mainland north of Caracas, the Los Roques archipelago comprises a beautiful collection of coral atolls with white-sand beaches, fringed by extensive coral reefs. Protected as a national park, the islands support a great density and diversity of tropical marine life, making for fantastic snorkelling and diving. Nor are the waters crowded – expensive accommodation and the cost of reaching the islands by plane or yacht help keep visitor numbers low.

• **Gran Sabana** South of Angel Falls and set within the same massive Parque Nacional Canaima, the beautiful and remote Gran Sabana is a vast, rolling plateau covered with savannah grassland and tropical rainforest, from which rise over a hundred flat-topped mountains known as *tepuis*. Inhabited by scattered indigenous groups, the region is rich in wildlife, and the tops of the *tepuis*, where plant species have evolved in isolation, are amongst the most unique natural habitats in Latin America. The largest of the *tepuis* is the 2810-metre Mount Roraima, which sits on the three-way border with Guyana and Brazil and can be climbed on a tough five- to six-day trek.

• **Parque Nacional Morrocoy** With its clear blue waters, near-deserted beaches and islands, and extensive coral reefs, Parque Nacional Morrocoy covers an idyllic stretch of the Caribbean coast west of Caracas, and is an excellent place for snorkelling, diving or just chilling out on the beach. It's best visited by taking day-trips by boat from the towns of Tucacas and Chichiriviche, though if you take your own camping equipment and supplies you can arrange to be dropped off on one of the deserted islands and enjoy a few days of blissful isolation.

• **Mérida** Set at an altitude of 1640m within sight of Venezuela's highest mountain peaks, the friendly city of Mérida is the best base for exploring the Venezuelan Andes, which stretch for some 400km along the western side of the country. From the city you can take the world's longest and highest cable car ride up to the 4765-metre summit of Pico Espejo for fabulous views of the mountains all around. Mérida is also home to a well-developed tour industry, which makes it easy to organize trekking, mountain-biking, whitewater rafting and horse-riding trips into the surrounding mountains, large areas of which are protected by Parque Nacional Sierra Nevada.

Also recommended

• **Orinoco Delta** The Orinoco Delta is a massive wetland region of swamp and rainforest where the waters of the mighty River Orinoco – the third biggest in South America – weave their way through an intricate system of waterways before reaching the sea. The delta supports a rich and varied range of wildlife, and is also home to the indigenous Warao, who reside in houses raised on stilts on many of the innumerable forested islands, and live largely by fishing from dugout canoes. You can visit this great wilderness on organized tours from the riverside town of Tucupita, staying in lodges on the delta.

● **Coro** The peaceful little port town of Coro, on the Caribbean coast about 180km west of Parque Nacional Morrocoy, was one of the first Spanish settlements in South America, and is home to the finest colonial architecture in Venezuela.

● **Colonia Tovar** Set in the forested mountains west of Caracas, the Colonia Tovar was founded in 1843 by a group of German settlers who proceeded to live in near total isolation from the rest of Venezuela for almost a century, marrying only amongst themselves and maintaining their German cultural traditions and language. This isolation faded from the mid-twentieth century with the introduction of Spanish and the construction of a road link with the rest of the country, and the colony has since become a major attraction, but its distinct cultural background is still very much evident in the Aryan looks and German accents of most of the inhabitants, and in their rich agricultural produce.

● **Isla de Margarita** The Isla de Margarita is Venezuela's biggest island and a major holiday resort, attracting large numbers of package tourists with its combination of beautiful beaches, modern hotel complexes and duty-free shopping. Despite the impact of mass tourism, however, the island's many beaches are so extensive that you can still find relatively peaceful stretches, especially if you avoid the main Venezuelan holiday periods (around Christmas and Easter), making it an excellent place to relax by the sea for a few days after some hard travelling elsewhere.

Routes in and out

Caracas is a major regional hub for air travel, with regular flights to most South American capitals, and is also generally the cheapest place to reach in South America from Europe or the US, with regular flights from major cities in both continents. By land, there are four major crossings between Venezuela and Colombia, the easiest, safest and most scenic of which runs through the Andes between Cúcuta and San Antonio del Táchira. You can travel between Venezuela and Brazil along the recently opened road through the Gran Sabana, across the border at Santa Elena de Uairén and south to Boa Vista and Manaus in Brazil. There are no land crossings between Guyana and Venezuela; the only way to travel overland between the two is to go via Brazil. You can also enter and leave Venezuela by ferry between Isla Margarita and Trinidad and Tobago. Note that though you generally don't need a visa if you're flying into Venezuela, most nationalities do need one to enter the country overland, so check to make sure you can get one in a neighbouring country, or ideally pick one up before you leave home.

Itineraries

One week

● Head west from Caracas to Chichiriviche and spend a few days exploring the beaches and islands of Parque Nacional Morrocoy, then either travel up into the Andes to Mérida and spend the remainder of the week exploring the city and taking the cable car up into the high mountains, or fly down to the village of Canaima in Parque Nacional Canaima and take a one-day trip by plane to the Angel Falls.

Two weeks

● Follow the one-week itinerary at a slightly more leisurely pace, perhaps continuing further west along the coast to Coro, before heading up to Mérida or taking a couple of extra days once there to trek in the mountains, then return to Caracas and fly down to the village of Canaima in Canaima National Park and take a three-day canoe trip to Angel Falls.

One month

● Follow the two-week itinerary and arrange to be dropped off in the historic city of Ciudad Bolívar on the banks of the Orinoco River on the way back from Angel Falls. From there, head east by road via the new city of Ciudad Guayana to Tucupita to take a two- or three-day tour into the Orinoco Delta. Return to Ciudad Bolívar, then either head south by road to San Fransisco de Yuruaní

in the Gran Sabana and spend your last week trekking up Mount Roraima, or return to Caracas and fly out to the Archipelago Los Roques and spend the week snorkelling or diving on the coral reefs and relaxing on the beach. If you have a couple of days left over at the end of the month, visit Colonia Tovar from Caracas before you leave.

Venezuela online

Think Venezuela
Ⓦ **www.think-venezuela.net**
Comprehensive online tourism directory, with excellent information on Venezuela's main attractions and on practical details like accommodation, transport and tour companies, plus a good selection of links to other relevant sites.
Venezuela Analysis
Ⓦ **www.venezuelanalysis.com** Political news and comment on Venezuela from around the world, almost all of it from a pro-Chavez perspective – a useful antidote to the strong anti-Chavez bias in much of the media.

First-Time Latin America

The big adventure

1	Planning your route	127
2	Studying, volunteering and working in Latin America	159
3	Documents and insurance	172
4	When to go	186
5	How much will it cost?	199
6	Guidebooks and other resources	211
7	What to take	225
8	Your first night	239
9	Culture shock	250
10	Getting around	270
11	Accommodation	294
12	Staying healthy	308
13	Keeping in touch	327
14	Crime, safety and sleaze	336
15	Coming home	354

1

Planning your route

L atin America is a vast area, encompassing nineteen countries, two ocean coastlines, one of the world's mightiest rivers, the Amazon, and a mountain range, the Andes, which stretches well over 4000 miles. With a multitude of different landscapes and cultures – including Amerindian, colonial European, African – to experience, choosing exactly where to go is no easy decision.

Built-in constraints like time and budget will help you to whittle down the myriad possibilities, but there are other factors to consider. Think about making your itinerary as varied as possible: spend time in the mountains, the rainforest and by the sea, as well as mixing the experience of rural indigenous life with peaceful colonial towns and big-city bustle. On the other hand, don't make the mistake of trying to see too much in a limited time – you'll return home with very little impression of your travels.

Try to be as flexible as possible when planning your route. Until you arrive you won't really know how much you're going to like (or dislike) the places you're visiting, so build enough time into your itinerary so that you're able to extend your stay if somewhere particularly takes your fancy.

See "When to go" (p.186) for more detailed information on climate and specific holiday seasons.

Itineraries

The following itineraries describe some of the classic Latin American journeys and are intended to give you some ideas of how to structure your trip, whether you want to hike up Andean peaks, explore the ruined cities of the Maya or Inca, or simply lounge around on a Caribbean beach. Additional itineraries for individual countries are provided in the country profiles on pp.19–123; many of these can be connected into longer, multi-country trips.

Ruta Maya

One of the world's most fascinating ancient cultures, the Maya civilization left behind the often spectacular remains of hundreds of cities – the majority still unexcavated – across southern Mexico, Belize, Guatemala, Honduras and El Salvador. While the Ruta Maya (or Mayan Route) is essentially a tourist board invention, it makes an excellent itinerary for exploring parts of Mexico and Central America. The most important – and magnificent – sites are at Palenque, Uxmal and Chichén Itzá in Mexico, Tikal in Guatemala and Copán in Honduras; it's possible to see all five in three or four weeks, as well as explore the surrounding region, which includes the gorgeous Caribbean coast of the Yucatán Peninsula in Mexico, the coral reefs and islands of Belize and Honduras, and the dense jungle surrounding Palenque and Tikal.

A good starting-point for visiting the Maya region is Cancún, on the northeastern tip of Mexico's Yucatán Peninsula, partly because you can fly there direct from the US, partly because it's close to two of the most significant Maya sites – Uxmal and Chichén Itzá. From the Yucatán, you can cross the border at Chetumal into Belize, whose Caribbean cayes make an idyllic spot for some welcome relaxation after exploring a few ruins, before continuing on to Tikal in northern Guatemala, perhaps the most impressive of all Maya sites. From Tikal, head southwest into the highlands of Guatemala, still largely inhabited by pure-blooded descendants of the ancient Maya, who preserve their traditional customs and colourful costumes. From Guatemala, you can cross the border into Honduras to visit Copán, the last of the big five Maya sites, renowned for its carvings. Finally, if you'd rather venture a little way off the well-trodden trail, there are plenty of less tourted but rewarding Maya sites to visit, such as

Caracol, Lamanai and Xunantunich in Belize, Ceibal and El Mirador in Guatemala's Petén region, San Andrés in El Salvador, or the vast site of Calakmul in Mexico.

Central America

The seven compact countries that make up Central America are conveniently linked in a long narrow isthmus, and form an easily negotiated, ready-made itinerary. Essentially a bridge between the temperate climate of North America and tropical South America, Central America is blessed with a geographical diversity that belies its tidy proportions. With terrain ranging from the cloudforests of Costa Rica and Panama to the swampy flatlands of Mosquitia in Honduras and Nicaragua and the Caribbean coral atolls of Belize, and a central chain of volcanoes – over 250 in all, a number of them active – running the length of the isthmus, this region has much to offer to outdoor enthusiasts. Culturally, too, Central America is rich in diversity, its peoples ranging from the deeply traditional Maya groups of the Guatemalan highlands to the English-speaking African-descended population of the Caribbean coast.

It's possible to travel through the whole of Central America, north to south, in two or three months. Belize is a good starting point, especially since it's easy to reach overland from Cancún in Mexico, which has direct flights from the US and Europe. From Belize City, you can head out to Caye Caulker in the Caribbean for some great snorkelling and then move down the coast to the Garífuna (black descendants of African slaves with their own language and culture) communities of Dangriga and Hopkins to listen to some distinctive local drumming and music. Then cross the country westwards towards Guatemala and the magnificent Maya site of Tikal, before heading southwest into Guatemala's Western Highlands. Spend some time exploring the indigenous lakeside villages of Lake Atitlán and their colourful markets before crossing the border into tiny El Salvador. Then travel on to Honduras, where there's superb snorkelling and diving in the Bay Islands, before crossing the border to visit Lago de Nicaragua. From Nicaragua, head on into Costa Rica, the most developed of the Central American countries, with a range of ecotourism opportunities and over 850 species of birds, then finish off in Panama, which has a similar wealth of natural attractions but fewer tourists. Panama City is one of the most vibrant of Central American capitals, a melting pot of different immigrant and domestic cultures situated on one of the great crossroads of the world. This location makes the city a keen commercial centre, long established as a trading post with sophisticated and open-minded inhabitants less interested in the rest of the country than the rest of the world.

The Caribbean coast

From the Yucatán Peninsula of Mexico south through Central America and curving east along the northern edge of South America, Latin America forms the western edge of the Caribbean Sea. If you're looking for palm-fringed beaches or coral-fringed islands, this is the place to come. With clear aquamarine waters and the world's second largest barrier reef, the scuba diving and snorkelling are excellent; for those who'd rather just lie in the sun, there are endless little beach communities. In terms of culture, Latin America's Caribbean stretch has its own distinctive feel – thanks to a mixture of the Afro-Caribbean (descendants of slaves brought in by the Spanish to work on plantations) and mestizo (European-Amerindian) populations of the interior. You're as likely to hear reggae and soca rhythms as Latin American salsa, English is widely spoken in some places, and the region's cuisine is often spiced up with ingredients like coconut milk and chilli.

There are two strands to this itinerary, which can be joined together if you've several months' travelling time. The first is to fly to Caracas in Venezuela, a major air-hub with direct connections to the US and Europe, and then make your way along a stretch of Venezuela's 2800-metre coastline (the longest in the Caribbean) to Colombia. Heading west from Caracas brings you to the travellers' hot spot of Choroní, reached via a spectacular bus ride through the cloudforest of the Parque Nacional de Henri Pittier. Other highlights of this coastline include the paradisical islands of the Parque Nacional de Morrocoy – you can charter a boat here without breaking the bank and even camp overnight on some islands.

Once over the border in Colombia, you'll want to make your way to the city of Cartagena via the popular Parque Nacional Tayrona, a collection of white sandy beaches where you can hang a hammock or camp. From here consider embarking on the spectacular five-day trek to the Cuidad Perdida in the Sierra Nevada de Santa Marta mountain range. Cartagena itself is one of the loveliest colonial cities in Latin America and probably the most interesting destination on the coast, with remnants from its past as the biggest port in northern South America. From Cartagena either head south into Colombia towards Ecuador, or fly to Colón in Panama to explore Central America.

The second strand of the itinerary encompasses the Caribbean coast of Central America and especially its offshore islands. These include the San Blas archipelago of Panama, home to the indigenous Kuna; the Bay Islands of Honduras, one of the cheapest and most popular spots to learn to scuba dive; and the cayes of Belize, which lie right on the edge of a lengthy coral reef. It's not possible to hop from one chain of islands to another, though – you'll have to return to the mainland and travel to the next departure point (see above for details of the Central America itinerary). Highlights inland are Costa Rica's Parque Nacional Tortuguero, especially in turtle-hatching season, and surfing spot Puerto Viejo; the wild swamplands of the Mosquitia region in Nicaragua; and the Afro-Caribbean Garífuna villages of Honduras.

△ The Bay Islands, Honduras

The Amazon

Covering over half of Brazil and significant parts of The Guianas, Venezuela, Colombia, Ecuador, Peru and Bolivia, the Amazon basin is one of the world's defining landscapes. It's the largest tropical rainforest on earth with the greatest biodiversity: more than 6000 known species of plant (and doubtless many more unknown), 15,000 animal species and a fifth of the planet's birds can be found in the Amazon; the river itself extends 6500km from source to mouth and has over a thousand tributaries. The basin also supports hundreds of thousands of indigenous peoples, living deep within the forest and largely undisturbed by outside influence. That said, it's not easy to penetrate the jungle – your best bet is to visit the region as part of a guided tour or on a boat trip along the river.

Popular starting points for organized trips into the Amazon are Iquitos in Peru, Tena and Misahuallí in eastern Ecuador, and Rurrenabaque in Bolivia – the last is the base for the cheapest trips into the Amazon (from US$20 a day). All these towns are easily reached by land, offer accommodation in jungle lodges and established routes down rivers and into the forest. With less infrastructure and fewer tourists but similar environments are Leticia in Colombia (which you'll have to fly to within Colombia – there's no road access), Puerto Ayacucho on the Venezuelan border with Colombia and Puerto Maldonado in Peru. Several national parks close to Puerto Maldonado, the Tambopata-Candamo Reserved Zone and the Manu Biosphere Reserve are in a region which is arguably the most biodiverse on Earth and the absence of city noise and light make them perfect places to experience the unique fauna, flora and atmosphere of the jungle.

A quintessential Amazon journey is the Brazilian trip from the mouth of the Amazon River at Belém to Manaus, right in the heart of the rainforest, a boat journey of five days. Because of the massive width of the river between these points (you can't see both its banks when you're on it), you won't see a lot of wildlife, but it's a classic adventure all the same, with accommodation in hammocks, river dolphins playing in the boat's wake (if you're lucky), and local people paddling past in canoes, selling jungle fruit. From Manaus you can make boat trips on the Amazon's tributaries – such as the Río Negro, which winds northwards to Colombia, or the Río Madeira, which makes its way down towards Brazil's border with

Bolivia – many of which are sizeable rivers in their own right but offer better opportunities for spotting river wildlife.

The Andes

The longest chain of mountains in the world at 7200km, the Andes run the length of western South America, from the southern tip of Chile to Venezuela in the north, and include some of the highest peaks outside the Himalayas. Made up of dozens of parallel mountain ranges or *cordilleras*, the Andes provide some of the most spectacular scenery in Latin America. These mountains were home to the great Inca race and to others before them – Chavín, Nazca and Tiahuanuco, to name three – who left behind a string of dramatic ruined cities and trading routes that now form memorable hiking trails. Today, the rural highlands are still inhabited by indigenous peoples, principally the Quechua and Aymara, who wear traditional costume, farm the terraced slopes much as their ancestors did and come together to trade in colourful weekly markets.

The classic Andean itinerary runs between Quito in Ecuador and La Paz in Bolivia via Peru – this is the most visited region in Latin America and not without reason known as the Gringo Trail. It's easy to escape other travellers, though – apart from the resorts and attractions on the well-worn route (listed below), the Andean region is still largely overlooked by tourists.

Quito, capital of Ecuador, is an attractive colonial city with an old centre – known as the Old Town or *El Centro Histórico* – packed with churches, monasteries and a wealth of seventeenth- and eighteenth-century religious painting. With its easy-going charm, spring-like climate and good tourist facilities, the city makes an excellent starting point. The country's central sierra, site of the so-called Avenue of the Volcanoes, has some spectacular trekking and climbing opportunities and is also the indigenous heart of Ecuador. Heading south towards Peru, highlights include Baños, a small thermal spa town with a subtropical climate; Cuenca, an even finer example of colonial architecture than Quito – and without the capital's noise and traffic; and Vilcabamba, a gringo hangout set in a beautiful valley and close to the cloudforests of Parque Nacional Podocarpus. Crossing into Peru, head for the Cordillera Blanca, the highest tropical mountain range in the world with spectacular scenery, glacial lakes and pre-Inca ruins, before making for Cusco.

A delightful colonial city with a lively backpacker scene, Cusco is the gateway to the Inca ruins of Machu Picchu, Latin America's biggest tourist attraction, set on a terraced plateau between two prominent mountain peaks; one of the most popular ways of reaching it is the Inca Trail, a strenuous three- to five-day hike. Bolivia's Andean highlights include the clear blue waters of Lago Titicaca, which straddles the border between Bolivia and Peru, the legendary silver-mining city of Potosí, and La Paz, Bolivia's de facto capital and a bustling cultural melting pot situated at an altitude of over 3500m. Close to the city, Huayna Potosí is one of the few peaks in South America over 6000m that can be climbed by people with no mountaineering experience. To cover this stretch of South America, you should allow two to three months.

If you have more time to spare – at least a fortnight though ideally a month – consider exploring the mountain regions of Chile and Argentina. Moving south from Bolivia, you'll cross into the Chilean Altiplano, a high mountain plain with starkly beautiful scenery punctured by turquoise lakes and snowcapped Andean volcanoes. The main tourist centre of the region is San Pedro de Atacama, a friendly village with adobe houses and a large backpacker scene, sitting at 2400m between the desert and the Altiplano. Trips from the village go to the eerie lunar landscape of the Valle de la Luna, the salt flats of the Salar de Atacama and the fuming geysers of El Tatio. Another attractive settlement in the Chilean Altiplano is Parinacota, a typical *pueblo altiplánico* with a bright, whitewashed church. Parinacota is headquarters for the Parque Nacional Lauca, a starkly beautiful place where herds of vicuña (a llama relative) roam near the shores of the wide Lago Chungará and nearby stands one of the highest peaks in Chile, Volcán Parinacota.

Chile's eastern border with Argentina is a natural one, formed by a 5000m long *cordillera* of the Andes, and it's on the Argentine side of this border that Aconcagua, the highest mountain outside the Himalayas (6959m), juts above an array of impressive neighbouring peaks. Although you shouldn't consider a trek to its summit unless you're an experienced mountain climber, the region around the peak, Alta Montaña, is very picturesque with good skiing and hiking available for sports lovers. From here you could head into Argentina's Lake District and onto Patagonia (see opposite) or loop back into Chile and head south to explore the Carretera Austral, a 1000m road that winds through a lush green wilderness laced with national parks.

Patagonia and Tierra del Fuego

Patagonia, a huge and remote wilderness in the far south of South America, encompasses more than a third of Argentina along with the southern tip of Chile. Of its several distinct landscapes, the central region is a vast dry steppe with little of interest for tourists; western Patagonia, however, comprises the dramatic terrain punctured by the huge Andean peaks, glaciers and lakes commonly associated with the region, while the eastern coast boasts a rich marine wildlife. There are almost no indigenous peoples in Patagonia: the native Tehuelche tribes, nomadic hunter-gatherers, were wiped out by European settlers in the nineteeth century. Bizarrely, though, Patagonia's Chubut Valley became home to a Welsh Nonconformist community in 1865, whose descendants continue to farm the land today.

In this scarcely populated region, distances between areas of interest are immense – you'll either have to fly from place to place or be prepared to spend days in either a bus or rental car. Still, with its world-class trekking, mountains and national parks – and no large cities to speak of – Patagonia will satiate even the hardiest of outdoors types.

This also goes for the archipelago of Tierra del Fuego to the south, again split between Argentina and Chile, and quite literally the end of the earth. Tierra del Fuego's principal island, Isla Grande, has one main draw that lures people enormous distances to see: Ushuaia, a town dramatically wedged between the mountains and the sea. From here Parque Nacional Tierra del Fuego is within easy reach, with its diversity of landscapes ranging from subantarctic tundra to intricate lakes and swampy marshland, all offering some great trekking. The island's central landscape comprises rolling hills covered with beech woodland, at its prettiest in autumn (late March to late April), while the north of the island consists mainly of pasture grazed by sheep – though it does have some superlative fly fishing on the Río Grande.

An exhaustive trip starts with flying into Buenos Aires, then heading south to Chile, a journey of over 1500km. Other highlights of the region not listed above include (from north to south) the Península Valdés, with its colonies of penguins, killer whales and other marine wildlife; the 10,000-year-old handprints on the walls of the Cueva de los Manos Pintadas; and the Perito Moreno Glacier, with its sixty-metre cliffs of ice. Cross the border into Chile at Tierra del Fuego and take the two-day ferry ride from Puerto Natales, conveniently near to Parque Nacional Torres del Paine, through the Chilean fjords to Puerto Montt and on up the scenic Carretera Austral to points north in Chile and the other Andean countries.

You'll need several weeks to fully explore the region. Bear in mind that roads here are often not in the best of conditions – particularly large stretches of the fabled RN-40 in Argentina – and that during the winter months of June and July temperatures drop to as low as -25°C/-13°F.

Themed trips

If you've a particular interest, be it wildlife, or ancient civilizations, or activities such as whitewater rafting, trekking or scuba diving, Latin America is certainly a place where you could plan your trip around a theme instead of basing it on a strictly geographical itinerary.

Adventure sports

Latin America, with its diverse, grand and unspoilt landscapes, has an extremely impressive range of adventure sports on offer, many of which are far more reasonably priced than what you're accustomed to at home; bear in mind, though, that safety standards may not be what you'd expect at home either. If you have your own equipment, consider bringing it along, in case the quality of gear available isn't up to scratch.

● **Mountaineering and rock-climbing** There are superb climbing opportunities in the Andean countries of South America, ranging from some of the world's most challenging ascents to relatively easy ones that can be tackled by anyone with a reasonable level of fitness (remember, though, that you'll need to be properly acclimatized, or you risk developing the potentially fatal acute mountain sickness – see p.319). John Biggar's *The High Andes: A Guide for Climbers* is an excellent, comprehensive climbing guide to the region. Amongst specific destinations, Bolivia's spectacular Cordillera Real, close to La Paz, has six peaks over 6000m, one of which, Huayna Potosí (6088m), can be climbed by people with absolutely no mountaineering experience. For experienced climbers, *Bolivia: A Climbing Guide* by Yossi Brain, is an essential read. Ecuador's Avenue of the Volcanoes, south of Quito, also offers a wealth of climbing opportunities (see *Climbing and Hiking in Ecuador* by Rob Rachowiecki, Mark Thurber and Betsy

Wagenhauser for further details). The *departamento* of Ancash in Peru, particularly the Huarez valley of the Cordillera Blanca, has some of the best mountaineering in the Americas. Huascarán (6768m) is Peruy's tallest peak and the climb to the top is challenging and for serious mountaineers only. Less difficult peaks to scale are Pisco and Urus; for all these climbs you'll need local guides. In Argentina, the main climbing centres are the city of Mendoza, close to South America's highest peak, Aconcagua (6962m); the holiday resort of Bariloche in the Patagonian Lake District; and western Patagonia, particularly the Fitz Roy Massif in the Parque Nacional Los Glaciares and the Volcán Lanin (3776m).

- **Skiing** Argentina's main resort is Las Lenas in the southwest of Mendoza province, which attracts a chic South American crowd as well as northern hemisphere skiers looking for some summer (June–Oct) action. Chile has the best skiing in South America, with very dry powder snow; the main resorts – El Colorado, La Parva and Valle Nevado – are all roughly 40km from Santiago.

- **Whitewater rafting** and **river kayaking** Latin America has some championship-level locations for whitewater rafting and river kayaking. In Chile there are two world-class rafting rivers (graded III–IV) in spectacular settings, with backdrops of volcanoes, waterfalls and lush forest: the Bío Bío on the southern edge of the Central Valley; and the Futaleufu down by the southern Carretera Austral, occasional venue of the Rafting World Championships. Gentler waters can be found on the Río Maipo near Santiago, the Rio Trancura near Pucon and Río Petrohue near Puerto Varas. Peru also offers some of the best whitewater rafting in the world, the main centre being Cusco, from where you can organize trips to the Urubamba and Vilcanota rivers; the Cotahuasi and Colca river canyons close to Arequipa are also popular. For a thrilling account of a 1986 journey by kayak from the Amazon's source to its mouth (2500km later), read *Running the Amazon* by Joe Kane.

- Other adrenaline highs include **bungee-jumping** in Costa Rica, from a bridge over the Río Colorado in the Central Valley, and also in Guatemala, over one of the ravines near Guatemala City or on the Río Dulce; **hang-gliding** from the Parque Nacional de Tijuca in Rio de Janeiro, where a spectacular tandem flight takes you 520m down to the beach at São Conrado; and **mountain biking** on the road which runs dramatically from the mountains of La Paz to the jungle lowlands around Coroico in Bolivia.

Scuba diving and snorkelling

The Caribbean coast and islands offer the best scuba diving and snorkelling in Latin America, with great visibility. The year-round warmth and calm waters of the Caribbean Sea, protected by its circular shape, make this a particularly good place for beginners and those keen to learn to scuba dive. There is a wealth of marine life including the world's largest fish, the whale shark; parrot fish; eagle rays and stingrays; barracuda, hammerhead and nurse sharks. Courses range in price from fairly expensive in Mexico to very cheap in Honduras. There are various isolated snorkelling and diving spots in South America, too, principally the Galápagos Islands.

● **Mexico, Belize and Honduras** Lying offshore from the Caribbean coast of the Yucatán Peninsula in Mexico is a huge coral reef which offers some world-class scuba diving, particularly around the island of Cozumel and further south around the pristine Banco Chincorro. The cayes of Belize and Bay Islands of Honduras, set on the same 290-kilometre-long coral reef that begins in Mexico, also have wonderful diving, along with idyllic island settings. There are three atolls in Belize alone and the renowned Great Blue Hole, a vast collapsed cave made famous by Jacques Costeau. The Bay Islands are especially popular with backpackers – Utila has the cheapest diving courses in Latin America. Recommended specialist guidebooks are: *Diving and Snorkeling Guide to Cozumel* by George S. Lewbel, *Diving in Belize* by Ned Middleton, and Cindy Garoute's *Diving the Bay Islands.*

● **Colombia** The tiny coral islets called the Islas del Rosario, just off the Caribbean coast at Cartagena, are teeming with brightly coloured fish – dive operators in Cartagena take trips out to the islands. Further out in the Caribbean, the island of Providencia also has wonderful scuba diving and snorkelling in pristine turquoise sea.

● **Ecuador** The waters off the Galápagos Islands are home to unique marine species including marine iguanas, the Galápagos fur seal and the stalkeye scorpion fish, and offer some of the world's best diving (and snorkelling), although colder temperatures, strong swirling currents and low visibility mean that this is for experienced divers only, and rates are not cheap.

● **Brazil** The Atlantic coast of South America has crystal-clear waters and good scuba diving around the marine park island of Fernando de Noronha in northeastern Brazil. Its position, 340km from the nearest land, means that abundant marine life is largely undisturbed and includes turtles, stingrays and spinner dolphins. There are numerous caverns, submerged rocks and several shipwrecks including the *Corveta* V17, a cargo ship with structure intact. Other notable places to scuba dive are Abrolhos, an archipelago off the coast of Bahia with one of the largest and healthiest coral reefs in the South Atlantic and visited by humpback whales between June and December and Arrail do Cabo Marine Reserve near Rio de Janeiro where divers can spot seahorses, moray eels and Queen Angelfish.

Surfing

The entire Pacific coast of Latin America is dotted with surfer communities, with a high concentration in Mexico and Costa Rica, and several in El Salvador and Nicaragua – these are populated mostly by well-organized and friendly American expats. In South America the scene is much more homegrown, with large domestic surf scenes in Peru and Brazil. Renting reasonably priced boards and equipment is possible in all these places. Check ⓦwww.surfline.com and ⓦwww.surflink.com for detailed reports on the best breaks.

- **Mexico** The Pacific coast has the best waves and the most established surfer communities, notably the laid-back town of San Blas and the larger resort of Puerto Escondido. The Baja California peninsula also has lots of more remote surfing beaches including Punta El Conejo and El Martillo (The Hammer) on the Islas de Todos Santos.
- **Costa Rica** With some famous breaks on both coasts, Costa Rica has a big surfing scene. The Pacific side attracts more visitors – with a whole series of top spots including Boca Barranca, Jaco and Dominical – while Puerto Viejo on the Caribbean is home to the *salsa brava*, one of the country's few really big waves.
- **Peru** Peru has some of the longest waves in the world, with quality surf spots around Lima, particularly Punta Hermosa, 50km south of the city, and also in the far north of the country.
- **Brazil** The best surfing in South America is on the southern beaches of Brazil, though Brazilian surfers have a terrible reputation for aggressive riding and stealing waves. The island of Santa Catarina in the state of the same name is famous for its waves and hosts the Brazilian national championships every January.

Wildlife

With the incredible variety of flora and fauna and a rich diversity of habitats, largely undeveloped and unspoilt by mass tourism, Latin America is one of the world's leading destinations for ecotourists and wildlife enthusiasts. Of course, the Amazon rainforest has no equal in terms of its profusion of animal and plant species, but the region holds numerous other habitats – such as flat grasslands, mountain forests, alpine lakes and seas – which are also strikingly fertile. Indeed, every Latin American country offers good opportunities for spotting wildlife, but some – notably Belize, Costa Rica and Argentina – have better organized networks of national parks and reserves, which can make a wildlife-themed trip a lot easier and more rewarding. Animals you might see include anteaters, tapirs, pumas and jaguars; howler monkeys and sloths; giant turtles, caymans and anacondas; poison dart frogs and leafcutter ants. The region is also a paradise for birdwatchers, both in terms of quantity – there are more species of bird in Brazil and Colombia than in any other country in the world, while Guatemala and Costa Rica aren't far behind – and celebrated species – condors, scarlet and hyacinth macaws, toucans and quetzals all reside here. *Andes to Amazon: A Guide to Wild South America* by Michael Bright and John C. Kricher's *A Neotropical Companion: An Introduction to the Animals, Plants and Ecosystems of the New World Tropics* are recommended guidebooks to the flora and fauna of Latin America. There are also dozens of specialist books on birds – *A Field Guide to the Birds of Mexico and Central America* by Meyer de Schauensee and L.I. Davis's *A Guide to the Birds of South America* are the most comprehensive. Below are just a few of the best destinations – other than the Amazon (covered on pp.132–133) – for spotting wildlife in Latin America.

- **The Petén** In northern Guatemala, the Petén comprises a mixture of low-lying swamp, savannah and rainforest, and includes the Maya Biosphere Reserve, the largest tropical forest reserve in Central America. The most accessible area is that surrounding the Maya site at Tikal.
- **The Darién Gap** Straddling the border between Panama and Colombia, much of the Darién Gap is currently off-limits thanks to the activities of guerrillas and drug runners (see p.153). However, parts of this great, untouched natural wilderness can be explored from the Panamanian side, where large tracts of forest are protected by the Parque Nacional Darién.
- **Los Llanos** A vast area of plains between the Andes and the Río Orinoco basin in Venezuela, Los Llanos is flooded annually in October and November, when wildlife spotting is at its best – species include river dolphins, alligators, puma and howler monkeys.
- **The Pantanal** The open swampland of the Pantanal in western Brazil is not easily reached independently, but there are dozens of tour operators in Corumba running trips into the area. The flatness of

the Pantanal (and its lack of inhabitants) means that sighting wildlife is more likely than almost anywhere else in Latin America – with luck you might see anteaters, armadillos, rare blue macaws, toucans, jaguars and anacondas.

● **The Galápagos Islands** Never mind that the cost of reaching the famous Galápagos Islands, 950km off the coast of Ecuador, is enough to put a sizeable hole in all but the deepest of budgets – there can be little doubt that it is money well spent. The abundant marine fauna of one the world's pre-eminent wildlife destinations leaves an unforgettable impression, not to mention the rare chance to glimpse a venerable giant tortoise.

● **Península Valdés** One of the most important marine reserves on earth, the waters around the arid Península Valdés in Argentine Patagonia are home to an array of arresting animals – from southern right whales to pods of killer whales known to momentarily strand themselves as they hunt for young sea lions and elephant seals idling at the foot of the peninsula's cliffs.

Trekking

Even if walking and outdoor activities are normally anathema to you, you'll probably be tempted by the dramatic beauty of Latin America's mountains, rainforests and Inca trails to do some trekking on your trip. Try always to stick to established paths and, if you're walking in an area with a guerrilla or paramilitary presence (such as Colombia or Chiapas in Mexico), check first with the locals about the current situation and err on the side of caution. Never go trekking alone – even a sprained ankle could prove hazardous if you're stuck on your own in a remote region.

If you're planning on doing several long treks (three or more days), consider taking your own camping and water filtration equipment. Detailed topographical maps can be purchased from the relevant Instituto Nacional Geográfico/Militar (normally located in capital cities). Several well-worn routes in Latin America (notably the Inca Trail, see p.142) can only be done in organized groups with registered guides – these regulations are to protect you as well as the landscape and should be respected. Even if a guide is not strictly necessary, you should always consider the option when trekking in lesser known areas and particularly in the jungle, where dense vegetation makes getting lost a real possibility. If your plans entail hiking for several days in a national park you may have to book your place well in advance. And finally, if you're trekking in the Andes, bear in mind that at high altitudes there's an enormous difference in temperature between sunny and shady areas during the daytime – and once the sun sets it gets very cold indeed.

Guidebook publishers Bradt are experts in trekking and have some excellent guides to climbing and trekking in Latin America. There are spectacular opportunities for trekking in every country in Latin America – listed below are just a few of the best.

- **Guatemala** The Western Highlands of Guatemala provide a variety of trekking experiences through lush green hills dotted with traditional Maya villages and volcanoes. The Ixil triangle in the Cuchumatanes mountains is another of the region's picturesque walking areas, while the northern Petén region offers an arduous two-day trek with pack horses through remote jungle to the remote Maya ruin of El Mirador.

- **Costa Rica** Costa Rica's many national parks and nature reserves are home to numerous excellent, well-organized walking trails. Some of the most popular include those in the famous Monteverde Cloudforest Reserve (and in the less tourised Santa Elena Reserve nearby), the trek along the coast of the pristine Osa peninsula in the Parque Nacional de Corcovado, and the challenging climb to Costa Rica's highest point at 3819m in the Parque Nacional Chirripó.

- **Colombia** Starting from the Caribbean coast, the five- or six-day trek to the Cuidad Perdida of the Tayrona Indians in the Sierra Nevada de Santa Marta is one of the country's highlights, while the mountainous Parque Nacional de Puracé, in southern Colombia, offers a rewarding day's trek up Volcan Puracé, with the possibility of spotting condors, bears and tapirs.

- **Venezuela** Climbing the *tepui* or flat-topped mountain of Roraima at the eastern edge of the Gran Sabana is strenuous and takes at least five days, but the eerie landscape at its summit, with a black craggy surface split by fissures and weirdly shaped rocks, makes the climb well worth it.

- **Bolivia** Bolivia's most popular trekking region is the Cordillera Real, which is blessed with high Andean scenery and easily reached from La Paz. Three different Inca trails run from close by La Paz across the mountains and down to the tropical valleys of the Yungas – the most spectacular, the Takesi Trail, takes two to three days and is easily done by less experienced hikers without a guide.

- **Peru** The Peruvian Andes are home to Latin America's most popular trek, the three- to five-day Inca Trail to the legendary ruined city of

Machu Picchu. There are many other good trekking opportunities in the surrounding Sacred Valley, while Huaraz in the Cordillera Blanca, north of Lima, is the starting point for serious mountain-hiking.

- **Brazil** Parque Nacional de Chapada Diamantina in Bahia, northeastern Brazil, is laced with caves, waterfalls and dramatic rock formations rising from flat grasslands. The full day's trek from the colonial mining town of Lençois to the hamlet of Capão is one of many spectacular walks in the park.

- **Argentina** Most visitors to Argentina head to Patagonia to trek and particularly the Fitz Roy region around El Chatén. Other popular trekking areas include Nahuel Huapí Nacional Park, just south of Bariloche. In the north of Argentina both Jujuy and Salta provinces offer a wide range of walking terrains, from subtropical to cloudforest and high mountain valleys.

- **Chile** The meadows, lakes and forests of the Chilean Lake District make it the most popular trekking region of the country, along with the spectacular mountain peaks of the Parque Nacional Torres del Paine in Chilean Patagonia.

Ancient civilizations

Long before the Spanish and Portuguese colonizers arrived in the Americas in the sixteenth century, much of Latin America's Amerindian population had organized itself into a series of complex and fascinating societies with their own languages, culture and political and belief systems. Although much of what these ancient civilizations – such as the Maya, Inca and Aztec – created was razed to the ground by tribal wars and systematically destroyed by the European invaders, some surprisingly intact remnants – including cities, temples and burial grounds – are scattered across Latin America. With new archeological discoveries still being made, these civilizations and their enduring cultural heritage together are one of the region's defining attractions.

Good sources of background information, current news and essays on the pre-Hispanic civilizations of Latin America are Mesoweb (Ⓦwww.mesoweb.com), Archnet (warchnet.asu.edu) and the Archaelogical Institute of America (Ⓦwww.archaeological.org) which organizes pricey but very professional archeological tours of Latin America. The Lanic (Latin American Network Information) website (Ⓦlanic.utexas.edu) has dozens of links to relevant societies, online magazines and websites.

The Maya, Inca and Aztec

- **The Maya** Perhaps the best known of Latin America's ancient civilizations is the Maya. Over three thousand years ago nomadic tribes began to settle in the rainforests of middle (or meso) America, over a landmass that includes the countries now known as Mexico, Guatemala, Belize, Honduras and El Salvador. They established the most sophisticated pre-Hispanic civilization in Latin America, one that, with its complex structures and incredible prowess in engineering, architecture, mathematics and astronomy, rivalled those of contemporary Europe. Even though all their cities had been mysteriously abandoned by 1200 AD, Maya culture lives on, particularly in Guatemala which has a majority population of pure blooded Maya.

  A detailed itinerary, covering the major sites of the Maya World, is listed on p.128. For those interested in background information, both Michael Coe's *The Maya* (Thames and Hudson) and Robert J. Sharer's *The Ancient Maya* (Stanford University) should be considered required reading.

- **The Inca Empire** The Inca Empire was once the largest in the world. Much later in formation than the Maya civilization and much shorter in length (three hundred years rather than two thousand), it began in 1200 AD and was centred in the valleys around Cusco in the Peruvian Andes. At its height the Inca Empire covered around 980,000 square kilometres linked by 30,000km of roads and stretched from southern Colombia down to northern Chile. Its most fabled city was Machu Picchu, a three- to five-day hike from the Inca capital of Cusco. Around Cusco there are several other impressive Inca sites including the megalithic fortress of Sacsayhuaman and the sacred spots of Qenko and Salapunco, both marked by rocks carved with Inca patterns, pumas and snakes. Close to Machu Picchu are the ruins of Pisac and Ollantaytambo and hundreds of lesser known Inca trails which wind through the mountain scenery. Further north, close to Lima in the Rimac valley, are the impressive Inca remains of Pachacamac, once one of the most famous shrines in the Inca Empire. On the shores of Lago Titicaca is the Incan Templo de Fertilidad which has a hundred stone phalluses jammed within its walls, and on the Bolivian side of the lake is the Isla de Sol, the birthplace of the sun, the mythical father of the Inca race. In Ecuador, Ingapirca, a city in the southern sierra, is the country's only notable Inca ruin with a striking temple forming the centrepiece of the site.

  Most visitors to Latin America explore Inca culture as part of a trip to the high Andes of South America. The Andes itinerary (see p.133) joins together various places of interest in this area though you may want to concentrate your time on Peru where all the major Inca sites are located.

The *Conquest of the Incas* (Papermac) by John Hemming is widely considered to be the authoritative account of the end of the Inca Empire, brought about by the Spanish conquest of Peru. Michael E. Moseley's *The Incas and Their Ancestors* (Thames and Hudson) is a good overview of the civilization.

● **Aztecs** Like the Incas, the Aztec civilization arose late and was short lived (1200–1521 AD), and in Mexico is overshadowed by the more lasting legacy of the Maya. Still, the Aztecs, or Mexica, gave Mexico its name and were in their time the most formidable of all Mexican empires, dominating the whole of central and southern Mexico in less than a hundred years. Their capital city, Tenochtitlán, was vast and so impressed Cortes and his Spanish army when they arrived to conquer the country that some of them thought it a mirage. The modern day Mexico City sits above the Aztec's capital and remains, albeit small, can be found dotted all round the city. Beneath the main square or *zocaló* is an Aztec temple, Templo Major, and on the outskirts of the city are the ruins of Tlatelolco where the beleaguered Aztecs made their last stand against Cortes in 1521.

Aztec culture didn't expand beyond Mexico – those interested in exploring it in depth would be best served by basing themselves in Mexico City. Essential reading on the Aztecs includes *The Aztecs* (Thames and Hudson) by Richard F. Townsend and Warwick Bray's *Everyday Life of the Aztecs* (P Bedrick).

Other ancient civilizations

Apart from the Maya, Inca and Aztec civilizations, there are dozens more in Latin America that have also left their legacy on the landscape. Listed below are the countries where you will find the most fascinating examples.

● **Mexico** Mexico has, by a large margin, the richest cultural history in Latin America. Apart from the legacies of the Mayans and Aztecs, there are remains throughout the country left by the Olmec, Zapotec, Mixtec, Toltec and Teotihuacán cultures, among others. A good starting point for exploring these civilizations is in the well laid out rooms of the Museo Nacional de Antropología in Mexico City, one of the world's foremost museums. Major sites include the great pyramids of Teotihuacán just outside Mexico City and also at Cholula; the Toltec city of Tula, also near Mexico City, with its famous atlantes, five-metre statues of fabled warrior prince Quetzalcoatl; El Tajín, close to Veracruz on the Gulf of Mexico, one of the most enigmatic of ruined cities with an unknown provenance and seventeen ball courts; Monte Alban in Oaxaca state, built by the Zapotecs and a masterpiece of engineering with a mountain top flattened by hand to create a massive plateau on which the Zapotecs built palaces, pyramids and astronomical observatories. Nigel Davies' book *The Ancient Kingdoms of Mexico* (Viking) is an excellent introduction to the 'other' ancient cultures of Mexico.

- **Colombia** There are two ancient cultural sites in Colombia that warrant a visit: San Agustín and Tierradentro. Both are in the far south of the country, and are difficult to get to, involving several bus journeys from the nearest town. Still, the trip is well worth the effort – San Agustín is an attractive place and its Parque Archaelógico is home to over a hundred standing statues, many zoomorphic, of mysterious origin. There are hundreds more statues dotted across the neighbouring hillsides – you could easily spend a week visiting them. Tierradentro consists of a series of circular burial caverns, some as deep as seven metres and decorated with unusual geometric designs. The surrounding countryside is a walkers' paradise with hiking trails to Indian villages and waterfalls in the hills.

- **Peru** Like Mexico, Peru has been host to many important ancient civilizations other than its greatest, the Inca, though we still know very little about them. Perhaps the most important archeological site in the country is a recent discovery – the pyramids of Caral. The oldest pyramids in the world, which date from 2600 BC and were functioning 100 years before the Great Pyramid at Giza, Caral is situated just north of Lima and is still being excavated. Visitors need special permission to visit from INRENA – Peru's main conservation agency – in Lima. In Lima itself are the ruins of Huaca Pucllana, a vast pre-Inca adobe mound and one of thousands of *huacas* (sacred places) in Peru. South of the capital is the consecrated citadel Pachacamac ("the Earth's creator") which was occupied well before 500 AD and later used by the Incas as a shrine. Other major sites in Peru include the world-famous Nazca Lines, a series of geometric shapes and animal figures, some 200m in length, drawn in the desert landscape of Pampa de San José; Chavín de Huantar, a temple complex in the Cordillera Blanca which had over three thousand resident priests and temple attendants in its heyday of 300 BC; Chan Chan, the capital city of the Chimu Empire, an urban civilization which appeared on the Peruvian coast around 1100 AD; and Kuelap in the north of Peru, a ruined city with 20m limestone walls and round stone houses decorated with a distinctive zigzag pattern.

Both Richard Keatinge's *Peruvian Prehistory* (Cambridge University Press) and *Ancient Civilizations of Peru* by J. Alden Mason (Penguin) are recommended reading if you're interested in learning more about the pre-Hispanic history of Peru.

● **Chile** Although tiny Easter Island, or Rapa Nui, is part of Chilean territory, it is actually located almost 4000km from the Chilean coast (a five-hour flight from Santiago) in the Pacific Ocean. Its isolation has given it a unique atmosphere – much more South Pacific than Latin American – which is augmented by the famous standing stones or *moai* which line the island's shores. The source of endless speculation – Who built them? And why? – the stones are discussed in several scholarly books, the best of which is *Easter Island* (André Deutsch) by Belgian anthropologist Alfred Métraux though it is currently out of print.

Indigenous culture

Long before the earliest classic civilizations of Latin America began to organize themselves into empires, its original inhabitants, now known as Amerindians, migrated to the continent from Asia. It is widely – though not universally – believed that the ancestors of Latin America's present-day indigenous population crossed the Bering Strait from Siberia to America during the last Ice Age (17,000 – 11,000 years ago) and then filtered its way down through the American landmass. While in some regions these people developed advanced civilizations, many groups remained semi-nomadic, hunter-gatherers living in the rainforest or other wildernesses. Although the Spanish and Portuguese colonizers wiped out much of the indigenous population, vibrant Amerindian communities remain, some living in much the same way as their migrant ancestors. Appallingly treated by past – and present – governments, indigenous Latin Americans are engaged in a constant struggle for land and human rights.

The growing trend of responsible tourism (see Chapter 9), which encourages tourists to contribute positively to the places and people they're visiting, makes it increasingly possible to catch more than a cursory glimpse of the indigenous culture of Latin America. This obviously requires some sensitivity since many of the existing tribes or groups of Amerindians are traditionally wary of outsiders. If you are interested, it's best to seek out eco- or community-based tourism or volunteer projects, either from home or on the ground once you arrive. These will encourage you to get involved and learn from your experience rather than just taking a tour to "gawp at Indians", a hideous practice which should be avoided at all costs. Taking photographs and any kind of unwelcome intrusiveness is often a no-no – always ask first and accept the answer "no" with good grace.

△ Kuna women, Panama

Good web resources on indigenous Amerindians include ⊛www .nativeweb.org, ⊛www.rainforestfoundation.org, ⊛www.cs.org and ⊛www.survival-international.org. Recommended books are *Fate of the Forest: Developers, Destroyers and Defenders of the Amazon* by Susanna Hecht and Alexander Cockburn (Penguin); *Tristes Tropiques* by Claude Levi-Strauss (Penguin): *One River* by Wade Davis (Simon and Schuster); *Savages* by Joe Kane (Pan/Vintage); *Indians of the Paraguayan Chaco* by John Renshaw (University of Nebraska); *Eduardo El Curandero: The Words of a Peruvian Healer* by Eduardo Calderon (North Atlantic Books) and *Sastun: My Apprenticeship with a Maya Healer* by Rosita Arvigo (Harper).

There are groups of surviving indigenous people in almost every country in Latin America. Listed below are just some of the places where there are well-conceived opportunities to explore indigenous culture. A decent guidebook will also detail these places as well as the best way to visit them.

- **Mexico** The Huichol, numbering 100,000, live in the isolated mountain regions just north of Guadalajara, and are possibly the indigenous group least affected by colonization and the modern world in Mexico. Although you need permission to visit their lands and there are no facilities for visitors, the Huichol Centre for Cultural Survival in nearby Santiago Ixcuintla is a co-operative enterprise selling distinctive Huichol woven paintings which depict animals, suns, moons, fertility and birth. It also has an extensive ethnographic archive with photos and taped interviews of Huichol leaders and particularly shaman, who use the hallucinogenic cactus *peyote* to reach the spirits. On the shores of Lago Zirahuen in Michoacan there is an eco-cultural village where Huichols run workshops in traditional crafts and natural medicine.

    Much further south in Chiapas, the Lacandón Maya (also known as the "Hach Winik" or "True People"), distinctive with their long white robes and pageboy haircuts, are also one of the most isolated groups of Amerindians. Close to the Maya ruin of Bonampak, Lacanhá Chansayab is a Lacandon village with campsites and local guides who will show you the waterfalls and rivers in the area and sell you well-crafted *artesanía* (clay and wood figurines, wooden bow and arrow sets). The best place to visit to learn about the Lacandón is Casa na–Bolom in San Cristóbal de las Casas. Once the home of Danish/Swiss anthropologists Frans and Gertrude Blom, it is now renowned as a centre for the study of the region's indigenous cultures, particularly the Lacandón.

- **Costa Rica** Close to Puerto Viejo de Talamanca on Costa Rica's Caribbean coast, is the KéköLdi Indigenous Reserve, home to two hundred Bríbrí and Cabécar people. The best way to visit the reserve is on one of the tours offered by the *Asociación Talamaqueña de Ecoturismo y Conservación* (ATEC; ✆www.greencoast.com/atec.htm). Tours usually consist of guided treks in the Talamanca mountains on Bríbrí trails with traditional medicinal plants pointed out along the way and folklore explained by indigenous guides.
- **Panama** Stretching some 375km along the northeastern Caribbean coast of Panama, Kuna Yala is the autonomous home of the Kuna (or Dúle), and one of the only regions in Latin America populated and governed exclusively by indigenous people. Living mostly on 40 of the islands of the San Blas archipelago, the Kuna survive on fishing and selling *molas*, brightly coloured fabric pictures in reverse-appliqué. It is possible to visit the islands, either independently or on a tour although all visitors are expected to abide by strict codes of conduct. Homestays with local families are popular, and once you've arrived on an island and asked permission to stay from the village elder or *sahila*, a guide will usually be assigned to you and a place to stay arranged.
- **Venezuela** In the Orinoco Delta of Venezuela there are numerous river lodges close to the isolated communities of the Warao. Activities whilst staying there include visiting Warao villages, canoeing and even piranha fishing.
- **Ecuador** The Oriente, or Ecuador's slice of the Amazon basin, hosts one of the fastest-growing "ethnotourism" scenes with plenty of well-organized opportunities to explore indigenous communities. One of the most attractive is in the village of Añangu, on the south shore of the Río Napo, where the Quichua people have built their own visitors' lodge. Jungle walks and canoe rides are led by expert guides, and there are visits to parrot licks where a wide variety of parrots and parakeets come, in a frenzy of sound and colour, to feed. For more details, *Defending Our Rainforest: A Guide to Community-Based Ecoturism in the Ecuadorian Amazon* by Rolf Wesche and Andy Drumm is packed with useful information.

Where shall I go first?

Once you've thought about which part of Latin America you'd like to go to, you'll need to think about where exactly to begin your trip so that you can start booking tickets and buying guidebooks.

Bear in mind that if you fly in on a long-haul flight you'll be suffering from jet lag and may not be ready to face the full force of culture shock. To ease yourself into your trip gently, choose a relatively safe and easy-going city or a well-established resort town to arrive and acclimatize in. Good starting points include Cancún in Mexico, San José in Costa Rica, Santiago in Chile and Buenos Aires in Argentina. Quito in Ecuador is also relatively small and trouble-free, although its high altitude may mean that you suffer from headaches and nausea for your first few days.

If you're thinking of starting your trip in Rio de Janeiro, Bogotá, Caracas or Mexico City, take heed that while these cities are undeniably exciting they are also large, noisy and not always safe (in Mexico's case, there are many smaller and safer cities which are accessible from the US by plane). The capital cities of Central America – with the exception of San José in Costa Rica - are also not known for their safe streets, cleanliness or tranquillity. Many tourists choose to enter Central America from the Yucatán region of Mexico.

And on a slightly different note, flying directly into La Paz in Bolivia, the world's highest capital city at 3500m above sea level, will almost certainly give you a bout of altitude sickness (see Staying Healthy for more details). You might want to consider flying into Bolivia's second city, low-lying Santa Cruz or (since flights to Bolivia from Europe are the most expensive in Latin America) coming overland from Peru, Chile or Argentina.

For more general information on helping you to plan where to go and in what order, see the itineraries and themed trips listed in this chapter.

Getting there

By air

There are plenty of options when it comes to flying into Latin America – major gateway cities include Mexico City and Cancún in Mexico, San José in Costa Rica, Caracas in Venezuela, Lima in Peru, Buenos Aires in Argentina, and São Paulo and Rio de Janeiro in Brazil. Major cities across the US – notably New York, Miami, Houston and Los Angeles – have a wide range of connections to Latin America; Miami offers the greatest choice, with several daily flights not just to capital cities, but to smaller destinations as well, and Houston has almost as many.

In Europe, there are direct flights to most South American capitals and to Mexico City from London, Paris, Amsterdam, Frankfurt and, especially, from Madrid. There are also direct flights to Central America from Europe – though not from London any longer (Cancún in southern Mexico is the nearest point via nonstop plane from the UK though these are charter flights and often only valid for two weeks).

There are also direct flights from Australia (Sydney) and New Zealand (Auckland) to major Latin American air-hubs (Mexico City, Buenos Aires, São Paulo and Rio de Janeiro). For more advice on buying a plane ticket to Latin America, see pp.176–182.

Overland from the US

If your home country is the US (or, less practical given the vast distances involved, Canada), you might consider travelling overland to Mexico and beyond – though there aren't as many advantages to this as you might think. Greyhound bus services (⊛www.greyhound.com) run to all the main border crossings (there are more than twenty in total between the US and Mexico) and some of these will take you right into Mexico and drop you conveniently at the local bus station for onward routes. Additionally many Mexican bus companies cross the border into the US, so that you can now pick up a bus back into Mexico as far north as Houston or Los Angeles. Distances can be huge, though – 60 hours travel time from New York to the Texas–Mexico border and 15 hours from San Francisco to the Baja California border – and you'll need a further day to get from the border to Mexico City. You might save some money travelling overland since bus journeys are generally cheaper than flights (New York to Texas return, for example, costs from US$105 by bus and around US$270 by plane), you'll get to see a lot of both countries from the bus window, and have plenty of time to acclimatize to your new surroundings.

Another overland option is to travel by car. This gives you complete freedom of movement and means that you have access to those off-the-beaten track places you might otherwise never find. If you're planning on camping or carrying a lot of gear, taking your own car or van removes the stress of lugging all your stuff around on public transport. Taking a car into Mexico, however, is a complicated process. You'll need to buy a temporary importation permit (approx US$25 and only valid for six months) at the border and show your registration and title for the car as well as your driving licence (US, Canadian, British, Irish, Australian, New Zealand and most European driving licences are valid in Mexico) and passport. You'll also need to leave a credit card imprint to stop you selling the car in Mexico or a neighbouring country. Additionally US/Canadian car insurance isn't valid in Mexico so you'll need to take out Mexican insurance from one of the numerous agencies who line either side of every border crossing. And all this before you deal with the state of the roads, Mexican and Central America driving, corrupt traffic cops and the possibility of car theft.

If you do decide to travel overland by car, make sure that everything is in order before you leave, that you have all the relevant paperwork and a good set of road maps (the American and Canadian Automobile Associations produce maps and route planners specifically for travel to Mexico; ®www.aaa.com, ®www.caa.ca). The *Rough Guide to Mexico* has more detailed information on red tape and crossing the border with a vehicle.

Crossing the Darién Gap

Connecting Central and South America, the so-called Darién Gap is the name given to the region of jungle wilderness that straddles the border between Panama and Colombia. There are no roads across it – the Pan-American Highway, which runs the length of the Americas from Alaska to Tierra del Fuego – here suffers its one and only interruption (hence the "gap"), meaning that travel from Panama to Colombia is by plane, boat or on foot only. Previously, the overland crossing of the Darién Gap was one of the classic Latin American adventures (although risky at the best of times), whereas these days the presence of Colombian guerrillas, paramilitaries and drug traffickers means it's now extremely dangerous, with a significant risk of kidnap or murder, and should on no account be contemplated.

Nowadays, most visitors cross the gap by plane – you can fly from Panama City to various cities in Colombia, with Cartagena being the most popular option. A more adventurous crossing is by sea, most easily done by travelling on one of the private yachts that sail regularly between Colón and Cartagena, a three- to four-day trip. The *Voyager International Hostel* (®www.geocities.com/voyagerih/english.html) in Panama City usually has up-to-date information on which yachts are carrying passengers on this route; otherwise ask around at the yacht clubs in Colón or Panama City.

Border crossings

Unless you're planning to visit just one country or to fly everywhere, you will find yourself at some point experiencing a land border crossing. These vary enormously from country to country. Some of them, like the main ones from the US into Mexico, are highly organized with clearly laid out procedures, officials in uniforms and surrounding communities designed to service the travellers' every need. Others, like Punta Gorda in Belize, consist of a ramshackle hut and a sleepy immigration officer. Some are scruffy, confusing and down at heel – Paso Canoas, between Costa Rican and Panama for example – and others, like Sixaola, also between Costa Rica and Panama and which involves crossing a long rickety bridge over the river are dramatic and picturesque. There are several border crossings in Latin America on the water – rivers or lakes (like LagoTiticaca which divides Peru and Bolivia, the Río San Juan between Nicaragua and Costa Rica or the Cruce Internacional de los Lagos which connects Chile and Argentina).

However informal the border, you should always have your wits about you – and your manners. As with immigration at airports, border guards have the right to refuse you entry to their country for any reason. Be polite and have your passport and all documents (plane tickets, proof of funds and any visas necessary) ready for inspection.

Also do your homework in advance – some border crossings don't have the right paperwork to permit entry and you'll need to pick up entry cards or immigration forms in the nearest big town – or even capital city – to the border before you arrive. Many smaller border crossings close at night so make sure you arrive in daylight. Others have idiosyncracies – while you won't need a visa for Venezuela if you fly in, for example, crossing its land borders does require one. See individual country profiles in the "Where to go" section for details on all the main border crossings.

By sea

Travelling to Latin America by sea may sound exciting, but in reality it's usually expensive (costing at least three times as much as flying) and time-consuming – if you're coming from Europe, voyages across the Atlantic take three weeks or more. Cargo ships take a limited number of passengers, while the fares are high and the journey long.

It might also be possible to reach Latin America across the Atlantic for free by working your passage as a crew member. In Europe the best place to hitch a ride is Gran Canaria in the Canary Islands, where lots of commercial shipping stops en route to the Caribbean islands or the Venezuelan coast. Once in the Caribbean, there are plenty of boats between islands and over to Central America (particularly Panama, a good place to find onward rides and yachting work in general: visit the Panama Canal Yacht Club in Colón) and the coasts of Colombia and Venezuela. Ask around at any major port or large marinas. If you're keen on setting up lifts before you set off, you could check the classified ads sections of boating magazines or one of a number of crewfinding websites (@www.crewfinders.com, for example).

A shared experience?

Once you've decided to travel to Latin America you need to think about whether you want to go on your own, with friends or a partner, or even on an organized tour. Don't make this decision lightly, because the people you travel with will greatly affect the kind of experience you have and the success of your trip.

There are obvious advantages in going with other people. Travelling in a couple or a group is cheaper than travelling alone, since you're able to share the cost of hotel rooms, taxi fares and many other expenses. Travelling with a friend means you'll always have someone to eat with and talk to, offering some protection against loneliness and homesickness. You'll feel safer and possibly more adventurous with people you know by your side, and you'll also have someone to look after you if you get ill. And at the end of it all you'll have someone who was also there to share in the memories. Having said that, travelling with people from back home can insulate you somewhat from the countries you've come to visit, so that you're less tempted to explore, and you might meet fewer locals. There's also always the possibility that you might fall out with each other.

Going solo

Travelling alone in Latin America is still uncommon. If you do go solo, your trip will be more expensive and more challenging, and you'll also be seen as an oddity by gregarious Latin people (and, if you're a woman, as very perverse indeed). Nevertheless, if you're brave enough to take the plunge, the rewards are huge. You'll be much more deeply immersed in local culture than if you're travelling with someone else from back home, while the locals will find you much more approachable, and may well take you under their wing.

You might even find that the greater challenges you face will uncover previously unknown reserves of ingenuity, strength and courage, so that you return as a much more confident and self-aware person.

Travelling with friends

If you've decided to visit Latin America with friends, take a long hard look at the people and personalities involved: travel in Latin America is often uncomfortable, chaotic and stressful, and you'll be asking a lot more from your friends than is customary back home – and they in turn will expect support from you. Ask yourself if your friendship is strong enough to withstand the occasional disagreement, the extra time spent together, whether you'll be able to share responsibilities and decision-making, and whether you trust them to look after you should the need arise. It's important to establish whether or not you have similar expectations and goals – there's no point in going trekking in the Andes with a friend whose ideal trip is a couple of weeks clubbing in Ibiza or lying on a beach in Hawaii. Be wary, too, about travelling with someone who has a significantly different budget – if you don't agree similar budgets right from the start, you'll find yourselves rapidly parting ways. Finally, consider how many of you are going together: three is an awkward number unless you all know each other very well, while larger numbers are difficult to manage and usually split up into smaller groups.

There are lots of ways of finding a travel companion if you don't want to travel alone but don't know anyone who's able to come with you. Your best bet is to check out the numerous Internet bulletin boards or forum sections of travel websites (see pp.374–375 for details) and perhaps post a message yourself. Alternatively, the classified ads in travel magazines often have sections dedicated to finding travel companions – Wanderlust (@www.wanderlust.co.uk) is particularly extensive. Make sure that you meet potential fellow travellers as many times as possible before you set out, and discuss your expectations about the trip with them in detail.

If you don't manage to find anyone to travel with before you set out, don't despair. Once in Latin America, there's a good chance of hitching up with other travellers – popular travellers' cafés, hostels and resorts are all good places to meet up with like-minded people. Though of course, the same rules apply as when travelling with people from home.

Travelling with partners

Although lots of things are taken for read with couples travelling together – budgets, common goals, mutual levels of trust and care – the intensity of the experience and an unexpected sense of isolation that many couples feel as a self-contained unit on the road can cause irreparable damage to even the strongest of relationships. Go on a brief, less challenging holiday together at least once before you set off and try to remain open to meeting others, and even occasionally spending time apart on your trip. On a positive note, travelling in Latin America can be incredibly romantic, and you'll have time together that you won't have at home. Assuming all goes well, you'll possibly finish the trip much closer.

Travelling with kids

Latin Americans love children, and if you're travelling with kids you're likely to be the object of special attention and care. Locals will ensure you get a place on the bus, women will talk to you in regions where they're otherwise wary of tourists, and waiters and shopkeepers will coo and flirt. And of course, the children will come back with unforgettable memories.

Bear in mind, though, that if you're flying from anywhere other than the US, you'll have to endure a long-haul flight. Additionally, conditions in Latin America are often less than comfortable and sanitary; if you're travelling on a tight budget, it may not always be easy to find somewhere that feels clean and safe enough. You'll also need to be careful to make sure your children stay healthy in the face of risks ranging from contaminated water to obscure tropical diseases.

Organized tours

Dozens of travel companies run trips to Latin America (see the list of specialist tour operators on pp.364–367), with endless variations in terms of destinations, length, theme and style of travel. Many of these tours are imaginative and well organized, accompanied by guides who have in-depth knowledge of the area, offering a painless and potentially insightful introduction to the region without any of the hassles suffered by independent first-time visitors.

If you do decide to go on an organized tour, choose the company you go with very carefully – as always, the best recommendations are via word of mouth. Bear in mind, also, that the majority of these tours are much more expensive than travelling independently, and much of what you'll see is on well-established tourist trails. Don't be afraid to ask lots of questions before booking a tour – in particular, try to get some idea of the size (8–10 is a good number) and average age of your group, the pace of the trip (many organized tours run at breakneck speed) and the exact details of your itinerary.

2

Studying, volunteering and working in Latin America

While many visitors to Latin America will be dreaming of gathering thrilling experiences, seeing new and exotic locales, meeting people from all over the world or even just enjoying an extended holiday, you might want to immerse yourself in Latin American culture in a more long lasting manner. There are several ways of doing this – learn the language of the countries you're visiting, study a subject like conservation or archeology, work as a volunteer or even find paid work to subsidize your trip while you're there. With the growing trend of "gap year" travels, university students electing to study a semester or year overseas and an increasing number of people inclined to take a break from their career, there are literally dozens of websites dedicated to helping people find courses and work – unpaid or paid – abroad: ⓦwww.gapyear.com, ⓦwww.gapyeardirectory.co.uk, ⓦwww.bunac.org, ⓦwww.workingabroad.com, ⓦwww.ciee.org and

ⓦwww.transitionsabroad.com are just some of the best. There are also several good books on the subject: *Gap Years for Grown Ups* and *Work Your Way Around the World* both by Susan Griffith and *Work Abroad: the Complete Guide to Finding a Job Overseas* (Transitions Abroad Publishing) are all recommended.

Learning a language

One of the strongest bonds between the countries of Latin America is their shared linguistic inheritance, with Spanish being the principal language in most of the region's nations. If you don't already speak a bit of Spanish and haven't attempted to learn it at home (see "Guidebooks and other resources", p.211, for details), you could arrange your trip around taking a language course in Latin America itself. This has long been a popular way to begin travelling in Latin America, and most towns on the Gringo Trail have at least one language school, while some have become specialist centres with dozens of establishments to choose from.

Unlike in Asia or Africa – and even most parts of Europe these days – in Latin America many people do not speak English or any language other than their own. Most written information is in the national language only – for tourists who don't speak the relevant language, this is particularly frustrating in museums and places of cultural and historical interest – and even guided tours (particularly those off the beaten track) are sometimes not translated. Even learning the rudiments of Spanish, Portuguese or an indigenous language like Quechua (spoken in Peru and parts of Bolivia) will vastly enhance your travelling experience. The locals will take you much more seriously and respect your attempt to communicate, you'll be able to express yourself properly and get about without the complications caused by a language barrier and you'll understand and be integrated into the culture you're visiting much more deeply. Additionally, learning a language in its own country means that you'll have instant access to the way it's used by native speakers – just walking through the streets on your way to school will immerse you in the sounds and cadences of the language and going about your daily business – shopping, eating out and travelling on public transport – will give you opportunities to practise and improve what you are learning in a classroom.

While language courses in Latin America will invariably cost less than at home, they're not all good, and some are actually pretty shoddy. Do some research before you choose your school (there are dozens – if not hundreds – of websites dedicated to learning a language abroad), check out the classes before you sign up or, best of all, get a personal recommendation. Language courses usually take the form of four hours a day, five days a week and last anywhere from a week to several months according to your needs (and budget). Some schools will arrange extracurricular activities in your spare time, and almost all will be able to place you with a local family for the length of your course, so that you can practise what you've learned.

Though by no means the only place in Latin America to learn Spanish, Guatemala is by far the most popular and consequently has the widest range of options, with at least sixty well-established schools and very reasonably priced courses. What's more, Guatemalan Spanish is spoken slowly and clearly (partly because the largely Mayan population themselves speak Spanish as a second language). This is also the case in Ecuador, another favourite place to learn Spanish. For those of a poetic or musical nature, the most beautiful – rather than the most easily understood – Spanish spoken in Latin America is said by many to be that which is spoken by Argentines, while the most expressive (and also considered to be highly comical) is Mexican Spanish – instantly recognizable with its drawn-out nasal cadences.

Should you be interested, it's also possible to study several indigenous languages in Latin America. In Bolivia, which has the largest indigenous population in South America, you can study Aymara in La Paz and Quechua in Cochabamba. The small town of Joyabaj in the Western Highlands of Guatemala has a language centre where you can learn Quiché.

Studying other courses

Visitors to Latin America wanting to study will find themselves almost invariably studying Spanish. However, if you already speak Spanish and want to study something different there is a wide range of other options available. Like learning a language, taking a course at a university or cultural centre is a fantastic way to meet Latin Americans and extend your knowledge of local culture.

Language schools

Argentina There are half a dozen language schools in Buenos Aires and almost as many in Argentina's second city, Cordobá, as well as Bariloche and – rather bizarrely – Ushuaia, the world's most southern city at the tip of Tierra del Fuego. Recommended is the ILEE Spanish Schools network (⊛www.argentinailee.org) which is long established and ensures that standards in its regional centres (those listed above) are as good as those of its main school in Buenos Aires.

Bolivia Centrally located Sucre and Cochabamba are both popular places to learn Spanish in Bolivia. The Escuela Runawasi (⊛www.runawasi.org) in Cochabamba has classes in Quechua and Aymara (learning even a few words of either will elicit gasps of astonishment and delight from locals and is well worth the effort) as well as Spanish.

Brazil Because it is the only Portuguese-speaking country in Latin America, there is a greatly reduced demand to learn the language of Brazil. Nevertheless there are language schools – many aimed at businessmen rather than tourists – in Rio de Janeiro, Sao Paulo, Salvador, Florianopolis and Maceio. Check the websites ⊛www.amerispan.com/country/Brazil and ⊛www.firststepworld.com/language_schools/portuguese for further details.

Chile The vast majority of language schools in Chile are based in the capital, Santiago, though there are also courses available in Iquique, Pucón, Valparaiso and seaside resort Viña del Mar. Bellavista Language School (⊛www.escuelabellavista.cl) in Santiago has small class sizes – no bigger than five students – and a good reputation.

Costa Rica The country's capital, San José, is the centre for Costa Rica's language schools: they're mostly US-owned and comparatively expensive, though very well organized. There are also classes in the student town of Heredia and on the beach at Quepos. The Costa Rican Academy of Language (⊛www.crilang.com) in San José is a small Tico-owned school with a friendly atmosphere and a conversational approach. Outside the city in the Valle Central, the Montaña Linda Language School (⊛www .montanalinda.com) is located in the pretty village of Orosí with excellent local teachers, a charming informality and the cheapest rates in the country.

Ecuador Ecuador's capital, Quito, is easily the most popular place to study in South America, with over sixty language schools, cheap courses and immersion in the particularly clear local dialect; there are other language schools in Cuenca. Both the South American Spanish Institute (⊛www .southamerican.edu.ec) and Bipo and Toni's (⊛academia.bipo.net) are rated by ex-students; the latter regularly donates a portion of its profits to environmental projects.

El Salvador While there aren't a great deal of language schools in El Salvador, the well-run El Salvador Spanish Schools organization (⊛www .salvaspan.com) has schools in San Salvador, Santa Ana and two beach destinations – with optional surfing lessons.

Guatemala Antigua, one of the most impressive colonial cities in Latin America, is now one of the most popular places in Latin America to learn Spanish, although you may not be able to see (let alone practise on) the locals for the crowds of tourists. Further west, the city of Quetzaltenango is less pretty but boasts some equally good schools in a far less touristy environment. Rapidly growing in popularity for Spanish classes is the backpacker haven of San Pedro La Laguna on the shores of Lago de Atitlán. There are also a number of language schools in the Petén region, within striking distance of Tikal. With so much choice, the website ⓦwww .guatemala365.com serves a useful purpose in listing the best and most professional schools as well as providing tips about the relative advantages of different study centres. If you're interested in learning Mayan, the Centro Maya de Idiomas (ⓦwww.centromaya.org) in Quetzaltenango has classes in five Mayan dialects – K'iche', Q'anjob'al, Kaqchikel, Tzutujil and Mam.

Mexico The attractive colonial city of Cuernavaca, 50km south of Mexico City, makes a good base for exploring the capital, the pyramids of Teotihuacán and the silver town of Taxco. The place for learning Spanish in Mexico, particularly popular with young Americans, it has lots of language schools and teaching of a high standard. Other places to learn Spanish in Mexico are the equally attractive colonial cities of Guanajuato and San Miguel de Allende. The longest-standing and most professional school in Guanajuato is the Centro de Idiomas at the University of Guanajuato (ⓦwww.ugto.mx). In San Miguel de Allende the most prestigious place to study is the Instituto Allende (ⓦwww.instituto -allende.edu.mx).

Nicaragua Although the colonial cities of Granada and León have several language schools, the pleasant university town of Estelí in the north has the longest established and most professional places, originally set up in the 1980s for the visiting supporters of the Sandinista revolution. Courses here are probably the cheapest in Latin America at around $150 per week, including full board and lodging with a local family. The most popular school in Estelí is Escuela Horizonte (ⓦwww.ibw.com.ni/u/horizont) which is particularly known for its excellent teachers. For those who'd prefer to study in Granada or on the coast in San Juan del Sur, Nicaragua Spanish Schools (or NSS; ⓦpages.prodigy.net/nss-pmc) has schools in three places and is a co-operative venture run by Nicaraguans.

Peru Backpacker hot spots Cusco and Arequipa both have several language schools, as does the more commercial city of Huancayo in the foothills of the Andes. In Cusco the Amigos Spanish School (ⓦwww .spanishcusco.com) is a not-for-profit organization which ploughs all its profits into food and education for local poor families. Also recommended is the Academia Latinamericana de Español (Ⓔlatinocusco@goalsnet.com.pe).

University and post-graduate studies

If you're studying Spanish, Portuguese or Latin American Studies at university you will be, in all likelihood, spending a year studying in Latin America as part of your course. If you aren't, all is not lost. Many Latin American Studies centres and universities with connections to Latin America (this, for obvious geographical reasons, applies particularly to universities and educational institutes in the USA; in the UK check LAB at ⊛www.lab.org.uk and the Society for Latin American Studies or SLAS at www.slas.org.uk) have summer programmes for students of other subjects or even people who are no longer studying. These are not cheap; course fees rarely start below $2000 (even for just a month of study) but sometimes include accommodation and living expenses. Additionally you will probably be studying at a Latin American university, with access to its facilities and plenty of opportunity to meet young Latin Americans. American undergraduate students can also earn credits which count towards their degree if they choose a well-considered course in Latin America – check with your university when planning your coursework. Note, however, that university courses will require at least a basic grasp of Spanish and more likely a good working knowledge of the language – if you don't speak any at all you won't be able to take up a place.

The best place to look for these kinds of course is on the Internet – there are literally dozens of websites and organizations dedicated to academic study in Latin America (see Directory for details). *Peterson's Study Abroad* by Joseph Krasowski, *Study Abroad* by Michele-Marie Dowel and *Study Abroad 101* by Wendy Williamson are all informative books on the subject.

Courses in Latin American culture

If your interest in studying in Latin America is less academic or you would like to explore the region's culture in a more light-hearted fashion, there is no shortage of options. Again, the Internet is the best starting point for finding a suitable course. Cultural Travels (⊛www.culturaltravels.com) lists over 2000 travel agencies and other set-ups which offer "educational holidays" by theme: these include art, archeology, architecture, cookery, history, marine biology and sport.

Another place to search for cultural courses in Latin America is your guidebook, which will detail organizations offering training to visitors. These include national parks, environmental agencies, community centres and the odd eco-lodge or hostel.

Volunteering

A great way to give added purpose to your trip is to work as a volunteer. You'll be getting directly involved in local communities and experiencing Latin America in ways you can't possibly as a tourist. You'll see firsthand how many Latin Americans struggle to survive on a handful of dollars a week and learn about the devastating effects a lack of decent infrastructure and sanitation bring. But you'll also – in all likelihood – share your working days with local people, learning their particular sense of humour and expressions, what they eat for lunch and what concerns them most in their daily lives. Chances are you'll be invited to your colleagues' homes for special occasions or just to meet their families. You'll learn far more about local culture – flora and fauna, history and society – than you ever could if you were just passing through town as a tourist. And

△ Studying at the Univeristy of Buenos Aires, Argentina

Courses

Listed below are just some of the courses – both academic and non-academic – available at the time of writing.

Archeological dig Two weeks working on an archeological site in the Peruvian highlands with field trips to Cusco, Machu Picchu and La Paz. Contact Spanish Abroad (🌐www.spanishabroad.com).

From Coffee Beans to Ecotourism and Microchips An in-depth examination of the Costa Rican economy with fieldwork and tours to local businesses and industrial sites. Contact Cultural Experiences Abroad (🌐www.gowithcea.com).

Lens on Latin America: Video and Media Production An opportunity for students in video and media production to learn from award-winning Bolivian documentary producer Ismael Saavedera. Courses are based in Cochabamba and include a visit to the Bolivian film archives in La Paz. Contact the School for International Training (🌐www.sit.edu).

The Maya World: Culture, Society and History Immersion in the daily lives of Guatemalan Mayans and the chance to learn about the Mayan worldview, mythologies and spiritualities and contemporary efforts to promote indigenous rights. Contact the Center for Global Education (🌐www.augsburg.edu).

Mexican cuisine Learn how to cook classic Mexican dishes such as *mole poblano* and *chiles en nogada* in an attractive colonial house in the small town of Tlaxcala in the centre of Mexico. Contact the Mexican Home Cooking School (🌐www.mexicanhomecooking.com).

Permaculture Investigate new ways of creating sustainable human habitats at Ecoversidade, a grassroots ecological institute in tropical Brazil. Contact Living Routes (🌐www.livingroutes.org).

Revolution, Transformation and Civil Society An educational tour with expert local historians and guides of key sites in Nicaragua where Spanish colonial powers, the Sandinista revolution and a brief Contra war have left their legacies. Contact the School for International Training (🌐www.sit.edu).

Tango Learn the most sensuous and complicated of Latin dances in one of Buenos Aires' best dance schools, the Escuela Argentina de Tango. Contact the Grupo de Intercambio Cultural or GICArg (🌐www.gicarg.org).

Teacher Training Practical experience teaching primary schoolchildren in rural Ecuador with community politics and on-the-job training. Contact Fundación Brethren y Unida (🌐www.fbu.com.ec).

Wildlife and Wildlands of South America A chance to study firsthand Chile's wildland habitats and the diverse species they support. Contact Study Abroad (🌐www.studyabroad.com).

you'll have the satisfaction of helping Latin Americans and their environment in ways that go beyond parting with a few bucks. With any luck, you'll establish life-long connections with communities, projects and people vastly different from those back home.

Volunteering opportunities usually follow one of two themes: working with nature (generally conservation or scientific research) or working with people (for example, building homes, caring for the homeless, sick or drug-addicted, or teaching). In most cases volunteers have to commit themselves for a certain amount of time (at least one to three months). Once you've enrolled, you'll be expected to work hard, and for no pay – volunteer organizations don't take kindly to their workers choosing their own hours, partying all night and sleeping the day away. If you have specialist knowledge – medical, engineering, scientific – you may be able to find volunteer positions which will give you basic living expenses and "pocket money"; otherwise the majority of volunteer schemes (particularly those organized at home) expect their participants to pay to take part in exchange for board and lodging. Often these fees are not cheap (running to several thousand dollars) though prices vary enormously and can cost as little as a few hundred dollars.

Dozens of international volunteer organizations have programmes in Latin America (see pp.367–368 for more details), while there are many more local community and government-sponsored projects. Although in theory you could just turn up while in Latin America and offer your services to a suitable organization, fixing work in advance guarantees you a position of your choice and gives the organization a chance to check your details and make sure that you're placed in the most suitable project. If you're on a budget, however, it's far cheaper to volunteer on the hoof – the more informal and locally run schemes that are likely to welcome you won't charge huge fees for the privilege although you'll still have to cover your living costs while you're volunteering. Some projects require volunteers with specific skills; others will take on anyone with enthusiasm and energy. The *International Directory of Voluntary Work* (Vacation Work) will give you lots of ideas on what kind of work is available as will *Worldwide Volunteering* (Worldwide Volunteer Organisation). Online, the Lima-based South American Explorers Club (@www.samexplo.org) has a database for members called Volunteer Resources, which hooks up organizations and potential volunteers, as well as providing up-to-date feedback from people who've taken part in various projects. Amerispan (@www.amerispan.com), chiefly a language school organization, also has a section on volunteer opportunities in Latin America. Additionally, all the gap year websites (see p.159) have links to voluntary projects and organizations, as does @www.volunteerabroad.com and @www.planeta.com.

Educational institutes with Latin American studies centres are also an ideal starting point for investigating volunteer opportunities – Stanford University's CLAS (Center for Latin American Studies; @www.stanford.edu/group/las) is a good option, as is the UK-based

Volunteer projects and organizations

Listed below are just some of the myriad organizations and volunteer projects throughout Latin America that you can – at the time of writing – get involved in.

Belize The Cornerstone Foundation (@www.peacecorner.org/cornerstone.htm), based in San Ignacio, runs volunteer projects such as working with HIV/Aids sufferers and the disabled and teaching English. Based in San Pedro on Ambergris Caye, Green Reef (@www.ambergriscaye.com/greenreef) volunteers help protect the caye's marine environment and also run bird sanctuaries. The Belize Aubudon Society (@www.belizeaudubon.org) runs nine of Belize's protected areas and takes on volunteers to help with warden duties and education programmes.

Bolivia An animal rehabilitation centre, Refugio Bolivia (@www.intiwarayassi.org) in the Inti Wara Yassi community in Bolivia is always looking for extra help; volunteers can just turn up.

Brazil US-based non-profit organization Globe Aware (@www.globeaware.org) uses volunteers on short-term placements (1–2 weeks) to help out with its community project in Bahia, where it is building a community centre, teaching children basic computer skills, growing a vegetable garden and working with alcoholism.

Colombia Peace Brigades International (@www.peacebrigades.org/colombia.html), an organization which maintains observer teams in areas of conflict, currently has volunteers in four parts of Colombia – Barrancabermeja, Bogotá, Urabá and Medellín. The Inter-cultural Youth Exchange (@www.icye.co.uk) organizes several projects in Colombia, including a school for deaf students and caring for the elderly.

Ecuador AmaZOOnico (@www.amazoonico.org), an animal refuge and rehabilitation centre on the Río Napo, accepts volunteers to help tend rescued forest animals and show visitors around. The Fundacion Jatun

Latin America Bureau (LAB; ⊕www.lab.org.uk). Finally, check your guidebook – many have sections on voluntary work, complete with listings.

Working

If you run out of cash and don't want your adventure to end you could always try looking for a job. Bear in mind, though, that unemployment runs as high as eighty percent in some parts of Latin America and if there aren't jobs for the locals, chances are there won't be jobs for foreigners.

Sacha (⊕www.jatunsacha.org) accepts volunteers to work in one of its ten biological stations in the Amazon, Andes, coastal lowlands and the Galápagos Islands. Workers get involved in field research, community service, agroforestry and environmental education.

El Salvador CIRES (Comité de Integración e Reconstruccion para El Salvador; ☎503-298-9410) is a development organization which works in housing, potable water and primary-health care schemes in 50 areas in the country. Volunteers should have relevant medical, technical and administration skills. The AMOR project (⊕www.churchinwales.org.uk), based in Wales is a church organization which runs a day centre for street children in San Salvador as well as outreach programmes.

Guatemala The Phoenix Project (⊕www.volunteerguatemala.org) works with over 300 deprived children living near Guatemala City's main garbage dump. Volunteer Petén (⊕www.volunteerpeten.com) is an environmental NGO based in San Andres and has projects for volunteers including park maintenance, reforestation and animal husbandry.

Guyana Canadian organization Youth Challenge International (⊕www.yci .org) sends young volunteers to Guyana to work on a number of projects, including HIV/Aids education and women's groups.

Nicaragua International conservation body Fauna and Flora International (⊕www.fauna-flora.org) needs volunteers to help protect endangered species and habitats on the remote Pacific coast. Most towns in Nicaragua have a local IXCHEN *casa de la mujer* (women's centre) which women volunteers with some Spanish skills are welcome to visit and help out.

Panama International volunteer organization Amigos de las Américas (⊕www.amigoslink.org) has teamed up with the Panamanian Ministry of Health (MINSA) to work in the state of Veraguas with young people, to foster leadership spirit and build integrated communities.

Obviously, if you speak Spanish or Portuguese you'll massively improve your chances of employment. That said, most job opportunities exist in one of two areas: ELT or tourism. ELT (English Language Teaching), is the most widespread work available for foreigners in Latin America. *Teaching English Abroad* by Susan Griffith is a good starting point if you're planning to take up ELT. More and more locals are keen to learn English and every capital city will have scores of English schools as well as private classes held at large businesses or in individual's homes. Generally the hourly rate of pay is quite reasonable, although your hours (usually before and after the working day) won't be convenient. Although it's not mandatory, having an ELT qualification – a CELTA (Certificate in English Language Teaching to Adults), TESOL (Teaching English to Speakers of Other Languages) or TEFL (Teaching English as a Foreign Language) will greatly improve your chances of employment and increase your status and wages. The best qualification to go for is the RSA/Cambridge Certificate in English Language Teaching to Adults; the course takes a month to complete and is recognized worldwide. Courses are widely available in most parts of the developed world and cost around US$2500 (see Directory for details); once qualified you can work anywhere in the world. Generally acknowledged as the best ELT training centre, International House (@www.ihworld.com) has branches in many countries including the US, Canada, Australia, New Zealand and most of Europe. You can also kill two birds with one stone and do the ELT course at one of three International House centres in Mexico – or take your qualification and teach at an IH centre in Mexico or Argentina (students who've studied at International House are naturally always favoured over other prospective ELT teachers). Alternatively you could try just turning up at an English-language school on spec – particularly in places less popular with tourists, there might well be vacancies for English teachers, and all you may be asked for in terms of qualifications is to be a native speaker. There are also occasional admin jobs at English Language schools or work as student coordinators. The British Council's website (@www.britishcouncil.org/work/job) and the TEFL website (@www.tefl.com) both have lists of English-teaching vacancies worldwide.

Additionally, you may find work in tourist resorts, especially if you have a special skill or qualification in something like scuba diving, sailing, whitewater rafting or mountain-climbing – ask around at likely spots. Otherwise, you might find a job in a hotel as a chambermaid, waiter or even receptionist. Backpacker hostels, especially those run by gringos, often hire broke guests to help serve food and drinks or clean in exchange for board and lodging, although this won't be of much use if you've already run out of cash and need to earn more money, rather than just having a place to stay.

If you have any kind of talent for writing or taking photographs you may also find paid employment working for one of the English-language newspapers based in Latin America – most countries have at least one, based in capital cities or major tourist resorts; worth contacting are San José, Costa Rica's *Tico Times* (⊛www.ticotimes.net) which sometimes offers four-month internships with a small monthly stipend; *The Buenos Aires Herald* in Argentina (⊛www.buenosairesherald.com) and Mexico's *The News* (⊛www.thenewsmexico.com). Alternatively you could work freelance, sending in articles and images as you travel – the Lanic website (⊛lanic.utexas.edu) has links to dozens of newspapers in Latin America as does World Newspapers (⊛www.world-newspapers.com).

Whatever sort of work you find, however, it's likely to be of an unofficial nature. Work visas for Latin America are difficult to obtain: you'll need a contract of employment and endless patience to negotiate the relevant bureaucratic hurdles. Fortunately, many employers will turn a blind eye to your lack of papers.

Teaching English

While studying Spanish in Antigua, Guatemala, I was recruited by a language academy to work in El Salvador. Most of my fellow teachers were American – perhaps the reason why the students loved my English accent. I fielded innumerable questions about the royal family, Michael Owen, David Beckham and the Spice Girls. In return, I learned a huge amount about postwar society in Central America and the economic and social disparities.

A few adventurous travellers passed through and stayed to teach and share our house – located opposite the presidential palace. I taught government ministers, Latin American diplomats and the captain of the national women's soccer team. After classes, teachers and students would hit the bars and at weekends we'd hit the beach or climb volcanoes.

But the best bit? Undoubtedly teaching English slang to the youngsters. Imagine the thrill of listening to kids running out of class calling each other "geezer" and "bloke".

Gary Bowerman

3

Documents and insurance

O nce you've decided where you're going, there are several essential documents you'll have to organize, including a plane ticket, insurance, and any visas you might require. You'll also need to make sure your passport will remain valid for the entire length of your stay and beyond – officially, all countries in Latin America require you to hold a passport which still has at least six months before it expires. Renewing your passport is fairly straightforward – in most cases you can apply for a new one at your local post office or online. Don't leave it to the last minute, though, or you may have to pay much more than the standard fee for rapid processing.

Visas

Very few Latin American countries now require visitors to get a visa before arrival. Current entry regulations are given in the box on p.173, but bear in mind they do change, and it's always worth contacting the relevant embassy or consulate to check the latest situation. If you do need a visa, you'll have to apply to the relevant embassy or consulate in your country – which can mean hours of queueing, armed with photos, a return air ticket and proof of funds.

Don't leave this until the last minute: well before you set off, find out how long your visa will take to process (although it rarely takes longer than two weeks). In some cases there won't be a consulate in your country, so you may have to write to one abroad – the only European consulates for Suriname, for example, are in Holland and Germany.

Visas usually have a time limit: you'll have to use them within three to six months of their being issued. If you're planning a long trip, this might make it impossible to collect all your visas in advance, in which case you'll have to wait until you arrive in a neighbouring country and apply for a visa there (take all the necessary documents with you, including passport photos). If you do have to do this, remember that Latin American bureaucracy is notoriously inefficient and frequently corrupt. You might be given incorrect information, the office may have run out of the relevant pieces of paper, or its staff might not know how to deal with you. Always give yourself plenty of time to cope with any problems that might arise. It's also probably worth applying for a multiple-entry visa if you think you might want to leave and re-enter a particular country; though this usually costs more than a single-entry visa, you could save yourself a lot of time and paperwork.

Entry cards and stamps

On arrival, your passport will be stamped and you may also be given an entry card – known variously as a *tarjeta de turismo* (tourist card),

---

Visa requirements for Latin America

At present, the following countries require certain visitors to hold a visa:
Brazil: citizens of the US, Canada, Australia
Colombia and Panama: citizens of the Republic of Ireland
El Salvador: citizens of Australia and New Zealand
Paraguay: citizens of Australia, Canada, Republic of Ireland and the US
Suriname: citizens of the UK, US, Canada, Republic of Ireland, Australia and New Zealand
Venezuela: anyone entering via a land border

Note: Citizens of the Republic of Ireland should pay special attention when checking entry requirements. These differ sometimes from those of all other members of the EU (see above) and are much more prone to change.

tarjeta de embarque (embarkation card), *tarjeta de entrada* (entrance card) or *tarjeta de ingreso* (entry card). To obtain your entry card, you'll have to fill out a form. Although you may not know where you'll be staying it's always best to fill in the destination address box on the form (a blank space can make officials nervous) – if you don't have a hotel, pick one, preferably well-known, from your guidebook; no one will check whether or not you actually stay there.

On arrival you'll have to present your completed form to an immigration official who, all being well, will stamp your passport and give you one half of the entry card, if you're being issued one (he'll keep the other half). In several Central American countries you'll have to pay a fee on arrival; this will be in dollars (or local currency), so keep at least US$10 to hand. Take special care of your entry card – it's regarded as being as important as your passport, and officials will not take kindly to you being without it if you're asked to show your documents whilst in the country (although they won't bother to tell you this at immigration). You'll have to surrender it on departure, so have it ready when leaving.

Although in theory there are complicated regulations regarding the length of your stay according to your nationality, in practice the decision is left to individual officials. It's always worth asking, as politely as you can, for the standard maximum of ninety days (note: this is theoretically limited to 30 days for citizens of particular countries – check with the relevant embassy before you plan your trip), although you may not get it – it's infinitely preferable to have more days than you'll need rather than to have to extend your stay, which is generally a costly and time-consuming procedure.

Extending your stay

In theory, it's almost always possible to renew your entry stamp if you decide to stay longer. The procedure involves going to the nearest immigration office (*migrácion*) or police station (*policia*) with your documents – passport, return ticket, proof of funds – and asking for a *prórroga* (extension) *de turista*. Bear in mind that although extensions are nearly always granted, you're not guaranteed to be given one – dress smartly and be polite. In many cases, it's possible to add an extra ninety days to your original ninety (though you'll never get more than 180 days in total); however, you may only be given another month or two. Extensions cost anything from a few dollars (US$10 in Ecuador, US$12.50 in Belize, US$27 in Peru) up to US$100 (in Argentina and Chile) – as a rule of thumb, the more expensive the country generally, the more expensive a visa extension is liable to be.

An alternative way of prolonging your stay – especially in Central America, where distances are relatively small – is simply to cross briefly into a neighbouring country and then return over the border, where you'll be given a brand-new entry stamp.

Overstaying

If you stay beyond the date stamped in your passport or written on your tourist card, you'll have to pay a fine when you leave the country. This is usually calculated on a daily basis of a few dollars per day,

△ Peru passport stamp

though some countries operate a fixed fine (US$40 in Costa Rica, US$50 in Argentina and US$100 in Chile, for example) irrespective of how long you've overstayed. If you know you're going to over-stay your visa, make sure it's not going to cost an arm or a leg first – if the fine is cheap it may be worth paying it rather than going through a costly extension process or having to leave and re-enter the country. Bear in mind, though, that overstaying your welcome is a risk – although most Latin American countries will just fine you and let you go with no problems at all, there's always the possibility that you might be refused entry to that country in the future.

Tickets

In all likelihood, your biggest single expense will be your airline ticket to Latin America. Whichever country you're planning to fly into, there will be a variety of routes and fares, so give yourself plenty of time to shop around and make sure you do your homework: a few hours' research should give you a good idea of current prices and routings. It's also best to adopt a flexible approach so that you're able to take advantage of any special deals which crop up, even if this means, say, starting your trip in a city or country other than the one you had in mind – for example, there are cheaper and more frequent connections to Lima in Peru or Santiago in Chile than to La Paz in Bolivia. As a rule of thumb, more affluent cities with well-established tourist attractions or business links with Europe, North America and Australasia will have better plane services and therefore potentially cheaper deals. These include Mexico City, São Paulo and Rio de Janeiro, Buenos Aires and Santiago.

Fares vary according to the season. High season in Latin America runs from mid-November to mid-January (fares are particularly high over Christmas), Easter, July and August. If you're determined to fly at Christmas or Easter, be prepared to pay premium prices and book months in advance. By contrast, flying in low season can knock several hundred dollars off the cost of your flight. The most direct flights are faster but usually more expensive, and you can save cash by taking an indirect flight.

Finally, remember that it's best to avoid arriving in Latin America at night. Banks, bureaux de change and tourist information desks may well be closed, and if you don't have a hotel or hostel booked you won't want to start wandering through a strange city in the dark.

Types of ticket

One-way

The idea of a one-way ticket, leaving you completely free to decide when and from where you're going to return (if ever), might sound romantic, but in real terms it's not very practical. For starters, one-way tickets usually cost around two-thirds of the price of a return ticket, so aren't very economical. Then you'll have to deal with immigration on arrival: without an onward or return ticket, proving that your stay is temporary will be virtually impossible, and you might even be refused entry. Additionally, when you do eventually decide to return you'll find that your flight will cost much more than you would have paid back home – there are none of the discounted ticket deals you'll find in the UK or North America, so you'll be paying full fare, and with Latin America's often exorbitant departure taxes on top.

Return

Mile for mile, return tickets are a much more economical option than one-way fares. However, flying in and out of the same city does restrict your movements, and you may find yourself either having to take a local flight to get back to where you started or wasting valuable days retracing your steps.

Open-jaw returns and circle tickets

A useful alternative to a straightforward return, especially if you're on a longer trip, is an open-jaw return, which allows you to fly into one city and return from another – ticket prices aren't much more than a standard return. A slight variation on an open jaw is a circle ticket, which involves flights linking more than one destination – for example London–Caracas–Bogotá–London. This may sound ideal if you want to travel large distances and on specific stopover routes, but choosing several cities to fly between months in advance really does set your itinerary in stone, and a certain amount of

Sample return fares

The following sample fares are for flights during low season.

To Mexico City	
From London	£450–560
From Los Angeles	US$299–440
From New York	US$375–525
From Toronto	C$835–940
From Sydney	A$2000–3200
From Auckland	NZ$2200–2700

To Lima	
From London	£530–580
From Los Angeles	US$510–635
From New York	US$550–685

From Toronto	C$780–1000
From Sydney	A$1900–3000
From Auckland	NZ$2050–3600

To Rio de Janeiro	
From London	£540–600
From Los Angeles	US$695–905
From New York	US$657–820
From Toronto	C$1250–1900
From Sydney	A$1800–2800
From Auckland	NZ$2000–2800

backtracking is required on each leg, since you'll have to return to the city you arrived in to fly on to the next.

Round-the-world (RTW) tickets

If Latin America is part of a longer trip, you might consider a round-the-world (RTW) ticket, which is often excellent value for money. Unfortunately, the countries of Latin America aren't included on many standard RTW itineraries – which tend to focus on Asia and Australasia – and where they are, they tend to be on the more expensive routings. The most frequently featured Latin American cities are Mexico City, Lima, Buenos Aires and Rio de Janeiro. The situation is slowly improving though – deals at the time of writing include a Classic Circle Atlantic fare at US$1997 for Miami–Lima–Sao Paulo–Rio de Janeiro–Lisbon–London–Paris–Miami with Airtreks (⊛www.airtreks.com), or £1319 for UK–Rio–overland–Buenos Aires–Santiago–Easter Island–Tahiti–Auckland–Sydney–Hong Kong–Bangkok–UK with STA travel (⊛www.statravel.co.uk). Several RTW companies also do Latin American routes – sample itineraries include the Conquistador trip, Dallas–Guatemala–Costa Rica–Panama–Dallas that costs US$1099 with Circle the Planet (⊛www.circletheplanet.com). Other renowned companies that offer RTW fares are Star Alliance (⊛www.staralliance.com) and One World (⊛www.oneworldalliance.com). The BootsnAll website (⊛www.bootsnall.com) has an excellent section on RTW tickets as does ⓦwww.roundtheworldtickets.com and most of the online student travel agencies and gap year websites.

Charter flights

There are almost no charter flights to Latin America from the UK, although there's a reasonable selection from North America. Virtually all charters go to tourist resorts in Mexico, Costa Rica or Brazil; although they're often much cheaper than scheduled flights, tickets are only valid for a maximum of three weeks. One possibility, if you can manage to find a charter return which is less than half the price of the standard fare (not as unlikely as you'd imagine), is to buy two and ditch the half of each you won't be using – your local travel agent may be able to come up with a good deal.

Courier flights

On a courier flight, you'll get a deeply discounted ticket – always at least half the price of an average return ticket, and often considerably less – in exchange for accompanying business cargo (which means checking freight in as excess baggage and carrying the relevant shipping documents). Unfortunately, despite their obvious attraction courier flights aren't very practical for long-haul flights, since couriers can only take hand luggage and tickets are usually only valid for a fortnight (and never more than a month). Even so, you may be able to save money by organizing a courier flight out to your destination and then purchasing another ticket when you want to come home. For more information, read the *Courier Air Travel Handbook: Learn How to Travel Worldwide for Next to Nothing* by Mark I. Field (Perpetual Press) or *Winning the Airfare Game* by Charles McCool (Hawk Ridge Press). Alternatively, check out ⓦwww.aircourier .co.uk or ⓦwww.aircourier.org.

Airpasses

Given the size of Latin America, at some point you might want to take an internal flight. Most Latin American airlines offer airpasses, either covering a single country or a particular region – these are more economical if you're planning a series of short flights within a single country or region of Latin America. Airpasses usually include a set number of flights for a certain fee (3 or 4 usually) plus the option of buying a limited number of additional flights at a reduced rate (a maximum of 8 or 9 in most cases). Airpasses must always be purchased outside the country they serve, and in conjunction with an international air ticket: routes and dates must be fixed on purchase, although they can later be altered for a fee (US$15–70). Tickets are completely non-refundable. Passes are considerably cheaper if your international flight is with the relevant national airline. It's best to contact a specialist travel agency if you want to buy an airpass (see Directory for details); there are many options which change frequently and the regulations regarding each airpass are varied and complex.

The most popular single-country airpasses – the ones which make the most sense time-wise and financially – cover the region's largest countries, Argentina and Brazil. These are offered by Aerolineas Argentina with its Visit Argentina airpass and national carriers Varig and TAM in Brazil. Note that the sheer size of Brazil means that two connecting internal flights to your planned destination only count as one flight – for instance, if you fly from Rio to Brasilia via São Paulo. Other single-country airpasses cover Mexico, Costa Rica, Colombia and Chile. Prices for singe-country airpasses start at US$199 for the smallest countries (Costa Rica) to US$399 for the largest (Brazil).

Perhaps more useful than single-country airpasses are regional airpasses. The Mexipass International is particularly good, taking in all the Latin American cities served by the domestic Mexican airlines AeroMéxico and Mexicana as well as North American cities – this makes particular sense if you're flying through Latin America from the US. Similar deals are offered by both Grupo Taca, based in Costa Rica and Copa Airlines, Panama's national carrier. In South America, the Mercosur airpass covers Argentina, Brazil, Uruguay, Paraguay and Chile while the Lan Visit South America airpass joins up countries on the Lan network (Chile, Ecuador and Peru as well as Argentina and Venezuela). Prices for regional airpasses start at US$200 and go up to US$750 for long-distance flights with several stopovers.

Buying a ticket

From travel agents and wholesale consolidators to booking online, there are a number of ways to buy a ticket. On the whole, you'll get a better price if you book your ticket several months in advance, since cheaper seats usually go before more expensive ones. If you book your ticket less than two weeks before departure, you may end up paying over the odds, unless you're lucky enough to find a special last-minute flight deal (more likely in low season). In addition, unlikely as it sounds, it's worth trying to bargain, particularly with bucket shops. Discounted ticket prices are not fixed, and if you tell the person you're speaking to that you've been quoted a lower price by another agent you may find that price being matched or even undercut.

When you find the right ticket, remember that discounted tickets are nearly always non-refundable and non-transferable. Check that you can alter your return date should you need to, and find out exactly how much you'll be charged for doing so. On some airlines your travel agent can reserve you a seat and on all of them you can request special meals (vegetarian, halal, kosher) in advance. Very few now permit smoking – if you won't be able to last a long flight without lighting up, ask your agent which carriers still take smokers, or stock up on nicotine gum. Finally, pay for your ticket as soon as you can. A small deposit (US$75) will usually hold a reservation, but won't guarantee the price you've been quoted.

Discount and specialist travel agencies

The most obvious, though often also the most expensive, way of buying a plane ticket is to contact the relevant airline directly. In most cases the airline will just quote you their standard scheduled fares, although they do occasionally have special offers which are worth checking for. In general, however, it's cheaper to go via a discount ticket agent – known as "bucket shops" in the UK and flight consolidators in North America. Discounted tickets are sold in blocks by airlines to these travel agents, who pass on most of the discount to their customers. What you actually pay depends on the mark-up added by the travel agents, as well as the price they originally paid for the tickets (you'll invariably find the person on the plane beside you has paid a different price to you).

Discount agencies are often listed in the classified ads of newspapers' travel sections, and in free or listings magazines. These include, in the UK, the *Sunday Times* travel section, the *Evening Standard* or, best of all, London's *Time Out*; in the US, there's the *Village*

Voice in New York, the *Chicago Tribune* and the *Los Angeles Times*; in Australia, try the *Sydney Morning Herald* or *TNT* magazine. Ring around as many as you can and compare prices, which can vary dramatically. If you do decide to buy your ticket from a bucket shop, check that they're bonded with ATOL (Ⓦwww .atoldata.org.uk) or ABTA (Ⓦwww.abtanet.com) in the UK, or with AFTA (Ⓦwww.afta.com.au) in Australia. This means that if the company goes bust you'll be refunded in full – it also tends to indicate a decently run and professional operation. There is no such organization in the US, but you can protect yourself by paying with a credit card (this applies worldwide); again, you'll be refunded in full if your ticket agent goes bust.

Even better is to find a specialist travel agency with expertise in Latin America (see the list in Directory on pp.364–367). Most of these have expert staff with first-hand experience of the region, and they can often match the cheapest flights found in bucket shops – as well as giving you the lowdown on airpasses, visas and perhaps even inoculation requirements.

The Internet

Booking airline tickets on the Internet cuts out the travel agent or middleman, and if you search thoroughly you may find some great bargains. The Cheap Flights series of websites (in the USA, UK, Canada and Australia) compares prices on a wide range of airlines, and is particularly competitive. Auction websites sell flights at up to forty percent discount though you'll have to bid hard. Booking online also has the disadvantage that you'll usually need to specify both outward and return dates and you won't get the specialist knowledge a decent travel agent can offer. See pp.361–364 for a list of online discount travel agents.

Insurance

Having some form of travel insurance is absolutely essential. Although the vast majority of travellers to Latin America return home safe and sound, accidents do happen, and without insurance you could be faced with huge medical or legal bills that you can't possibly pay for. As with airfares, it's worth doing a little research on travel insurance before you buy a policy.

Insurance is a very lucrative – and hence highly competitive – business, which helps keep prices low. Premiums vary depending on the level of coverage selected, ranging from around £50/US$80 to £70/US$130 for six weeks, and approximately £115/US$220 to £250/US$450 for six months. Some travel agents will try and sell you their own insurance policy when you buy your ticket – these are usually as good as any you can find yourself, but check the details before you sign up. The specialist travel agencies listed in Directory (see pp.364–367) also offer insurance. Other insurers advertise in the travel sections of the publications listed in "Buying a ticket" on p.181, and on the Internet.

Choosing a policy

All insurance policies provide slightly different types of cover, though all include some form of medical coverage and some protection against loss of personal effects (unless you choose to go without this part of the policy – see below). Other eventualities usually covered standard by travel insurance policies are unavoidable missed flights or cancelled trips, legal expenses, hijack and kidnap, though you won't be covered in the event of a natural disaster or the outbreak of war. Consider the following before you buy your travel insurance:

- Every policy is slightly different, both in the cover it offers and the way it's written, and it's important to read every last detail. The small print (usually "conditions and exclusions") will tell you exactly what you can and can't claim for – there are virtually as many exclusions as inclusions on most insurance policies.
- Almost all travel insurance policies are one hundred percent refundable within a week of purchase, provided you haven't set off yet. If you decide you're not happy with yours, send it back.
- Dangerous sports, such as rock climbing, skiing, scuba diving and whitewater rafting, often aren't covered by insurance policies unless you pay an additional premium – even fairly innocuous activities like horse-trekking are sometimes not covered. Pay particular attention to the small print in this section to see what's included and what's not.
- Check that you're able to extend your policy from abroad if you decide to extend your trip – this usually just takes a phone call.

Once you've bought insurance, it's essential to make a note of your policy number and the emergency 24-hour telephone helpline (most travellers take their insurance certificates with them, although this isn't usually strictly necessary). You'll have to quote your policy number in any contact you have with your insurance company. If something does happen to you, hold on to copies of all medical bills, receipts or other official documents – without them you won't have a claim.

Finally, remember that insurance companies are notoriously reluctant to pay out; if you do make a claim, the onus will be on you to prove that whatever happened was unavoidable and in no way caused by your own actions. In other words, being insured doesn't give you a licence to jump off cliffs, get into fights or leave your possessions lying around. Take the same amount of care of yourself and your things as if you weren't insured.

Medical coverage

By far the most important part of your travel insurance is the medical coverage. In a worst-case scenario, you may have to be airlifted to hospital and perhaps even repatriated with a trained medical team. Very few people could afford the vast cost of doing this, which is where your insurance company steps in. Less dramatic expenses – medicines and doctor's fees – are also covered. The exception is if you have any existing medical condition which leads to you being treated or hospitalized abroad, in which case you will not be able to make a claim.

Check what the procedure is should you need emergency medical treatment: some companies require you to pay first and then reclaim the costs on your return; others will pay your bill directly to the relevant hospital or doctor. You may also be required to phone (collect call) first to speak to a company-approved doctor to check that you're being offered the correct treatment.

Personal effects

Although the medical component of your insurance is the most important part, the most common cause of insurance claims is theft – most insurers now offer a discount of around twenty percent if you choose to leave out this area of cover and take your chances.

Rough Guides travel insurance

Rough Guides has teamed up with Columbus Direct to offer you travel insurance that can be tailored to suit your needs.

Readers can choose from a number of different travel insurance products, including a low-cost backpacker option for long stays; a short break option for city getaways; a typical holiday package option; and many others. There are also annual multi-trip policies for those who travel regularly, with variable levels of cover available. Different sports and activities (trekking, skiing, etc) can be covered if required on most policies.

Rough Guides travel insurance is available to the residents of 36 different countries with different language options to choose from via our website – ⓦ www.roughguidesinsurance.com – where you can also purchase the insurance.

Alternatively, UK residents should call 0800 083 9507; US citizens should call 1-800 749-4922; Australians should call 1 300 669 999. All other nationalities should call +44 870 890 2843.

Coverage for personal effects usually includes the loss of a certain amount of cash, passports and other essential documents, but there's usually a maximum amount you can claim for any one item – roughly US$250–500 – meaning that you may not be able to claim for the full value of expensive items like cameras which exceed this limit. You might need to invest in a household insurance policy which covers them outside the home or get specialist insurance – camera insurers sometimes advertise in photographic magazines.

4

When to go

Obviously, planning when to go to Latin America is largely dependent on your own circumstances, and when you're able to find the time and the money to get away. These constraints aside, it's important to have an idea of what the weather will be like in the areas of Latin America you're planning on visiting, and to understand how seasonal variations in climate are likely to affect your travels – with a little planning, it's possible to organize an extended itinerary through the region that makes the best of the weather conditions in each country you're visiting.

However, it's also worth bearing in mind that, in any particular region, the time of year which enjoys the best weather will almost inevitably also be the peak tourist season, particularly if it coincides with the December-to-January, Easter, and June-to-August holiday periods in the US and Europe. Prices for everything from international airline tickets to accommodation are at their highest at these times, and popular destinations can get uncomfortably crowded. If you're prepared to put up with a little rain and visit outside these periods, you'll often be rewarded by lower costs and fewer crowds.

Weather aside, you may also want to arrange your visit around one of Latin America's major fiestas. These extravagant festivals encapsulate the heart of Latin American culture and are amongst the most colourful and exciting experiences the region has to offer, so it's well worth making the effort to coincide with one of these, as it's likely to prove one of the highlights of your travels.

If you're travelling for a few months or so, bear in mind that it's also a lot more pleasant to be away during the winter and to return home in the spring or summer.

The climate in Latin America

Most of Latin America lies within the tropics, the zone on either side of the equator between the Tropic of Capricorn in the south and the Tropic of Cancer in the north. There's no real difference between winter and summer in the tropics, and seasonal variations in temperature are minimal – Belize City, for example,

The best time to visit

What follows is a very broad guide to the best times of year for travelling to each country in Latin America ("best" meaning the driest and mildest conditions). This summary is meant only as a general introduction to help you plan your route; for more detail, check the relevant guidebooks, tourist offices and other sources of information.

Argentina	Dec–May
Belize	Late Dec to March
Bolivia	May–Sept
Brazil	Feb–June
Chile	Nov–March in the south; year-round elsewhere
Colombia	Nov–March
Costa Rica	Nov, April & May
Ecuador	June–Aug in the highlands; Dec–April on the coast
El Salvador	Nov–April
Guatemala	Feb–May
The Guianas	Feb & March, July–Nov
Honduras	March–May
Mexico	Nov–Feb
Nicaragua	Dec–March
Panama	Dec–April (the dry season)
Paraguay	May–Sept (the cooler winter months)
Peru	May–Sept in the highlands and Amazon (the dry season) and Dec–March on the coast
Uruguay	Sept–April
Venezuela	Nov–June (the dry season)

is 27°C/81°F in January and 31°C/88°F in July. Despite the relatively stable temperature, there are considerable seasonal variations in rainfall and humidity that may affect your plans. Most tropical regions have wet seasons, when heavy rain can make travel difficult and uncomfortable.

However, despite the fact that most tropical regions receive extremely high annual rainfall, even in the rainy seasons this tends to be concentrated in torrential bursts lasting a few hours or so (in some places, afternoon downpours are so predictable you can almost set your watch by them), after which the skies clear and the sun comes out. In some tropical lowland regions – particularly in the rainforests of the Amazon and the Colombian Pacific coast – it can rain almost every day (it's not called rainforest for nothing), so the occasional soaking just goes with the territory and will only really spoil your trip if roads are washed out, making bus travel impossible.

That's not to say tropical Latin America is uniformly hot, however: altitude is a huge factor in determining local climate, particularly in the Andean countries, which sit astride the highest tropical mountain range in the world. Temperatures decrease by about 6–7°C/11°F with every 1000m you ascend, so that in the Ecuadorian capital Quito, for example, which is set at an altitude of 2800m, the year-round daytime temperature never really exceeds a spring-like 20°C/68°F (with much cooler nights), even though the city sits almost directly on the equator. In mountainous countries you can take advantage of local differences in climate caused by altitude: if you can't stand the heat and humidity of the lowlands, you can always escape to the comparatively cooler highlands (it's no coincidence that many Spanish colonial cities were founded at higher altitudes), while if the bitterly cold nights in one of the cities of the high Andes get too much to bear, you can always jump on a bus and head down into the sweltering lowlands for a day or two.

South of Latin America's tropics, the temperate "Southern Cone" region – comprising Argentina, Chile, Uruguay and southern Brazil – experiences far greater annual variations in temperature, with seasons similar (but in reverse) to those of the northern hemisphere. However, it's only in the far south of the Southern Cone that the cold weather and short days of the southern-hemisphere winter (June–Sept) can limit your options and make travel unpleasant.

Whilst taking seasonal variations into account, you shouldn't let the prospect of very wet or cold weather put you off altogether, so long as you're prepared for travel arrangements to be less reliable and for certain outdoor activities, such as trekking, to be less enjoyable.

Mexico and Central America

Northern Mexico is the only part of Latin America north of the tropics, but the region is so hot and arid that rain and the northern hemisphere winter are no real impediment to travel, though it can get pretty cold at higher altitudes between December and February. Southern Mexico lies within the tropics and shares the same

El Niño

Every two to seven years, weather patterns across much of Latin America and beyond are transformed by a natural phenomenon known as El Niño, with devastating results. The phenomenon was first recognized by Peruvian fishermen in the nineteenth century, when unusually warm waters appeared off the coast of Peru, displacing the colder, nutrient-rich Humboldt Current, with catastrophic effects on fish catches. They christened the phenomenon El Niño – meaning "Little Boy" or "Christ Child" – because it usually appears around Christmas time.

This shift in Pacific Ocean currents is caused by a slackening of the trade winds and resultant warming of the surface layer of water in the eastern and central Pacific, accompanied by sharp swings in atmospheric pressure. As well as disrupting vital fisheries, El Niño provokes sudden and often disastrous changes in weather patterns, bringing floods to some parts of Latin America and drought to others. The last time El Niño struck, in 1997–98, it wrought havoc throughout Latin America, particularly in Peru and Ecuador, where massive floods killed hundreds, devastating crops and infrastructure and inflicting many millions of dollars worth of damage. Nor is El Niño's impact limited to Latin America: scientists now believe it also changes weather patterns worldwide, and may be responsible for droughts and floods in places as far apart as the US, Australia and East Africa, as well as for increasing the strength and frequency of hurricanes in the Caribbean. Scientists are also becoming more concerned that the frequency and severity of El Niño may be growing as global temperatures rise, possibly as a result of human activity. If so, the consequences for millions of people in Latin America could be dire indeed.

As a traveller to Latin America, it's worth keeping an eye on news reports to see if your visit coincides with a possible El Niño year. If it does, be prepared for freak weather conditions and severe disruption. For a wealth of information on El Niño, including the latest predictions, stop by the US National Oceanic and Atmospheric Administration website at Ⓦ www.elnino.noaa.gov.

△ The Pacific coastline, Costa Rica

First-Time Latin America | **WHEN TO GO**

seasonal climate patterns as the countries of Central America, which are generally hot and humid year-round (though, again, cooler in highland regions), but have seasonal variations in rainfall and humidity. The best time to visit southern Mexico and Central America is during the dry season, which runs roughly from November to March. The rainy season runs from around May to October, but even then it doesn't rain all the time, and you'll often get a fine sunny morning followed by a few hours of rain in the afternoon. Along the Caribbean coastline of Central America, rain and humidity continue year-round with only slight seasonal variations.

The tropical Andean countries

Running the length of the western side of South America, the Andes are the second-biggest mountain range in the world, and the highest range in tropical latitudes. In the five tropical countries the Andes pass through – Venezuela, Colombia, Ecuador, Peru and Bolivia – the extreme variations in altitude created by the mountains produce an astonishing number of different climatic zones within a surprisingly small area. The eastern slopes of the Andes, in particular, are so steep that it's possible to experience both sub-zero conditions and extreme tropical heat in the same afternoon, even if you're travelling on foot. Colombia is home to so many different microclimates as to make generalization almost impossible, while Peru embraces perhaps the greatest extremes of climate of any country on earth, ranging from the world's driest desert on its Pacific coast to the glacial peaks of the high Andes and the hot and humid lowlands of the world's largest tropical rainforest in the Amazon basin. This enormous variety means that whatever time of the year you happen to be in one of these countries, the weather conditions are likely to be ideal in at least some regions (though it's equally likely to be pouring with rain elsewhere).

That said, there are some broad seasonal differences that you should be aware of when planning your trip. In so far as it's possible to generalize, Venezuela and Colombia broadly share the same dry season as Central America, particularly along the Caribbean coast, so November to March is the best time to visit. The rest of the year tends to be much wetter (though rain falls throughout the year in the lowland rainforest regions in both countries and along Colombia's Pacific coast). Further south, the Andean countries of Ecuador,

Rainy days in Chocó

The region of Chocó in northwest Colombia is among the world's rainiest – unless you go there in its "dry" period (Dec–March) you're likely to get drenched. When I arrived in the region's capital, Quibdó, it wasn't actually raining; the streets were full of colourful fruit stalls and locals sitting idly along the riverfront, shooting the breeze. That evening, though, when I went to bed, the rain began – my modest hotel had a flat tin roof, as did all the other buildings in Quibdó, and the violent drumming noise, like a thousand tap-dancing giants, kept me awake all night. In the morning the streets had been churned into muddy rivers, the rain was still falling heavily and the sky was sporadically lit up with dramatic white flashes of lightning. The locals, used to the weather, had donned wellies and were splashing happily through the water – I had come unprepared and so stayed in my hotel all day watching the rain from the reception and only periodically rushing out to the nearest café to eat and then race back again. All day it rained and all the next night and then all day again. I couldn't sleep or sightsee or even just stroll through the streets as I would usually have done. The level of noise, both the crashing rain and the cracks of thunder, was incredible – I could barely get myself heard, let alone read in peace. Slowly the water began to seep under the front door into the hotel and the corridors were filled with sodden clothing drying out and a damp cloying mist. After several days the rain stopped – for a while – but by then it was time to move on. When people ask me what Quibdó is like I can only shrug and say "wet".

Polly Rodger Brown

Peru and Bolivia experience more defined seasonal differences. In the highlands, the dry season runs between May and October, with bright, dry, sunny days, though nights can be cold, particularly at higher altitudes. This is obviously the best time to visit, particularly if you want to do any trekking or mountaineering, though it also coincides with the peak tourist season from June to August. The rainy season runs roughly from November to April, with the wettest weather in January and February, and is generally a less favourable time to visit. Heavy rains can cause floods and landslides that damage or completely block the generally poor mountain roads, causing frequent travel delays. Rain can also make mountain trekking pretty miserable, with cloud obscuring the best views, while some high-altitude routes become cut off by snow. However, those difficulties aside it rarely rains so much in the highlands as to spoil your day, and the landscape is arguably more beautiful than during the dry season, with crops high in the fields and the mountainsides green with vegetation, rather than parched and brown.

Though the Amazon Basin is pretty wet all year round, along its western edge in Peru and Bolivia it is also affected by the Andean rainy season, so between November and April the Amazon regions of both countries see heavy rain and can be impossible to visit, as roads are washed away and large areas are flooded (though, conversely, river transport can be easier). The Pacific coast of Ecuador and Peru is affected by a very different set of seasonal variations. The period from around December to March generally sees hot, sunny days along the coast (in comparison to the rains that affect the highlands), but for most of the rest of the year the region is covered by low coastal cloud or mist known as *garúa*, which makes for grey days and cold swimming, even though it rarely ever rains along the entire length of the Peruvian coast.

Brazil

Given its vast size, it's no surprise that Brazil's climate varies considerably between different parts of the country. The entire country lies within the tropics, so it's generally hot and humid year-round, and in most areas rain can fall at any time of the year, though rarely for long enough to affect your travel plans – in general, most of the country can be visited at any time. The main exception to this is the far south of the country, where the climate is more temperate and seasonal variations are more marked; here, the southern-hemisphere winter months from June to August see cooler temperatures and heavy rains which can make travelling miserable, while the peak summer months of January and February are particularly hot and humid and coincide with the main holiday period for Brazilians.

The Southern Cone

South America's Southern Cone, comprising Argentina, Chile and Uruguay, lies almost completely outside the tropics and enjoys a temperate climate with more marked seasonal differences in climate between the winter (June–Aug) and summer (Nov–Feb) – the fact that these seasons are the exact opposite of those in the northern hemisphere means that if you time your trip right you can enjoy two summers in one year. Uruguay and the northern parts of Chile and Argentina can be comfortably visited at any time of the year, though the winter months are cooler and drier than the summer, which can be unpleasantly hot: the optimum times are spring (Sept & Oct) and autumn (March & April). The further south you travel in Chile and Argentina, however, the better it is to avoid the winter months, when the days become short and it gets very cold and wet; in addition, heavy snow can prevent access to mountainous national parks and block some passes between Chile and Argentina (though, of course, this is the perfect time to go skiing). In the far south, the summer offers the added advantage of long summer evenings, allowing far more time to enjoy the sights.

Fiestas

Latin Americans welcome any excuse for a party, and most countries host a large number of national, regional and local fiestas. These are amongst the most vibrant and exciting spectacles Latin America has to offer, and can be worth planning your trip around. For many Latin Americans, fiestas are the most important events of the year and are taken very seriously, often involving lengthy preparation and considerable expense, with the largest featuring thousands of costumed dancers, massed bands, fireworks, copious food and drink, and unrestrained revelry that can continue for a week or more.

The most famous fiesta is without doubt the *Carnaval* in Rio de Janeiro, one of the biggest parties in the world. It's worth remembering that Carnival (originally a religious festival marking the start of Lent) is also celebrated throughout Brazil and the rest of Latin America, albeit on a less spectacular scale, and smaller celebrations often have a more intimate, authentic and less commercial feel.

Like Carnival, many of the major fiestas mark important dates in the Roman Catholic religious calendar, so the dates they're held on can vary from year to year – tourist offices should be able to give you precise details of major events. As well as religious occasions like Carnival and Semana Santa (Easter), many national and regional public holidays mark significant events in Latin America's post-conquest history, such as the gaining of independence, famous battles or the foundation of particular cities; though still treated as an excuse for a party, these tend to be somewhat stuffier affairs, involving interminable civic and military parades.

During major fiestas, transport and accommodation can be very difficult to come by and prices increase dramatically, so it's worth booking well in advance. Even when they don't coincide with an

Semana Santa

Semana Santa – Holy or Easter Week – is Latin America's biggest festival, even more ubiquitous than Carnival, with celebrations taking place in every city, town and village from Mexico to Argentina. Firstly it's a public holiday, when locals head in droves for the beach, national parks and other resorts or else back to their hometowns. Hotels are booked out, buses and domestic flights are crammed full – anyone planning to travel during this period will need to book in advance. More significantly, though, it's a deeply religious occasion with a series of packed masses over the week leading to Easter Sunday and churches lovingly decorated with extravagant flower arrangements. Though ceremonies vary from region to region, they usually include solemn parades of church statues through the town centre and vivid Passion Plays with real blood and suffering – the man playing Christ often wears a genuine crown of thorns, staggers under the weight of a solid cross and is sometimes even nailed to it with real nails. The sanctity of the occasion is lightened with street food stalls, traditional live music and noisy firework displays.

The most impressive Semana Santa celebrations in Latin America occur in the colonial city of Antigua, Guatemala, and attract tens of thousands of visitors. Locals spend hours carpeting the streets with elaborate patterns of flowers, coloured sawdust and pine needles for the Good Friday parades where life-sized images of Jesus Christ and the saints are carried through the town on massive cedar platforms to an accompaniment of brass band dirges and thick clouds of incense. Elsewhere, some of the best places to witness the festivities include San Miguel de Allende in central Mexico, Popayán in southern Colombia and Ayacucho in the Peruvian Andes.

official public holiday, major fiestas tend to result in pretty much everything shutting down for at least a day or two, so they're not a good time to buy an airline ticket, change money in a bank, or get a visa extension. The same is true of national public holidays, particularly the Christmas and New Year period, when buses and trains get very crowded as people travel to visit relations, and international flights are often booked up months ahead by expatriate Latin Americans returning home for the holidays.

As well as major national and regional celebrations, most towns and villages have their own annual local fiesta (some have several), usually held on the day of its patron saint. These celebrations can be much more fun to visit than major fiestas in larger towns, particularly in rural areas of countries with a large indigenous population such as Guatemala, Peru and Bolivia, where they can last over a

Our favourite fiestas

We've listed some of our favourite fiestas below; any guidebook or local tourist office will suggest many others. It's also worth looking at *Wild Planet! 1001 Extraordinary Events for the Inspired Traveller* by Tom Clynes (Visible Ink Press), which has details of dozens of celebrations throughout Latin America and the rest of the world, or check out the websites ⓦwww .whatsonwhen.com and ⓦwww.worldparty.co.uk, which list hundreds of events by country and by month.

Feria de Alasitas La Paz, Bolivia (last week of Jan). This unusual festival sees the streets of central La Paz filled with stalls selling miniature models of items as varied as cars, houses, livestock, wads of dollar bills, and even computers and university degree certificates. Locals buy these to offer to Ekeko, the household god of abundance (portrayed as a diminutive, smiling, moustached man), in the belief that whatever they give him in miniature will be given back to them for real before the year is out.

Carnival (late Feb or early March). Beginning on the Friday before Ash Wednesday, the pre-Lenten *Carnaval* in Rio de Janeiro is without doubt the world's most famous party, a five-day extravaganza that attracts over a quarter of a million foreign visitors each year. The highlights are the processions of the samba schools, each made up of thousands of costumed dancers and myriad decorated floats, who parade along the main avenues and around the purpose-built Sambódromo, competing both to impress the *Carnaval* judges and the huge crowds. The manic celebrations continue through the night at numerous themed *Carnaval* balls, unrestrained parties that start a week before the main event.

Carnival is also celebrated throughout the rest of Brazil and Latin America, albeit on a smaller and less dramatic scale than in Rio, though usually involving the same ingredients of music, dance and licentiousness. If the sheer scale and commercialism of the Rio *Carnaval* puts you off, you may be better off joining a smaller but arguably more authentic celebration somewhere else – many people rate the celebrations in Salvador de Bahia, with its strong Afro-Brazilian traditions, more highly than Rio. Elsewhere, the Carnival in Baranquilla, on the Colombian Caribbean coast, is renowned for its raucousness, while Carnival in the bleak Bolivian mining city of Oruro is amongst the most colourful folkloric fiestas in all Latin America.

International Caribbean Music Festival Cartagena, Colombia (March). For two weeks in March the beautiful colonial port city of Cartagena, on Colombia's north coast, is taken over by bands and musicians from all over the Caribbean who come to perform in one of Latin America's best live-music events. All the region's rich musical heritage is featured, including reggae, soca, salsa, merengue and vallenato.

Semana Santa (March or April). Semana Santa – the Easter Holy Week – is marked throughout Latin America with colourful religious processions. The celebrations in the city of Ayacucho in Peru and in Antigua in Guatemala are particularly fervent and dramatic. For more on Semana Santa, see the box on p.195.

Qoyllur Riti Peru (May or June). Held at the foot of a glacier in an isolated valley in the Andes south of Cusco in the week before Corpus Christi, this is one of the most exciting fiestas in Latin America, a celebration of ancient Andean beliefs centred on mountain gods and natural cycles, covered with only the thinnest veneer of Catholicism. Thousands of indigenous peasants make the pilgrimage to a bleak spot at well over 4000m, many of them marching through the night, and costumed dances, accompanied by traditional music and dynamite explosions, continue for three days and nights. On the last night, young men dressed in ritual costumes stay up on the high glacier, marching down at first light bearing hunks of ice on their backs, which are melted down and taken to their home communities to improve fertility. This is primarily an indigenous fiesta and though a few Cusco tour agencies take groups, it's only for the adventurous, as you'll have to hike there and camp out at high altitude.

Inti Raymi and Corpus Christi Cusco, Peru (June). Inti Raymi (June 24) is a popular and commercial re-enactment of the Inca Festival of the Sun, performed by costumed actors in Sacsayhuaman, the massive Inca fortress that towers above Cusco. The fiesta draws thousands of tourists to the city, and hotels and flights fill up, but it's far from the most authentic of Cusco's many fiestas – that honour belongs to Corpus Christi. Taking place nine weeks after Maundy Thursday (usually in mid-June), this event involves mass processions of saints' effigies accompanied by costumed dancers, traditional music and street markets selling traditional food.

Yamor Fiesta Otavalo, Ecuador. Held in the first two weeks of September, the Yamor Fiesta is the main annual festival in the Ecuadorian town of Otavalo, best known for its craft market. The indigenous people of the region come into town for several days of bullfights, food, drink, music and dance, in celebration of a pre-Columbian fiesta revived in the 1940s.

Day of the Dead Mexico (Nov 1 & 2). Fervently celebrated throughout Mexico on All Saint's Day, and through the night into the following day (All Soul's Day, the Day of the Dead proper), the Day of the Dead is a time of remembrance that is at once sombre and festive. People converge on cemeteries with food and drink to party with their deceased loved ones and ancestors. In the run-up to the event throughout the country shops and market stalls sell special foods and macabre decorations in the shape of skulls, coffins and the like, which are used to adorn graves, and ceremonial offerings arranged in honour of the dead, who are believed to return to the land of the living and visit their former homes for the day. Precise customs vary from region to region within Mexico – one of the most dramatic places

Our favourite fiestas (*continued...*)

to witness the occasion is on the Lago de Pátzcuaro, about 200km east of Mexico City, where locals converge on an island cemetery in canoes carrying candles and floral offerings. The Day of the Dead is also celebrated in similar fashion in Guatemala, most spectacularly in Todos Santos Cuchumatán, where days of Maya music, drinking and dance culminate in a riotous horse race. The Day of the Dead is also marked throughout the Andes, though on a more restrained scale and without the bizarre ritual paraphernalia of Mexico.

Día de la Tradición Argentina (around Nov 10). Also known as the Fiesta del Gaucho, this is a celebration of Argentina's most powerful cultural icon, the gaucho (cowboy) of the pampas grasslands. Centred on the town of Santiago de Areco, the festival involves traditional gaucho folk music and dance, rodeos and horse-riding displays, and the consumption of large quantities of the finest beef in the world, much of it cooked in the traditional gaucho style: roasted on a spit over an open fire.

Día de la Virgen de Guadalupe Mexico (Dec 12). Mexico's patron saint's day is celebrated with extravagant processions and a mass pilgrimage to the Basílica de Guadalupe, outside Mexico City, with many of the thousands of celebrants advancing to the shrine on their knees.

week and involve traditional music and colourful costumed folkloric dances. Be prepared to change your itinerary at short notice if you hear of a good local fiesta going on anywhere near where you are – it's an opportunity not to be missed.

5

How much will it cost?

The cost of travelling in Latin America varies wildly: from ultra-cheap countries like Nicaragua or Bolivia to places like Chile or Costa Rica, where living costs can be similar to those in Europe or North America. Overall, though, travelling in Latin America is much less expensive than travelling in your own country. Having said this, you're going to come across the kind of opportunities on your trip that you don't normally come across – staying in a remote eco-lodge in the Amazon, hang-gliding over Rio, riding with gauchos in Argentina – and these opportunities all have a price tag. While you might baulk at the cost of all this, actually doing any of these things will give you memories which will last well beyond the pain caused by prising open your wallet. Just accept, even before you set off, that visiting Latin America is going to cost you – if this really is the trip of a lifetime, then it's worth doing it properly.

Obviously, your budget is vital in determining what kind of trip you have, and it's important before you set out to have at least a rough idea of how much you'll need. If you do have a very limited budget, then think about taking a shorter but more satisfying trip. Nothing is more frustrating than not having enough cash to really enjoy your holiday. Imagine getting all the way to Venezuela and not being able to afford the flight to the Angel Falls, or going to the Caribbean islands of Mexico, Belize or Honduras and sitting forlornly on the beach while everyone else goes snorkelling or scuba diving.

However tedious it sounds, once on the road, it really does help to keep a record of your expenses so that you always know how much money you have to play with. It's all too easy to run out of cash well before the end of your trip, or (much less likely) forgo a special outing because you're saving money when actually you don't need to. Don't be alarmed if you spend a lot of money in your first few days, however – it's well worth the investment just to feel safe and properly acclimatized. If you're on a tight budget, consider flying into one of the cheaper Latin American countries and then taking on the more expensive ones once you're an old hand at cutting corners.

If you're planning to get involved in voluntary, ecology or community projects whilst away, you may be eligible for some kind of grant or sponsorship – check the *Directory of Grant Making Trusts*, *The Grants Register* or *The Australian Grants Register* in your local library. These publications list businesses which regularly give funds to or sponsor all kinds of projects and individuals, including small-scale schemes which involve travelling abroad.

Cost of living

It's difficult to generalize about the cost of living in Latin America, which can vary wildly even between adjacent countries – travelling in Costa Rica costs two or three times more than in neighbouring Nicaragua, for example, whilst crossing the border from Bolivia into Chile will immediately double your expenses. In general, the richer, more westernized Latin American countries are significantly more expensive to travel in than the poorer, less developed ones, and knowing roughly how much you'll need in each one will allow you to prepare for sudden changes in living expenses. For more details, see the box on p.203.

Bear in mind that parts of Latin America have been – and may again be – subject to periods of economic meltdown and hyper-inflation, as demonstrated by recent fiscal woes in Argentina, which have had a topsy-turvy effect on that nation's cost of living.

Making savings before you go

With a little careful planning, you can start cutting the cost of your trip immediately.

- Begin planning well in advance of your departure date – if you leave everything to the last minute you'll invariably pay over the odds. Do some research on basic expenses like airfares and insurance so you know, before you start, how much you should be paying.
- Wait for the sales to buy your equipment or surf the net for special deals. Alternatively, borrow gear from friends and family – backpacks, in particular, are often bought, used and then thrown into the back of the wardrobe – and consider buying secondhand stuff (although you should check important pieces of equipment like backpacks or boots carefully), such as clothes, which you can then ditch on your way home. Alternatively, you could wait to buy basic clothing until you arrive in Latin America, where it's invariably cheaper than at home.
- Make sure you buy those day-to-day items which cost considerably more abroad before you go – these are usually things that the locals don't use as much, such as camera film, batteries, suntan lotion, moisturizing cream and tampons.

Making savings on the road

Despite the unavoidable expenses when on the road – mainly consisting of lodging, eating and transport – there are plenty of ways to cut costs. The following tips will help you minimize expenses.

- The slower you travel the cheaper your trip will be. Not only will you cut down on transport costs, which in some countries can be considerable, but with each day you spend in one place you'll be discovering new budget restaurants, and you should also be able to get a reduced rate on accommodation if you're staying more than a few days – always ask.
- Travel during the low season, when hotel and tour prices drop (sometimes dramatically) and when the relative lack of tourists gives you more bargaining power. Conversely if you're staying in a holiday resort or popular spot over a local holiday period you'll pay premium rates – if you don't mind missing the party avoid going to the beach or the UNESCO World Heritage Site at weekends or on public holidays.
- Form groups with other travellers for arranging tours, hiring transport and even getting good deals on accommodation. The more there are

of you, the cheaper things get. Once you've got your bargain, you can always split up into your original smaller units.

- Always ask the price of things before you start. Be very wary of menus with no prices, agree fares with taxi drivers before you get in (and get the driver to repeat it back to you so there can be no confusion).
- Do as the locals do. Take local buses, eat in markets or informal cafés and choose the daily set meal.
- Travel at night. In the larger countries of South America, many journeys can be taken at night, saving you the cost of a night's accommodation (but check before you go that the journey isn't prey to thieves or guerrillas – some, unfortunately, are).
- Stay in hostel dormitories. They're often the cheapest accommodation available, and most also have kitchens where you can cook your own meals. You might even want to take a tent – you can often camp in the gardens of hostels or cheap hotels, or in national parks – or buy a hammock, which you can sling up on a willing hotel proprietor's porch for a very small fee.
- Take a water filter or some other method of purifying unclean water. Tap water in Latin America is usually not safe, and bottled water, not something the locals buy, can cost as much as other drinks including beer, sometimes more – buying several litres every day will hike up your daily budget.
- Home stays – staying with a local family – are good for practising your Spanish or Portuguese, a great way to get involved in the community and, above all, cheap.

Tourist prices

You may as well accept right from the start that you'll be paying more for most things than the locals – annoying as you might find this, there's very little you can do about it. In some parts of Latin America, tourists are officially charged more than nationals for things like entrance fees to museums and art galleries, national parks and sites of historic and archeological interest. Arguing until you're blue in the face won't make any difference; if you want to visit these places then you'll have to pay the extra.

Much more widespread is the unofficial hike in prices that happens when a tourist comes to town. Market food, taxi fares and perhaps even hotel rooms and meals will invariably cost more. However, you should refuse to pay anything that seems outrageous, not only for the sake of your own funds, but also because tourists

Sample budgets

The following sample budgets are linked to a few of the itineraries suggested on pp.128–136. They do not include international or domestic flights, insurance or any other pre-trip expenses. Minimum daily living expenses (which cover staying in cheap hotels/hostels, eating *comida corriente* and travelling by local bus) for individual countries are listed on the opening pages of the profiles in the **Where to go** section (see p.17).

Three weeks on South America's Caribbean coast

Though both Venezuela and particularly Colombia are inexpensive to visit, anywhere on the Caribbean tends to cost more than inland destinations. Still, US$400 will cover your expenses and include a couple of snorkelling or short boat trips (US$25–50). If you want to splash out and spend the odd night in a decent hotel (US$30–50) and eat an occasional posh meal (US$5–15) you could fit that into your budget as well.

One month on the Ruta Maya

Ten days in this part of Mexico and Belize will be relatively expensive – count on US$30 per day to cover fairly basic eating and sleeping arrangements with travel included. The rest of this trip – twenty days in Guatemala, Honduras and El Salvador (where accommodation can cost as little as US$2 a night, as does eating, US$2–3 for a substantial *menu del dia* lunch) – will cost much less. Altogether, count on spending US$600 for the month with entrance to the Yucatán's Maya cities (US$5–10) but no frills added. If you want to scuba dive (from US$75 for a one-day "exploratory" course) in Belize, tuck into Mexican "haute cuisine", take an organized day-trip or visit one of the Ruta Maya's amusement parks (such as Xelha) you'll need an extra US$150–200.

Three months in the Andean highlands

While Chile is one of the priciest countries in South America, the other places on this itinerary – Peru, Ecuador and particularly Bolivia – are among its cheapest. For this trip reckon on a minimum budget of US$1500 which will cover food, accommodation and travel on a fairly tight budget. If you want to ski in Chile (prices start at US$800 for an all-inclusive week-long package), visit upmarket beach resort Viña del Mar or spend any longer than three weeks in the country you'll need to increase your budget. On the other hand both simple accommodation and eating out rarely cost more than a few dollars in the other Andean countries – a month in Bolivia could cost as little as US$300–400.

who pay silly money push up the cost of living for the locals – after all, why sell something to a local when you can get five times its value from a rich visitor? Very soon locals become second-class citizens – which naturally fuels resentment, making things even worse for visitors.

Having said that, bear in mind that what is small change to you might be a lot more important to the seller. There is nothing uglier than a tourist with a thousand-dollar camera round his neck quibbling with a *campesino* over the price of an orange.

For more on spending money responsibly, see the section on ethical tourism on pp.267–269.

Bargaining

One way to cut costs and reduce the effect of tourist prices is to master the fine art of bargaining. Latin America's more developed countries tend to be relatively closed to bargaining, whereas those with a large indigenous population have a long tradition of flexible pricing. Markets are the best place to start, since virtually all prices in these are open to negotiation. The quoted cost of hotel rooms, tours and private transport (including taxis and boats) can also sometimes be lowered. Don't assume, however, that all prices are open to negotiation in every country – they're not, and there will be much rolling of eyes if you pick the wrong place to have a go. Places where bargaining is off limits are fairly obvious: supermarkets, smart clothes shops and chemists all have fixed prices; equally, you can't bargain for airline or bus tickets, or reduce the cost of items on restaurant menus.

Before buying anything, have a look around and compare prices to give yourself an idea of prices. When bargaining, retain a sense of humour at all times and be as charming as you can; be complimentary, polite and patient, and bear in mind that this is not a matter of life or death – at least, not to you. If you think your chosen stallholder is trying to rip you off or you're just not happy with the way things are going then walk away – the simple act of leaving might trigger a better offer. If you're planning on buying a lot of last-minute presents or souvenirs you might save some money by buying them all in the same place. Don't appear too keen when bargaining, and if you've almost sealed the deal, get out the relevant cash: the sight of your money might encourage the seller to close out the deal at a slightly lower price.

Splashing out

In Latin America, quite possibly for the first time in your life, you'll be considered rich. And, like it or not, by most Latin American standards, you are – compare the cost of your return airfare with wages in the poorer parts of the continent of as little as US$15 a week (coupled with 75 percent unemployment rates) and you begin to get the picture. Instead of fighting this and irritating the locals by continuing to insist that actually you're an impoverished student struggling to make ends meet, why not make the most of your temporary wealth?

In some parts of Latin America, US$30 will buy you a night in a plush hotel room with all the frills. On the Atlantic coast of Nicaragua you'll pay less than US$7 for a slap-up meal of freshly caught lobster. You can learn to scuba dive in the Bay Islands of Honduras for as little as a third of what it would cost elsewhere – and the same holds for learning Spanish in Guatemala, whitewater rafting in Peru or mountain-climbing in Bolivia.

Occasionally there may be times on the road when you need to indulge yourself. Long bumpy bus rides; lack of sleep caused by poor hotels; bad food; mosquito bites; extremes of heat and cold – all these can take their toll and leave you exhausted. Instead of staggering on until you grind to a halt or fall ill, it's a good idea to take time out by paying more than normal for a decent night's sleep and a proper hot meal. And when it comes to your personal safety, no price is too high to pay. If the only budget hotel in town is down a dark alleyway, don't book in; if the cheapest local guide is clearly a bit of a cowboy, don't hire him; and if the third-class boat you're planning to board looks like it might sink, don't get on it. You'll feel very foolish if something awful happens simply because you were cutting corners.

How to take your money

The best way to keep your money safe is to take it in as many different forms as possible – cash, travellers' cheques, and credit cards. In addition, be sure to check exchange rates on the Internet (Ⓦwww.oanda.com or Ⓦwww.xe.com) or in a newspaper before you go so that you'll know roughly what you should be getting.

US dollars

The US dollar rules supreme in Latin America – it's actually the official currency of Panama, Ecuador and El Salvador; in Panama's case since independence in 1904, in Ecuador as recently as 2000 and even more recently in 2003 El Salvador also adopted the dollar as national currency. Every country in the region accepts dollars as payment as well as its own currency, and you should never be without some. Generally speaking, the more expensive the service or goods you're buying, the greater the chance that you'll be able to pay in dollars, while the further away you get from tourist areas, the slimmer your chances of paying in dollars become.

Buying dollars before you leave home is the same as for any other foreign currency. In case you run short, you can also get dollars from ATMs in some parts of Latin America – this is easiest in Mexico.

Cash

The easiest and cheapest – though least secure – way to take your money is as cash, either in local currency or as US dollars. Don't change too much cash all in one go, though. You'll miss out on local currency fluctuations, which often favour established hard currencies

△ Casa de cambio, Mexico

like the dollar and the pound. More importantly, you won't get cash back if it's stolen unless you've invested in a more comprehensive insurance scheme.

Travellers' cheques

Travellers' cheques (*cheques de viaje*) are by far the safest way of carrying cash abroad, and come with a guarantee that they'll be swiftly replaced in full should they be stolen (assuming you've kept a record of the lost cheque numbers). The price for this security is the commission you pay to buy them (usually 1–1.5 percent), as well as a possible commission when you change them and, in many cases, a lower exchange rate.

For Latin America, you should always buy travellers' cheques issued in US dollars; any other currency renders them virtually useless. Also ask for a variety of different denominations: larger ones will save you commission fees and endless visits to the bank, while smaller ones are good for changing in places where you'd rather not carry heaps of cash. American Express travellers' cheque are recognized almost everywhere, while Thomas Cook cheques are also well known – other types of cheque may not be accepted.

The standard procedure for using travellers' cheques will be explained to you in full when you buy them. You'll also be given a

Keeping an emergency stash

On your travels through Latin America, be sure to keep a stash of US dollars for unforeseen emergencies. Although I started my trip with one, soon it was all but spent after giving in to far too many ice cream urges and overloading on trinkets. In time I would come to regret this.

Mexico, like almost every other Latin American country, requires that travellers pay an airport departure tax, and, furthermore, that it be paid in US dollars. I was fully aware of this in the days leading up to my flight home, although I was unsure of the exact amount. The afternoon before my flight back to London I popped into a reputable travel agency in Playa Del Carmen to ask, and was assured by three separate agents that the amount would not exceed US$25. Splendid, I thought – I could enjoy my last night in Mexico.

The following day, clutching my US$25, I arrived at Cancún airport. I struggled over to an airport official, my rucksack bulging from one last souvenir binge the previous evening. "Forty-five dollars please," the airport official barked. Needless to say, I didn't have it. I then had to wait for a shuttle bus to take me and my increasingly unwieldy rucksack back to a distant terminal where the only airport cash machine was located, withdraw money on my credit card, and then wait for a second shuttle bus to take me back to my point of departure. I just made my plane, but only because I had arrived at the airport with time to spare. I was lucky. An emergency stash would have spared me the fretting, backaches and heart-racing panic.

Faye Cook

record of purchase as well as a list of the serial number of each cheque you've bought. Keep both these documents safe and separate from the cheques themselves – a record of purchase is sometimes requested by the bank changing your money as a security check, and if you do have travellers' cheques stolen you'll have to quote the numbers of those missing. Tick off each number on your list as you change them.

If your cheques are stolen, you'll have to make your way to the nearest American Express or Thomas Cook agent. If you ring in advance your replacement cheques may well be waiting for you when you arrive – make sure you carry the free hotline number on you at all times. You will be expected to take the necessary precautions to avoid being robbed and, if you are, to have a plausible explanation of the circumstances.

Credit and debit cards

Credit and debit cards are the most convenient, if not necessarily the cheapest, way to carry funds in Latin America. Most banks will give you an advance on your card, and there are increasing numbers of ATMs across Latin America where you can withdraw the local currency (and sometimes even dollars) – you can check the location of ATMs in Latin America at ⓦwww.visa.com or ⓦwww.mastercard .com. In lots of places, you can also pay for higher-end hotel rooms, meals, airline tickets and other large purchases using plastic.

It's worth remembering, however, that using a credit or debit card is far from cheap. When it comes to withdrawing money from an ATM, the average cost for using both types of card includes a 2.75 percent handling charge plus a further 1.50 percent commission on foreign exchange – in total, a whopping 4.25 percent (on the plus side, however, ATMs often offer far better exchange rates than local banks or *casas de cambio*). With credit cards, you'll also be paying interest on any money withdrawn from the moment you take it out. Additionally, if you're paying for a room or a meal with plastic you may be stung with an additional charge levied by the hotel or restaurant owner to cover the commission that the proprietor will have to pay to the card issuer – such additional charges are completely unregulated, and can potentially be as high as fifteen percent. Always check in advance if you're intending to pay by card.

In terms of security, avoid withdrawing cash from an ATM at night and exercise due caution at all times – choose machines in busy public places and don't hang around after your transaction. If your card is stolen, ring the emergency phone number (which you should always carry with you) as soon as possible to cancel it. Assuming you report the theft promptly, you won't be liable for a thief's spending spree.

The most popular credit cards in Latin America are Visa and Mastercard – Visa is the more widely accepted of the two, though it's worth carrying both. If you're travelling for a while, you'll need either to set up a direct debit or ask a friend to pay off your account. It's also possible to get Visa debit cards: these work in most Latin American ATMs (as do other debit cards linked to the Cirrus or Plus networks). Don't take a debit card issued by your bank unless it carries a Visa, Mastercard, Cirrus or Plus symbol, or it will probably prove useless.

For UK citizens, the current best debit card deal is with Nationwide (ⓦwww.nationwide.co.uk). A FlexAccount debit card carries no charge for taking money out when abroad and the rest of your funds remain in a fairly high interest-bearing account.

An alternative way of carrying funds is Visa TravelMoney. This is a disposable debit card which you can use in any ATM which accepts Visa cards. You can buy cards loaded with prepaid funds from most branches of Thomas Cook and Citicorp. Once the funds you've loaded on to the card run out, you simply throw it away. You can also request up to nine cards to access the same funds – very useful for couples or groups travelling with a common kitty.

Changing money

The easiest form of money to change is dollars: in many parts of Latin America virtually everyone you come across – hoteliers, restaurateurs, shopkeepers, local business people, market traders – will be more than happy to change them for you at the going rate. There are also moneychangers (*coyotes*) on the streets in most Latin American countries who'll change dollars for rates slightly better than banks, and without commission. They normally hang out in commercial areas, like shopping malls or around markets – you'll recognize them by the wads of cash they flick through and wave in your face. Some are licensed, while some are unofficial – be very careful if you decide to deal with the latter, who are adept at all kinds of scams. By contrast, official licensed moneychangers (look for the badge) are often trustworthy, though it's worth checking locally first.

You can also change money at banks and *casas de cambio* (exchange bureaux, usually street booths); some will also change travellers' cheques and give advances on credit cards. In some places, banks offer better rates than *casas de cambio*, while in others, the reverse applies. Whatever the case, banks are potentially much more frustrating places than *casas de cambio*, with long queues (although tourists are sometimes ushered to the front) and inflexible set hours for changing money. *Casas de cambio* are generally more user-friendly, with many opening late and over weekends.

Change is in very short supply in many Latin American countries so whenever you're changing money always ask for small-denomination notes and check that they're in fairly good condition – torn or even just grubby notes may be refused by traders (this goes for dollars too). Once you've completed your transaction, be it with a moneychanger, *casa de cambio* or bank, count your money carefully. You might prefer to go straight back to your hotel, just to be on the safe side, rather than wandering around with a pile of money.

Emergency funds

The easiest and fastest way of getting emergency funds is to have someone wire money. The two main operators are Western Union (ⓦwww.westernunion.com) and Moneygram (ⓦwww.moneygram .com), both of which have branches all over the world – even quite modest-sized towns in Latin America have an office of one or other (Western Union is more prevalent). Someone at home will have to take the money to the local branch, which is then wired immediately (taking no more than fifteen minutes) to the office you have specified. Remember, though, that wiring money is hugely expensive – costing anything up to fourteen percent of the sum being wired – and should be considered a last resort.

6

Guidebooks and other resources

Whatever the nature of your trip, the chances are that the more you know about Latin America, the more you'll enjoy your time there. Having some idea about the history, politics and culture of the countries you'll be visiting will whet your appetite for travelling and place what you see in some kind of larger context.

There are lots of ways of learning about Latin America. The Internet is an excellent resource; connect to a powerful search engine like Google (Ⓦwww.google.com), type in the subject or place you're interested in and you'll get hundreds of useful links to websites, online articles and photo essays (see p.374–375 in the Directory and the individual country profiles for some recommended websites). Cities with large Latin American populations in North America, Europe and Australasia all have specialist resource centres with libraries and collections of useful videos; they also run courses, lectures and publish useful leaflets and magazines (see p.376 for details). Their staff are often experts in Latin America. Specialist travel agencies (see pp.364–367) and national tourist boards should also be able to advise you, particularly on the practical aspects of your trip.

Guidebooks

A decent guidebook is an essential tool in planning your trip. Not only is it a source of all kinds of practical information – from how to buy a plane ticket to how to ask for a sandwich in Portuguese – but it will also give you a reasonable grasp of a country's or region's culture and history. Bear in mind, though, that it's impossible for guidebooks to be one hundred percent accurate – prices change constantly, restaurants open and hotels shut down every week. Guidebooks also, inevitably, reflect their authors' bias, and though decent editing should ensure a degree of objectivity, your own opinions will inevitably clash at some point with those in your book. The other disadvantage of slavishly following a guidebook, especially a popular one, is that you'll constantly bump into other readers following the exact same route as you. Places given an endorsement by best-selling guidebooks can become overpriced and rest on their laurels, leading to a decline in standards. Conversely, places not listed may be perfectly decent, and actually make more of an effort to provide a good service.

Choosing a guidebook

When it comes to choosing a guidebook, go to a large bookshop and browse through all the relevant titles; compare the way different guidebooks write up a particular destination, and see what sort of hotels and restaurants they list to work out how relevant they're likely to be to your budget. And don't leave getting a guidebook till the last minute – good guides are full of useful pre-trip advice. Compendium volumes which cover several different countries in one area (the *Rough Guide to Central America* or Lonely Planet's *South America on a Shoestring*, for example) are obviously popular, since most travellers to Latin America will visit more than one country. Bear in mind, though, that tight editing means that they contain much less information than single-country guides. If you're planning to go to just two or three countries it might be worth taking a separate guidebook for each one – any more than that and you should opt for a compendium. You might be able to sell guidebooks you've no further use for while travelling, or even swap them for books on the region you're heading to – check the noticeboard in backpackers' hostels and book exchanges. If you've planned your trip round a particular theme or activity – whether scuba diving, bird-spotting or trekking

– you might want to also take a specialist guidebook; the best of these are detailed in Chapter 1 under the relevant theme or itinerary.

Maps

Although your guidebook should have maps of cities and particular regions, these will inevitably be fairly basic, given the constraints of book format. Although it's not strictly necessary (unless you're travelling under your own steam), it's worth thinking about taking a proper map with you. This will give you a much better overview of where you're going, with enhanced road details and contour markings, so you'll get a much clearer picture of the land through which you're travelling. For a list of good map shops, see pp.373–374.

The best travel maps of Latin America are published by International Travel Map Productions, Vancouver, Canada (🌐www.itmp.com), who are specialists in the region. Their maps are renowned for their accuracy, for being regularly updated, and for their wealth of detail (including symbols for caves, lighthouses and even oil pipelines). ITMP have the largest-scale maps for most countries in Latin America, including less-visited destinations like French Guiana and Uruguay, as well as maps of particular regions, such as the Amazon Basin, the Galápagos Islands and Cusco/Machu Picchu. Additionally, Rough Guides, in partnership with the World Mapping Project, produces its own set of country and regional maps. The maps are highly detailed and printed on waterproof and virtually indestructible paper. There are currently Rough Guide maps to eight countries and regions in Latin America – Argentina, Baja California, Chile, Costa Rica and Panama, Guatemala and Belize, Mexico, Peru and the Yucatán Peninsula. Maps produced by Berndtson and Berndtson (🌐www.berndtson.com) – which are laminated for extra durability – and GeoCenter (🌐www.geocenter.de) are also good.

If you're planning on trekking, most Latin American capital cities have an Instituto Geográfico Nacional or Militar that sells detailed topographical maps of the country.

Background reading

While your guidebook is a good starting point for learning about Latin America, to really flesh out your knowledge of the region's history, geography, politics, society and people, you'll need to consult other sources.

Magazines

There is a wide range of travel magazines, from the very chic (*Condé Nast Traveller*) to the very adventurous (*Outside*), which have articles on Latin America on a regular basis. Most feature general information on travelling as well as reviews of the latest equipment and books, plus current travel news. Published in the UK (but available worldwide on subscription), *Wanderlust* (@www.wanderlust.co.uk), *Traveller* and *Global Adventure* feature off-the-beaten-track destinations with great photographs and well-written articles. Comprehensive sections in all three list websites, road-test new equipment and review the latest travelogues and guidebooks. *Wanderlust* also has a useful classified sections with adverts for travelling companions. *Adventure Travel* (@www.at.co.uk) is written with hikers and mountain climbers in mind, though it too has a wealth of more general travel information. *Geographical* (@www.geographical.co.uk), the magazine of the Royal Geographical Society, has special features on exploration and ecological/environmental issues. In North America, the best magazines on adventurous, independent travel are *Outside* (@outside.away.com), *Blue* (@www.bluemagazine.com) and *National Geographic Adventure* (@www.nationalgeographic.com/adventure); in Australia, *Backpacker Essentials* (@www.backpackeressentials.com.au), the magazine of the Australian Youth Hostel Association, is packed with useful travel tips plus features written by backpackers; *TNT* (@www.tntmagazine.com.au) runs articles on budget travel and is a good source of practical information on cheap flights and insurance policies.

There are a number of magazines devoted to Latin American society and politics, which are available to read in specialist libraries (see p.376) and on subscription. The best of these are printed in the US: the bimonthly *Americas* (@www.americasmagazine.oas.org) is published by the Organization of American States and has clearly written features on history, film and food; *Report on the Americas* (@www.nacla.org), published by the left-wing North American Congress on Latin America, is more highbrow, though still highly readable. The *Latin American Weekly Report* (available on subscription – and online – from Latin American Newsletters, 61 Old Street,

London EC1V 9HW; ®www.latinnews.com) offers a useful overview of political, economic and financial happenings in the region.

Online magazines

There are now hundreds of online travel magazines or (webzines) – some require a paid subscription but many have travel articles that can be browsed for free. Among the best for independent travellers are Travel Mag (®www.travelmag.co.uk), Destinations Elsewhere (®www.destinationselsewhere.com) and High on Adventure (®www.highonadventure.com).

There are a couple of good online magazines which focus on travelling in Latin America: *Latin Travel* (®www.latintravel.com) which has news stories, expert advice, destination guides and travel features and *Aventura* (®www.aventura-mag.com) which specializes in adventure sports travel in Latin America.

For links to hundreds of magazines published in Latin America – on ecology, history, sport, fashion and pretty much everything else – check ®www.zonalatina.com. Links to online versions of the magazines are conveniently listed country by country.

Books

Although Latin America is not as widely visited or written about as Europe or Asia, there are still dozens of good books on all aspects of the region which will whet your appetite for the countries you're going to visit – if you don't get time to read them before you go you might want to take some of them with you. Recommended bookshops with comprehensive travel sections are listed in Basics (see p.373). Detailed below are a few of the best books on Latin America, as well as some of our particular favourites.

Travel writing

● Sybille Bedford: *A Visit to Don Octavio*. Wonderfully idiosyncratic and vivid account of a visit to Mexico in the 1950s. While some of the book portrays a Mexico long since gone, other passages feature scenes of everyday life – chickens on buses, colourful markets – which are still familiar sights today.

● Bruce Chatwin: *In Patagonia*. Inspired by tales of his grandmother's cousin, a sailor who settled in Punta Arenas after his ship sank in the

Straits of Magellan, Bruce Chatwin set off in 1975 to explore the strange and wild plains of southernmost Latin America – this award-winning travelogue, with its unerring eye for human and historical eccentricity, was the result.

● Peter Ford: *Tekkin' A Waalk*. Taking a break from city life in Managua, journalist Peter Ford walked the length of the wild and swampy Caribbean coast from Belize to Panama in the mid-1980s, describing aspects of the unique Garífuna and Miskito cultures he came across along the way.

● Charles Nicholl: *The Fruit Palace*. A humorous and thrilling investigation into the 1970s cocaine trade, exposing the ubiquitous corruption and craziness that underscore Colombian life and business.

● Peter Robb: *A Death in Brazil*. Genre-defying book which blends history, food, politics and culture to create an absorbing portrait of Brazil, past and present. Robb has lived in the country for many years and his research and observations are deftly woven with his own vivid experiences of life there.

● Salman Rushdie: *The Jaguar Smile: a Nicaraguan Journey*. Invited to Nicaragua by the Sandinista Association of Cultural Workers, writer Salman Rushdie spent three weeks in the country in 1986 and returned to write this thought-provoking account of his brief stay.

● John Lloyd Stephens: *Incidents of Travel in Central America, Chiapas and Yucatán*. Classic account of two trips made in the late 1830s by the American ambassador to Central America and keen amateur archeologist, John Lloyd Stephens, in search of the lost cities of the Maya. Together with draughtsman Frederick Catherwood, whose elegant drawings illustrate some editions of the book, Stephens provided the outside world with the first detailed descriptions of Uxmal, Palenque, Copán and Chichén Itzá, as well as vivid scenes of everyday life in the Maya villages of the region.

● Paul Theroux: *The Old Patagonian Express*. A decidedly bad-tempered, misanthropic but keenly observant Paul Theroux leaves his native Boston and travels all the way through Latin America to its southernmost tip by train – a journey made particularly poignant because, with the abandonment of almost all train networks on the continent, it's no longer possible to follow in his footsteps.

● Hugh Thomson: *The White Rock: An Exploration of the Inca Heartland*. Filmmaker Thomson is a self-confessed Inca addict, obsessed with the ancient Peruvian civilization and its legacy. *The White Rock* details the gripping history of the explorers who set out to discover ruined Inca cities as well as vividly describing several of Thomson's own visits to Cusco and the surrounding region.

Politics and social sciences

- *In Focus Guides*. Published by the Latin American Bureau in London, this excellent series of individual country profiles covers more than half of the countries in Latin America, each consisting of a collection of short and clearly written essays organized by theme – history, politics, environment and society.

- Eduardo Galeano: *Open Veins of Latin America: Five Centuries of the Pillage of a Continent*. Written some 25 years ago by Uruguayan journalist Eduardo Galeano, this groundbreaking treatise lays the blame for Latin America's ills squarely on its sixteenth-century European colonizers and, more recently, on the creeping globalization initiated by the US.

- Duncan Green: *Faces of Latin America*. Comprehensive and lively introduction to Latin American politics, economics and society, illustrated with deftly chosen accounts drawn from personal experiences.

△ Booksellers, Mexico City

- Joe Kane: *Savages*. Deeply depressing but excellently researched tale of the environmental destruction of parts of the Ecuadorian Amazon by US oil companies and the attempt to fight back by the forest's Huaorani people.
- Claude Lévi-Strauss: *Tristes Tropiques*. Seminal work by the legendary French anthropologist describing a working trip to Brazil in the 1930s to study the Nambikwara and Tupi-Kawahib Indians, describing with wit and insight the ups and downs of travelling in a strange culture.
- Gabriel García Márquez: *News of a Kidnapping*. Using interviews and diary entries, Márquez skilfully recreates the stories of several brutal kidnappings (Colombia is the kidnap centre of the world, with over a thousand annually) by infamous drug lord Pablo Escobar – by turns gripping and grimly illuminating.

History and culture

- Michael D. Coe: *The Maya*. Celebrated general introduction from a renowned Maya expert to one of Latin America's most sophisticated indigenous cultures.
- Charles Darwin: *Voyage of the Beagle*. The journal of young naturalist Charles Darwin recording his five-year trip around the southern end of South America (1831–36), a journey which inspired his evolutionary theories, with an obvious – though not exclusive – focus on flora and fauna.
- John Hemming: *The Conquest of the Incas*. Clear and easily digestible history of the Spanish victory over the Incas, using a vivid narrative style woven together from original accounts from both sides of the battle.
- Bartolomé de Las Casas: *A Short Account of the Destruction of the Indies*. Written by a Dominican cleric and "Defender of the Indians" in 1542, this furious letter (addressed to the then king of Spain, Philip II) records Las Casas' horror at his fellow Spanish colonists' appalling treatment of the native people of Cuba and other parts of the New World.
- *Salsa: Musical Heartbeat of Latin America*. Attractively presented and illustrated history of the ubiquitous Latin American dance-music style and its offshoots – rumba, mambo, cumbia and merengue.
- Chris Taylor: *The Beautiful Game*. Fascinating and thoroughly researched history of Latin American football along with an examination of the vital role football plays in the region's culture, politics and society.

Latin American literature

Latin American literature is known principally for its evolution of a literary style which has influenced writers worldwide: magic realism. A seamless blend of fact and fantasy, magic realism often takes as its themes the absurdity of murderous dictatorships, brutal regimes and eccentric family life. Latin American writers also have a particularly strong political commitment – both Mario Vargas Llosa (see below) and Chilean poet Pablo Neruda ran for the presidencies of their respective countries. Detailed below are some of the most celebrated Latin American novelists.

- The literature of Nobel prize winner **Gabriel García Márquez** (1928–) is one of Colombia's most famous exports. *One Hundred Years of Solitude* is the seminal work of magic realism, telling the story of the pioneering Buendía family and the history of their strange little town, Macondo, in the South American outback. *Love in the Time of Cholera* is the romantic and humorous love story set on the steamy Caribbean coast. *The General in his Labyrinth* is the spare and wonderfully poetic story of the tragic dying days of Simón Bolívar, El Libertador.

- Peru's most famous author and former presidential candidate, **Mario Vargas Llosa** (1936–) is a ubiquitous figure in Peruvian society. *Aunt Julia and the Scriptwriter* is a partly autobiographical and very amusing account of a young radio soap writer's life in which fact and fiction become marvellously confused. Set in the Brazilian backlands in 1897, *The War of the End of the World* is a fictionalized account of the charismatic leader Antonio Conselheiro, his short-lived utopian commune at Canudos, and the brutal suppression of his followers, which left thousands dead.

- Niece of assasinated Chilean president Salvador Allende, **Isabel Allende** (1942–) is the author of several of the most recent popular examples of Latin American magic realism. *House of the Spirits* is a fantastical saga of the wealthy Trueba family which follows the lives of matriarch Clara and her eccentric, unusual children and grandchildren. *Of Love and Shadows* is set against the background of a brutal military dictatorship whose unexplained disappearances mirror those in Chile under Pinochet.

- **Jorge Amado** (1912–2001) was a lavish chronicler of life and culture in the colourful tropical state of Bahia, northeast Brazil. In *Dona Flor and her Two Husbands*, Dona Flor marries a sensible pharmacist after her roguish husband drops dead at *Carnaval*, only to find her previous husband returning as a ghost. When *Gabriela, Clove and Cinnamon* was made into a TV film in Brazil, the entire country, including the government, downed tools to tune in. Here Amado chronicles the growing prosperity of the Bahian town of Ilheus in the 1920s, thanks to the creation of vast cocoa plantations as seen through the eyes of a young mulatto girl, Gabriela.

- **Jorge Luis Borges**'s (1899–1986) *Labyrinths,* a collection of short stories and essays, is a compact introduction to the inventive and philosophical world of Argentina's – and perhaps Latin America's – most esteemed writer. With his original style, comprising an erudite mixture of wild fantasy and intellectual rigour, Borges has often been called the father of magic realism.
- The work of Guatemalan **Miguel Angel Asturias** (1899–1974) interweaves the past, present and future and is often seen as a precursor of magic realism. Asturias's main theme was the deep-rooted and continuing value of indigenous Latin American traditions. In *Men of Maize* he tells the story of a backlash by the Maya against the intended cultivation of maize – a crop woven into their culture and folklore – for profit by outsiders. *The President* chronicles the machinations of a ruthless dictator who plans to rid himself of a political opponent in an unnamed country generally considered to be Guatemala.

Fiction set in Latin America

- Joseph Conrad: *Nostromo.* Conrad's 1904 masterpiece records the story of a silver mine in the imaginary South American republic of Costaguana, brilliantly depicting the damage done by corrupt Latin American politicians and big business, as well as the continuing North American obsession with controlling its southern counterparts.
- Graham Greene: *The Power and the Glory.* Based on Greene's own travels in Chiapas (described in his travelogue, *The Lawless Roads*), *The Power and the Glory* takes as its theme the anti-clerical purges in the southern states of Mexico during the 1930s. It tells the story of an outlawed priest on the run, a drunken anti-hero who redeems himself through a dogged sense of duty and eventual martyrdom, and wonderfully evokes the tropical torpor of Mexico's backwaters.
- Malcolm Lowry: *Under the Volcano.* Set in Cuernavaca, Mexico, over the course of a single day in 1938, this wonderfully written novel painstakingly unravels the last hours of alcoholic British Consul Geoffrey Firmin's life through a haze of mescal and the macabre celebrations of the Day of the Dead.

Memoirs

- Ernesto 'Che' Guevara: *The Motorcycle Diaries* and *Back on the Road*. In 1951 Che Guevara set off on a motorbike with his friend and fellow medical student Alberto Granado to discover the countries of South America. This journey, witnessing the extreme poverty and hardship of many Latin Americans, shaped the revolutionary that Guevara famously became. Now important social documents, the diaries are reassuringly adolescent with tales of pretty girls and drunken nights. *Back on the Road* describes a later trip that Guevara made into Central America, and is witness to his life-changing meeting with Fidel Castro in Mexico and his final emergence as a committed Marxist rebel.

- Subcomandante Insurgente Marcos: *Our Word Is Our Weapon*. A collection of writings from Subcomandante Marcos, the famously erudite and poetic leader of the Mexican revolutionary movement, the Zapatistas, who are fighting for land rights for the indigenous peoples of southern Mexico.

- Rigoberta Menchú: *Rigoberta Menchú – An Indian Woman in Guatemala*. "This is my testimony. I didn't learn it from a book and I didn't learn it alone . . . My personal experience is the reality of a whole people." So begins the story of a young Quiché woman as told to a French anthropologist in 1983, which details the atrocities of Guatemala's civil war and the complex culture of the Quiché, one of 23 Maya groups in the country. When her brothers and parents were murdered by paramilitaries, Menchú became the leader of her community and went on to win the Nobel Peace Prize. These memoirs brought her international fame and are a fascinating social document, though some writers have attempted to discredit them as being riddled with inconsistencies.

- Diego Rivera: *My Art, My Life*. Between 1944 and 1957, Mexican painter Rivera dictated over two thousand pages of idiosyncratic recollections and opinions on the three things that mattered most to him – art, sex and politics. This vivid "autobiography" – an edited transcription of Rivera's choicest sayings, complete with black-and-white photos of his work, wives and colleagues – is the result.

- Caetano Veloso: *Tropical Truth: A Story of Music and Revolution in Brazil*. Among the most influential and popular of Brazilian musicians, Caetano Veloso was one of a group of friends from Bahia in north-eastern Brazil who invented tropicalismo, an avant-garde musical form. This poetic memoir is the story of the heady late Sixties in Brazil, the birth of tropicalismo amid a stifling military dictatorship and Caetano's own deportation from Brazil and subsequent exile in London.

Background viewing: Latin America on film

Three countries have long dominated Latin American cinema: Argentina, Brazil and Mexico. Brazil's *cinema novo* was one of the world's most vibrant film movements in the 1960s. After quieter years – which coincided, not surprisingly, with military dictatorships in both Argentina and Brazil – all three countries are currently undergoing a cinema revival with slick modern films which have attracted critical acclaim and are being shown in mainstream cinemas.

An annual Latin American film festival is held in London every November (⊛www.latinamericanfilmfestival.com), while there are numerous festivals in the US, including ones in Washington (⊛www .oas.org); Austin, Texas (⊛www.cinelasamericas.org); Chicago (⊛www.latinoculturalcenter.com); and Miami (⊛www.hispanicfilm .com), among others. If you become seriously interested in Latin American films, *Mediating Two Worlds: Cinematic Encounters in the Americas*, *The Cinema of Latin America* and *South American Cinema: A Critical Filmography* are all recommended anthologies.

Latin American films

The following films are some of the most memorable movies made in Latin America in either Spanish or Portuguese.

- *Black Orpheus/Orfeu Negro* (1958). Set amidst the Rio *Carnaval*, this is a vivid reworking of the ancient Greek legend of Orpheus and Eurydice, a fatalistic love story with a tragic ending. The city's dramatic setting is beautifully though rather sentimentally filmed – Rio's *favelas* (slums) look almost pretty – and is accompanied by a best-selling soundtrack by Antonio (Tom) Jobim and Luís Bonfá which ushered in a new type of Brazilian music: bossa nova.
- *Central Station/Central do Brasil* (1998). This colourful and heart-rending film tells the story of Dora, a lonely and cynical older woman who spends her days writing letters for illiterate customers at Rio de Janeiro's Central Station. Things begin to change when she reluctantly befriends a homeless orphan and agrees to help him search for the father he's never known. Features a wonderful performance by acclaimed Brazilian actress Fernanda Montenegro.

- *City of God* (2002). An extremely stylish – and fictional – portrayal of life in the slums or *favelas* of Rio de Janeiro, *City of God* nevertheless pulls no punches. The film spans two decades, and follows the lives of a gang of children, two in particular, who grow up in the infamous City of God and deal with their hardships in very different ways. Absolutely gripping and horrifying by turns.
- *Like Water for Chocolate/Como Agua para Chocolate* (1992). Set during the Mexican revolution, this award-winning film, adapted from a best-selling novel by Laura Esquivel, follows the story of three sisters and their separate but entwined destinies. Tita is denied the man she loves who marries her sister instead and, stuck in the kitchen, uses food to vent her anger and frustrated passion – with magical results.
- *Maria Full of Grace* (2004). Grimly depressing and stark fictional account of the lives – and deaths – of Colombian drugs mules who carry cocaine to the USA. Catalina Sandino Moreno deservedly won an Oscar for her spirited performance in this joint American and Colombian venture.
- *The Motorcycle Diaries* (2004). Adapted from Che Guevara's diaries which describe a trip he made through South America in 1951, this is a beautifully shot though occasionally sentimental film. Current Mexican heart-throb Gael García Bernal pulls off a fine performance as the fledgling revolutionary though the film's real star is South America itself, which looks dazzling.
- *Nine Queens* (2000). An ingenious con-man comedy set in Buenos Aires over the course of 24 hours, *Nine Queens* also reflects the cynicism and suspicion of Argentines towards their thoroughly corrupt institutions. A remarkably prescient film, made shortly before the country's economic meltdown in 2001.
- *Pixote* (1981). The story of a homeless urchin in São Paulo, *Pixote* is a fictionalized account of the appalling lives of Brazil's numerous street children, and won many awards for its affecting and graphic depiction of a world which, lamentably, still very much exists.

Films set in Latin America

Predictably many films set in Latin America are made in the US and tend to focus on cowboys, lost-in-the-jungle action movies or civil war. The following include some more critically acclaimed offerings, as well as a couple of documentaries.

- *Aguirre, Wrath of God* (1972). Werner Herzog's crazed masterpiece tells the story of a band of Spanish conquistadors who go up the

Amazon in search of El Dorado, the fabled city of gold. Led by the megalomaniac Aguirre, self-styled "Wrath of God", the trip rapidly descends into chaos and death as the group travel from the high Andes into primeval forest.

- *Missing* (1981). Based on true events during the Chilean coup of 1973, *Missing* tells the story of an American journalist who "disappears" and of his family's subsequent search for him, taking a dark look at the human tragedy of murderous dictatorships like Pinochet's, and evocatively portraying a society coming apart at the seams.

- *Salvador* (1986). Arguably Oliver Stone's best film, *Salvador* features James Woods as washed-up American journalist Richard Boyle, who travelled to El Salvador in 1980 in search of a story and instead found himself in the middle of a civil war. Co-written by Boyle himself, the film has brilliant action sequences underpinned by a forceful and sometimes moving polemic.

- *Carla's Song* (1996). Left-wing filmmaker Ken Loach's examination of the civil war in Nicaragua centres around the love affair of a Glaswegian bus driver (played by Robert Carlyle) and a Nicaraguan refugee – the film's witty depiction of the Nicaraguan's humour and playful language had the audience at its Managuan premiere in fits of laughter.

- *The Battle of Chile* (1973). Patricio Guzman's three-part documentary on Allende and the Chilean coup d'état is widely feted as among the best documentaries ever made. The three films cover events in chronological order, mixing trenchant political analysis with revealing interviews with some of those who took part in the events described.

- *Señorita Extravida/Missing Young Woman* (2001). Moving and lyrical documentary made by Chicano film-maker Lourdes Portillo about the more than two hundred young women who have been kidnapped, raped and murdered in the border town of Cuidad Juárez, Mexico. Portillo has also made films about the Day of the Dead and the women who march weekly in Buenos Aires for their "disappeared" children.

- *Los Olvidados/The Forgotten* (1952). One of surrealist filmmaker Luis Buñuel's best films and his own personal favourite. *Los Olvidados* is a stylish though gritty narrative about the miserable lives of two street urchins living in Mexico City and is in many ways a forerunner to *City of God* (see p.222).

- *¡Qué viva México!* (1931/1979). Never finished in his lifetime but finally pieced together by the original cameraman, this is Russian director Sergei Eistenstein's poetic meditation on the potency of Mexican culture. The film consists of a series of six non-fictional and fictional episodes which link Maya civilization with the Spanish conquest and the Mexican Revolution.

7

What to take

T he short answer to the all-important question "what shall I take?" is as little as possible. If there's one piece of indispensable advice when embarking on a long journey it's to travel light. Once you realize just how often and how far you're going to have to lug your gear around, you'll understand why it's a very good idea to reduce your packing to the bare minimum. There's nothing like an hour wandering with all your stuff around a hot and unfamiliar town looking for a hotel to make you curse your backpack and everything in it. Remember too that public transport in most Latin American cities and towns consists of a motley collection of beaten-up tin buses, vans and trucks. These are invariably crammed to the gills, and in many cases there literally may not be room for you and your enormous backpack. In addition, the larger your pack, the more likely you are to be marked out as a gringo no matter how well you know the country or how good your Spanish or Portuguese. The size of your luggage will signal the fact that you've just arrived, making you a sitting target for every wide boy, con artist and thief in town.

Having said that, there is a certain amount of travel kit that you will need to take, unless you want the hassle of having to constantly buy stuff as you go along (or, worse still, scrounge off fellow travellers). Travelling light is smart; travelling with too little is not smart.

Backpacks

Your backpack is the single most important piece of kit that you'll take – if you've got any money to spend on equipment, this is the time to splash out. Backpacks vary in price from £80–195/US$140–350, and generally you get what you pay for. Shop around various specialist travel, camping or adventure-sport shops – the best shops have knowledgeable staff who have travelled widely themselves (see pp.377–378 for listings of recommended retailers).

Backpack sizes are measured in litres (since their actual weight depends on what you put in them). A medium-sized, 50-litre pack is the most popular size, and you'd be mad to carry anything bigger than 65 litres, even if you're taking camping gear. If you're a really ruthless packer, you might manage with 25–30 litres, the size of a largish daypack. Experts recommend that the total weight of your pack doesn't exceed one-fifth to a quarter of your body weight. In practical terms, this means that most men shouldn't try to carry more than 18–22 kilos, whilst women ought to stick to 13–17 kilos.

The most important element of a backpack is its harness. The best harnesses are fully adjustable and have padded shoulder straps, a wide hip belt (essential for transferring weight from your back) and compression straps on the side of the pack which push its contents tightly into your back. If your backpack doesn't come with a built-in harness cover (backpacks usually don't; travel packs usually do – see below), you should consider buying one – this is very useful for airplane holds and other luggage racks because it avoids straps being torn and damaged by baggage handlers (the most frequent source of backpack damage); following complaints, airlines now sometimes insist that backpack straps are tidied away with a harness cover or outer sack; alternatively, they may charge you to wrap it properly themselves.

The way the pack is divided into compartments is also important. Outer pockets are useful for quick access to essential items, though these are hard to secure properly. Too many outer pockets will make your backpack bulky – the narrower your pack, the easier it will be to manoeuvre while wearing it, and to store it in tight spaces when you're not.

It's essential to try on a backpack before you buy it to check that it fits properly and feels comfortable. First, though, find a knowledge-able shop assistant who will measure your back length (from the top of your hip bone to the seventh vertebra) – this is vital in determining the right size of pack. Backpacks should never be tried on empty – get a shop assistant to fill it with a suitable weight – and you should then walk around the shop to ensure that the pack is stable. A properly fitting pack has a good harness (see above) with shoulder straps and a hip belt which fits snugly and doesn't dig. Other features to look for are a ventilated or mesh back system which will help reduce sweating, long-lasting and tightly woven fabrics, and triple-sewn seams (stress points should have five lines of stitching). Most manufacturers make backpacks specially designed for women; these have straps which are closer together to fit narrower shoulders, making them significantly more comfortable.

Toploader and travel packs

There are two basic types of backpack: choosing the right one depends on what kind of trip you're planning. A toploader or traditional backpack opens principally at the top, though most

△ Backpacking in Patagonia, Argentina

brands also have side pockets and a bottom compartment. The long, narrow shape of toploaders gives them an effective weight distribution and makes them particularly comfortable to carry – useful if you're planning on doing any serious trekking, mountain-climbing, or even if you just expect to have to lug your pack around a lot.

The newer type of backpacks, known as travel packs, are wider than traditional toploaders, with horseshoe-shaped zips, meaning that almost all the pack can be easily accessed (although this does mean that it's less secure), whilst clothes can be packed flat as in a traditional suitcase. Most travel packs also come with a zip-on daypack (see below) and built-in harness covers. If you're not planning to carry your pack around a great deal, a decent travel pack will suffice.

Weatherproofing

Surprisingly, most backpacks aren't entirely rainproof. You can remedy this by waterproofing your backpacks with a can of waterproofing spray; these can be bought at most camping and outdoor shops. Use the spray outside, however, and apply it well before you leave – it smells horrible at first and gives off toxic fumes (though these wear off after the first few days). Alternatively, you could buy an elastic backpack raincover or a waterproof backpack liner. If you're on a really tight budget you can either line your pack with a binliner or simply pack your stuff in a series of plastic bags before putting it in your pack.

Security

Keeping your backpack and its contents safe is a major concern. Essentially, it's impossible to completely secure a pack against a determined thief, and the best way to avoid losing valuables while travelling is not to take them in the first place. That said, most thieves are opportunists, and any attempt to make their job harder and slower will probably encourage them to look elsewhere.

One traditional way of stopping thieves slashing your pack open is to line it with chickenwire, which is cheap and fairly tough and can be bought at most hardware shops. It's still a good deterrent – try to get wire with the smallest holes. There are several other ways of making your pack more secure. You can now buy something called

PacSafe, which works on the chickenwire principle – it's a sheet of very strong metal mesh which fits over the outside of a backpack; it also comes with a padlock so that you can attach your pack to a luggage ruck or other fixed object. Although PacSafe is heavy and not totally foolproof (it can be cut with wirecutters), it does at the very least make getting into your backpack a job for professional rather than amateur thieves.

A further option is a cable lock: a long length of thick wire which can be used to lock your pack to fixed objects. Some cable locks come with sturdy combination locks and a built-in alarm which goes off if someone touches or tries to move your pack – particularly useful if you're travelling alone and have no one to help keep an eye on your stuff. Finally, you could also take small padlocks to slot through backpack zips and secure openings, but their size and limited strength make it relatively easy to snap them open.

A cheap option for making your backpack slightly more secure and protecting it at the very least from the elements is to carry it in a large grain sack, available from local markets in Latin America. This "disguise" may not fool many locals for long but it just might stop your backpack being identified immediately as such and the tough covering will keep it free from dust, rain and mud.

Daypacks and shoulder bags

Once you've arrived at your destination, found a hotel and dumped your backpack, you'll still need a daypack to carry essential items – guidebook, water, camera, extra clothing – in. Daypacks are essentially just smaller versions of a backpack (between 15 and 30 litres). Most travel packs now come with matching daypacks zipped onto the front. If you're buying one of these, make sure you unzip the daypack and examine it properly before you buy it – some are sturdier than others.

If you're buying a daypack separately it's as important to choose it as carefully as a backpack. You're likely to use your daypack on a daily basis, and it needs to be tough, with strong padded straps and sturdy zips. Some travellers prefer to take a different kind of day bag. This has the advantage of making you look less like a tourist when you're strolling round town. A good choice is a nylon shoulder bag (which can be worn across the body for extra safety) or a local bag, something that the locals use to carry their shopping in – all over Latin America you can buy extremely tough, brightly coloured, very cheap nylon mesh bags from the market; they weigh almost nothing and last forever. Anything made of leather is obviously much bulkier and weighs more, as is anything woven (although hand-woven bags are also widely available in Latin America and make great souvenirs). None of these options, though, will be as comfortable to carry or as secure as a proper daypack.

Money belts

You need somewhere safe to carry your documents and money – don't under any circumstances keep valuables in your back pocket or in an outside compartment on a pack. Many tourists still carry their cash in a bumbag (fannypack), worn around the waist outside clothes, but there really couldn't be a less discreet way of carrying your stuff. If you must wear one, don't use it for valuables.

Most travellers nowadays keep their documents and cash in a slim money belt with two zipped compartments (one the size of a passport, the other big enough for credit cards), which is tucked away underneath your clothing. The most popular type of money belt goes round your waist; other types can be found which hang round your neck; which are strapped under your arm or round your calf; or which hang from your regular belt inside your trousers. Another recent innovation is an apparently ordinary buckled belt with a narrow, zipped pocket inside where you can hide folded banknotes (though obviously it's no use for larger items like passports).

Obviously, wearing your belt around your waist makes it more accessible, though sweat can be a problem (it's a good idea to keep documents, travellers' cheques and notes wrapped in plastic to avoid them getting soggy). Choose a belt made from cotton to keep as cool as possible – it's amazing how much hotter something light round your waist can make you feel. Additionally, a skin-coloured or beige belt is far more discreet. Bear in mind also that thieves in Latin America are all too aware now that foreigners carry their valuables in hidden money belts, although on the positive side they take too long to remove to be regularly stolen.

If you're travelling alone, something else to consider is a water-safe or plastic container to keep money and keys in if you want to go for a swim without leaving them lying on the beach. These are worn round the neck and range from fairly bulky containers to slim, wallet-shaped affairs with watertight zip locks.

Documents

It's a good idea to take photocopies of important documents, such as your plane ticket and the personal pages of your passport, with you. Keep these copies with you but separate from the originals (it's also worth leaving another copy with a friend back home); having a copy of the information-bearing pages in your passport hugely speeds up the process of getting it replaced if it's stolen. Alternatively, as a further precaution you could email a scan of them to your on-the-road email address (see p.327) to download in case of emergency. Other useful documents to take with you include your driving licence and an international student card, which entitles you to various discounts. Passport photos are handy for visa extensions or any permits or passes that you might need.

Clothes

Before packing, lay out all the clothes you think you'll need, and then halve the amount – remember that you can buy much of what you'll need (and generally more cheaply) once in Latin America. Trainers/sneakers, T-shirts and trousers are sold everywhere, while in Andean countries like Ecuador, Peru and Bolivia you can buy very cheap and wonderfully warm alpaca sweaters, gloves and socks. It's also worth leaving your favourite clothes at home: if they're not lost or stolen, they'll likely be reduced to shreds by the wear and tear of constant travelling. Instead, pick up bargain bits and pieces at cheap chain stores, charity shops or jumble sales, which can be dumped when they've worn out or you no longer need them.

Remember when you're packing to allow for Latin America's extremes of temperature, from the high Andes to sizzling Caribbean beaches. Unless you're only going to one region in one country you'll probably need clothes for both hot and cold weather, and it's always worth erring on the side of caution – even in the warmest climates, you might find yourself on overnight buses with freezing air conditioning. If you're heading into the Andean highlands or

Patagonia in winter you'll need to have adequate clothing to deal with temperatures that can fall well below freezing. Don't assume that because these places suffer freezing temperatures they have indoor heating systems – most parts of Bolivia, for example, don't. Conversely, in a city like Manaus in Amazonian Brazil, where it's too hot to move by 10.30 in the morning, even cotton can seem too warm and clothes need to be light and loose.

For more on Latin American dress codes, see p.256.

- **Dress** A cool, loose sundress is an excellent piece of all-round clothing: they're generally light, easy to pack and can function for more formal occasions as well as fun nights out.
- **Fleece** Fleece jackets are an absolute godsend: they weigh nothing and are very cosy, so you won't need to take another jacket or jumper. Although the best are expensive (£50–110/US$90–200), they're worth every penny. High-street stores sell fleeces in all shapes and sizes, though they're not as effective as those made by adventure sports manufacturers (see Directory).
- **Hat** A small, foldable hat is a great idea, both for keeping the sun off your head when it's hot and helping retain body heat when it's cold (when a fleece or woolly hat is invaluable).
- **Waterproof jacket** Unless you can afford an expensive breathable Gore-Tex jacket, raincoats are too sweaty to be comfortable in Latin America. If you're planning on doing some serious trekking in the rainy season, however, you will need a decent waterproof jacket. Tropical rain can be torrential, and you'll be wasting your money if you buy anything that's not hardy enough.
- **Socks** Take several different thicknesses – lightweight for deterring mosquitoes in the tropics and a thermal pair for the mountains and long, chilly bus rides.
- **Shirts and trousers** Avoid taking jeans: they're bulky, heavy, difficult to wash and take forever to dry. Much better to take something like cargo pants, which are lightweight, tough and comfortable, although be careful with combat trousers – the soldier-boy look doesn't always go down well in countries which have suffered brutal military dictatorships or, like Colombia, are still in the throes of civil war. Specialist manufacturers make practical travelling trousers which are made from breathable fabric, dry out very quickly and zip apart to make a pair of shorts. A pair of loose drawstring trousers, cool in the heat and doubling up as pajamas (recommended if you're sleeping outside in a hammock) is also a good idea. Shirts should also be loose and lightweight – a loose shirt can be much cooler than a T-shirt. Take

one with long sleeves for protection against mosquitoes, in case you get sunburnt or need to cover up.

- **Tights** If it gets cold, a pair of tights worn under trousers can add a valuable extra layer of insulation.
- **T-shirts** A long-sleeved T-shirt is a good idea for chilly nights, while a short-sleeved T-shirt will be useful during most days. Bear in mind, if you're a woman, that wearing very tight or low-cut T-shirts will attract ogling men.

Footwear

Shoes and boots are obviously a vital part of your kit, but don't take more than two pairs because that's all you'll need and they take up lots of room. A pair of sturdy walking boots is essential if you're planning on doing some serious trekking, and recommended even if you're not. Modern brands are incredibly lightweight and last forever, and a good pair is a great investment. The best come with special gripping soles, supported sides (to protect your ankles) and waterproof lining so that your feet don't get wet. Specialist shops (see Directory) sell a wide range of walking boots, but

you won't find them on sale in many places in Latin America, so buy them before you leave. Many travellers take a pair of trainers or sneakers instead – these are cheaper, do pretty well on the road and are easily replaced.

Your other pair of shoes should be sandals, which are hard-wearing and waterproof. Again, they're most easily found in adventure sport shops. Leather sandals are sold everywhere in Latin America – in fact shoes of every kind are a Latin American fetish – and are cheap and well made. Flip-flops in every shape and colour are also available absolutely everywhere (though not if you have big feet – Latin Americans are normally short with small feet and footwear caters accordingly).

A clothing checklist

- Three or four pairs of underwear
- Thermal underwear (if you're visiting the Andes)
- Swimwear
- Two or three pairs of socks
- One pair of longish shorts
- Two T-shirts (one long and one short-sleeved)
- Two shirts (one long and one short-sleeved)
- Two pairs of trousers
- One or two dresses
- One lightweight jumper
- Fleece jacket
- One pair of trainers or walking boots
- One pair of sandals
- Hat
- Waterproof jacket

Essentials

Below is an alphabetical list of items (apart from documents and clothes) that you're likely to need.

- **Alarm clock** Take the smallest one you can find and make sure it has a light. Alternatively take a watch (not expensive) with an alarm on it.
- **Batteries** Standard batteries are available everywhere (though they're often expensive), but you may have difficulty finding more obscure camera or watch batteries – take spares with you.
- **Cable lock** More useful than a padlock: with a good cable lock you can attach your backpack to fixed objects; fancier models come sealed into a natty hardwearing case with combination lock and with a 100-decibel alarm. You can hang them from hotel doors and windows – particularly useful if you're a lone woman traveller – so that you'll know if someone is trying to get into your room while you're sleeping.
- **Cigarette lighter** Surprisingly useful even if you don't smoke, and much better than matches (which are sometimes so flimsy that

they're virtually useless) for lighting mosquito coils, camp fires and candles during power outages.

- **Contact-lens solution and glasses** Contact-lens solution can be difficult to find outside big cities; take supplies with you. If you wear glasses, take a spare pair and your prescription.
- **Contraceptives** Condoms are available pretty much everywhere, but may not reach the same rigorous standards as those at home. If you're on the Pill, take a supply with you – you may not be able to find your prescription in Latin America.
- **First-aid kit** See p.310 for details.
- **Flashlight (torch)** An important piece of kit, since there are still large parts of Latin America without any electricity, while power cuts are also common.
- **Guidebook** See pp.212–213.
- **Liquid soap** Special, all-purpose liquid soap (available in specialist adventure shops) can be used to wash yourself, your hair, your clothes and even fruit and vegetables.
- **Penknife** Take a good penknife with a sharp blade, bottle opener and corkscrew (and remember not to fly with it in your hand luggage).
- **Sarong** A sarong is extremely versatile and can be used as an emergency towel, a bedcover, a scarf, a skirt and so on. They're widely available in beach resorts, though you might prefer to bring one with you.
- **Sheet sleeping bag** Useful in hostels where they don't provide sheets and in cheap hotels (if you first spray it with a solution of Permethrin) to ward off fleas, lice and bed bugs. You can easily make one yourself from a folded sheet sewn across the bottom and down the side.
- **Sunglasses** Vital for protecting your eyes from the sun (and also from snow-glare in the mountains). Make sure you get proper UV-resistant lenses – a pair of cheap sunglasses is useless.
- **Sunscreen** Sunscreen is available in big cities and tourist resorts, but the locals don't use it, so it's expensive and sometimes not of the best quality. You'll need at least factor 15 to start with.
- **Tampons** Not available in every country in Latin America (the less industrialized the country, the less chance of finding them), although most capital cities and, especially, large tourist resorts and gringo hangouts have them.
- **Toiletries** Keep your washbag supplies to a minimum and transfer things like shampoo and moisturizing cream into smaller travel bottles which you can buy at chemists or in camping shops. Avoid bottles with pop-tops which tend to open in depressurized environments (such as aircraft holds) and will then leak everywhere. The heat and

fierce sun mean that one thing you will need loads of is moisturizing lotion; in some parts of Latin America this will cost more than your lunch.

Non-essentials

- **Binoculars** Great for bird- and wildlife-spotting. The latest models are tiny and very light; you ought to be able to get a decent pair for US$30.
- **Books** Although there are innumerable book exchanges at backpacker's hostels and cafés across the continent, the quality of books on offer is often pretty dire, so you'll probably want to bring plenty of reading matter of your own.
- **Camera** Most people now take a digital camera travelling. The simplest of these replicate auto-focus ("point and shoot") cameras; they are small, light and virtually idiot-proof but are considerably more expensive than auto-focus (US$100 for a decent model). A good digital camera costs £100–300/US$175–520 but its advantages are manifold. You won't need to buy camera film, you can erase any unwanted pictures immediately and you'll be able to download your images onto computers and send them home to your friends and family as you travel. You can also save the images in disc format and either mail these home or travel with them.

  For non-digital camera users, standard camera film is widely available (though prices vary widely), but you should take a supply of slide and/or black-and-white film if you use these, since they're not always easy to get hold of in Latin America. It's also worth taking plenty of high-speed film (400 ASA), which is best for naturally dark environments like the rainforest.
- **Camping gear** Obviously, taking camping gear opens up lots of extra possibilities in terms of trekking and saving on hotel costs, although it also means you'll have to say goodbye to travelling light and carry a much larger pack.
- **Compass** Important if you're planning on trekking, and useful anywhere to get your bearings. A more advanced option is a portable GPS (global positioning system) which works with satellites and gives clear instructions on which route to take to reach your required destination.
- **Earplugs** Latin Americans love noise and scarcely seem to notice it, but you might not: a decent pair of earplugs is a godsend if you find yourself in a hotel next to an all-night bar or sitting beside the sound-system on a bus.

- **Games** A pack of cards or a travel chess or backgammon set can help while away the hours waiting for buses, on buses or sitting indoors during rainy season days.
- **Map** A decent map can add hugely to your appreciation of the country you're travelling through, both as a guide during long journeys and as an aid in planning itineraries.
- **Mosquito net** Even if your hotel does have mosquito nets, they may well have holes in them, which makes them pretty useless. Take your own. Some come impregnated with repellent; if not, you can treat it yourself with Permethrin.
- **Neck cushion** An inflatable neck cushion is great for long bus and plane journeys.
- **Needle and thread** Useful for mending clothes and sewing buttons back on.
- **Notebook** Most people keep some kind of diary of their trip – very valuable years after the event when you've forgotten the small details of life on the road that once seemed so crucial.
- **Padlock** Handy for hostel lockers and for locking the door of your room in cheap hotels.
- **Personal stereo** Great for lazy days in a hammock and long boring bus journeys. If your personal stereo has a record feature you can tape live music, local sounds and your own audio diary.
- **Photos and postcards** Photos of your family and home town are a great way of breaking the ice with curious locals. Postcards from your home country make good presents – children, in particular, love them.
- **Plug** A universal plug is useful, since most sinks and baths in cheaper hotels have lost their plugs.
- **Plug adaptor** Sockets in Latin America are the same as those in North America (ie they take two flat prongs); if you're from anywhere else you'll need an adaptor, available from camping shops or at the airport.
- **Radio** Lets you tune into local radio stations and sounds; with a short wave radio you can get the BBC World Service/Voice of America and keep up with news back home.
- **String** Often useful for running repairs, and can also serve as an emergency washing line.
- **Toilet paper** Although toilet paper is sold everywhere in Latin America, it's often not supplied in toilets, so carry your own roll.
- **Towel** If you'd like something more absorbent than a sarong to dry yourself, don't take an ordinary bath towel – they rot easily, smell horrible and take up far too much room. Instead take a special travel towel which looks more like a duster, folds away to almost nothing,

is made from incredibly absorbent fabric and can be packed when damp.

- **Water bottle** Take a sturdy water bottle (with a carrying strap) if you're planning on camping, trekking or exploring the wilderness.
- **Water sterilizing kit** A valuable money-saving device – see Staying Healthy for details.

8

Your first night

E ven for seasoned travellers, arriving in Latin America after a long flight is a daunting prospect. The noisy and chaotic scene that is likely to greet you is hardly an ideal situation when you're feeling exhausted and vulnerable, and it's often difficult to retain a positive attitude and a sense of humour. With just a small amount of organization, however, you can make sure your introduction to Latin America is as painless as possible.

Booking hotels in advance

Chances are that you'll be flying into one of Latin America's capital cities, some of which – such as Mexico City and São Paulo – are vast. It will take you days to orient yourself, and half an hour after flying in is not the time to start. Booking a hotel in advance is quite possibly the best five minutes you'll spend on planning your trip, and will stop you fretting all the way through the flight (it might even make your mother fret less, too). Your guidebook should list the phone number and fax or email details of a wide range of hotels, as should the relevant tourist board and a host of Internet sites (see Basics for details). When choosing a hotel, consider the following:

● Decide on the part of the city you want to stay in, as well as a particular hotel. Most cities have two distinct hotel areas – expensive and budget. While expensive hotels are often located in leafy suburbs adjacent to the city centre, budget hotels and hostels are frequently right in the heart of the city or, alternatively, near bus stations and/or markets. It's also best to pick a hotel close to several others so that you can swap easily should you want to. And try to avoid choosing a hotel miles out of the centre.

● This is the time to spend more than your allotted daily budget. After a lengthy flight you'll be in need of a comfortable bed and a hot shower, two facilities missing from the very cheapest hostels. Also, a hotel that serves breakfast and has a bar and restaurant will save you wandering the streets of a strange city unnecessarily.

● Consider booking not just your first but also your second night's accommodation. Otherwise, if you arrive late in the day, you'll have to get up early (checkout time is usually noon) and spend your first morning looking for another hotel – sounds fine now, but you might not want to do it with jet lag or altitude sickness.

When it comes to booking a room by phone, you'll find that even small hotels in Latin America often have a staff member who understands English – assuming, that is, you don't speak enough Spanish or Portuguese to make yourself understood. Easiest of all, choose a hotel with a fax number or an email address. Alternatively, some travel agents (see pp.361–364) have a hotel-booking service and can book hotels for you – if you're booking your flights through them, they might do this for free, although the hotels on their lists will probably be three-star or better and cost at least $50 a night. You can also book a bed through various international youth hostelling associations (see Directory).

Long-haul flights and how to survive them

Unless you're flying from the southern US to Mexico or Central America, to reach Latin America you'll have to endure a long-haul flight – up to fifteen hours – even before stopovers. Even if you love flying, hours and hours spent in a cramped pressurized container is bound to take its toll. There are lots of ways of avoiding feeling utterly dreadful on arrival, though.

First, arrive as early as possible at your departure airport. Most international carriers ask that you be at the check-in desk at least two hours before take-off, although in practice they often begin checking in passengers an hour before that. The earlier you arrive, the better choice of seats you'll get, unless you've been able to reserve them in advance through your travel agent or personally by phone to the relevant airline (see "Buying a ticket", p.180) – otherwise you'll have to take potluck at check-in.

The position of your seat is very important in determining how comfortable your flight is. A window seat gives you a great view during take-off and landing, and you'll have somewhere solid to lean your head if you want to sleep, and a little more privacy. If you think you're going to want to get up and move around during the flight, then choose an aisle seat. You can also ask your check-in official if there are any seats available by the emergency exits – these have loads more legroom (understandably, these seats are often given to particularly tall people, if they haven't already been snapped up). In addition, the so-called "bulkhead" seats, situated in the front row of each section of the plane, have significantly more legroom – you could try asking for one of these, though they're often reserved for families with babies. It's also worth checking in early if you're travelling with a bicycle or surfboard.

During check-in, the official dealing with you will tear out the outward voucher(s) of your ticket. Very occasionally a careless official will tear out the return portions as well – when your ticket is given back to you, check that these are still there or you'll find yourself in big trouble. If you're taking several different flights you may either be checked in to all of these or just the first. Ask your official to explain which is relevant to you – if you're "checked through", your luggage will automatically be sent on with you to your final destination. If not (most likely if you're travelling with several different airlines), you'll have to collect your luggage at your next port of call and then check in again.

Once you've checked in you'll be given a boarding card for your flight (plus additional boarding cards for any connecting flights you've been checked on to). Hold on to these: they have your designated seat number as well as your boarding time (approximately half an hour before take-off). In large airports these are often a fair way from check-in – give yourself plenty of time to get there.

Secondly, pack your piece of hand luggage very carefully. You'll have to lug this around the airport so don't make it too heavy, but do think about taking the following:

- Your guidebook, so that you can bone up on the city you're flying into.
- Novels and magazines help pass the time, as does listening to a personal stereo.
- A jumper and possibly socks: long-haul flights can be surprisingly chilly (on the other hand, your destination may well be very hot, so you'll need to dress in removable layers).
- Several items of "bathroom" kit. A toothbrush and toothpaste – cleaning your teeth really does make you feel better. Moisturizing cream helps combat dry plane cabins. Take some aspirin both to combat headaches and to guard against deep-vein thrombosis – and any other drugs you need to take regularly. If you wear contact lenses you'll want to take them out – dry air will make your eyes sore – so carry your glasses with you.
- Any documents you'll need on arrival, plus foreign currency, hotel address and telephone number, and booking confirmation.
- Anything valuable and/or fragile, like your camera or sunglasses.
- A large bottle of mineral water – air stewards will offer you drinks from time to time, but it's often not enough, and though you're perfectly entitled to ask for extra drinks, it's easier to take your own.

Once on board, there are several things you can do to give yourself a head start on arrival. Drink as much liquid as possible, preferably water, and try to avoid alcohol, which has much more effect at high altitude and exacerbates the effects of jet lag. Get up and move around every few hours to avoid stiffness. Use the time to prepare yourself mentally by reading your guidebook or learning a few words of Spanish or Portuguese. An hour or so before landing, go and wash your face and clean your teeth, which will make you

Post-September 11 security

Following the terrorist attacks of September 11, 2001, both airport and airline security have been dramatically increased. Passengers are no longer allowed to carry any sharp or potentially dangerous objects in their hand luggage (these include Swiss Army knives, scissors and nail files). If you're taking anything of this kind, pack it in your hold luggage or be prepared to have it confiscated. You'll need official clarification if you're carrying needles or a syringe. Generally speaking, checking in is now more thorough, as are boarding procedures – you might well be frisked and/or have to open up your hand luggage. If you're concerned for any reason, ring your travel agent or the relevant airline to check current procedures before you fly.

feel much more alert and prepared for the challenge of arriving in a strange country.

Arrival

Once off the plane follow the signs – and everyone else – through immigration, baggage reclaim, customs and the arrivals hall (always in that order) and then out onto Latin American soil. This is where culture shock kicks in: you'll probably be jet lagged, and as a tourist you'll be prey to every hustler in the building. Don't let anyone bully you into something you don't want to do or distract you – instead, try to keep focused on getting out of the airport, and at least look as though you know what you're doing.

Immigration

You shouldn't have any problems at immigration, assuming you've filled in all the forms correctly (these likely will have been given to you on the plane) and have all the relevant documents to hand, including your passport, return ticket and proof of funds. Your entry stamp will have a number of days written on it by the official dealing with you – make sure you get the days you need for your stay; if you don't, point this out very politely and ask for the right amount. Most immigration officials speak a little English, but will always appreciate the effort if you speak even just a few words of Spanish or Portuguese. Remember there's no absolute guarantee that you'll be allowed into your chosen country, even if you have a visa. The decision to let you enter rests with whichever immigration official deals with you upon your arrival. Although it's pretty much unheard of for anyone to be refused entry without a very good reason, it doesn't hurt to be on your best behaviour.

Baggage reclaim

Baggage reclaim is usually where the chaos begins – this may be the moment to start getting used to Latin American spontaneity and disorder. Keep your eyes peeled for your backpack, and once it arrives don't ever leave it unattended until you reach the safety of your hotel room. Beware of any distractions, particularly strangers rushing up to you and shouting in your face – this is a well-known ruse to distract you while a thief makes off with your stuff.

Customs

Unless you're travelling with specialized equipment, you won't need to declare anything at customs – obviously, it's not recommended that you bring in weapons, large amounts of alcohol and recreational drugs (unless you relish the prospect of being locked up in squalor for a very long time). In all likelihood you'll be allowed to walk straight through customs past a couple of bored officials; if you've been given a customs declaration to fill in on the plane, this is where you hand it in, having presumably ticked no to every question – are you bringing in contaminated liquids? Explosives? Infected meat? No, no and no.

Arrivals hall

This is where your journey finally begins. Once you've emerged into the arrivals hall – usually not as grand as it sounds – you're now officially on Latin American soil and what you do next is entirely up to you. You might have first to wade through an excited throng waiting for long-lost relatives to emerge, followed by an unholy scrum of airport hustlers pressing in on all sides. Ignore them, and head for a relatively quiet space to orientate yourself and work out where what you need is situated. This is likely to be a *casa de cambio* and the taxi rank. You might also want to make a phone call, book a hotel, use the bathroom to tidy yourself up or buy a drink. Don't spend more time in the arrivals hall than you need to, however – like any transport hub anywhere in the world, airports are a favourite hangout for all kinds of unsavoury characters who prey on the vulnerability of new arrivals.

Airports always have somewhere to change money, although if you arrive at night this might be closed. It's a good idea to have a rough idea of the exchange rate before you change your money, and bear in mind that airport facilities often offer a poorer rate than elsewhere, so only change enough to tide you over until the next day, unless you're arriving at the weekend, in which case you'll obviously have to change a bit more. Make sure that the notes you're given are in good condition (politely ask for them to be replaced if they're not), and check you've been given the correct amount before you walk away. Ask for some coins if you want to make a phone call. Once you've counted your cash, put it away safely in your money belt apart from whatever small amount you might need immediately. If the *casa de cambio* is closed, don't despair – there can't be an airport taxi driver in Latin America who doesn't accept dollars, and all you really need to pay for at this stage is a ride to your hotel.

Some airports also have ATMs: these offer better exchange rates than the *casas de cambio* and you won't have to speak a foreign language to get your cash. Be careful when using them though, especially if there are no security guards or policemen nearby. There's also likely to be some kind of tourist information booth at the airport. Though these are often fairly useless, staff do usually speak some English and can tell you how much you should pay for a taxi ride into the city. They should also be able to recommend a hotel (though these will be mid- or top-range places) if you haven't already got a reservation, and book a room for you. Some might even have a basic city map.

Some travellers arriving in the middle of the night prefer to wait in the airport until daybreak. Note, though, that some airports close after the last arrival; at others, security guards might ask you to move on. If you do spend the night in the airport, pick a well-lit, secure spot and tie your luggage onto something solid. Having said all this, it really is much easier to fork out for a taxi to take you to a hotel where you can dump your bags and get a much-needed first night's sleep.

Getting into town

Your next challenge is to find a way of getting from the airport to your hotel, whether in a taxi, *colectivo* or bus. Airport taxi runs are extremely lucrative and are usually controlled by hard-nosed taxi unions who seemingly set the fare by thinking of a reasonable price and then trebling it; their members are the only drivers licensed to take you directly from the airport taxi rank. If you want a safe ride there's little you can do about this – take consolation from the fact that in almost all cases, the ride from the city back to the airport with a regular cabbie will be half or less the price you paid on arrival. Most Latin American airport taxi ranks are at least properly regulated. You'll first have to pay your fare at a ticket booth in the airport (you'll be given a receipt or coupon to hand to your taxi driver) and then have to wait in line at the taxi rank. You can pay in dollars, though prices are fixed and not open to negotiation.

Many taxi drivers speak a little English, and are generally friendly and honest, but there are a few things to watch out for. The most common is that your driver, after asking you where you're staying, will tell you that the hotel or area you're going to is dangerous and that he knows somewhere much safer. Always stick to your guns – this is a well-rehearsed ploy to take you to his aunty/mother-in-law/good friend Miguel's hotel, or indeed anywhere where he'll get a slice of your money. Secondly, if you haven't bought a coupon at the airport, always agree the price of your journey first even if the taxi is metered (meters are often doctored) and absolutely refuse to pay any more if your driver tries it on. Thirdly, don't get in any cab if there's someone else riding up front, and never get out of the taxi until you arrive at your destination for whatever reason (in Bogotá, taxi drivers claim that the engine has stopped and that they need your help pushing the car, which then miraculously springs back into life leaving you standing in the middle of the road without your luggage). Be careful, too, that taxi drivers don't drive off with your luggage at the end of your trip when you get out of the vehicle.

As well as private taxis, you may well find shared taxis or *colectivos*. These are usually minibuses that, once full, drive round town dropping everyone off at their various destinations. *Colectivos* are much cheaper than private taxis, stringently regulated and more secure – in sum, a much better option. Again you'll purchase a coupon from an official booth in the airport.

Another alternative (but only if you arrive in daylight) is to walk out of the airport to the nearest main thoroughfare and hail a regular taxi; these will charge you much less than the airport taxi service. A decent guidebook will tell you where to head for, but don't wander aimlessly, and try to make sure you get into a licensed cab (identified by a certain make of car in a certain colour, such as the green Volkswagen Beetles used in Mexico City). A riskier alternative is to go with one of the touts in the airport to his vehicle, which will be parked outside the jurisdiction of the official airport taxi union. These unlicensed taxi drivers are often perfectly decent citizens trying to make a living – but who's to say if they're not? You could be mugged, dumped somewhere dangerous or worse – if you do take a ride with a tout you have only your instincts to decide whether he's honest or not.

If you arrive in daylight, you might find a bus that goes into town from the airport or close by, but you'll need to have a good idea of where you're going and some small change to pay your fare. Local buses are frequently rife with pickpockets, and if you have a huge backpack they may refuse to take you or simply not have enough room. In general airports that don't run a *colectivo* service will instead run airport shuttle buses. These take you on a set route, usually to the city centre or to hotel districts. Shuttle services are more expensive than ordinary local buses but are also safer, and frequently come equipped with air conditioning and comfortable seats.

△ Bolivian hostel

Jet lag

To those who have never suffered it, jet lag might appear to be nothing more than a rich kid's whinge, but unfortunately it's all too real, as you're likely to discover for yourself after your arrival in Latin America, unless you've flown from North America. The condition affects the vast majority of all long-distance travellers, and unless you're one of the lucky few who are immune, it's an inevitable hazard of flying long distances. Jet lag results from the disruption of the human body clock which is caused by rapidly crossing world time zones. If you cross more than three time zones (ie if the time in your departure city is more than three hours different from that at your destination), chances are you will experience jet lag. You're likely to suffer less from jet lag when travelling west rather than east, so Europeans have it easier on the way out to Latin America, while Australasians will have less jet lag going home. The good news for North Americans is that if you're flying directly south from the US or Canada to Latin America you may not even cross a single time zone, thus avoiding jet lag altogether.

Symptoms of jet lag include extreme fatigue, disorientation, lack of concentration, disrupted sleep and dehydration. In the days following your arrival you're likely to feel light-headed and unable to go to sleep and wake up at the appropriate times. Sitting bolt upright in bed at 4am and falling asleep in your breakfast may sound amusing, but disrupted sleep patterns can wreak havoc on your health and wellbeing. According to NASA, for each time zone crossed, you'll need a day before your body clock is properly adjusted – this means that if you're flying from London to Santiago, for example, it'll take six days. And jet lag doesn't really kick in until the second day of your arrival, so don't congratulate yourself on avoiding it prematurely.

There are all kinds of bizarre jet lag treatments available on the market. Some, like melatonin, a synthetic version of the hormone which is secreted into the bloodstream when it's time to sleep, have large followings (though its effectiveness is doubted by as many others, and there's no standard dose) – it's available in health-food stores in the US but not Europe. A herbal remedy from New Zealand called No-Jet-Lag (Ⓦwww.nojetlag.com) is said to work (though it's easy to get hold of in North America and Australasia it's not licensed for sale in Europe) as is intensive light therapy (Ⓦwww .bodyclock.com). In general, though, the best way to minimize the effects of jet lag is to follow the points below:

- Try to avoid 24-hour partying the night before you leave and last-minute panicking – stress and hangovers will only exacerbate jet lag. It's possible to "save up" sleep by having several decent nights of it before you fly, which will help you to deal with the loss of sleep that comes with jet lag.
- Once on board, set your watch immediately to your destination time zone and start to adjust to the new time. Try to stay awake and sleep at the relevant hours.
- Drink loads of water, avoid alcohol and caffeine, and eat light meals. Don't take conventional sleeping pills, which are dehydrating.
- Once you've arrived, continue to follow the local time even if your body is desperate for sleep. Go to bed when the locals do, eat meals at the right time and avoid sleeping during the day.
- Get out into the fresh air and spend as much time in bright natural light as possible – daylight alleviates jet lag by helping to reset your body clock.
- Take some gentle exercise as soon as possible – swimming or walking will combat the stiffness which results from sitting in one place for a long time and may also alleviate symptoms of jet lag such as disrupted sleeping patterns.
- Take it easy for your first few days – put off any non-urgent decisions, since your mental processes will be impaired by jet lag. Now is the perfect time to go to the beach, where the sunshine will aid your recovery.

9

Culture shock

Don't worry if you find you don't much enjoy your first few days in Latin America. You may well find the change in climate and food and the sheer strangeness of the place overwhelms you, leaving you feeling anxious, disoriented, paranoid, self-conscious or simply exhausted. You may even find yourself wishing you'd never come, shocked by the poverty, appalled by the pollution, confused by the language and disconcerted by the apparent chaos all around you. These are all common symptoms of culture shock, a perfectly normal reaction that almost every traveller experiences to some degree. Even experienced travellers sometimes undergo the same feelings of anxiety and alienation when they return to the region after some time away; in many ways, these feelings are part of the exhilaration of travel: if it didn't feel slightly dangerous, alien and exotic, it wouldn't be an adventure.

Culture shock often goes hand in hand with homesickness, and some people find it comes and goes in waves during long trips, so that the very same things which one week you find exciting about the country you're travelling through – be it the food, the local culture, the pace of life – can the next week seem deeply frustrating and annoying, making you wish you were back home surrounded by the safe and familiar. Fortunately, though, culture shock usually fades very quickly after arrival, generally giving way to excitement as you settle in and begin to enjoy all that Latin America has to offer. The following tips should help you overcome any initial culture shock and get through the confusion and strangeness of the first few days.

- If you're gong on a long trip taking in several different countries, consider starting in a country that's relatively easy to travel in, such as Chile, Argentina or Costa Rica, before taking on somewhere more challenging, such as Peru or Colombia.
- Take it easy for the first few days after arrival: you may well be jet-lagged after a long flight, exhausted and struggling to cope with a very different climate.
- Start exploring gradually rather than diving into your travels headfirst. Take time to get your bearings and visit a few easy and accessible places before heading off to more remote and adventurous destinations.
- Try and speak a few words of the local language, even if you only know enough to order a beer: this will make you feel less of an alien and make the locals much more approachable.
- Call or write home about your initial experiences – often just telling someone about what you're adjusting to can make it feel much more manageable.
- Chat to other travellers, as they've invariably been through the same thing and can offer useful support and advice, and help you see the funny side of things you might otherwise find exasperating.
- Don't feel obliged to have a completely "authentic" experience right from the start, no matter what other travellers tell you. If you want to stay close to your hotel and eat only familiar food for the first few days, then go ahead – there will be plenty of time to explore further afield and eat more adventurously once you've settled in.
- If after a few days the symptoms of culture shock don't go away, it may simply be that you don't like your first port of call. Try moving to another city or region where the climate or culture makes you feel more comfortable.

Different countries, different customs

Though when you first arrive in a Latin American capital it may seem disappointingly familiar, with its high-rise business district, rushing commuters and international corporate advertising hoardings, it won't be long before you realize that the Westernization of the region is only skin deep. Beneath the sometimes banal globalized

Blockbuster movies

When you're travelling, cumulative cultural dislocation can make you take a sudden dive for the nearest Burger King, blockbuster movie, or other culturally familiar things you might never consider doing at home. I never see American blockbuster films at home, of course, being a snob. But it's quite entertaining, not to mention instructive, seeing *Speed III* or *Godzilla* in a Central American cinema, surrounded by the increasingly Americanophile teenage sons and daughters of the local scions (cinemas are sometimes too pricey for the average family). The parking lot is full of four-wheel drives, and the foyer stuffed with girls admiring each other's outfits (*Que chivo!, que barbaro! – roughly, Cool!*). You can learn a lot of Spanish by reading the subtitles and comparing them with what comes out of Keanu Reeves' mouth – or perhaps that's not such a good example…

Jean McNeil

veneer, traditional Latin American culture runs deep, and it will quickly become clear that you are in the midst of a society with a very different approach to life and view of the world to what you're used to back home. Religion – above all Roman Catholicism – and extended families play a far greater role in Latin American culture than you're probably used to, and you may find many of the attitudes you encounter surprising in comparison to those commonly held in Europe or the US. Traditional Latin American values, especially those related to gender roles, inequality and social conformity, may seem stiflingly conservative or even outrageously oppressive. Many Latin Americans will find your behaviour equally strange – the very fact of your travelling to far-away countries simply for pleasure may be viewed as an irresponsible eccentricity, while to be unmarried and childless in your mid-twenties will strike many as at best bizarre or at worst indicative of some underlying misfortune.

Though there have been important steps towards more equal rights in recent decades, the culture of machismo is alive and well in Latin America. This tradition of gender stereotyping sees men as strong and dominant and women weak and subservient, and many women find it the most challenging aspect of travel in Latin America. Advice on coping with sexual harassment is given on pp.348–349, but you should also be prepared to cope with more general gender prejudices. If you're a woman travelling with a man – be it a husband, partner or friend – most conversation will be addressed to him, even if you're the one who speaks the local language; if you're a woman travelling alone, meanwhile, many Latin American men will assume it's because you can't find a man back home, and act accordingly.

Gay and lesbian travellers

Traditional macho attitudes to gender roles combined with the influence of the Roman Catholic Church make much of Latin America fairly hostile to homosexuality. In some countries homosexual acts have only recently been decriminalized, and gays and lesbians across the region still face considerable discrimination. For gay and lesbian travellers, it's safest to follow the example of local gay couples and avoid flaunting your sexuality. In rural areas in particular, open displays of affection between two men or two women can still provoke a hostile reaction. You'll find a more tolerant attitude in the cities, particularly in Brazil. Rio de Janeiro, São Paulo and Salvador all have thriving gay nightlife scenes, as do Buenos Aires in Argentina and Santiago in Chile. The website of the International Gay and Lesbian Travel Association (🌐www.igtla.com) has listings of gay-friendly accommodation and travel agents throughout Latin America.

Other aspects of Latin American culture that you may well find frustrating include a near-complete disregard for timekeeping, widespread corruption, shocking levels of poverty and inequality and interminable bureaucracy. However infuriating these aspects of Latin American culture can be, there's almost nothing you can do to change them, so railing against them is a waste of time and energy that can really spoil your trip. It's much better to accept such traits as part and parcel of what you came to experience, and adapt accordingly; keeping a sense of humour and perspective about things also helps.

On your best behaviour

However much you may dislike the idea of being an ambassador for your country, this is how many Latin Americans will see you, just as your view of their country will be shaped by how the locals treat you, so it's important to act with respect towards the cultural and social norms of the country you're in. No one expects you to transform yourself overnight into a Latin American, but adapting your behaviour to the country you're visiting is polite, makes local people more receptive, and generally makes travel easier and more enjoyable. Mastering the full range of social niceties in any country takes considerable time, but there are a few general behaviour codes you should definitely try to follow.

Even if you're only travelling for a few weeks, it's essential to learn at least a few basic words of Spanish or Portuguese. As well as being practical, making an effort to speak the local language makes locals react more favourably towards you, even if it's no more than basic greetings. Although few Latin Americans speak good English,

△ São Paulo, Brazil

many understand enough to know if you're talking about them, and certainly recognize common English obscenities, so be careful what you say.

Though it varies in degree from country to country, Latin Americans generally attach considerable importance to politeness and formality. It's normal to shake hands and use a formal greeting such as "good morning" or "good afternoon" before engaging someone in conversation – failure to do so will make you appear rude and can cause offence, or at least make people less helpful. It's also a good idea to use formal titles like *señor/señora* or *don/doña* and, if speaking Spanish, to use the formal *usted* rather than *tú* when addressing older people or those in authority. Politeness is particularly important when dealing with officials such as police officers, for whom the respect accorded their uniform or position is one of the few compensations for low pay and poor conditions. If you're rude or disrespectful, they can make things very difficult for you.

Though you're likely to see a few locals doing it, getting angry and raising your voice will seldom produce results, and is more likely to cause

A few pisco sours too many

The conversation around the table has come to an abrupt halt. The old man in the cravat smiles weakly as his leather-faced wife glares at me like an Easter Island statue in Chanel. My new-found drinking companions are turning against me. I try to replay the last few sentences to come out of my mouth but my brain isn't cooperating. Those pisco sours are really moreish.

I'd travelled up from the Central Valley having spent a busy week attending tours entitled "Getting to Know Chilean Wine", even though we'd been acquainted for some time. In search of something stronger I arrived in the idyllic village of Pisco Elqui, home to Chile's oldest pisco distillery. The guided tour I took there was informative but merely foreplay to the tasting session that followed. It started with the weakest, the Seleccion, then gently eased through the Reservado onto the Especial, and finally finished with the strongest of them all, the aptly named Gran Pisco. These were all sampled neat and were really good, but were trumped marvellously by what followed: pisco sours, a delicious cocktail of crushed ice, pisco, lemon juice, sugar, egg white and angostura bitters. And they are lethal. Intent on furthering my education, I headed out to the first bar I could find.

So all of them are just sitting there looking at me, not saying a word. And I honestly can't remember what I have just said to cause offence. Earlier they seemed happy to accept my devastating critique of Pablo Neruda's infantile love songs. Some of them, the two gauchos, were even nodding. Is that a hunting knife hooked onto his belt? I wrack my brain some more and catch a faint echo. I think I just mouthed off about Pinochet. I can't believe I've broken one of the Golden Rules – namely do not be drunk, English, totally uninformed and launch into a rant about a much-loved fascist dictator. I can't have done something that stupid. Stupid pisco sours.

Ross Monaghan

further antagonism, particularly when dealing with people in authority. This doesn't mean you can't be firm and assertive – just do it in as calm and civil a manner as you can manage. Getting involved in any kind of fight is a very bad idea, as the use of fists can easily provoke a reaction with a knife or gun.

Dressing the part

Latin Americans also attach considerable importance to appearance. Even if they are so poor they only have one set of clothes, they're still likely to be clean and relatively smart. Although the prejudice against people perceived as hippies is not as strong as it once was, dressing in untidy or dirty clothes is usually viewed unfavourably, whilst having at least one set of reasonably smart attire can get you into places where scruffier backpackers wouldn't be admitted.

It's a good idea to observe local dress codes as much as possible. Short shorts, sleeveless shirts and bikinis are fine on the beach, but in towns and cities they are usually frowned upon, and in some isolated rural communities can cause serious offence and even provoke stone throwing. Wearing part or all of the traditional costumes of local indigenous groups, on the other hand, provokes ridicule at best and grave offence at worst, so save them until you get home. Military clothing, particularly anything camouflaged, is also a bad idea, especially in countries with recent experience of armed conflict.

The Roman Catholic religion is taken seriously across Latin America, so it's particularly important to dress appropriately and behave respectfully when visiting churches or attending religious ceremonies or fiestas.

Harsh realities

Unless you've travelled to other developing countries before, the thing you'll find most shocking when you arrive in Latin America is likely to be the extreme poverty endured by much of the region's population. Most major cities are ringed by slums and shantytowns which lack even basic amenities such as water, electricity and sewerage, and whose populations are constantly increasing as a result of migration from rural areas where poverty is even more desperate. Unemployment levels are very high, and wages so low that even those who do have jobs (including professionals such as teachers) often struggle to make ends meet. This poverty is even more shocking in comparison with the extreme wealth enjoyed by small sections of the population: Latin America is home to some of the most unequal societies in the world, and the gap between rich and poor is distressingly pronounced.

The most visible manifestation of poverty you'll come across is undoubtedly the large number of beggars on the streets of almost every city. Many Latin Americans of all social classes give generously to beggars, particularly to the old and sick, and their donations act as an informal welfare system in countries where generally there is no universal health provision or financial support for the unemployed. Many tourists are unsure how to deal with beggars in Latin America, and you wouldn't be the first to mask your discomfort by averting your gaze while marching by. Obviously, giving is a personal decision, and you may prefer to give to a charity instead, or even to get actively involved in a local charity for a while. If you do decide to give money, you may want to follow the example of most locals by targeting the old, disabled and sick rather than those beggars who could otherwise be working for a living. There are also other ways of giving to the poor: the locals you see paying for the services of the countless shoe-shine boys and girls in every city centre do so not just because they want immaculate footwear; paying for small services like this is also an informal way of giving money to the poor whilst encouraging hard work and self-reliance in street children who might otherwise turn to begging or crime. Having your shoes shined will also deflect the often annoying pestering to which the shoe-shiners will subject you, at least until the next day.

Mañana, mañana

One of the most striking cultural differences between Latin America and countries in the developed world is in their attitude to time. Whereas back home turning up fifteen minutes late is considered at best thoughtless and at worst rude and unprofessional (if you do it persistently, it can even lose you your job), in most of Latin America arriving hours or even days late for a meeting barely warrants an explanation, never mind an apology. This relaxed attitude to time, whereby almost anything can be put off until tomorrow (*mañana*) and punctuality is considered of little or no importance, is one of the aspects of Latin America that most tourists and travellers find most frustrating. In part, dictionaries are to blame. Take a look in an English–Spanish dictionary and you'll probably read that *ahora* means "now". Though technically correct, in practice this translation is way off the mark: in Latin America *ahora* means sometime in the future, possibly today; the diminutive *ahorita* (literally "right now") means fairly soon; only when you start using terms like *inmediatamente* (immediately) or *ahoritita/ahorita mismo* (absolutely right away) is any sense of urgency communicated – and even then, it's likely to be ignored. Latin Americans are usually aware of this trait (though that doesn't stop them setting very exact agendas which they've no hope of meeting) and often rather bemused by gringos' bizarre obsession with punctuality. Indeed, when they really, truly mean an exact time, they'll emphasize it by using the expression *hora inglés* ("English time").

That they're aware of it, however, doesn't mean they're going to change just for you, and the bottom line is that there's nothing you can do about it. Getting angry because a bus leaves a few hours after the official departure time isn't going to make things happen any faster, so to avoid frustration it's best to allow extra time for every journey and leave enough space and flexibility in your travel plans to accommodate the inevitable delays. It also helps if you can adopt the same laid-back approach to time as the locals, and enjoy the relaxed unpredictability it adds to life: after all, if you want to travel in a country where the trains run on time, you'd be better off going to Switzerland. Finally, it's worth bearing in mind that, according to Latin American travellers' lore, the only time a bus or train does leave on time is when you arrive at the terminal five minutes late.

Being a gringo (what they think of you)

Wherever you go in Latin America, it won't be long before you hear locals refer to you as gringo or (if you're female) gringa. Strictly speaking, the term originally only applied to people from the US, and this meaning is still retained in most of Mexico, but elsewhere in Latin America "gringo" is used to describe anyone from rich, developed and largely white countries in Europe, North America and Australasia – in parts of the Peruvian Andes, it's even used to refer to lighter-skinned people from elsewhere in the country. The origins of the word are thought to lie in the nineteenth-century US–Mexican War, either drawn from a slogan shouted at the invading green-uniformed US troops ("Green Go Home!"), or derived from the song "Green Grow the Rushes, Oh!" to which those same troops apparently marched. It can have negative connotations – in Colombia, for example, the expression *hacerse el gringo* ("to act like a gringo") is used to mean "play the fool" – but generally speaking it's not an insult, just a description of which ethnic or cultural group you belong to in Latin American eyes, so it's not worth getting upset about. Latin Americans are equally blunt in describing people of Chinese, African and indigenous descent as *Chino*, *Negro* and *Indio*, and while there is a degree of racism in this system of categorization, with the exception of *Indio* these terms are not generally considered racist in themselves – it depends on the tone and context. If you're black or of Asian descent but from a gringo country you'll find Latin Americans have some difficulty categorizing you, but generally speaking you'll suffer less discrimination than local members of these ethnic groups can face in Latin America.

While gringo is not in itself a derogatory term, you will find that Latin Americans are prone to making assumptions about foreign travellers, just as Latin Americans are often stereotyped in the media back home as superstitious, shiftless, corrupt and prone to thieving and drug-trafficking. Gringos in Latin America are in turn often stereotyped as being ignorant, clumsy, arrogant, rude,

Latin American attitudes to people from the US – often referred to as Yanquis (Yankees) no matter what part of the States they're from – are a complex mixture of love and hate. On one hand, Latin Americans generally admire the wealth, dynamism and material success of the US. Millions have friends and relatives who live, work and study in the US, and millions more would like to join them and live the "American dream" in what's seen as a land of milk and honey. However, this admiration is tempered by widespread political resentment of the US government's long record of support for brutal military regimes in Latin America, its ongoing political and military interventions in the region, and its deeply hypocritical approach to the so-called "war on drugs", not to mention the rhetoric of the "war on terror". The US is also widely blamed (not without some reason) for the poor economic situation in many Latin American countries, especially where the Washington-based International Monetary Fund and World Bank have insisted on swingeing government spending cuts that have crippled social services. In addition, there are few political crises that are not blamed in some quarters on supposed CIA conspiracies and US "imperialism". These resentments are particularly strong in countries that have borne the brunt of US intervention in recent years, such as Nicaragua, Bolivia and Colombia. Some US citizens go so far as telling casual acquaintances they are Canadian when travelling in Latin America, but in fact these political resentments are rarely directed towards individual travellers and are unlikely to affect you as long as you stay out of heated political discussions and keep a relatively low profile in countries and regions where tension is high. The one glorious exception to this is the indigenous territory of Kuna Yala on Panama's Caribbean coast, where people from the US are referred to respectfully as *Merki* (from American), a prestigious term that dates back to US intervention in the early twentieth century in support of Kuna autonomy.

naive, sexually promiscuous, obsessively uptight about time, unable to string two words of Spanish or Portuguese together, and, above all, as inordinately wealthy. However, like all stereotypes, these are easily broken by engaging in a little direct human contact. Often, just making an effort to speak the local language, eating the local food, sharing a drink or a joke, revealing a little about your real life and showing a modicum of interest in local culture or respect for local social norms is enough to shatter these clichés and make local people realize you're not some ugly stereotype that's stepped out of the latest Hollywood movie, but an ordinary person much like themselves, albeit from a different country and with different experiences of life.

Making that contact is also pretty easy, as generally speaking Latin Americans are just as fascinated by you as you are by them, and wherever you go you're likely be engaged in conversation and bombarded with questions. "Where are you from?", "Where are you going?", "What do you think of my country?", "How much did it cost to fly here?", "How many children do you have?" (and if you have none, why not) – the same enquiries will come again and again, but though the constant repetition and the assumptions that underlie these questions can be irritating, they're usually just conversational openers. Particularly in areas that see little tourism, a foreign traveller passing through can be an exciting event for the locals, an opportunity to practise their English and satisfy some of their curiosity about the outside world, something few Latin Americans are able to do by travelling themselves. Some travellers like to carry photos of their friends and family to show curious locals, and coins or postcards of typical scenes back home to give as presents as a good way of making friends and giving a clearer picture of what their life back home is really like.

Being a wealthy tourist

All over Latin America, the most common assumption you'll confront is that as a gringo you are, by definition, extremely wealthy. You'll find people constantly asking you how much your flight cost and what the minimum wage is in your home country, then gasping in amazement as their preconceived view of your inordinate personal wealth is apparently confirmed. What makes this stereotype almost impossible to dispel is the fact that it is, by and large, entirely accurate. However low your economic position may be back home and however tight your budget, compared to the average Latin American earning just a few dollars a day you're very rich. Not only do you come from a wealthy country, you can even afford to take time off work and travel long distances for pleasure, something most locals can only dream about. Small wonder that many Latin Americans can't understand why so many travellers dress in scruffy clothing – surely if you can afford a flashy camera and a long-distance air ticket, you can stretch to a decent set of clothes? You can counter this assumption of endless wealth to a certain extent by explaining how long you had to work to raise the money for the trip, or how prices back home are much higher, but in the end you're unlikely to convince anyone that you're not comparatively rich, because all the evidence points in the other direction.

And why bother, when this comparatively wealthy status, however unusual you find it at first, was probably one of the reasons you chose to go to Latin America in the first place. After all, unless you're used to being relatively rich, it can be very enjoyable suddenly to be able to take a taxi whenever you want rather than waiting for a bus, to eat in restaurants every day, and to take part in all kinds of activities that would be too expensive to contemplate back home. Whilst enjoying the freedom wealth allows, however, you should be aware that your (probably new-found) wealth involves some responsibilities, too. As a person with cash to spend you can drive up local prices just by paying over the odds for a taxi fare or a beer – and many locals will encourage you to do this – as traders may then overcharge future custom-ers, driving inflation up. In the worst cases, goods and services in popular tourist destinations can become so expensive that locals can no longer afford them. Ask locals about prices before buying and try to pay a reasonable price, but conversely don't worry too much about being slightly overcharged: as a relatively rich person in a poor country you can afford to be slightly magnanimous, and getting angry and frustrated over a few cents really isn't worth the energy. In some countries and regions local traders operate an informal two-tier price system whereby foreign tourists are charged more than locals – some buses in Guatemala, for example, or hotels in Nicaragua. This can be quite annoying, but there's usually not much you can do about it, so it's not worth getting upset about – think of it as an unofficial subsidy for the locals who struggle to afford the same service.

For more on tourist prices and bargaining, see pp.202–204.

Food and drink

Getting used to the local food and drink can be one of the trickiest cultural transitions to deal with while travelling, but in comparison to Asia or Africa, Latin American food and drink isn't so very different to what you find at home, and there are only a handful of dishes – such as iguana eggs, guinea pigs or the dried ants popular in eastern Colombia – which you're likely to find totally alien. In cities and towns you'll find that familiar foods like pizza, burgers and fried chicken are widely available, and in areas popular with budget travellers you'll find restaurants and cafés specializing in the kind of food backpackers eat the world over – muesli, banana pancakes and the like. If you're travelling on a tight budget, you're better off sticking to local food, particularly the very good-value set lunch and dinner menus available in most countries, though you may find you eventually tire of regional staples like rice and beans, maize tortillas, or starchy soups. However, you'll be really missing out on one of the great pleasures of travel in Latin America if you don't sample the local specialities in the countries you visit: from Peruvian *ceviche* (cool, spicy raw fish) and Mexican *mole poblano* (turkey in a spicy chocolate sauce) to Argentine steaks (the best in the world) and Brazilian *feijoada* (a meaty black bean stew), the region is a cornucopia of culinary delights.

The one thing to be wary of is the fondness of people in some countries (above all Mexico and Peru) for particularly spicy food – Latin America is, after all, the original home of the red-hot chilli pepper. Fortunately for those without the fire-eating habit, chilli is usually served in a side dish, either chopped raw or blended into sauces with all kinds of other ingredients. Be cautious in applying this to your food, as it could well be hotter than anything you've tasted back home; the best remedy if your mouth is on fire is bread or something sweet rather than cold water. In addition, always wash your hands after handling chillies, as otherwise touching your eyes or other more sensitive parts of your body can give you a culture shock of a particularly agonizing kind.

The only reason you're likely to have difficulty with food is if you are a vegetarian. Latin America is very much a meat-eating society, and most Latin Americans who can afford to do so eat meat with pretty much every meal. All kinds of fruit and vegetables are of course available, but outside tourist areas they rarely make it onto menus as main dishes. Telling a waiter you're vegetarian is quite likely to produce a blank stare, while insisting you don't eat meat will probably be interpreted as meaning you don't eat beef, but pork or chicken is okay. If you're a strict vegetarian, be warned that ostensibly vegetarian dishes such as beans are often cooked in pork fat for

Some of the best Latin American food and drink

These are just a few examples of Latin America's many culinary delights. You don't have to spend much to eat very well, and the best food can turn up in the most unlikely places.

Argentine beef Good steak features regularly on menus throughout Latin America, but nowhere does it match the quality of Argentina's, where preparing the world's best beef has become an art form unto itself. Ordered from a complex diagram of bovine anatomy, Argentine steaks come in many different cuts and have many different names, but they're invariably large and almost always delicious.

Ceviche Peru's unmissable national dish, a cool and spicy combination of fresh fish and seafood marinated in chilli, onions and lime juice, best washed down with an ice-cold beer. Anything served under the same name elsewhere in Latin America seldom lives up to the exquisite Peruvian version.

Chilli sauce The chilli pepper originates in Latin America, and as well as being one of the regions greatest gifts to world cuisine, it's an indispensable everyday condiment in almost every Latin American country. Whether mass-produced in a bottle or handmade to a family recipe, chilli sauce is always on the table and can liven up even the blandest food. In Mexico in particular, the variety of chillies available is amazing. The hottest varieties can bring tears to your eyes, but once your taste buds are accustomed you may find you can't eat without it.

Colombian coffee Coffee may come from Africa originally, but Latin America now has a strong claim to producing the world's finest beans, as well as being home to some of the world's most enthusiastic coffee drinkers. The best is arguably found in Colombia, where sweetened black coffee known as *tinto* is always available, served from thermoses by wandering vendors.

Cuy Bred as livestock for thousands of years, the guinea pig remains the favourite party dish for indigenous people in much of the Peruvian Andes.

extra flavour. With a little persistence and determination, however, it is possible to be a vegetarian in Latin America. Most large towns and cities have at least one vegetarian or health food restaurant (often run by Hare Krishnas), and tourist restaurants usually have several vegetarian options. If you stick to local places, however, you may well find yourself consuming a lot of eggs. Shopping for fruit and vegetables in the local market – where a huge range of both is almost always available – and cooking or preparing it yourself is one way to supplement the rather meagre fare available to vegetarians on the road.

If you can get past the fact they look like rats once roasted and are better known as children's pets elsewhere in the world, cuys are a tasty treat and certainly something to write home about.

Empanadas A classic snack available throughout Latin America in a variety of guises, empanadas are small pies or pasties, filled with meat, chicken, fish cheese and or vegetables and either baked or fried.

Feijoada No visit to Brazil is complete without tasting this classic dish. *Feijoada* is a rich black-bean stew laden with chunks of meat and sausage that's served throughout the country, either as a side dish or, accompanied by rice, as a meal in itself.

Fruit juice Latin America's astonishing variety of sumptuous tropical fruit is best enjoyed juiced and blended with ice. Known by various names including *zumo*, *suco*, *vitaminha*, *batido* and *licuado*, fresh fruit juices are available almost everywhere, providing a delicious, refreshing and inexpensive way to stay healthy on the road.

Mole poblano Only in Mexico, where chocolate originated, could they get away with using it to make a spicy sauce for turkey. But strange as it may sound, the subtle blend of bitter chocolate with several varieties of chilli that is *mole poblano* is excellent. The food of the gods – as the Aztecs considered it – is also used more conventionally in contemporary Mexico, grated from natural blocks to make delicious hot chocolate drinks.

Tortillas You can love them or loathe them, but you certainly can't escape tortillas if you travel in Mexico or Central America. These flat pancakes of maize or wheat flour are the traditional equivalent of bread, served with almost every meal. At their worst they're soggy, dull and repetitive. But at their best – made from hand-ground corn and baked on a stone by a wood fire – they're the very essence of Central America. And as a key ingredient in a host of dishes – tacos, burritos, enchilladas – they're an essential part of Mexico's varied and distinctive cuisine.

What kind of meat?

On the inland roads of the Yucatán, hitchhikers are common, trying to get from the middle of nowhere to the edge of nowhere. I pick up nice-looking women and children to break up the monotony of the greenery and practise my Spanish.

One day, into my car climbed a little bundle of Maya cheer, clad in a traditional flowery dress and toting three huge mesh bags. After the conversational preamble – her Spanish was about as fluent as mine – she asked me, "So, what kind of meats do you eat in your village?" It was such an odd question that I made her repeat it – and I'd already told her I was from New York ("Díos mio!" she gasped), so her saying "pueblito" was also confusing. Baffled, I began to list all the meat words I could think of: *pato, pavo, pollo...* But she quickly interrupted – this was a question she wanted to answer. In her village, they eat special animals that you only find in the forest, such as...and she rattled off several of them.

To illustrate one, she reached in a bag and pulled out the back half of a forest critter's carcass, splayed out flat and all black from roasting. The little feet were still on, with delicate toes and nails. This was an *uhum*, she said – it had (once upon a time) a long tail and pointy nose. According to her, it was a great little animal, but they'd been hunted for so long there were hardly any left.

And then she encouraged me to sample some of these endangered hindquarters. A difficult task while driving, but I got a few shreds, and it was quite tasty, though I think that had more to do with the pit-cooking than its innate *uhum*-ness.

Zora O'Neill

Taking photos

For many people, taking photographs or video footage is one of the great joys of travel and one of the best ways of preserving memories, and the sheer visual magnificence of so much of Latin America makes it an excellent place for photographers, whether you're fully kitted out with state-of-the-art professional equipment or snapping away with a cheap point-and-shoot. However, not all Latin Americans are happy to have their photo taken by tourists, and there are certain situations where you should be cautious about who or what you photograph. The following guidelines should help you get the picture you want without causing offence or getting into trouble.

- Always ask permission before taking pictures of people, as failure to do so is at best rude and at worst deeply offensive. Remember that you're not in a theme park, and think how you would feel if strange foreigners began taking your picture without so much as a by-your-leave. Be particularly cautious in isolated indigenous communities, where taking people's picture is sometimes considered akin to theft.

- Sometimes you may find people ask you to pay them a small fee in return for allowing you to take their photo. Some travellers view such demands with outrage, but in fact they represent a perfectly reasonable exchange – you get the picture, the usually poor subject earns a little money which may make him or her more receptive to tourists in the future, and locals are encouraged to maintain the colourful and unique costumes and traditions which are probably the main reason you wanted to photograph them anyway.

- Locals will often ask you for copies of the pictures you take of them or their families, as many can't afford cameras or development costs themselves. Though the quality of prints is usually not as good as back home, getting pictures printed locally and giving away a few copies to the people you've photographed makes the whole process a much more equal exchange, and the delight a few pictures can bring to people who have perhaps never seen a photo of themselves can be very satisfying. Don't promise to send people photos if you're not going to follow through, as this will make them less receptive to future photo requests.

- Always ask before taking pictures in churches and during religious processions and fiestas, as it may be considered disrespectful. Flash photography is often banned in churches as it can damage ageing oil paintings and other decorations.

- Don't take pictures of border posts or any kind of military installation, as this can result in you having your film or camera confiscated or even in your being arrested by paranoid military personnel. Always ask permission before taking photographs of police or soldiers or, better still, avoid doing so altogether.

Responsible tourism

Culture shock works both ways, and with the number of tourists visiting Latin America increasing all the time, it's important not to underestimate the impact the tourism industry has on local cultures, particularly in popular destinations. One of the most alarming aspects of reverse culture shock is the tendency for big businesses to take over local enterprises in resort areas, preventing the economic dividends of tourism from reaching local communities. As a first-time traveller you'll probably be on a fairly tight budget and so unlikely to be patronizing international hotel chains, but you may well be tempted to stop off at familiar multinational takeaway food outlets. Where possible, it's much better (as well as cheaper, more enjoyable and more authentic) to support local shops, restaurants and hotels instead. That way, the money you spend stays within the community and local residents retain control over their own neighbourhood, ensuring that the place keeps its original character – which is, after all, what you travelled so far to experience. In this way, budget travellers can have a beneficial effect on the countries they visit: though they spend less money than wealthier tourists on short, all-inclusive tours, most of the money they do spend tends to go to small local businesses, and so has a far more positive impact on local economies than the major tourism developments beloved of bankers and government officials.

It's also important to support local initiatives when it comes to visiting traditional indigenous communities, so that the people you go to see – be it Quechua-speaking llama-herders in the Andes or semi-nomadic tribes in the Amazon – see some economic benefit from your curiosity. All too many tour companies sell trips to visit isolated indigenous groups without giving travellers any chance to communicate with them, turning communities into little more than human zoos and exotic photo opportunities where traditional culture is parodied rather than respected. Where possible, try to organize a tour with a tour guide or agency from within the community you wish to visit, or at least endeavour to actually meet and interact with the people you've travelled so far to see. Tourism can have a dramatic negative impact on remote communities, in some cases plunging them suddenly into an unfamiliar market economy and materialist society. However, if conducted in a sensitive manner, tourism can have a positive effect, reviving local economies and keeping local traditions alive. A growing number of community-based guides and tour operators are springing up all over Latin America, offering a far more authentic and positive experience of traditional societies than you'll get with many more mainstream tour agencies. If you can't find any useful leads in guidebooks or the websites listed on pp.372–373, check out the *Good Alternative Tourism Guide*, published by Earthscan for the campaigning organization Tourism Concern, which lists a selection of successful local tourism initiatives in Latin America and the rest of the world. Tourism Concern also have a website at ⓦwww.tourismconcern.org.uk.

As a responsible tourist, you should also try to reduce your impact on the environment, particularly in national parks and other protected wilderness areas, where you otherwise risk damaging the pristine natural beauty you've travelled so far to see. In practice, this can mean everything from being careful about rubbish disposal to following strict national park rules. Even if the locals appear unconcerned about litter, it doesn't mean you should be. In particular, don't dump non-biodegradable stuff like plastic, cigarette ends and dead batteries in rural areas: if you can manage to carry it in with you, you can certainly take it out again. Don't buy souvenirs made from endangered species such as black coral, and avoid eating endangered species such as turtle, which often make it onto tourist menus. When visiting protected natural areas, try to follow the mantra: "leave nothing but footprints and take nothing but memories (and photographs)".

In recent years Latin America has seen an explosion in ecotourism, which in theory involves tourists visiting fragile natural environments such as rainforests and coral reefs whilst minimizing the negative impact their visit has on them and their inhabitants. In the best cases, ecotourism can even have a positive impact, encouraging environmental protection by allowing local communities to make a living through conserving rather than exploiting natural resources. In many instances, however, tour agencies claim to practise ecotourism to attract clients but in fact do little or nothing to reduce the negative impact of their tours, a process known as "greenwashing". Where possible, you should treat such claims with caution. Advice on getting involved in nature conservation work in Latin America is given in Chapter 2, and you'll find a list of relevant organizations in Directory on pp.372–373. You'll also find plenty of information and advice on ecotourism on the websites ⓦwww.planeta.com and ⓦwww.ecotour.org.

10

Getting around

ravelling in Latin America can be wonderful and frustrating, often at the same time. The extremes of terrain, poor infrastructure and the enormous distances involved mean that simply getting people from one place to the other is an enormous challenge, but it's one that Latin American transport operators overcome every day, moving millions of passengers around using the wide range of transport including planes, trains, passenger ships, river boats, motorized dugout canoes, tourist buses, local buses, open-top lorries, pick-up trucks and shared taxis.

Road transport is the main way of getting around throughout the region, though the quality of this varies enormously. In relatively rich and developed countries such as Argentina and Venezuela, most main roads are well paved and buses are often modern and reliable. In poorer countries, however – and particularly in sparsely populated regions with swampy or mountainous terrain – most roads are unpaved dirt highways in very poor condition which are only kept open by constant labour against floods and landslides, and by the determination, skill and sheer bloody-mindedness of bus and lorry drivers.

Throughout the vast, rainforest-covered basins of the Amazon and Orinoco, meanwhile, roads are few and far between and the mighty river systems form the main highways, served by a variety of boats ranging from large ships to canoes hewn from single tree trunks. In many coastal regions, too, ferries and fast launches are the main means of hopping along the shore or reaching nearby islands. Throughout Latin America local flights, whether in airliners shuttling between major cities or light aircraft skimming over the treetops, offer a quick and easy way of getting around, saving many hours or even days of hard overland travel at a relatively reasonable price.

All this exciting variety must be set against discomfort, poor safety conditions and often appalling driving, delays and sometimes unbelievable unreliability, all of which are enduring characteristics of travel in Latin America. While back home a five-hour bus ride in a comfortable seat may seem interminable, and a fifteen-minute delay a serious inconvenience, if you want to travel in Latin America for any length of time you'll find yourself making a lot of twelve-hour bus journeys in cramped seats and confronting delays of many hours, often for no apparent reason. If you look on the travel itself as part of the adventure, you'll have a better chance of keeping things in perspective. The twelve-hour bus journey that turns into a three-day marathon may be a gruelling experience at the time, but when you get home you'll probably look back on it as one of the most memorable adventures of your trip. On most journeys, too, the spectacular scenery you'll pass through and the colourful antics of your fellow passengers are usually compensation for the arduousness of the trip.

Public transport in Colombia

As the crow flies, it was a distance of 100km from where I was staying to the Caribbean coast of Colombia – a leisurely morning travelling, you might assume. There was no direct route, though – so the journey took a lot longer than I'd imagined. From inland Mompos I took a crammed jeep – "When does it go?" I asked the driver, who was ordering breakfast from a street stall. "It goes when it's full" was his reply, grunted between mouthfuls of empanada – to the river, then a speedboat to Magangue, a dusty town from where I took a minibus and arrived in Sincelejo in time to find a room for the night. A dawn start the next day began with another minibus ride, which got me at last to the coast – but not the village I was heading for. In Tolu the roads petered out and I climbed into the back of a truck – the only form of public transport other than the local "taxis", bicycles with rickety seats custom-built over the front and back wheels – with the aid of a handy wooden stool that was whipped out by the driver's assistant at every stop so that passengers could climb. These included local farmers wearing straw stetsons and carrying chickens, businessmen with mobile phones, school girls, and smart women adorned in flowery frocks and gilt jewellery. Another truck ride and then the luxury of a proper bus and I finally arrived in San Bernardo del Viento – seven bus/truck rides, one boat trip and two days later.

Polly Rodger Brown

Planes

Almost all countries in Latin America have an internal air network of some sort, and flying is by far the fastest way to get around. It's also by far the most expensive, and only a very small proportion of Latin Americans can afford to travel this way. However, the prices of flights are generally a lot cheaper than in Europe or North America, and flying is an excellent way of avoiding exhausting overland journeys and saving time if you're trying to fit a lot into a relatively short trip – a one-hour flight between Lima and Cusco in Peru, for example, can cost as little as US$60, not much when you consider that the alternative is an exhausting bus journey lasting at least thirty hours. And although you'll miss out on many of the scenic views at ground level, many flights – especially those passing over the high peaks of the Andes or across the endless green carpet of the Amazon rainforest – offer breathtaking bird's-eye views.

You can often book internal flights from home when you book your outward flight (see p.180): though this will cost more than booking in Latin America itself, it's worth doing if you're short on time and want to travel on popular routes, which may be booked up well in advance. Several airlines offer internal airpasses at good rates to tourists, which can be worthwhile if you're intending to cover a huge amount of ground in as short a time as possible (for more on airpasses, see p.179).

As well as domestic commercial carriers, in some countries the airforce also operates passenger services as a means of subsidizing the maintenance of their aircraft and connecting isolated regions. These military flights are usually slightly cheaper than commercial flights. In some remote regions like the Amazon you can also travel in small light aircraft that carry only five to twelve passengers. Though expensive, this is an exciting way to travel and can save days of arduous overland travel; in some cases it's also the only way to reach the most remote (and therefore most pristine) national parks and wilderness regions.

When using Latin American airlines, the following tips should make your trip easier:

- Some of the airlines flying internal routes are small operators with minimal back-up both on and off the ground, so don't expect them to be as efficient or punctual as airlines back home.

- Not all Latin American airlines have the same safety standards as what you're accustomed to at home, and some have poor records: if in doubt, check with your embassy before you book, or visit Ⓦwww.airsafe.com, which lists the safety records of many Latin American airlines.

- It's often easier to book air tickets through a reliable local travel agent for a small fee.

- Having booked a seat, you often need to reconfirm with the airline before travel. Check before you book, and make a careful note of the number you'll need to ring to reconfirm.

- Flights are often cancelled or delayed at short notice due to weather conditions or due to technical problems or lack of aircraft. Build as much flexibility into your itinerary as you can, and, if possible, avoid relying on an internal flight to get you back to the capital on the day your international flight home departs.

- Overbooking – where more tickets are sold than there are seats on the plane – is also often a problem, so make sure you reconfirm, and check in as early as possible as boarding passes are usually issued on a first-come-first-served-basis.

- Follow the advice on hand baggage on p.241 – just because a flight is internal doesn't mean you can't get delayed or they won't lose your baggage.

- In most countries you have to pay a domestic airport tax before flying. This is often payable only in cash, so make sure you have enough with you before heading to the airport.

Hitching a ride in a Cessna

In Central America it can be quite cheap to hire a small plane and its pilot, if there are four or five of you – although it's best to ask around for recommendations and to press for credentials, as light aircraft accidents are distressingly common. But for those who like to fly, it can be literally awesome, flying above volcanoes (perfect views of the craters and the lagoons) and over carpets of low rainforest, mangroves and the lazy rivers and man-made canals that dot much of the east coast in the isthmus. I used to hitch rides with a pilot friend of mine in his Cessna, and we'd fly quite low, so that we could see fishermen out for their morning catch, or even herons lazily launching themselves from the riverside, and arrive at small hamlets with an airstrip and little else. In countries like Costa Rica and Nicaragua, flying is the fastest way by a long chalk to get to the Caribbean coast, and small planes can be a revelation after travelling in commercial jets. You see much more of the wildlife and landscape, and it's pleasant, rather than scary, to feel the various updrafts and air currents.

Jean McNeil

Long-distance buses

Most Latin Americans rely on long-distance buses when it comes to making extended journeys, and travelling this way is one of the most enjoyable (and also sometimes the most exasperating and exhausting) experiences the region has to offer – all of human life is jammed together, often with a few chickens or pigs thrown in for good measure, travelling at a pace slow enough to really appreciate that landscape you're passing through. The buses are often a sight in themselves, painted with bright slogans and designs and with lavish handmade consoles around the driver, complete with statues of Christ or the Virgin Mary that light up when the brakes are applied. Bus travel is also extremely good value – for example, travelling from one end of Peru to the other, a distance of about two thousand kilometres, will cost you less than US$30. In some countries there's an annoying custom of charging foreign tourists slightly more for bus travel, although this is only a small amount and not worth getting angry about – just think of it as a subsidy for poor locals, for whom that US$4 bus fare is a major expense.

The quality of buses varies enormously both within and between countries. The best ones – variously described as *Pullman, primera clase* or *de lujo* – are modern vehicles with air conditioning or heating, comfortable reclining seats, plenty of legroom, chemical toilets, television and video, and even waitresses serving drinks to passengers. These are more common on major inter-city routes and in wealthier, more developed countries. They tend to be fairly punctual, particularly in more developed countries like Chile or Argentina, and also make fewer stops, meaning that they're faster. Obviously, these types of buses cost a bit more than slower and less comfortable vehicles.

At the other extreme are ageing buses with dodgy engines, cracked windscreens, ripped seats and balding tyres; many are old school buses from the US, or even flat-bed lorries fitted with seats. When there are a number of different bus companies operating the same route, it's worth trying to get a look at the bus before buying a ticket and choosing the one that looks in best condition. These buses tend to stop frequently en route to pick up passengers, who are crammed into every available space, both on extra benches or folding seats which fill the aisles or standing (or even hanging) out of the door or perched on the roof – this latter option should be

△ Bus, Panama

"Fe en conductor"

Antigua's bus station is located at the market, and it's a hectic place. There are no first-class buses here, only crazily painted old school buses, known fondly as "chicken buses", that make their way around locally or (by some miracle) to far-flung places. Suffice it to say, the adage "Old buses don't die – they go to Guatemala" rings true. It is a common belief that Guatemala's bus drivers have death wishes. With names like Fe en Dios (Faith in God) and Mi Esperanza (My Hope) painted on the windshields, it's easy to wonder if you'll make it to your destination in one piece.

When the bus to Guatemala City pulled away from the curve, there were eight of us in my row – three on my side, and a family of five on the other. The other rows were just as packed, and there were a dozen people standing. It wasn't until there were about seventy people on the bus – including the very uncomfortable 6' 7" gringo with whom I was travelling – as well as a baby chick (honest), that the driver felt he had enough passengers.

A good part of the road from Antigua to Guatemala City is curvy, with some incredibly steep grades. As we sped along I grabbed the only free spot on the seat in front of me and held on for dear life; I felt many things – disbelief, discomfort, amusement, fear, nausea. After a while, I put my faith in the driver (Fe en conductor), as one has no choice but to do, and within an hour, we were nearing my stop. When the moment of truth came, I shoved my way past several tightly packed people and practically fell out the back door onto the street, so very happy to be alive, as the bus pulled away.

Julie Feiner

avoided if at all possible; if you do sit on the roof, keep a careful lookout for overhanging branches. A popular joke asks: "How many passengers fit in a Peruvian [or Bolivian, etc] bus?", with the inevitable answer, *unito mas* – "just one more!"

Seats at the back are always the bumpiest, while those at the front afford the best view of the driver's technique and an earful of his favourite music. Frustratingly, while you will want to enjoy the views, the Latin American sitting beside you will likely want to draw the curtains to block out the sun and the (to him or her) mundane scenery and concentrate on the trashy B-movie on the video at the front of the bus. Latin American buses are generally designed for smaller physiques – many are made in Japan but refitted with smaller seats to allow for extra passengers – so don't underestimate the stamina required for long journeys, particularly if you're relatively large.

Any journey over four hours or so is likely to involve a meal stop at a roadside restaurant. You'll rarely be told how long this will last, so watch what the driver and other passengers order and keep an eye on the bus lest it leaves without you. Unless you're on a luxury bus with a chemical toilet, these meal stops are usually the only opportunity you'll get to relieve yourself, so think carefully before drinking that extra beer or cup of coffee. Anywhere the bus stops it's likely to be boarded by people selling drinks, snacks, sweets, complete meals and whatever is the local speciality or produce of the region you're passing through, as well as hawkers of miracle cures, poets, musicians, beggars and even magicians hoping to entertain the passengers in return for a few cents – this can often be an enjoyable part of the whole experience. It's worth carrying some food and drink with you on long journeys, however, as you may not like or trust what's on offer at the roadside, and you never know when a breakdown or other delay might leave you stranded and hungry. It's also worth keeping some warm clothing or even a sleeping bag or blanket with you on the bus, even if it's extremely hot when you set off – nightfall or a climb in altitude can send temperatures plunging, and in luxury buses powerful air conditioning can leave you shivering even as the temperature climbs above 30°C/86°F outside.

Generally speaking, journeys are measured in time rather than geographical distance. On well-paved roads between major cities and in more developed countries, buses make good time, but elsewhere roads are often simply rough tracks or mud and rock, and mountainous terrain often means that what looks like a short distance on your map actually takes far longer to cover than a much greater distance on a good road through flat country. Punctuality varies greatly between different countries – Chilean buses almost always leave on time, for example, whereas buses in rural Peru frequently leave hours after the man who sells you the ticket tells you they will. Often buses will leave only after hours of futile driving around town hooting loudly to conjure up nonexistent passengers. Sometimes it can appear that buses leave on time only if you arrive five minutes after the official departure time written on your ticket, and if they're full of passengers they may even leave early.

Once underway, further delays can be caused by poor road conditions, landslides, police or customs searches, or simply by the driver's desire to spend an hour with his girlfriend in a town en route. All this can be very frustrating, of course, but if you can it's best to take delays with the calm, fatalistic approach adopted by many Latin Americans – if you always expect journeys to take longer than expected, it's a pleasant surprise when you arrive as scheduled; if you really want to travel in a country where the buses always run on time, you're better off going somewhere like Switzerland.

On long inter-city routes you'll often have the option of travelling overnight. Many travellers favour this as a way of saving money on accommodation and making extra time for sightseeing at their next destination. Latin Americans often prefer it too, as it means they can travel to the city, spend a day conducting their business, then travel home the next night without splashing out on a hotel. However, travelling by night does mean that you'll miss out on the scenery, and unless you're in a luxury sleeper bus with fully reclining seats, it can be difficult to sleep in cramped conditions and on bumpy roads, leaving you tired and washed-out when you arrive. In addition, you're more vulnerable to theft, whether by bandits stopping the bus or sneak thieves filching your bag while you sleep, and drivers are far more prone to potentially fatal accidents when travelling by night.

On more luxurious inter-city buses, your luggage will usually be put in a locked compartment under the bus, and you'll be given a ticket with which to claim it at the end of the journey; the compensation this ticket entitles you to if your bag goes missing is paltry, but the system is usually pretty safe. On more basic buses in poorer countries or more remote regions, your bag will often be slung on the roof. If you like, you can climb up and padlock it to the roof rack yourself; otherwise, it's worth keeping an eye out of the windows when the bus stops to make sure no one takes it accidentally or on purpose. It's not a bad idea to cover your backpack with a sack (available in any market) to protect it from dust, rain, oil and prying fingers, and to disguise it from potential thieves, though you should mark the sack to avoid it being mistaken for someone else's potatoes. If you're travelling light, you can keep your luggage with you on your seat, and it's worth keeping valuable or fragile items with you in your hand luggage in any case. Be sure to keep it within sight, ideally with a strap looped around your leg, as otherwise it may disappear while you sleep, or you may unpack later to find someone has removed your camera and carefully closed the bag again afterwards. For more on backpack security, see p.228.

Most larger towns and cities have one or more bus terminals for long-distance buses (*Terminal de Buses* or *Terminal Terrestre* in Spanish, *Rodoviária* in Brazil), though in some places buses depart from various offices scattered around town. These are often on the outskirts of town, and worth taking a taxi to if you have heavy luggage; taxi drivers are also good people to ask if you're confused as to where you need to go to catch a bus to a particular destination. Bus terminals tend to have an information desk of some kind, as well as left-luggage offices, restaurants, and cheap (though usually insalubrious) accommodation close by. You'll often have to pay a small terminal tax on departure.

Generally speaking it's a good idea to book a seat in advance if you can, though on busy routes served by frequent buses this isn't always necessary – just turn up and buy a ticket for the next departure. On most bus trips you'll be allocated a numbered seat when you buy your ticket, so if you can it's worth having a look at the bus to choose a seat with a good view or more legroom. If you're travelling from a small town between major destinations or in a remote region where traffic is scarce, your best bet is often to flag down anything passing in the right direction, even though this may involve standing up for some time until a seat becomes available. During public holidays and fiestas people travel in great numbers, and bus tickets can be hard to come by even though prices are often higher.

In countries and regions where the tourist infrastructure is more developed, private companies operate special tourist bus services exclusively for foreign visitors. On these buses there's usually more

Best bus rides

The Carretera Austral Stretching over 1000km south in Chile from Puerto Montt to the remote settlement of Yungay, the Carretera Austral carves its way through great tracts of untouched wilderness, taking in soaring snow-capped mountains, ancient glaciers, narrow fjords, emerald rivers and swathes of temperate rainforest.

Cusco to Puerto Maldonado Linking Cusco, the ancient mountain capital of the Incas, with the remote jungle town of Puerto Maldonado, this route crosses stunning high Andean passes before plunging down into the dense rainforests of the Upper Amazon. In good weather the journey takes about two days, but rain can turn it into a week-long odyssey.

The World's Most Dangerous Road Descending more than 3500m over a distance of just 64km, the tenuous highway linking La Paz with Coroico in Bolivia is amongst the most spectacular roads in the world, plunging from the frozen high Andes down through dense cloudforest into the lush subtropical valleys of the Yungas. It's also extremely perilous – indeed the number of vehicles that plunge over precipices is so high that it's been dubbed it "The World's Most Dangerous Road".

space for luggage, and the vehicles are usually in better condition, but in other respects they are not much different from regular public buses. However, they do offer a direct, hassle-free and usually faster service between main tourist destinations. The downside is they're more expensive and they deprive you of the colourful (if sometimes infuriating) experience of sharing your journey with ordinary Latin Americans.

Lorries

In remote areas, and particularly in poorer countries, passengers often travel in heavy goods lorries rather than buses. Sometimes these are specially converted for passengers and fitted with basic seats, but usually you'll simply be standing in the back or sitting on top of the cargo or on a wooden plank placed across the top. On a good day, travelling in the back of an open-top truck with the wind in your face and 360-degree views is a fantastic experience – for the first hour at least. After that the dust, hard wooden seats (when there are any seats at all), exposure to the elements and extremely bumpy ride start to take their toll. Lorries are also slower and generally more dangerous than buses, and stop more frequently. Still, travelling by lorry is a quintessential Latin American experience that's worth trying at least once. For shorter journeys in remote areas, smaller pick-up trucks, known as *camionetas* in Spanish, also carry passengers; these share the same drawbacks and pleasures as lorries, but are slightly faster and less bumpy.

Is it safe?

There is no escaping the fact that road travel in Latin America is often a hair-raising experience. Buses and other vehicles often travel far too fast for the conditions – overtaking on blind corners is a regular occurrence – and drivers are often poorly trained and work long hours without sufficient sleep. Road conditions can be appalling and vehicles poorly maintained, so not surprisingly, accidents do happen – you only need to look out for the white crosses beside the road that mark where the victims of previous accidents have died to realize that bus travel involves a greater degree of danger in Latin America than it does at home. Statistically, however, the risk remains small, and you should remember that even after buying a ticket you can still choose not to climb on board the bus – if it looks too dangerous or the driver appears drunk, it's best to follow your instinct and stay put or travel in a different vehicle.

Trains

Travelling by train is often the safest and most memorable way of getting around Latin America, and usually considerably more comfortable than travel by bus. Unfortunately, however, railway travel is very much in decline across Latin America, and many networks have been abandoned, partly as a result of privatization and the withdrawal of government subsidies, partly because the industries like mining that once sustained them have fallen on hard times, but mostly because bus travel along the ever-increasing road network is generally cheaper and faster. Only rarely does rail offer a serious alternative for moving from one destination to another, but fortunately governments and tourist boards are waking up to the fact that many foreign visitors prefer to travel by train, and in many countries the most spectacular stretches of line have been preserved as tourist attractions even though most local cargo and passenger traffic now goes by road.

Though they vary between countries and lines, ticketing systems usually involve two or more classes: the most luxurious and expensive are tourist-only carriages featuring comfortable seats, heating or air conditioning, restaurant cars, waiter service and additional security; at the other extreme are second-class carriages with hard seats and few facilities which are usually packed to the seams with local passengers sitting, standing and hanging off the sides or on the roof. Buying tickets for the former is usually easy and can also be done through tour agencies as well, while getting tickets for the latter can involve arriving at the station before the ticket office opens and lengthy queuing to get a seat, especially at small intermediary stations. Security issues on trains are fairly similar to those on long-distance buses, except that you'll usually have your luggage in the compartment with you, in which case it's worth locking your backpack to the luggage rack and keeping small bags away from windows at stations.

Top train rides

Copper Canyon Railway Starting on the Mexican Pacific coast at Los Mochis, this line clings to the wall of the dramatic 2000-metre-deep canyon of the Río Urique, known as the Copper Canyon, as it climbs up to cross the continental divide amongst the peaks of the Sierra Madre before reaching the city of Chihuahua.

Cusco to Machu Picchu This train is the only way to reach the fabled Lost City of the Incas without walking the Inca Trail and is a spectacular journey in its own right, climbing up switchbacks from the city of Cusco and passing high Andean peaks that flank the Sacred Valley before plunging down the deep, narrow ravine of the rushing Río Urubamba to the foot of the ruins at Aguas Calientes.

The Old Patagonia Express A narrow-gauge steam train made famous by Paul Theroux's (rather disparaging) book of the same name, the Old Patagonia Express is a classic South American train journey, lurching across the arid steppe of northern Patagonia for a 1650-kilometre stretch between Esquel and El Maitén.

Panama Railroad The Panama or Trans-Isthmian railroad was the first railway to cross the American continent between the Atlantic and Pacific oceans when it was completed in 1855 at great financial and human cost. It now runs through pristine rainforests alongside the Panama Canal and has recently reopened as a tourist attraction, making it one of the best ways to experience that most impressive of waterways.

Uyuni to Calama Running from the railway junction of Uyuni in Bolivia, this route runs across the dramatic, bleak lunar landscape of the high Altiplano, passing the southern edge of the Salar de Uyuni, the world's largest salt lake and between snowcapped volcanic peaks before crossing the border and descending to the Chilean town of Calama.

Boats

Travelling by boat can be one of the most exciting ways to get around Latin America. In some regions – particularly among the many off-shore archipelagos along the Pacific and Atlantic coasts and throughout the Amazon Basin – it's often the only way of getting around without flying, and is usually cheaper than taking a plane. There's a huge range of memorable boat journeys you can make in vessels ranging from the modest motorized dug-out canoes which ply the Amazon backwaters to luxury tourist yachts and ships which cruise around the Galápagos Islands and the glaciers of Patagonia. Whatever kind of boat trip you take, however, bear the following points in mind:

- Be sure to take a sun hat, sunscreen and sunglasses, as reflected light off the water increases the effect of the sun while cool breezes can disguise its intensity.
- It gets cold at sea, so keep warm clothing close at hand. Waterproof clothing is also a good idea on sea, lake and river trips, as even if it's not raining, you can easily get soaked by spray.
- It's a good idea to take seasickness pills with you for sea voyages, even if you've never suffered before.
- Even if you're a strong swimmer, it is best to make sure life jackets are available before you depart. As with other forms of transport, boats are often overloaded, and accidents do happen. Providing life jackets is a legal requirement for public carriers in most countries, but one that is sometimes ignored.
- Put cameras and other valuables in plastic bags or other waterproof containers to protect them.
- On longer trips, take your own food and water, as the quality of what's available on board can be poor. Boats sometimes break down

Best boat trips

Amazon canoe trips For a closer look at Amazonian wildlife, you can't beat a trip in a motorized dugout canoe along one of the minor tributaries in the Upper Amazon – you can do this either by travelling in a canoe used for local transport, as part of an organized rainforest tour, or by hiring a boat yourself (though the high fuel consumption of outboard motors means this is expensive unless you're sharing the cost with several other travellers). Perhaps the most spectacular of these journeys is the trip down the Alto Madre de Dios and up the Río Manu into the pristine Manu National Park in southern Peru.

Galápagos cruise A week-long cruise exploring the unique and astonishing wildlife of the Galápagos Islands, 900km off the coast of Ecuador, is one of the world's finest boat trips, though the cost may stretch your budget to the breaking point.

Panama Canal A one-day cruise along the Panama Canal is the best way of appreciating the magnitude and surprisingly rugged beauty of one of the greatest engineering feats of all time. With a little luck you might even get taken on as a line handler on a yacht and be paid for the privilege of sailing down the canal.

San Rafael Glacier The 200-kilometre trip from the port of Chacabuco through the spectacular fjords and islands of southern Chile and along the seemingly unnavigable Río Tempranos into the iceberg-choked Laguna San Rafael, at the foot of the giant glacier of the same name, is one of South America's most magical boat journeys.

or get delayed by bad weather or other factors, so your journey may take longer than expected.

- On long river trips in the Amazon, you should take along your own hammock for sleeping in, ideally fitted with a mosquito net – both are available in most river ports. Most boat captains will let you sleep on board for a day or two while waiting for departure – a good way to save money on hotels.
- For Amazon river trips you may have to wait around a day or two (or longer in remote towns) for a departure. The naval port authority office can usually tell you which boat is likely to leave first.

City transport

Getting around the teeming cities of Latin America can be an intimidating experience. Most have grown incredibly quickly in recent decades, and underfunded and overloaded public transport systems struggle to cope with the near-impossible task of moving millions of people around every day. The capitals of more developed countries like Buenos Aires or Mexico City boast modern subway systems, but in most Latin American cities urban transport is dominated by a seemingly chaotic array of buses and minibuses.

However, despite any initial bewilderment, after a few days you'll most likely be able to work out which routes will take you where you need to go. Indeed the process of finding your way around by public transport can be a great way of exploring a new city, even if it means getting on the wrong bus a few times. If all this seems too daunting, or you're short on time or concerned about security, you'll be better off relying on taxis. These are generally plentiful and inexpensive, particularly if you are sharing the fare with one or more other travellers.

Local buses

Most Latin American cities are served by a mixture of large and small buses – often former US school buses or ageing colossuses which lumber around belching diesel fumes as they ferry people in and out of town from outlying suburbs. These are supplemented by an ever-increasing number of minibuses and vans known as *combis*, *micros* or *colectivos*, which race around shorter fixed routes, picking up passengers at every street corner.

Fares on all these vehicles are extremely low, but finding out which one will take you where you want to go can be very difficult – official bus stops are rare, and even then they're unlikely to display details of which buses stop there; bus timetables or maps of local services are even harder to come by, if they exist at all. Details of transport to popular tourist destinations, however, should be fairly easy to come by – ask at the local tourist office or in your hotel, or check your guidebook. Many buses have their main destinations written on the windscreen, while their conductors or fare collectors (often children) hang out of the open door at every stop shouting their destinations at the top of their voices. Drivers, conductors and other passengers are generally helpful, though rush-hour commuters around the world aren't known for their patience and Latin America is no exception. The following tips should help you survive the chaos:

● Before you set off, find out the fare system and how to pay.
● Carry plenty of small-denomination coins or notes, as getting change can be a nightmare.
● Give yourself as much time as you can and keep calm and you'll soon be nipping around town like a local. Don't worry too much about getting lost, as this is often part of learning to find your way around.
● Be wary of pickpockets and thieves who use razors or sharp knives to cut luggage straps and bags. Keep your valuables hidden away.
● Most buses and minibuses don't have room for any luggage: if you occupy space that could be filled by another passenger you'll be expected to pay double. If you're travelling with large bags you're better off taking a taxi for security reasons anyway.

Taxis

Taxis are plentiful and relatively inexpensive throughout Latin America – prices vary between cities and countries, but generally speaking a taxi ride in a city centre never costs more than a few dollars, offering a fast, convenient and relatively safe way of getting around, particularly if you're sharing the cost with one or more other passengers. In wealthier countries and larger cities taxis are licensed and marked as such, and have radio controllers, but in many places anyone with a car can become a taxi driver simply by putting a sign in the windscreen of their private car – often the two types of cab operate alongside each other.

Informal taxis tend to be cheaper but less reliable. Many Latin Americans from all walks of life moonlight as taxi drivers in their private cars to supplement their meagre incomes, which can make for far more interesting conversation than you usually get from taxi drivers at home. The Peruvian capital Lima, in particular, lays claim to having the best-educated taxi drivers in the world, and it's not unusual to find a doctor or university professor behind the wheel of your cab.

If you're travelling with heavy luggage, particularly when you've first arrived – and above all at night – it's a good idea to take a taxi straight to your hotel and dump your bags rather than risking public transport – think of the fare as an insurance policy. It's not unknown for taxis to be used by criminals as a means of robbing unwary passengers, but you can reduce the risk of this by telephoning for a cab from a reputable company. If your luggage is in the boot, it's best not to get out of the car until the driver does, as he or she may be tempted to drive away with your bags. In some cities taxis are equipped with meters, but otherwise fares are based on distance or a zone system, though they're generally negotiable. There's a strong tendency to overcharge foreign tourists, so it's best to agree the fare before you set off. You can get an idea of how much it should cost by asking other travellers or at your hotel. Fares tend to increase late at night and during public holidays, and taxis to or from international airports (see pp.245–246) usually charge fixed and relatively high fares. In some cities, special tourist taxis congregate outside upmarket hotels and major tourist attractions; these tend to charge far more than ordinary taxis.

If you want to see a lot of sights in a short time, it can be a good idea to hire a taxi for a few hours or a day (or even longer; see below) to take you around town – you can usually negotiate a reasonable rate, especially where business is slow, and with luck you may even find that your driver acts as a good impromptu tour guide.

In some countries taxis are treated almost as a form of public transport: fares are charged per person, and you may be asked to share your cab with a stranger, though you can always refuse this if it makes you uncomfortable. In some places you'll also find collective taxis (*colectivos*), which run along fixed routes picking up and dropping off passengers rather like a bus.

Motorbike taxis

In some cities and towns – especially in towns in the Amazon with poor or no road connections to the outside world – motor-bikes operate as taxis, offering an exciting but risky way of getting around. These are always cheaper than cars and often faster, and are a good option if you're travelling alone. Obviously they can't carry much luggage, though that rarely stops them trying – if you have a backpack you may have to carry it on your back while riding pillion, which is uncomfortable and precarious. Always negotiate the fare before you get on, as with conventional taxis, and always use a helmet if one is available.

Vehicle rental

Renting a car is relatively expensive in Latin America but does offer the freedom to visit areas that are otherwise difficult or impossible to reach by public transport. Costs vary between countries and regions, but generally speaking you'll be looking at around US$30–50 per day for a small car; much more for a large car or four-wheel drive (4WD). Most capitals have branches of international rental companies such as Hertz, Budget and Avis, which means you can book your vehicle in advance from home, but these places are usually more expensive than local companies. As with pretty much everything in Latin America, prices are flexible, so shop around for a good deal and be prepared to negotiate. Obviously sharing the cost and the driving with one or more other travellers makes renting a car cheaper and more attractive. To rent a car you'll need to be over 25 and to have an international driving licence. You'll also need a credit card or large quantity of cash as a deposit. Many companies require you to take out additional vehicle insurance as well as third party, so make sure you read the small print and know exactly what is covered and what you may be liable for in case of an accident.

Buying a car is only really a worthwhile option if you're staying in one country for a long time, ideally as a resident rather than on a tourist visa, and even then it involves considerable hassle, especially when you come to sell it at the end of your stay. It's possible to drive from the US into Mexico (beyond the immediate border area; see p.152) and on into Central America, but this involves considerable expense and bureaucratic hassle; shipping a car to Latin America entails even more trouble and expense, and really isn't worth it unless you absolutely must have your own vehicle.

If you do want to travel by car, consider hiring a local taxi driver to take you around for a daily rate rather than renting and driving yourself. This doesn't usually cost much more than renting a car, even though you'll have to pay for the driver's meals and accommodation costs on longer trips, and it means you can sit back and enjoy the scenery rather than concentrate on driving and worry about insurance and additional costs if anything goes wrong. A local driver will probably know the way (or be better at asking if he or she doesn't), and will often have good suggestions about side trips; with any luck, the driver will also offer a useful insight into the local area and people. If you do decide to drive yourself, the following tips should help:

- Make sure you know the legal speed limits and other requirements, and be aware that many local drivers regularly ignore road signs and traffic regulations, and may not even have driving licences, never mind insurance.
- Find out the local rules of the road. Your guidebook should have some information about these, although be aware that Latin American drivers often show scant regard for official rules – watch how people drive before attempting it yourself.
- Inspect the rental vehicle carefully before you accept it and make a note, signed by the owner, of any scratches or dents, so you don't get charged for these when you return it.
- Check things you would take for granted on a rental vehicle at home: the lights, horn, windscreen wipers, door locks, petrol cap, seatbelts, and so on.
- Make sure you know how to open the bonnet (hood) and check the spare tyre, jack and tool kit.
- Read the small print on the contract carefully, checking what the insurance covers and what the excess is – the amount you'll have to pay in case of an accident.
- Carry your passport, licence and all documents related to the vehicle with you at all times, as you'll often have to show them to police at roadblocks and impromptu checks. Failure to do so can lead to a bureaucratic nightmare, or at least having to pay a bribe.
- Make sure the rental agency gives you a 24-hour emergency telephone number.

- Secure parking is often a problem, so stay in hotels with garages or car parks. Don't leave a parked vehicle unattended for long, and never leave anything valuable in it. In many cities street children offer to watch over cars in return for a small tip, a service that's well worth taking up.
- Pay close attention when you buy gas, and make particularly sure that the pump gauge has returned to zero before you're served.

Motorbikes

Motorbikes are rarely available for rent in Latin America, and when they are it's usually on an informal basis, often from the same people who act as motorbike taxi drivers. All the tips for driving a car in Latin America also apply to motorbikes, with the added proviso that driver and passenger should always wear helmets and cover up, even if not required to by law. Pillion passengers also need to be careful to avoid leg burns from the exhaust pipe. Be aware that unpaved roads are difficult to ride on and can be very unpredictable, turning from dust to mud depending on weather conditions. Riding a motorbike in Latin America is not for beginners.

Bicycles

Bicycles are available to rent in a growing number of tourist centres in Latin America, with the emphasis particularly on downhill mountain biking, which involves taking a bus or truck ride up to a high pass on a mountain road and riding down the other side. This is easiest to do on a guided excursion with a tour agency, but you can easily do it yourself by renting the bike and using public transport. Unsurprisingly the Andean countries – Ecuador, Peru, Bolivia, Chile and Argentina – are the best and most popular places to do this, as they feature innumerable downhill rides, including some of the longest, most exciting and most scenic descents in the world.

For longer trips you're better off bringing your own bike from home, as buying a good-quality bike or renting one for long periods is likely to end up costing you more. Most airlines are happy to carry a bike, often for no extra fee, if you ask them in advance and pack the bike in a bike box. You should bring the best machine you can afford, plus extras like panniers, lights and a strong lock; make sure you also bring plenty of spare parts, and ensure that you're capable of carrying out minor repairs yourself. Though dust, wind, rain, heat, high altitude and unpaved roads mean bicycle touring is often hard work, it is nonetheless one of the most enjoyable ways of travelling around at a slow pace, giving plenty of contact with local people and allowing you to go pretty much at your own pace. If the going gets too hard, you can always stick your bike on top of a bus and relax for a while. For more information, see *Latin America by Bike, A Complete Touring Guide*, by Walter Sienko (Mountaineers Books, US, 1993).

Though common in smaller towns, suburbs and rural areas, bicycles are rarely used as a means of getting around in larger towns or cities, as almost no provision is made for cyclists and the snarling traffic makes riding very dangerous. If you do decide to ride a bike, whether for a day's easy riding, for a hardcore downhill run or for some long-distance touring, bear the following in mind:

- If you rent a bike, try it out before parting with your money, carefully checking the wheels, brakes and gears, and making sure the seat is set at the right height.

△ Mountain biking in Bolivia

- Most rental bikes come without lights, so be sure to get back before nightfall.
- Protect yourself from the sun and carry plenty of water – cycling is thirsty work.
- Ride defensively, as most drivers will behave as if you don't exist.
- Carry a pump and a puncture-repair kit or spare inner tubes.
- Local mechanics are usually masters of improvisation when it comes to fixing bikes, but spare parts are difficult to come by, so if you're bringing a bike from home, bring plenty of spares.

Hitchhiking

The cost of transport in Latin America is so low that hitching isn't really necessary for tourists, though in out-of-the-way places when the last bus has gone, no taxis are available and there's still a long way to go to your hotel it can become the only option. In such circumstances, local drivers who pick you up will anyway expect you to pay something close to what the bus fare would have been – the distinction between public and private transport is a hazy one in Latin America, and in remote regions private vehicles often carry paying passengers. Hitchhiking on roads where public transport is also available is unlikely to get you far for free and involves a greater degree of risk than doing the same thing at home. If you must hitch, never do so alone and, if you're a woman, never do so unaccompanied by a man. Don't suspend the instincts that keep you safe at home, and if you are in any way suspicious of a person offering you a lift, don't get into the vehicle.

Walking

With all these different means of transport available, don't forget the simplest and cheapest way of all – whether it's a short stroll around a city centre or a long hike in the mountains, walking is one of the best ways to enjoy Latin America and take in the sights. If you are planning to do much walking it's a good idea to bring hiking boots or at least robust walking shoes with you. When walking around in towns and cities, be very cautious when crossing roads, as Latin American drivers show scant regard for pedestrians and often ignore road signals. For longer walks in rural areas – even for just a few hours – it's important to be properly equipped with warm clothing, rain gear and/or sun protection, as well as food and plenty of water.

Organized tours

Throughout Latin America there are an ever-increasing number of national and local tour companies and travel agents offering all manner of organized trips, from brief city tours to hardcore wilderness adventures. You may leave home swearing to do everything independently, but once you're in Latin America you'll often find it's easy, convenient and relatively inexpensive to go on an organized trip. They're a particularly good way of visiting remote attractions that are otherwise difficult to reach – indeed, many of Latin America's finest attractions can only realistically be reached on a guided tour. Going with a local guide who knows the area and speaks the language can also make it far easier to visit regions where foreigners might otherwise be treated with suspicion or worse, and by acting as a mediator a good guide can give a much better insight into the lives of local people than you'll get travelling on your own.

Many tour companies also offer a range of excellent activities that are very difficult to do on your own or which require specialist equipment that you're unlikely to be carrying in your backpack, such as climbing, trekking, mountain biking, kayaking and white-water rafting. If you're contemplating taking an organized tour, bear the following in mind:

- A day or half-day city tour can be a very good way of orienting yourself in a place before setting out to explore on your own, and allows you to see far more than you'd manage in the same time travelling by public transport.
- Unless you have abundant cash, experience and equipment, an organized tour is often the only way to reach many of Latin America's most beautiful national parks and other remote wilderness areas.
- Not all tours are luxurious (and therefore expensive) – indeed many are budget trips aimed squarely at backpackers with limited cash.
- Going on an organized tour means you get to share the expense of things like local guides and boat or jeep hire which would end up costing you a fortune of you tried to do it on your own.
- With longer trips, be sure to find out the full details of the itinerary and exactly what's included before you sign up – make sure, for

instance, that a "four-day trip" doesn't leave after lunch on the first day and return early in the morning on the fourth.

● In popular tourist centres, tour agencies tend to be very competitive, so shopping around can get you a good deal. The best way to find out which agencies are reliable and have good guides is by asking other travellers who have just returned from a similar trip to the one you want to go on.

11

Accommodation

Some of your best and worst memories will be of the hotels or hostels you stayed in – these aren't just places to sleep, but also where you'll make contact with other travellers, where you'll hang out whilst recovering from long journeys or bouts of illness, or where you'll retreat to if you simply can't face the outside world or it's pouring with rain. Finding somewhere good to stay is a real bonus and might even shape your itinerary: it can be difficult to leave a place if you've made friends, if the hotel café has food you've been craving or you have a room with a great view for almost nothing. Conversely, if you've heard that a place has nowhere decent to stay, you'll probably be tempted to drop it from your plans.

Accommodation in Latin America ranges in price from a few dollars a night in a basic Guatemalan or Bolivian hostel up to several hundred in one of Mexico's chic *haciendas* or a flash hotel in Rio or Buenos Aires. However, it doesn't always follow that the cheapest countries to travel in have the best-value hotels: in general, the lack of demand and competition means that rooms in less-visited places will often be less keenly priced and often of a lower standard than places in popular tourist centres, which are usually packed with affordable and attractive hostels and hotels.

Accommodation costs will be a major part of your expenditure if you're on a tight budget. Even so, in Latin America you'll have the chance to stay in some amazing places for a fraction of the price you'd pay back home, and it would be a shame to miss out. Not only that, but there's nothing more guaranteed to restore the spirits after a few days of rough travelling than a decent hotel room with comfortable beds and an en-suite bathroom – try and factor the occasional posh hotel into your budget before you set out. If you're on a moderate budget you'll have a lot more choice, obviously – the difference between a US$10 room and a US$20 can be surprisingly large, although the downside of staying in mid-range hotels is that you might find yourself rather cut off from other travellers. At over US$20 per day, you can expect something very comfortable indeed, with all the modern amenities, including air conditioning, television and phone.

Finding somewhere to stay

The last thing you'll feel like doing when you stumble off a plane or bus at the end of a long journey is finding somewhere to stay. This is where a bit of pre-planning can save you unnecessary hassle, and where a good guidebook is at its most useful. Study the town map in your guidebook first and choose an area which has several appealing hotels close together so that if your first choice isn't right you can easily check out others – hotel accommodation is often clustered conveniently either around the major bus station or in the town centre.

It's important to remember, though, that guidebooks aren't infallible, since they rarely have enough space to list every hotel in town and inevitably go out of date between new editions. Once you get on the road, the travellers' network is the most up-to-date source of information about good accommodation. In particular, notice boards and visitors' books in gringo hangouts like hostels and Internet cafés usually have personal recommendations of places to stay.

At popular tourist destinations, you might be met by touts at the bus station. These will often be boys, and in most cases they're genuine and helpful, either taking you to a relative's hotel or to a hotel where the patron will give them a small fee for each guest checked in. Don't be instantly suspicious – many of the places you'll be shown will be fine, and if you don't like the place, you shouldn't be under any pressure to stay – and if you're lucky they might take you to an excellent local guesthouse not listed in any guidebook which you wouldn't otherwise have found. In addition, touts can also save you the bother of reading a map and finding your way around an unfamiliar town (although of course you should always try to keep your wits about you and retain some sense of where you are). The usual common sense applies when deciding whether or not to go with a tout: if it's the middle of the night, if you're on your own or if you just don't like the look of the tout, then politely refuse their services. You should be more wary of airport cab drivers in large cities, however, who are notorious for telling tourists that the place they're going to doesn't exist or is dangerous, and then suggesting other hotels, many of which are overpriced or miles out of the way (but which pay commission to the driver).

However you intend to find a hotel, it's best to arrive as early as possible at your destination – this will give you plenty of time to orientate yourself and find somewhere you like. Arriving early will also enhance your chances of getting into the better places – popular backpackers' hostels, particularly those in areas with little competition, often fill up as soon as the previous night's occupants have checked out, often around noon. It's worth phoning these places in advance to see if there's room before you go to the trouble of turning up in person. Looking for a hotel in the dark isn't much fun either – if your bus arrives in the early hours of the morning it might be safer to wait until daylight in the bus station (many stay open all night) before you begin your search. It's also worth waiting since if you check in before the dawn (usually 5–6am) you may have to pay for a whole night.

There are also times in certain towns during big festivals or public holidays (see pp.194–198) when every room gets booked out months in advance. If you're planning on visiting during these times, try to sort out accommodation as far in advance as you can. If you haven't done this, however, don't despair: enterprising locals often respond to tourist influxes by offering visitors rooms in their homes or turning their gardens into campsites.

Types of accommodation

Accommodation in Latin America covers a wide spectrum, from five-star hotels to backpacker dormitories; these are detailed below, in roughly descending order of expense.

Five-star hotels and boutique hotels

Latin America's five-star hotels tend to be part of international chains and are usually located in the hotel zones of capital cities and expensive tourist resorts such as Cancún in Mexico. Often looking like large tower blocks with hundreds of rooms, they have no shortage of creature comforts but little in the way of identifiable Latin American personality – you could be anywhere in the world.

Boutique hotels are a more attractive option, though rarely within the budget traveller's price range (many cost US$150 or over a night). These are always small, beautifully decorated – some by famous interior designers – and elegantly luxurious. Most boutique hotels are located in well-known areas of outstanding natural beauty, classy seaside resorts and quiet colonial towns. Some of the loveliest are restored *haciendas* in Mexico's Yucatán Peninsula.

Eco-lodges and estancias

Each year, more and more eco-lodges open for business in Latin America. These have become the region's quintessential accommodation choice, especially feted for their well chosen locations and convenient holiday packages which offer full board plus guided walks and other outdoor activities. Many are situated in places of great natural beauty or private wilderness reserves and the best really are worth splashing out for. Their remoteness means that you'll be expected to book in advance, partly so that you can be given a lift to the lodge. In theory, eco-lodges are environmentally friendly, though this is not always the case in practice – look out for those personally run by conservationists and ecologists. Eco-lodges tend to be on the expensive side, although some have a range of accommodation with much cheaper options, often in dormitories.

Another way of getting off the beaten track – and a distinctively Latin American one at that – is to stay at an estancia in Uruguay, Argentina and Chile. These are working cattle ranches where you can join in the daily life of the farm, riding round on horses and seeing the local gauchos (cowboys) at work. Although not cheap, estancias are usually fairly posh (often similar in style to a big farmhouse), and all meals are included in the price – you may also get treated to an *asado* (barbecue), with delicious beef roasted on a spit over an open fire.

Some of our favourite places to stay

- *El Panchan* is an eclectic collection of cabins and camping sites, individually run, close to the Mayan ruin of Palenque in southern Mexico. With a peaceful forest setting and New Age vibes, this is a great place to explore the mystical side of Mayan culture or just to soak up the chilled out atmosphere.

- The river pools of Semuc Champey are one of Guatemala's natural highlights and in the nearby village of Lanquin, *El Retiro* hostel has its own pretty setting in meadows by the river. Dorms are basic but the communal space is very attractive with great Gringo breakfasts and happy hour drinking sessions that run long into the night.

- In the highland Honduran village of Copán Ruinas (named after the ruined Mayan city close by), *Hacienda San Lucas* is a wonderful converted farmhouse with cosy rooms, delicious food and an engaging hostess.

- At one end of Little Corn Island, off the Caribbean coast of Nicaragua, the individual cabins of the *Hotel Casa Iguana* perch on the cliffs – most rooms are spacious and have porches with hammocks. Evening meals, held family-style in the hotel's reception lodge, are a great way to meet other travellers and swap stories

- *Reserva Selva Bananito*, on the Caribbean coast of Costa Rica between Puerto Limón and Cahuita, is a private rainforest reserve run by a family determined to protect their piece of the forest from loggers. With nothing but trees and dense vegetation as far as the eye can see, there's not much to do but swim, ride, climb trees, hike, or simply kick back and enjoy the green peace.

- Bizarrely situated in the metallic tower of a former US radar station, *Canopy Lodge* in central Panama sits high above the forest with bright comfortable rooms and superb birdwatching. The *Lodge* is especially popular in March and October, the migrating seasons of hawks and vultures, who pass over in their thousands.

- Some travellers end up staying for several weeks rather than days at the *Platypus* hostel in Bogotá, Colombia. The dormitory rooms are basic but the hostel's owner, German Escobar, is a mine of valuable information about the whole country, which makes this place an essential port of call if you're going to Colombia.

- One of Venezuela's loveliest stretches of beach, Playa Cepe on the northwest Caribbean coast, is the location for *Posada Puerto Escondido*.

Pensiones, residenciales and hospedajes

Latin America's mid-range and cheap hotels go under a bewildering variety of names: *pensión*, *posada*, *albergue*, *residenciale* and *hospedaje*.

Reached only by boat, the colonial house is set in a cacao plantation and you can arrange to snorkel or dive with the owner who is a dive master.

● *Karanambo*, the largest ranch in the Rupununi area of Guyana is also the first to offer nature-based tourism. Its owner, Diane McTurk, is known for her work rehabilitating the local giant river otters and boat trips to watch them play makes the long trip to the isolated ranch worthwhile.

● *Black Sheep Inn* is an eco-friendly guesthouse whose owners have a strong commitment to the environment. Lodging is in adobe huts, water and waste are all recycled and the food is organically grown in the inn's garden. The inn also has a stunning setting in the dramatic scenery of Ecuador's Central Sierra of Ecuador and is close to crater lakes, sleepy Andean villages and perfectly shaped Cotopaxi volcano.

● *Albergue Ecologico Chalalán*, Parque Nacional Madidi, Bolivia, was established as part of a sustainable living project for local people and is owned and managed by the Quechua-Tacana community of the Tuichi River. Rooms are in traditional Tacana style, with thatched wooden cabins and solar-powered energy, and the lodge overlooks a lake teeming with birdlife.

● *Hacienda Los Lingues* is possibly the grandest hotel in Chile. Still inhabited by the aristocratic family that owns it, staying here is much more like being a visitor in a large country house than a hotel guest. Rooms are furnished with antiques and family portraits, there are wine cellars, a chapel and library on site – all well used. The *hacienda* also breeds some of the finest horses in South America so there are plenty of horse-riding opportunities as well as trout fishing, visits to local wine estates and use of the swimming pool and tennis courts. Rates are high but weekend special offers are sometimes available.

● There are numerous eco-lodges in Brazil's Pantanal but *Réfugio Ecológico Caiman* is the most luxurious. Vast grounds host its own air strip and numerous activities for guests – nocturnal safaris, boat trips and cattle-drives.

● Close to the gaucho stronghold of San Antonio de Areco in Argentina's pampas is one of the country's loveliest estancias (cattle ranches), *La Bamba*. The main building is a classic example of early eighteenth-century rural architecture and one of the rooms for visitors is an adjoining watchtower. The Rio Areco runs through the grounds, so that guests can fish if they're bored of riding, and there's also a large swimming pool.

These names are often fairly meaningless, however, covering fairly basic establishments as well as some rather fancy examples. If you're using a guidebook to select a hotel, room rates are a much more useful indication of the type of service you should expect. The most commonly used name for this sort of cheap to mid-range accommodation is *pensión* (in Brazil, *pensão*) – these are usually small, reasonably priced guesthouses run by local families; they invariably have a lot more character than bigger hotels. Rooms vary enormously in quality, though you should get your own bathroom, towels and soap and have your room cleaned daily. Rates sometimes include breakfast.

Residenciales and *hospedajes* are generally cheap hotels with a range of accommodation in dormitories and double and single rooms. Many have shared bathrooms only, fairly basic facilities and desultory cleaning. Guests are usually a mixture of budget travellers and young locals on holiday.

Backpacker hostels

It's likely that you'll end up staying at least some of the time in a backpacker hostel – a place geared to the needs of foreign travellers on a budget (though they're not nearly as common in Latin America as they are in Asia, and as soon as you leave established tourist routes they are few and far between). As well as having some of the most competitively priced accommodation in town (usually a mixture of singles, doubles and dormitories), they're also a major source of information, with English-speaking staff, travellers' noticeboards and Internet access.

△ Eco-lodge, Kapawi Lagoon, Ecuador

In general, backpacker hostels offer a good way to ease your way into Latin America – or to retreat to if the going gets tough. Almost all offer good value for money and have staff who are used to dealing with budget travellers. Many also have lively on-site cafés with all the things you've been missing from home on the menu – bacon sandwiches, proper vegetarian food, pasta (even if you're staying elsewhere you'll usually be welcome to come in and check the noticeboard or visit the café). Don't assume, however, that these places are automatically cleaner or more comfortable than other hotels, and in terms of security you should look after your possessions as you would in any other hotel, and with particular care if you're sharing a dormitory.

Youth hostels

Youth hostels (*albergues juveniles* or *albergues de la juventad*) exist in Mexico, Costa Rica, Argentina, Uruguay and Chile, which all have youth hostels affiliated to the International Youth Hostel Association (⊛ www.iyha.org); if you have an IYHA card you'll be entitled to a discount. Standards vary, but most youth hostels are similar to those worldwide, with bunk beds in dormitories, shared cooking facilities and decent rates (under US$15 a night). Many travellers eschew youth hostels in favour of backpacker hostels (see above),

Home stays in Nicaragua

I arrived in El Castillo, a village on the Río San Juan in Nicaragua, intending to stay in a hotel. Over breakfast at a small café, the owner helpfully ran me through the various options. "And finally," he said, "if you want somewhere really clean for a good price you should stay with Doña Luisa, my wife's aunt." Doña Luisa had the prettiest house in the place, green- and blue-painted clapboard with potted plants in every corner. Though not a hotelier, she was happy to earn a little extra by putting up the occasional tourist – she gave me her absent youngest daughter's bedroom, which had a poster of the Back Street Boys on the wall, a shelf of white teddy bears and a pile of well-thumbed teen mags. It also had a priceless view right over the river and all for US$5 a night. Thinking I might be bored in the sleepy village, Luisa introduced me to her brother-in-law, who took me on a horse ride over the hills, and to one of her neighbours, who tried to teach me to fish. In the evening she cooked a delicious meal of freshwater lobster and home-made tortillas, while her husband Luis, home from his farm, talked of the old days, of shooting tigres (jaguars) in the woods and paddling a canoe downriver for two days to reach the nearest settlement – now a mere two-and-a-half-hour ride in a motorboat. When I left I knew I'd seen a slice of Nicaraguan life I couldn't have experienced in any hotel – and that I'd contributed directly to the local economy.

Polly Rodger Brown

though the former are often just as good value and a better place to meet young Latin Americans.

Dormitorios

Virtually every town in Latin America has one cheap hotel or *dormitorió* – these are often semi-permanent homes to migrant (male) workers who share rooms, string their washing through the corridors and stomp noisily off to work at four in the morning. Although you'll be welcome and rates will be very low, you might feel intimidated if you're female and you shouldn't expect high standards of hygiene – particularly in the shared bathroom. Occasionally, the town *dormitorió* is not just unsalubrious but also dangerous – in all cases, inspect the premises, management and clientele if possible before you check in, and if you don't feel safe, don't stay.

Rooms in private houses

Home stays – staying with a local family in their own home (*casas privadas*) – are popular in some parts of Latin America, particularly Guatemala and Nicaragua. This is a relatively cheap option (approximately US$10 for full board and lodging, or less than US$5 for room only), which contributes directly to local communities and – depending on the family set-up, of course, and how long you stay for – gives an insight into daily family life that you might not otherwise get.

Home stays are usually arranged in combination with a language course, so that you can practise what you've learnt outside the classroom, though it's also possible to arrange a home stay for a night or two without studying – either contact a language school in the area you're interested in, ask at the local tourist office for a list of local home stays, or look out for signs on private homes which say *hay cuartos, cuartos para alquilar, se alquila cuartos* (rooms to rent). Some home stays are formal arrangements where you'll get a room and have little or no contact with the family involved while in others, particularly those used by language schools, you'll eat three meals a day with your family, have your clothes washed and even go on outings with family members. In most cases, rooms in private homes are simple but scrupulously clean.

In various parts of Latin America without accommodation for tourists (such as the Solentiname Archipelego in Nicaragua) there might be an informal network of home stays. In this case you'll be met on arrival by family members, often children, who'll take you to their home – and if not, you could try asking around. You shouldn't assume, however, that families will always be willing to take in tourists if you offer to pay – where this is not the norm don't insist or you'll risk causing offence.

Short-stay hotels

Short-stay hotels, which charge by the hour and are euphemistically called "love hotels" or motels, exist all over Latin America. They're usually found on the outskirts of towns and advertise themselves with gaudy neon signs and lurid names. If you get stuck with nowhere to stay, don't rule out motels – the staff won't turn you away, and while they won't have the cheapest rates in town, rooms are often good value for money, with en-suite bathrooms and (not surprisingly) comfortable double beds.

Other hotels in Latin America used for short-stays include cheap hotels, particularly those situated around bus stations or the local market, which double up as informal brothels – this should be fairly obvious when you walk in though, again, you're unlikely to be turned away if you want to stay for the whole night. While some of these places are deeply insalubrious, others are clean and safe, if rather noisy.

Camping and sleeping in a hammock

Camping is obviously one of the cheapest forms of accommodation, although the inevitable hassle of having to carry a tent, sleeping bags, mats and cooking equipment might outweigh the savings you make. Remember too that organized campsites only exist in significant numbers in Costa Rica and the countries of southern South America (Brazil, Uruguay, Argentina and Chile). In these countries, where accommodation is relatively expensive and camping is popular with young locals as well as tourists, it's well worth considering – although also bear in mind that the south of Argentina and Chile are freezing cold in the winter (June–Sept). If, on the other hand, you're only going to the region's cheaper

Amazon accommodation

By mid-afternoon, on the first full day of my boat journey from Iquitos to Yurimaguas, the air was still and the deck had become uncomfortably hot. I tried to sleep because I couldn't bear to do anything else, but the children in the hammock "next door" had become restless. The baby was cranky, and in trying to cheer her up her older siblings had become rambunctious, banging me every so often, starting the domino effect; I banged my travelling companion, and he banged the next person, and so on. With so many hammocks crammed into such a small deck area, there was a lot of banging going on. Once in a while a little foot would pop over into my hammock, then an arm. Then I felt tiny little hands below me – the baby was underfoot, with her hair in a ponytail straight up on her head. Suddenly she was swept up and put in the hammock and covered up as if in a cocoon, where she squealed with delight, content with her game of hide-and-seek. Meanwhile her father slept beneath me on his plastic tarp, his head resting on my backpack. It was a lesson in patience, typical of Amazon journeys. Everyone pokes and prods and everyone gets poked and prodded, and people are amazingly tolerant. At bedtime, I realized my neighbours had shifted in such a way that their hammock (holding four of them) was practically on top of me. They were fast asleep, and I could feel the weight of their bodies no matter which way I turned. There was nowhere to go but up, so I raised my hammock and happily drifted off to sleep, no matter that I was completely lopsided.

Julie Feiner

Andean countries like Bolivia or Peru, then it's only really worth taking a tent if you're planning on doing a lot of trekking, given the cheapness of accommodation, the lack of proper campsites, and the challenging mountain temperatures. Likely locations for campsites are seaside resorts, national parks and popular scenic areas. Backpacker or youth hostels (see above) with gardens often keep some space free for tents.

Camping in the wild isn't recommended, since you risk upsetting local landowners (unless you specifically ask permission) and you put yourself at risk of robbery or attack. Never camp on a beach unless it's standard practice to do so. The exception is if you're on a guided trek, since you'll have safety in numbers and your guide should be able to find a good secure base for the night.

Even cheaper than camping is using a hammock. These are ubiquitous in many parts of Latin America – and if you're planning any long river trips you'll need to take your own. Hostels and other cheap hotels sometimes have a dedicated space for travellers to hang their hammocks or will be happy to let you hang it in a corridor, yard or garden for a few dollars a night. Laid-back beach resorts like Tulum in Mexico will have sets of bamboo huts or *cabañas* on the beach furnished with nothing but a pair of hammock hooks. Remember that you'll need to sleep diagonally across a hammock rather than along it if you want to avoid backache, so you'll need one that's a decent size – ask for a *matrimonial* (or couple-sized) hammock.

Inspecting the facilities

Never take a room without inspecting it first. Obviously, if you don't like a room you're shown you're under no obligation to stay, but try to avoid being rude when you leave in case, for any reason, you have to come back.

- Ask if the room you're being shown is the best room they have available. Hotel staff will often show potential guests the worst or most expensive room available first in the hope of getting rid of it. If you don't like the room you're being offered or can't afford the rate, ask to see another one – it's surprising how much rooms in the same hotel can vary in size and price.
- Try to avoid rooms next to shared bathrooms or communal areas unless you fancy spending your entire time listening to the sound of flushing toilets or blaring televisions.
- Check if the bathroom is clean, particularly if it's shared – some are filthy enough to put you off immediately. Also ask if there's hot water and for how long each day, and find out whether towels, soap and toilet paper are provided.
- Sit on the bed to see how comfortable it is – beds in cheap hotels often have thin foam mattresses which sag terribly and give you chronic backache if you stay for several nights.
- If there's a fan or air conditioning (fairly essential in a hot climate), turn it on to see that it works without sounding like a traction engine.
- Is the room secure? Make sure the windows close properly, particularly if you're on the ground floor, and that the room can be properly locked.
- Check whether there's a curfew: if you're out on the town, you might not be able to get back in until morning.

Room rates and checking in

Although room rates vary enormously, you ought to be able to find a bed in a hostel dormitory for US$10–15 per night in the most expensive countries in Latin America, while in the cheapest, the same sum will get you a comfortable en-suite room in a small hotel with breakfast included. Don't assume that room rates are standard across a country (sometimes a popular seaside resort will charge twice as much for its rooms as a small mountain village, or vice versa), and don't be surprised if the rates quoted in your guidebook no longer exist – waving your book at a bemused hotel owner won't usually get you anywhere. Having said that, rates are pretty flexible. If you're travelling in low season, if the hotel is almost empty or if you're planning to stay for several nights it's always worth bargaining; this may save you a dollar or so, although you won't get a huge discount unless you're staying for weeks.

Check-in procedure is fairly standard. If the hotel is full and you arrive before midday you'll have to wait until guests vacate the rooms before you can check in (Latin American hotels almost never operate the 24-hour checkout system favoured in some other parts of the world). Usually you'll be welcome to dump your bags so you can go for lunch while your room is cleaned. Otherwise it's simply a question of filling in a basic form with your name, address, nationality and passport number and, in most cases, paying in advance for the room. You shouldn't surrender your passport to hotel reception, and it's unlikely that you'll be asked to do so, unless you choose to put it in the hotel safe for security (for more on hotel security, see pp.338–342).

Showers and toilets

There are a few differences between the showers and toilets you'll be used to at home and those in Latin America. There's no hot water of any kind in many parts of Latin America, partly because of the climate, partly because hot running water is perceived as an unnecessary luxury. If you're staying in a cheap hotel in a warm part of Latin America your shower will invariably only have cold water, and although it's a shock to the system at first you'll quickly get used to it. Take showers during the heat of the day if it's too cool in the evenings or upgrade yourself to a more expensive hotel if you really can't bear it. Water pressure is often inadequate too, and hotels almost never have bathtubs.

In colder parts of the continent, cheaper hotels and hostels have come up with a device known to travellers as the "killer" (or "suicide") shower. This involves attaching a small electric unit to the top of the shower that heats the water as it passes through. Most are controlled by water pressure – the slower the flow of water, the hotter it will be. In most cases they're pretty unsatisfactory and provide a thin trickle of lukewarm water at best, and because they consist of a combination of water and electricity they're also highly dangerous and electric shocks are not uncommon. Be very careful when using them and if possible wear a pair of flip-flops or rubber-soled shoes – never fiddle with the electric unit while standing in the shower with the water on.

The other thing to know about Latin American plumbing is that it's pretty basic and you can't throw anything into the toilet bowl without risking it getting blocked. It's standard practice in virtually every country to put toilet paper, sanitary towels and tampons into a basket beside the toilet (these should be emptied regularly). Don't ignore this custom even if you find it distasteful – the other option, a blocked and overflowing toilet, is far worse.

12

Staying healthy

Despite dramatic extremes of climate, unclean drinking water and often poor standards of hygiene, visitors to Latin America are unlikely to suffer from anything more serious than a bout of diarrhoea or a touch of sunburn. All the same, it helps if, before setting off, you get yourself in the best possible shape, take care to get lots of sleep, good food and exercise and schedule a dental check-up.

Having said that, it's also worth remembering that the majority of travellers to Latin America inevitably suffer from the change in environment, usually manifesting itself as diarrhoea and/or nausea and vomiting – both can be very unpleasant, though far from life-threatening (if symptoms persist beyond a few days, though, they could be indicative of something more serious and you should see a doctor). Resign yourself to the fact that you may well lose a few days of your trip to illness, and make sure there's enough flexibility in your itinerary to ensure you don't have to travel when you're feeling awful. And just in case you have the misfortune to suffer a serious health problem, make sure you get a comprehensive insurance policy which covers all medical expenses in an emergency, including repatriation – see pp.182–185 for more details.

Although most countries in Latin America don't have free or subsidized health care, private health clinics of all kinds abound in large cities and are frequently very good indeed. And even the most expensive will be more affordable than their equivalent at home. The prescription system doesn't exist in Latin America, which means you can buy any drug over the counter. Locals frequently don't bother consulting a doctor but instead go straight to the pharmacy, where staff are often very knowledgeable and are used to offering informal diagnoses. If you're not convinced, shop around for the best pharmacist locally – even small towns usually have several. It's also worth memorizing the generic names of useful general antibiotics (such as metronidazole, trade name Flagyl – useful for clearing up giardia or dysentery), so that you can get the right drug fast.

Latin Americans love discussing medical problems in gory detail. If you do get ill, the staff at your hotel will all have an opinion on what you have, who you should consult and what to take. Most locals, particularly in the countryside, have some idea of natural or indigenous cures (usually an infusion made from local plants) – these often work wonderfully well. That said, it's important that you don't self-diagnose if you're feeling very sick – you must consult a professional doctor. Local medical services – public or private – in Latin America will be aware of the diseases listed in this chapter and should be able to treat them adequately.

There are lots of excellent sources of information on travellers' health (see Basics for websites). Books include Rough Guide's comprehensive *Travel Health*; *Bugs, Bites and Bowels*; and *Where There Is No Doctor*, which is particularly good if you're planning to stray far from accessible medical care.

Vaccinations

Unless you're a frequent traveller to the tropics, you'll inevitably need several vaccinations before you set off. Don't leave them to the last minute – some require more than one dose, others need to be given a few days apart from each other so that they don't cancel each other out or cause reactions, and all vaccinations need several weeks for full immunity to develop; it's best to start getting inoculated around three months before you depart. And don't freak out if you feel slightly unwell after your jabs – they do, after all, work by giving you a mild dose of the disease that spurs your immune system into action.

You will probably have been inoculated as a child against certain diseases, including diphtheria, polio and tetanus; in these cases you'll

First-aid kits

Travel clinics, adventure sports shops and large pharmacies all now sell comprehensive travel health kits with a combination of the following – alternatively, it's easy enough to put together your own:

- Anti-diarrhoeals, for emergencies only, such as unavoidable journeys
- Antihistamines, for itchy bites, rashes and allergic reactions
- Antiseptic cream, very important for the tropics where strong humidity exacerbates the infection of wounds
- Antiseptic liquid soap, the best way to ensure you're really clean
- Insect repellent with DEET
- Painkillers (Ibuprofen, for example)
- Band-aids/plasters in several sizes, and a length of bandage plus scissors
- Rehydration salts, for coping with the dehydrating effects of diarrhoea and sickness
- Sun block (SPF 15+)
- Sterile needles
- Tweezers, for removing splinters and sea-urchin spines

Antibiotics

Available only on prescription at home, though you may be able to persuade your doctor to give you a course of general antibiotics such as metronidazole or ciprofloxacin (both of which kill diarrhoea-causing bacteria) in advance. Or you could just buy them over the counter in Latin America if and when you need to. Remember that with antibiotics it's vital to take the whole course, and make sure you get your illness diagnosed before starting treatment.

Alternative medicine

Increasingly popular, alternative medicine offers, to various degrees of effectiveness, natural treatments – consult your local health food store or homeopath for detailed information. Particularly useful remedies to take include arnica or calendula cream for bruises and bites; echinacea to boost your immune system; citronella, eucalyptus or lavender oils to ward off mosquitoes and other nasty bugs; tea tree oil, which acts as an antiseptic; tiger balm for heachaches; and Rescue Remedy, a Bach Flower Remedy which calms the nerves in stressful situations. Additionally, if you're planning on wilderness trekking or going into the jungle for a lengthy period, vitamin supplements, particularly vitamins B and C, will help to keep you healthy.

require only a booster jab, if that. Other diseases that you'll need to be vaccinated against are typhoid and hepatitis. Combined injections now exist (ask your doctor about them), which lessen the ordeal.

Two more vaccinations you might consider having are yellow fever and rabies.

If your home country has some kind of public health service, you may be able to get some of your vaccinations (tetanus, for example) free or at a greatly reduced cost from your local doctor. Less commonly requested jabs (such as yellow fever) are not always available and will cost as much as going to one of the many private travel clinics (see Directory, pp.369–371, which deal exclusively with vaccinations and information about tropical diseases. The clinics have expert staff and generally offer much more rapid and convenient consultations, although prices for ordinary jabs can be much higher than your doctor charges. Additionally, there are several premium-rate phone lines in the UK, North America and Australasia that give specific health advice for travellers, plus various websites where you can pay for an online consultation (see pp.369–371 for details).

Diseases you should know about

- **Chagas' disease** (aka American trypanosomiasis) Transmitted by reduviid beetles, also known as "assassin bugs", Chagas' disease is rife in some parts of Latin America (particularly northeastern Brazil) and, though you're unlikely to be affected, can be fatal if left untreated. Try to avoid staying in the adobe or mud huts that the reduviid beetle lives in (if you can't, then be sure to sleep well away from the walls), and if you are bitten, disinfect the bite with antiseptic and don't scratch it. Should a fever develop within ten days, get a blood test as soon as possible – if you have the disease you'll need to be hospitalized. Other symptoms are localized swelling around the bite, swelling of the lymph glands and an itchy rash.
- **Cholera** Cholera is spread by contaminated water or by eating contaminated shellfish and manifests itself as a particularly nasty bout of diarrhoea and/or vomiting. There's currently no effective vaccine – the best way to avoid catching cholera is by being careful about the water you drink. Diagnosis is by stool sample and treatment is with antibiotics such as doxycycline.
- **Dengue fever** A virus spread by the Aedes mosquito, which bites in the early morning or late afternoon. Initial symptoms (similar to those of malaria) typically appear five to eight days after being bitten and include fever, headache, joint pains and backache, as well as

short-lived but severe diarrhoea and a fine rash. Diagnosis is made by blood test; you should check for malaria at the same time if you have this particular collection of symptoms. Dengue fever has no specific cure and is usually treated with bed rest. The disease can, however, develop into dengue haemorrhagic fever (though rarely – it most commonly affects children aged 15 and under), which is life threatening – seek immediate medical attention if you go into shock (characterized by clammy skin, a weak pulse and shallow breathing) or start to bleed from any orifices.

● **Hepatitis** Hepatitis (an inflammation of the liver) exists in several different forms. Hepatitis A is a virus spread by contaminated water or intimate contact; symptoms include nausea, loss of appetite, weight loss, fatigue and abdominal pain and, most distinctively, jaundice, which turns the patient's skin and eyeballs yellow. Hepatitis B is a more severe and longer-lasting form of the disease; it's spread by blood through sexual contact, sharing needles or blood transfusions. Both forms are usually treated with several weeks of bed rest. Effective vaccinations for both hepatitis A and B exist and can be given in one combined shot. Immunization is recommended.

● **Leishmaniasis** Found in many parts of Central and South America, leishmaniasis is transmitted by sandflies and exists in several forms. Most common in Latin America are the cutaneous and mucocutaneous strains: these cause the sandfly bites to develop into itchy red skin ulcers which can leave severe and permanent scarring. Diagnosis is made by a skin biopsy and treated with a ten-day intravenous course of drugs. There is no vaccine, although sandflies are low-flying, and sleeping above ground level will lessen your chances of being bitten, as will using an insect repellent. Mosquito nets, however, will not protect you, since sandflies are small enough to pass through the mesh.

● **Malaria** See p.314.

● **Rabies** Rabies is spread by the bite of an infected animal (usually a dog) and is a serious paralysing and potentially fatal disease that rapidly becomes incurable. Symptoms initially include fever, nausea and loss of appetite, muscle aches and sore throat; they may also include unpredictable or aggressive behaviour followed by muscle spasms, fear of water and paralysis. A three-dose vaccine exists which will partly protect you against the disease developing, but if you're bitten, even if you've been immunized, you must seek urgent medical attention. Treatment consists of a further course of injections. Thorough cleaning of the wound also helps to reduce the chances of becoming infected.

- **Schistosomiasis** (or Bilharzia) is now the second most prevalent tropical disease worldwide after malaria. Minute larvae that live in freshwater penetrate human skin, grow in the liver, mate and then release their eggs via faeces or urine. An initial itchy rash may be the only specific symptom of schistosomiasis, which can cause kidney failure and damage to the heart, lungs and central nervous system. The disease presents itself 2–12 weeks after exposure to contaminated water. There is no vaccine but the oral drug Praziquantel is an effective cure. Travellers who wade, swim or bathe in freshwater (lakes and rivers) in Latin America are at risk – if any of the above symptoms persist you'll need to undergo screening tests (blood and stools) to detect the disease before treatment.
- **Tetanus** Tetanus spores live in soil, dust and manure and infect humans through open wounds. Symptoms develop following an incubation period of between five and twenty days and include headache, fever, irritability and jaw-muscle spasms which spread to the neck, limbs and torso and may result in breathing difficulties. Tetanus is potentially fatal, with various complications including blood clots, pneumonia and heart problems; treatment requires hospitalization. Most people in the developed world are vaccinated as children, though you'll need a booster if it's been over ten years since your last immunization.
- **Typhoid** Typhoid is carried in contaminated water or food and, like cholera, is fairly widespread in unsanitary areas. Symptoms are similar to cholera and include fever, headache, lethargy and stomach pains. In some cases, coughing, temporary deafness and pink spots on the torso also occur, and what begin as mild symptoms may deteriorate over two weeks into serious illness. Diagnosis is through a blood or stool test, and the disease can usually be treated with antibiotics such as ciprofloxacin. An effective typhoid vaccine exists, and immunization is recommended.
- **Yellow fever** The yellow fever virus is spread by mosquito bites and is found throughout the Amazon region. Mild though sudden symptoms of fever, abdominal pain and vomiting often disappear rapidly, only to recur in fifteen percent of cases along with jaundice, kidney failure, bleeding and shock. This secondary yellow fever is potentially fatal and there's no specific treatment. There is a vaccine, however, and in various parts of Latin America (specifically Brazil, and in Amazonian areas in general – check with a travel clinic) you may be asked to produce an International Certificate of Vaccination proving that you've been immunized. If you can't, you run the risk of being immunized on the spot in potentially less than sanitary conditions. Immunization lasts for ten years and is recommended.

Mosquitoes and malaria

Malaria, a potentially fatal disease spread by the bite of the female Anopheles mosquito, is one of the world's most widespread diseases, with an estimated 300 to 500 million cases every year and between one and three million deaths. Although outbreak patterns change from year to year, parts of Latin America, particularly the Amazon region, are generally considered high-risk. There's no vaccine yet (although scientists are currently carrying out successful trials on a vaccine which they hope to have licensed by 2010) and anyone going to tropical or subtropical Latin America should take a course of preventative drugs and try to avoid being bitten.

The initial symptoms of malaria are worryingly similar to flu or more general fever. Typically, sufferers start feeling very cold and shiver, then develop a very high temperature and finally begin to sweat – these three stages continue in one- to three-day cycles. There are four different strains of the malaria parasite; the most dangerous, *p.falciparum*, can become potentially fatal in a matter of hours.

Your local doctor and specialized travel clinics, phone lines and websites (see pp.369–371) will have up-to-date advice on malarial areas and anti-malarial drugs. There is some controversy about anti-malarial drugs because of their side effects and efficacy (none is one-hundred percent effective), but all offer at least some (and usually much more) protection against contracting the disease.

Treatments

There are several anti-malarial drugs on the market; which one you take will depend on your medical history, where exactly you're going and for how long. The longest established anti-malarial, chloroquine, is also the most widely available, the cheapest and has no significant side effects (it can be taken continuously over a five-year period). However, its heavy use over the years has led to *p.falciparum* (see above) mutating to become chloroquine-resistant and thus rendering chloroquine ineffective in certain areas. In Latin America, *p.falciparum* exists throughout the Amazon Basin (which covers every country in South America apart from Paraguay, Uruguay, Argentina and Chile), and if you're travelling in this region you'll need another anti-malarial.

Of the other drugs currently available, mefloquine (Larium) is the most effective, can be taken for up to a year and works well against most strains of malaria – although strains are starting to become resistant to it. However, there have been reports of disturbing side effects, including hallucinations and psychosis, as a result of taking Larium – be aware of the risks if you decide to take it. It's also the most expensive anti-malarial. Doxycycline is effective against *p.falciparum* only, can be taken for three months though its side effects include increased risk of sunburn, nausea and vaginal yeast infections. It's not easily available in the USA. Malarone is the newest anti-malarial on the market, is effective against all strains of malaria and has few side effects – though it shouldn't be taken for more than 28 days.

All anti-malarial courses must be started before you reach the malarial zone, from two days for doxycycline to one to three weeks for mefloquine, and continued for up to a month after you've left. You'll have to pay full price for anti-malarial drugs (and most aren't cheap), but buying them before you set off is recommended since their availability and quality in Latin America can't be guaranteed.

In terms of alternative medicine, a Chinese remedy, *qinghaosu* (sweet wormwood) or *artemisinin*, has attracted much interest from the tropical medicine community and is now marketed in various forms (though it's not yet licensed for sale in Europe) – you can buy it online at www.OrganicPharmacy.org. Demal2000™ is a homeopathic anti-malarial which enables the immune system to develop antibodies to fight the infection. Developed in Indonesia and widely used in the region since 1989, the drug reportedly has very high success rates and is also available for sale online (www.blueturtlegroup.com).

How to avoid getting malaria

The best way to avoid getting malaria is to avoid being bitten (and bear in mind that as well as transmitting malaria, mosquitoes may also carry dengue and yellow fever). The following precautions will help when in malarial areas:

● Mosquitoes are mainly nocturnal – and malaria-carrying ones particularly love dusk, which is when you're most likely to be bitten. Cover up as much as possible, wearing long-sleeved shirts and trousers tucked into socks. Mosquitoes are drawn to strong dark colours – white is your best bet for keeping them at a distance.

- Buy an effective insect repellent and use it diligently. The best repellents contain varying levels of DEET (from 15 to 100 percent), and although it smells nasty, can sting sensitive skin, and actually melts plastic, it does work (but try not to apply it in a closed environment or near other people, unless you want to asphyxiate them). If you want to use natural repellents, citronella, eucalyptus and lavender essential oils (mixed into a base of oil or water) are effective for several hours. Bizarrely, Avon's Skin-So-Soft moisturizing lotion, available from drugstores in North America (and parts of Latin America), is one of the best repellents of both mosquitoes and sandflies. It's also claimed that mosquitoes love perfume, pregnant women and sweat, but hate the smell of garlic and vitamin B.
- Sleep under a mosquito net – it's best to take your own (those in hotels invariably have holes); good ones roll up into a small and virtually weightless pouch. In addition, soak your net in permethrin before you set off or choose one that's already been treated. You can also impregnate your travelling clothes with permethrin, which will act as a further line of defence.
- Burn mosquito coils in your room – they're the most popular local form of repellent and so are usually cheap and readily available.
- If you're not on a tight budget, choose a hotel room with mesh screens over the windows. Both air conditioning and powerful ceiling

△ Canoeing in the Amazon

fans prevent mosquitoes from getting near you because they find it hard to fly in circulating air currents.

- Even if you're not in a malarial area, mosquito bites can be distressing. If you are bitten, try not to scratch the bite – this only spreads any infection further. Calamine lotion, tea tree oil or an antiseptic cream may help to soothe the irritation; if the itching becomes unbearable, antihistamine tablets or cream will calm it considerably.

- The website ⊛www.malaria.org is a good source of information on the disease – otherwise check the general travellers' health websites.

Heat and cold

While all of Mexico and Central America – bar a few mountainous areas – enjoys tropical or semi-tropical weather, South America has extreme differences in temperature, from very hot and dry (in the Atacama Desert of Chile, for example, during the day) to humid (in the Amazon) through to freezing cold in the Andes and Patagonia. Whichever itinerary you plan to take, it's best to consider, and plan for, the intense heat and cold you could potentially encounter once in Latin America.

Sun exposure

Apart from stomach upsets, you're most likely to fall ill during your trip as a result of exposure to the sun. Remember that the sun is at its hottest between 11am and 3pm, and you should try to avoid being outside in direct sunlight for too long during these hours. You'll notice the locals keeping a low profile – copy them and have lunch in the shade or take a siesta. Bear in mind also that the effect of sun is stronger at high altitudes and anywhere where light is reflected, such as snow-scapes, or in and on the water; if you're on a boat, cooling breezes may mask the strength of the sun. Be extra careful in both these environments and cover up in a lightweight shirt and long trousers.

When you do venture out into the sun, always use a sunscreen, which will help protect you against skin cancer and premature ageing – however much you want to return from your trip with a healthy-looking tan, you could be seriously damaging your long-term health if you're not properly protected from the sun's ultraviolet rays. Use a sunscreen with at least SPF 15 and choose one that protects against both UVA and UVB rays and is waterproof. Apply it twenty minutes before you go out and reapply it diligently every couple of hours. Take a large bottle of sunscreen with you from home – it's often very expensive in Latin America – and once on the road, stock up in big cities since smaller places often don't have anything suitable. Also take a sunscreen stick for your lips – these are often neglected and burn or blister easily.

The other important item to take is a decent pair of sunglasses – cheap shades are little more than coloured sheets of plastic and can do more harm than good; get a pair of sunglasses with UV-resistant lenses. You may also want to take a hat to stop your head getting burnt. If you do get burnt, there's little you can do about it except slather yourself in a soothing after-sun lotion (anything with aloe vera in it is wonderfully cooling), increase your fluid intake (but avoid alcohol) and stay in the shade until the redness and soreness have gone.

Heat and humidity

As well as direct exposure to the sun, you'll also probably have to deal with the overall heat and humidity. Acclimatizing to these takes a while – weeks rather than days – so don't rush around or undertake strenuous exercise immediately after you've arrived. You should also increase your fluid intake, and if you do start to feel you're overheating, bathe frequently in tepid or cool water. Prickly heat or heat rash results from inflamed sweat glands, caused by over-exposure or over-exertion in high temperatures, and manifests itself as small itchy pink/red spots on the head, neck, shoulders and other sweaty parts of the body. As well as taking cool showers, treat heat rash by wearing loose lightweight clothing, using talc to keep dry and soothing after-sun creams to stop the itching. Heat stroke, by contrast, is a potentially life-threatening condition. If your body temperature rises significantly (above 40°C/106°F) and you experience nausea, sensitivity to light, rapid breathing and, most significantly, stop sweating, you need urgent medical attention.

Hypothermia

At the other end of the scale, in the Andes the temperature can fall well below freezing. It may be hot during the daytime in the mountains, but as soon as the sun sets the temperature drops alarmingly fast – if you're out hiking, take layers of warm clothes with you. At worst, severe cold can lead to hypothermia (when the human body temperature drops beneath 35°C/95°F). Symptoms include slurred speech, stumbling and shallow breathing; if untreated, hypothermia can lead to coma and then death. If you do get very cold, you can warm yourself up by consuming high-energy foods like chocolate and hot, sugary drinks (alcohol should be avoided because it dilates blood vessels near the surface of the skin, meaning you actually lose heat). Sharing your companion's body heat (and/or sleeping bag) is another highly effective way of increasing your own body temperature.

Altitude

Altitude sickness, known as *soroche* in Spanish, is caused by insufficient acclimatization to high altitudes (over 2500m) and the body's inability to cope with reduced levels of oxygen. You should be particularly wary of altitude sickness if you fly into La Paz in Bolivia (3636m), Cusco (3500m), Quito (2800m), Bogotá (2650m) or Mexico City (2400m) – plan on taking things easy for the first few days after your arrival if you're arriving at any of these cities from a low altitude. Symptoms of altitude sickness include persistent headache, vomiting, dizziness and breathlessness. Drinking lots of water will help enormously; in Bolivia, the local coca tea (*mate de coca*) is an effective remedy. There is also a homeopathic remedy, *coca,* which like other homeopathic remedies is not readily available in most parts of Latin America and should be purchased before you set off.

At very high altitudes (3000m or more, for example when climbing in the Andes) altitude sickness can worsen to become acute mountain sickness (AMS), which is much more serious and potentially fatal. Symptoms of AMS, caused by increased fluid and swelling on the brain and lungs, include lethargy and confusion, coughing and a bluish tinge to lips, nails and skin. If you're planning to climb in high altitudes you should be in good physical shape. Spend several days acclimatizing before you set off, limit your ascent to no more than 300m each day and keep hydrated by drinking at least three litres of non-alcoholic fluids a day. The only effective cure for AMS is to descend immediately – even several hundred metres will instantly make you feel better – although the drugs dexamethasone, frusemide and nifedipine (which should only be used under medical supervision) might buy you some time while you descend.

Water

Probably the biggest single health hazard travellers to Latin America face is contaminated water, the cause not only of travellers' diarrhoea and dysentery, but also of much more serious diseases like cholera, hepatitis and typhoid. Avoiding contaminated water, however, isn't that easy. With a very few exceptions (most of Argentina, Chile, Costa Rica), tap water in Latin America isn't safe to drink. Obviously, you should only drink and clean your teeth with bottled or purified water, as well as avoiding swimming in fresh water and (although it sounds stupid) taking a shower with your mouth open. In addition, avoid salads, which in most restaurants are washed in tap water, and check that ice and fruit juices (*jugos, licuados* or *batidas*) are made with purified water – this is increasingly the case in places popular with Western tourists.

Bottled water is widely available and inexpensive; alternatively, if you're on a very tight budget, in a remote area or camping, you can purify local water yourself with either chlorine or iodine drops that can be purchased back home in camping shops. Iodine can only be used for up to six weeks continuously although it has the advantage of killing the giardia parasite (see p.322), which chlorine doesn't. Both make water taste unpleasant, although you can add neutralizing crystals that mask most – but not all – of the taste (iodine tablets are available with neutralizers already added). Your other options are portable water filters or, better, purifying kits that both filter and sterilize water – although water filters won't get rid of every nasty organism, water purifiers clean water to a high level. They range vastly in price (US$25–100) and come in several sizes; consider weight, efficacy and ease and speed of use before you buy one. If you're carrying a camping stove it's easier to just boil water (for at least five minutes; longer at higher altitudes) to rid it of any harmful bacteria.

Food

Food that isn't properly cooked or is unhygienically prepared is another source of diarrhoea and sickness. When choosing where and what to eat, bear the following points in mind:

- Look at hygiene standards: if the floor is swept, tables wiped and ashtrays emptied regularly, chances are the same approach to cleanliness extends to the kitchen.
- You don't have to completely avoid eating street food – some stalls are scrupulously maintained, with ingredients covered and food freshly cooked. Look around for the busiest places – often the best way to tell if somewhere is worth going to.
- Conversely, don't assume that gringo cafés will be more hygienic than local places – they may not be.
- Choose places where food is cooked to order – food that's been left sitting around attracts flies and harmful bacteria.
- Undercooked meat and reheated rice could give you serious food poisoning and salad is often washed in unclean tap water – you should avoid all three. Be particularly careful with shellfish, which is prone to contamination because of the large amounts of polluted seawater they filter while feeding. Additionally a handful of people die every year in Chile from eating shellfish contaminated by the *marea roja* ("red tide"), a very poisonous algae – although the government does issue warnings when it's present. Also avoid fruit that you haven't peeled yourself, and unpasteurized milk and cheese.

Diarrhoea, vomiting, dysentery and giardia

However careful you are, chances are that at some stage in your travels you'll come down with some kind of stomach bug or bout of diarrhoea/vomiting – often shortly after arriving. This may be as much to do with a dramatic change in environment as anything, and the good news is that most cases of even severe diarrhoea and sickness clear up within days and can be easily treated without a visit to the doctor.

Diarrhoea and vomiting

If you do come down with something, try to rest for a few days until you feel better – you'll also make the experience less unpleasant for yourself (and other guests) if you check into a hotel with a private bathroom. You probably won't feel like eating if you're sick, and cutting back on food intake will give your guts a much-needed break, although the latest thinking is that it's best to eat at least something. Avoid anything spicy or strongly flavoured – stick to plain, freshly boiled rice, bananas and dry biscuits. Unless you have to travel, don't take anti-diarrhoea medication, which works by blocking you up, thus preventing your body from expelling the bacteria which caused your illness in the first place.

The most important thing, if you're suffering from diarrhoea and vomiting, is to ensure that you don't become dehydrated, since your body will be losing vital fluids. If you have a dry mouth and tongue, a loss of skin elasticity (you can test this by pinching the skin on the back of your hand: if it takes a while to return to its initial state then you're dehydrated), dark urine, headaches and backache, then you've already become seriously dehydrated and need to start rehydrating immediately – try to avoid reaching this stage by increasing your fluid intake as soon as diarrhoea and vomiting start. Adults need to take in 2–3 litres of liquid a day (not including alcohol, coffee or tea, which further dehydrate your system) – more in particularly hot or humid climates. Although in the worst stages of a particularly bad bout you may not be able to keep down anything at all, it's important to keep trying. Take sips of bottled water at frequent intervals; even better, add oral rehydration salts to boiled or bottled water to replace lost salt and sugar. If you don't have any in your medical kit you can prepare your own by adding half a level teaspoon of salt and eight level teaspoons of sugar to a litre of clean water. Alternatively, if you're feeling up to it, try drinking something fizzy (rather bizarrely, Coca-Cola is thought to soothe stomach upsets) and eating salty crackers. If more than three or four days pass without you being able to keep down liquids, or if you stop urinating altogether and start to feel drowsy, you may need an intravenous drip and should go to a hospital for treatment.

There are several homeopathic remedies for diarrhoea – *arsenicum album*, *china officinalis* and *veratrum album*. Ginger helps to alleviate feelings of nausea, while live yoghurt (not easily found in Latin America) or acidophilus tablets will repopulate your intestines with good bacteria after a serious bout of sickness. Locals may also have some ideas – this may well involve a herbal tea of some kind, usually foul tasting but often effective.

Dysentery and giardia

While most cases of diarrhoea and vomiting clear up within a few days, there are several more serious gastrointestinal illnesses which have similar causes and symptoms. The most notable of these are amoebiasis (amoebic dysentery) and giardia. Both are caused by parasites which enter the gut via contaminated water or food and are characterized by abdominal cramps, fever, nausea and weight loss. If you have amoebic dysentery, you may also be passing blood and in severe cases, where the parasite has reached the liver and caused an abscess, suffer intermittent pain on the upper right-hand side of the abdomen; giardia is very distinctive, with sulphurous or eggy burping and farts and a bloated stomach. Both can cause long-term intestinal damage (including lactose intolerance) if left untreated; treatment is with antibiotics (metronidazole).

Still more serious illnesses with similar symptoms to travellers' diarrhoea are hepatitis, cholera and yellow fever, amongst others (see pp.312–313) – if you continue to feel ill after five days, have a high fever (above 39°C/102°F) or severe abdominal pain, seek medical advice.

Footworms in Brazil

When you've finally reached that perfect beach – powdery white sand and palm trees – one of the first things you want to do is kick off your shoes and walk barefoot along the shore. So when I found my beach on an island in Brazil, that's exactly what I did. Two days later I had an itchy big toe and, on examination, a small swelling right by my toenail – it wasn't an insect bite, though. Jose, the man who ran my hotel, knew what it was as soon as he saw me scratching furiously – "Ah," he said phlegmatically – "you have a *bicho de pé*", which he went on to explain was a footworm, a small maggotty insect fond of crawling into the cracks between human toes and toenails and then moving into the bloodstream. Once I'd recovered from the shock, Jose explained that I'd have to remove it as soon as possible. "Oh God," I said, "and how do I do that?" Footworms, it appeared, have to be dug out with a thorn from a lemon tree – the native way – or with a sewing needle – the gringo method. However I did it, it wasn't the first and last footworm I dug out of my toe – every evening as sun set, examining my feet for the telltale signs became a nightly ritual – I could, of course, have just worn shoes on the beach like the locals did...

Polly Rodger Brown

Wildlife and parasites

You'll probably have the jitters about creepy-crawlies if you've never been to Latin America, and particularly if you're planning to visit the rainforest, but in truth you're extremely unlikely to be bitten by any poisonous creatures – they'll be trying harder to avoid you than you them. That said, there are many species of poisonous snakes and other unpleasant insects and parasites in the region, particularly in the Amazon, and it's worth following the points below to minimize the risk of being bitten.

- Tread carefully in jungle terrain and make as much noise as possible – which gives snakes, rarely aggressive, the chance to slither away. If you are bitten by a snake, get to a doctor as soon as possible and try to stay calm since panicking will pump the venom faster around your body. If you're able to kill the snake and take it to be identified, you may hasten the process of diagnosis and treatment. Attempting to suck out venom is not recommended.
- Avoid swimming in rivers, lakes and lagoons, particularly in tropical South America, where cayman (alligators), electric eels and piranha fish make their home. Although cayman aren't generally aggressive, they have been known to attack if protecting young or just plain hungry. The *candiru* fish is native to the Amazon and swims up the urethra and lodges there or in the bladder, which results in severe blood loss and infection and may be fatal; removal is by surgery. Other nasty parasites also live in tropical fresh water, such as those that cause schistosomiasis (also known as bilharzias; see p.313)
- Shake out your shoes every morning – they're a favourite habitat of scorpions and spiders. If you are stung by either (which is highly unlikely, and rarely fatal), apply ice or cold compresses to the bite and take antihistamines and pain relievers. Seek urgent medical advice if you show an allergic reaction to the bite.
- Avoid walking barefoot, especially on beaches or any other area where dogs roam freely (ie most of rural Latin America), no matter how tempting. Jiggers are small fleas that penetrate the skin, normally around the toenails, and lay their eggs. The only way of getting rid of them is to pick them out with a sterilized needle – not much fun. If you see and feel a dark itchy bump on one of your toes you must remove the flea or risk gangrene and septicaemia. Bathing your feet in hot water after walking in an infested area may help dislodge the fleas before they've become firmly attached, while the liberal use of insect repellent is sometimes effective. Locals will be able to keep you up to date about the prevalence of jiggers in their area – be wary if you see a lot of locals sitting around picking their feet.
- If a tick – which looks like an eight-legged woodlouse and can carry nasty diseases – attaches itself to you, remove it carefully using tweezers so that you don't leave part of it embedded in your flesh.

- Leeches are not dangerous and will drop off once they've satiated themselves on your blood, though if you'd rather not wait, applying a lit cigarette usually persuades them to leave sharpish. As with ticks (see above), don't pull them off.
- Try not to sleep in mud or adobe buildings. These harbour the assassin bugs that cause potentially fatal Chagas' disease (see p.311).

AIDS, HIV and contraception

AIDS (*sida*) is just as common in Latin America as in Europe, the US and Australasia – indeed Brazil has one of the world's highest number of infected people. All the usual precautions apply: never have unprotected sex or share needles. If you're planning on being sexually active, take a supply of condoms (*preservativos*) with you – the quality of those in Latin America may not be as good as you'd hope.

If you're on the Pill, take supplies with you, since your particular brand may be hard to find. Bear in mind that prolonged periods of diarrhoea and vomiting will affect the efficacy of the Pill, so take extra precautions following

A close encounter

Sitting around the campfire in the midst of the pristine Amazonian rainforest of Peru's Manu National Park, our tour guide, Barry, had warned us to watch out for the bushmaster. He said the most venomous snake in the Americas was also extremely aggressive, and had been known to pursue those who disturbed it, using infrared vision to track them down before delivering a lethal bite with its fangs. According to the locals, Barry said, the person walking third in line on a jungle trail was most at risk from the bushmaster: the first person passing by would disturb it, the second annoy it, and the third would pay the ultimate price. And so I was slightly concerned when, as we set out on a night walk through the forest an hour or so later, I found myself walking up a narrow trail with only Barry and one other ecotourist ahead of me. Within minutes, Barry suddenly stopped and took a step back, shining his torch at what looked like a stick lying across the path. "Bushmaster," he whispered, and I watched as one end of the stick rose vertically into the air, revealing it as a two-metre-long snake, angry and ready to strike. Even Barry seemed pretty unsettled at the sight, lighting a cigarette and puffing nervously as we peered over his shoulder. When asked what the striking range of the snake was, however, he was still cool enough to reply "Oh, he could get me from there." We waited at a safe distance until the bushmaster slithered into the forest and we could continue along the trail. I didn't realize quite how fortunate we'd been until a year later, when I ran into Barry in a Cusco bar. A few weeks after our trip, he told me, another tour group had run into a bushmaster in the same region. The snake had pursued one ecotourist and bitten him on the ankle. "What happened to him?" I asked, and Barry said he'd been lucky: after being airlifted to a Lima hospital, he'd lived to tell the tale, though only after having his leg amputated.

James Read

any gastrointestinal upset. Also be aware that taking the Pill does increase your risk of thrombosis, as does travelling at high altitudes – if you're planning on trekking above 4000m you should seriously consider coming off the Pill during this period (consult your doctor for advice). Alternatively, if you're planning some kind of adventure holiday and would rather not have to deal with periods, it's possible to prevent bleeding for up to three months with no problems by taking the Pill continuously and ignoring the monthly Pill-free week. If you're at all concerned, discuss your trip with your doctor before you leave.

13

Keeping in touch

Keeping in touch with home during your travels in Latin America is now relatively inexpensive and uncomplicated, largely thanks to the Internet, which has revolutionized communications in Latin America just as it has done everywhere else. Postal and phone networks too, though much less used by tourists nowadays, have been largely privatized and are now fairly reliable. There are obviously regional variations in communication networks – for specific details on keeping in touch check your guidebook, which should have a section covering the relevant issues in the country you're visiting. A few general points apply wherever you are, however. To begin with, don't fall into the trap of setting fixed times and dates in advance for ringing home or sending an email, since it's unlikely that you'll be able to stick to them – a delay in your itinerary, a power cut (frequent in some parts of Latin America) or a public holiday might all mean you can't send an email or get to a phone. However, if you find yourself anywhere near a natural disaster, airplane crash or political coup, get in touch with your family as soon as possible. Inevitably they'll have seen the details on the news, sometimes days before you, and will want to know that you're safe.

Email and the Internet

Internet access is widely available in Latin America. Every city and decent-sized town in even the poorest or least touristed of countries now has at least one Internet café – in fact, because many Latin Americans still don't have access to a computer at home or work, Internet cafés are far more popular with the locals than in the US or Europe. In addition, post offices, telephone centres, universities and libraries also often offer cheap Internet access – it's always worth asking at these places. Don't, however, assume that you can access the Internet everywhere. Many places in Latin America still lack electricity and phone lines. And the further off the beaten track you go, the more expensive using the Internet is likely to be.

If you don't already have an email account, there are now dozens of companies which offer free Web-based email accounts which can be accessed from anywhere in the world. Two of the most popular are Hotmail (⊛www.hotmail.com) and Yahoo! (⊛www.yahoo.com), which are both reliable, although with millions of subscribers using the service at any one time, logging on can be slow. Other recommended free Web-mail providers are Fastmail (⊛www.fastmail.fm) and Gawab (⊛www.gawab.com), which are among the fastest services available (though in terms of speed, it's worth remembering that the emptier your inbox, the faster you'll be able to log on to your account) and both have a massive 2Gb (gigabytes) of storage. Gmail (mail.google.com) is an experimental email account created by Google which has massive storage, no pop-ups and a unique way of filing – and accessing – messages alongside all replies sent. The Website ⊛www.emailaddresses.com has reviews of more than a hundred free email accounts, with useful comments and information on how to choose one which suits you.

Costs for Internet access in Latin America vary enormously – from US$0.50 in Ecuador to US$12 a hour in the Bay Islands of Honduras – though they average US$3 per hour; there's usually a minimum charge of ten or fifteen minutes. You may have to be patient, though – particularly in poorer countries and rural areas, connection times can be very slow, and occasionally you may not be able to get through at all. If you get stuck, many staff in places with Internet access speak some English. It's also worth knowing that the @ symbol (*arrobá* in Spanish) is not on many Latin American keyboards – you have to hold down the "Alt" key and then type 64.

To find out the locations of Internet cafés in Latin America, visit the comprehensive ⊛www.world66.com/netcafeguide, ⊛www.latinworld.com or ⊛www.planeta.com, or check your guidebook, which should have listings. In general the best areas to find Internet cafés are around universities and in heavily touristed towns; in addition, many backpacker hostels now have Internet access. If you get stuck in the middle of nowhere and need to use the Internet, you could always try asking around at local businesses or hotels (assuming there are any).

In some places you can also now make Web calls. These are effectively phone calls made through the Internet, and should cost the same per minute as being online (which is to say they're considerably cheaper than a standard international phone call). Bear in mind that there's little privacy in most Internet cafés (although the most go-ahead are starting to build individual booths for Web calls) and the Web-call process is still in its early experimental days – you may have badly echoing or crackling lines and long delays in getting through.

Another way of keeping in touch via the Internet is with instant messaging. This is, essentially, a text based conversation in real time – you sign on and type a greeting to an online friend or family member who receives it instantly and writes back; you can carry on your conversation for as long as you want. Like Web calling, the cost is the same as using the Internet, and you'll need a computer with instant messaging software – this can be downloaded free of charge from MSN, AOL, Yahoo or ICQ (®www.icq.com). An additional form of instant messaging is called Skype (®www.skype.com) and can also be downloaded for free. Computers with microphones or webcams attached make vocal and visual communication possible as well (meaning you can actually see and speak to your family and friends back home) – and all for the cost of using the Internet. If you

Email junkies

They sit in rows, hunched over computers, typing furiously – in Mexico, in Guatemala, in Colombia, Peru, Chile, in virtually every city in every country in Latin America. They'll tell you which cybercafé has the cheapest Internet rates in town, the fastest access, even which particular computer works best – they're email junkies and they need a daily fix. While Latin American life goes on outside, the bustle of markets and street life, the chaotic traffic and the noise, ruined cities, beaches, music, sunshine or torrential rain, email junkies are cloistered in cyber-cafés for hours on end, the low tip-tapping of the keyboard only sound as they indulge their obsession. All the way to Latin America to send an email, that's an expensive habit... And when you ask them in the evening what they've done with their day, they shrug a bit sheepishly – "Oh yeah, couldn't make it to Machu Picchu, had a few emails to send." "And tomorrow, do you want to visit Lake Titicaca?" "Hmm, nah, got to check if I've been sent any back."
Polly Rodger Brown

are interested in keeping in touch this way, you'll need to ensure that your friends and family are all signed up to instant messaging/Skype and that the Internet café you're using has all the necessary software and facilities.

Phoning home

Phoning home from Latin America is usually a fairly straightforward procedure, although you have several choices in how to make your call.

Telephone centres

All cities and towns in Latin America (and, nowadays, even some villages) have a telephone centre (*centro de llamadas* or *caseta de teléfono*; *locutorio* in Peru and Argentina; *posto telefônico* in Brazil) – generally a branch of the national telecom company. These usually have a series of numbered booths and an operator. You give the number you wish to call (preferably written in full with all the relevant codes) to the operator, who will dial it for you and then point you to a booth where you can make your call in private. You'll be charged by the minute, although there may be a minimum charge. Telephone centres vary enormously when it comes to rates – some charge no more than the cost of a call made in a public phone, while others hike up the prices substantially. Always check the prices of international calls first, since they can be exorbitant, and are always more than the cost of an international call from your home country. Generally, though, it costs about US$1–2.50 per minute to phone the US, US$3–4.50 to phone Europe, and US$6–8 to phone Australasia. Telephone centres may not always have the cheapest rates available (see below), but are often the simplest (and most private) way of making a phone call. In addition, telephone centres in larger towns and cities often offer a fax service and, increasingly, also provide Internet access.

Public phones

It's possible to make international calls directly from certain phones on the street; this is sometimes cheaper than using a telephone centre, although access to international phone lines is erratic at the best of times. You'll need to buy a phonecard (*tarjeta telefónica* or

△ Phoning home, Bolivia

carta telefônico in Brazil) – these are now used in most public phones in Latin America rather than coins, and are sold widely in grocery stores, pharmacies and newsstands (buy the highest-value card available if you're making international calls). The drawback is that public phones in Latin America are often situated in noisy public places, so if you do get through, you may not be able to hear anything.

Calling cards

Calling cards have lots of advantages when phoning from abroad: they're often cheaper to use than calling from a public phone or telephone centre, and can also be used when calling from private phones – including those in hotels – at no extra charge. While some calling card services are prepaid, the majority are now charged to a credit card account or home phone number, and you can top up the service as you go. The procedure is fairly straightforward – you dial a specified operator, quote your PIN number and then the number you wish to call. It's not always plain sailing though – sometimes lines are engaged or faulty and occasionally you may even be cut off.

Hundreds of telecom companies now offer calling cards: the best-established include AT&T, MCI and Sprint in the US and Canada; BT and Mercury in the UK; Telstra in Australia; and Telecom in New Zealand. Additionally, American Express offer a prepaid card, and it's also possible to use a Visa credit card (🌐www.visa.com). E-kit (🌐www.ekit.com) offer an advanced calling card service which offers a seventy percent discount on international calls, can be recharged online and has voicemail so that your friends and family can leave messages which you later pick up. With so many services to choose from, you should compare rates – US-based calling cards are often the best value and are increasingly available in Europe and Australasia. You can sign up for most calling cards via the relevant website.

Calling from a hotel

Phones in hotel rooms should be treated with caution, since rates for ringing from these are notoriously exorbitant (if you use a calling card you shouldn't be charged, although hotel staff don't always understand the system or might try to impose a surcharge). In dire emergencies you can always attempt a collect (reverse-charge) call (*llamada a cobrar)* through the international operator, and in some cases it may actually be cheaper to pay for the call when you arrive home than dialling directly from Latin America. Collect/reverse-charge calls can be made from telephone centres, the street or your hotel, although the country you're calling from will need to have a reciprocal agreement with the country you're phoning, and these don't always exist.

Mail

Unlike an email, a letter or postcard can be written anywhere and is a great way of whiling away long evenings. Postal services in Latin America are fairly reliable (though this varies from country to country: Chile and Belize have excellent postal services while Guatemala's is dire and hugely expensive) but slow (up to three weeks to Europe and longer to Australasia, although post to the US usually arrives within a week): always send letters airmail.

There aren't many mailboxes in Latin America; it's easiest to send mail from post offices. It's also best not to post mail from remote areas, where it may be collected only sporadically; wait instead until you reach a big town or city where post is sorted every day – your post home might arrive weeks earlier as a result. Stamps (*estampillas* in Spanish or *sellos* in Brazil) are available in general stores as well as post offices and are relatively expensive.

If you're having letters sent to you via poste restante, you can collect them at any post office: mail should bear your name followed by the words "Lista de Correos" (*Posta Restante* in Brazil; *General Delivery* in Belize), Correo Centrale, and then the town and country name. Every main post office will have a Lista de Correos section where they keep mail for at least a month. Letters are often filed erratically, however: ask the clerk to check under both your first name and surname. You'll have to present some form of ID (preferably your passport) when collecting post, and in some countries you'll also have to pay a small fee. It's also possible to pick up post from American Express offices – all big Latin American cities have them – though in theory you should be using an Amex credit card or travellers' cheques to qualify for this service. In practice this is often not necessary, though you might then be charged a few dollars to collect your post.

While letters usually get through safely, packages are likely to be tampered with or go missing – it's best to avoid having these sent to you at all via national postal networks. If you really need something sent to you, use a worldwide courier service (see below). To send a parcel, you'll need to find a large central post office, preferably in a capital city, where there'll be a special section. Take the contents of your parcel unwrapped – they'll have to be inspected by a customs official and you may then have to wrap them a certain way. Fortunately, all the materials necessary will be conveniently on sale, either in the post office or on the streets outside. Be aware, though, that parcels leaving Latin America are equally prone to disappear.

Alternatively, you can send anything home via an international courier company – both Fedex and DHL have offices all over Latin America and offer an expensive but efficient service. In some very touristy places, such as Antigua in Guatemala or San Miguel de Allende in Mexico, private shipping companies exist who will send home your souvenirs safely – for a price.

The media

As well as speaking or writing to your friends and family you might want to know what is happening in the news back home. If you're from North America, keeping in touch with the news is relatively easy, particularly in Mexico and Central America. Europeans and Australasians, however, may have a hard time finding newspapers and TV stations carrying news from home.

Newspapers

The most commonly found foreign newspapers in Latin America are all from the US and include the *Miami Herald*, the *International Herald Tribune* and the *New York Times*, which can be bought at newsstands in capital cities throughout Latin America. The news magazines *Time* and *Newsweek* and *The Economist* are also widely available, though expensive. If you're really desperate to know the news you're better off logging onto the website of your favourite newspaper back home. Alternatively, foreign embassies and consulates sometimes keep newspapers and magazines that you can go in and read.

Most countries also have an English-language weekly of some kind, usually found in capital cities and places with large expat communities who provide a ready market for English-language news, as well as contributing articles and columns. These papers tend to concentrate on local community issues and have little foreign news. The *Buenos Aires Herald* is the longest established English language paper in Latin America and is broad-ranging – so is the Cusco-based weekly, *New World News*; both have news gathered from the whole of South America as well as the rest of the world.

If your Spanish or Portuguese is up to it, you could try reading national newspapers, some of which are very decent, with foreign reportage, serious political analysis and commentary. The *Folha de São Paulo, El Mercurio* from Chile and Mexico's *La Jornada* and the relatively new *Reforma* are some of the best-regarded Latin American papers.

Television

Television is something of an obsession in Latin America, and increasingly numbers of Latin Americans are now subscribing to North American cable and satellite services, meaning that if you have a TV in your hotel room you'll probably have access to CNN, at the very least. In backpacker centres and big resorts you'll also find bars with sports channels, MTV and (if they're run by Europeans) the international BBC news channel, all in English.

Radio

Radio is also a good way of keeping up with news from home via the Voice of America (@www.voa.gov) or the BBC World Service (@www.bbc.co.uk/worldservice), but you'll need a good shortwave radio to pick them up. It's also worth checking out frequencies in advance – you can do this online – since these change with baffling rapidity from region to region and at different times of the day.

14

Crime, safety and sleaze

rom what you read about Latin America in newspapers back home, it's easy to get the impression that the entire region is dominated by earthquakes, floods, violent crime, drug-trafficking and civil disorder. In reality, although such problems do exist, they're unlikely to affect you – instead, you're much more likely to experience more mundane hassles like petty theft and con-tricks of one kind or another. The information in this chapter should help you avoid the pitfalls that await the unwary and ensure you join the great majority of those who visit Latin America without experiencing any problems with crime or personal safety.

It's worth reiterating that on no account should you set foot in Latin America without adequate insurance; see pp.182–185 for more information on this.

Avoiding trouble

In most of Latin America the threat of crime is not that much greater than in North America or Europe. The difference is that, whereas back home you blend in and can spot potential danger signs much more easily, in Latin America you probably stand out like a sore thumb – a very wealthy sore thumb, moreover, at least in the eyes of most Latin Americans. The most important rule is not to suspend the instincts that keep you safe at home. It's better to become slightly paranoid than to wander around oblivious to potential dangers: just because you're on holiday, it doesn't mean the crooks are. Once you get used to local cultural norms and, ideally, pick up some of the local language, you'll find you can judge whether or not to trust people just as effectively as you can at home. Latin Americans aren't all angels, but they're not all villains either, and you shouldn't let one bad encounter put you off the entire population.

It's also important to stay informed. Supplement what's in your guidebook with up-to-date information from newspapers, magazines and websites. Natural disasters, civil wars and the like don't make it into the pages of guidebooks until months or years after the event, but they'll be all over the international news media within hours. Travellers' newsgroups and bulletin boards on the Internet are also an excellent resource (see p.375 for a list of some of the most useful), and most governments have a department to advise on safety abroad (see p.371) – contact them or check their website to find out the current situation in countries you're planning to visit. In the event of an emergency while you're travelling, contact your nearest embassy or consulate (see pp.352–353 for details on how they can help you); the address should be listed in your guidebook. It's important to keep such information in perspective, however. If you hear about a guerrilla uprising or natural disaster in a country you're about to visit, be sure to check it out, but be aware that the problem may well be limited to a remote region hundreds of kilometres from anywhere you're intending to go – an outbreak of fighting in the southern Mexican state of Chiapas, for example, isn't going to affect your plans for a beach holiday in Cancún.

Once you're travelling, always heed advice from locals and other travellers, whether it's about a region affected by bandits, an area of a city affected by crime, a hotel where rooms are frequently robbed or a dodgy tour company. Such advice is often much more reliable and up to date than what's in your guidebook, though always be aware that some locals may themselves have an ulterior motive – telling you that a hotel has closed down, for instance, and directing you to their cousin's place instead.

Passports

In most Latin American countries
you are legally required to carry your
passport with you at all times; failure to produce identification when
asked for by a policeman can result
in arrest or lay you open to a bribe. A
photocopy of the personalized pages
of your passport makes it easier to
replace if lost or stolen, and in some
countries you can have the copy
authorized by a public notary for use
as a temporary form of identification if you leave your passport in
safe-keeping. If you're staying in the
same country for a while, consider
registering with your embassy; this
can also save lots of time if you have
to replace a lost or stolen passport.

Theft

Opportunistic theft of one kind or
another is the most common crime
tourists face. More often than not
it's simply the result of carelessness,
and by using common sense, staying alert and taking some simple
precautions you can greatly reduce
the chances of becoming a victim.
The following guidelines should
help reduce your chances of being
robbed, and make it easier to deal
with the consequences if you are.

● Keep a separate stash of emergency
  cash hidden somewhere about your
  person for use if your main money
  belt gets stolen.

- Make a careful note of your plane ticket numbers, the phone numbers you'll need if you have to cancel your credit cards, travellers' cheque numbers (always keep the purchase receipt separately) and insurance details, and keep all these separate from your valuables.
- Carry money, credit cards and vital documents like your passport and airline ticket close to your body and concealed under your clothes at all times. Money belts (see p.230) are good for this, but you can also buy secure wallets that hang under your shirt or from a loop on your belt under your trousers; a hidden pocket sewn inside your trousers, a leg pouch or a belt with a secret zip for cash are even more difficult for thieves to find. Some Latin American women hide cash inside their bras.
- Keep your day's cash separate from your main stash, so your hidden money belt isn't revealed every time you buy a cup of coffee. It's also good to have some cash to hand over in case of armed robbery, so the muggers don't start looking for your main money belt.
- You are at your most vulnerable, and have the most to lose, when you're on the move or arriving in a new town and have all of your luggage with you. Bus stations are a favourite hunting ground of thieves the world over: try not to arrive after dark, keep a close eye and hand on your bags at all times, and consider taking a taxi from the bus terminal to your hotel as a security precaution.
- Mugging and violent robbery usually occur at night, so try to avoid having to walk down empty or poorly lit streets in the early hours, particularly on your own. ATMs are an obvious target for robbers – don't use them at night, if possible. If the robbers are armed, do not resist.
- Unless you travel very light, when moving around by bus or train you'll often have to put your backpack into a luggage compartment or on the roof. This is usually safe, and some bus companies will give you a baggage reclaim ticket, but it's still worth keeping an eye out when the vehicle stops to make sure no one carries your bag off either by mistake or on purpose. It's also worth covering your backpack with a sack (available in any market) to make it less conspicuous – though mark it so you can distinguish it from others.
- Some travellers like to chain their bags together or onto an immovable object when waiting around transport terminals, and onto the roof of the bus or train luggage rack when travelling. You can also buy lockable lightweight metal meshes to fit over your pack for extra security, though this may be a little excessive.
- Transport terminals, markets, city centres, fiestas and other crowded public places are favoured by pickpockets and thieves. If you're

carrying a daypack, keep it in front of you where you can see it to avoid having it slashed; when you stop and sit down, loop a strap around your leg to make it more difficult for someone to grab.

- Better hotels often have a safe or strongbox at reception where you can deposit valuables. This is usually safe, though it's best to leave stuff in a tamper-proof holder (anything with zips which can be padlocked will do) or a signed and sealed envelope. In addition, make sure you get an itemized receipt for whatever you leave, and count cash carefully before and after. Leaving credit cards isn't a good idea – you may return home to find your card has been used up to its limit while you were off on an expedition and you thought it was safely locked away.

- A small padlock is useful for replacing or supplementing the one on your hotel room door if you're worried about security.

- Never leave cameras or other valuables lying around in your hotel room, and be cautious if sharing a room with people you don't know well – other travellers can be thieves too.

- Don't leave valuables on the beach when you swim. Most travel shops sell waterproof canisters which you can wear in the water; alternatively, just take enough cash for your immediate needs and keep it in a small plastic bag in a pocket in your swimming trunks or tucked into your swimsuit.

- Don't flaunt your wealth. Avoid wearing expensive jewellery, use a cheap watch and carry your camera concealed in your daypack rather than round your neck.

- Never carry important stuff in the pockets of your backpack: they're especially vulnerable to theft. You can always carry a small daypack on your front where you can see it.

- Beware of accepting food, drink or cigarettes from fellow passengers on journeys. Some thieves use these to drug their victims, making off with everything they own while they sleep it off. A variant on this, found particularly in Colombia, involves the use of a powder called Burundanga, which can make victims susceptible to hypnotic suggestion. Rather than just rob you, thieves may take you to a bank to withdraw cash on your credit card, or worse. When you come to hours or days later, you may have no recollection at all of what has happened.

- Though usually safer than walking, taxis can also carry an element of risk, as they're usually poorly regulated and drivers can be criminals too. If travelling alone, don't sit in the front seat, where you're vulnerable to attack from behind, lock passenger doors to stop people jumping in beside you, and be wary of cabs driving away with your bags – if your luggage is in the boot, wait for the driver to get out first. Where possible, it's better to order a cab by phone rather than flagging one down in the street.

- Don't automatically trust other travellers – a small minority fund their travels by ripping off others.
- Some travellers are tempted to make false claims of theft so as to claim money from insurance companies for items that have not, in fact, been lost. As well as being a criminal offence back home, fraudulent insurance claims can get you in a lot of trouble in Latin America. In popular tourist areas local police are often wise to this scam, and may well march you round to your hotel room to find your "stolen" camera.

Common scams

The common scams practised on tourists in Latin America change, evolve and become ever more elaborate, but never really go away. The best source of information about all the latest cheats and tricks is other travellers, so talk to other people on the road and learn from their mistakes. Here are a few classic scams you should watch out for:

- Thieves pose as plainclothes police officers, complete with fake documents, and ask to see your documents or check for fake currency, often calling on a "passer-by" (read accomplice) to verify their identity. Don't show them your valuables or get in a car with them, and insist on going to a genuine police station.
- Criminals pose as tour guides with the intention of robbing and/or raping you once they get you out in the middle of nowhere. Only go on trips with reputable tour companies and – particularly for trips to remote areas – with other travellers you trust.
- Your bag or clothing is mysteriously sprayed with mustard or the like. A "friendly passer-by" points this out and offers to help you clean it while his accomplice (who sprayed it there in the first place) picks your pockets or grabs your bag. If you are sprayed, walk away quickly and refuse his or her "help" – you can always clean up later.
- Something valuable – cash, a credit card – is dropped at your feet. A passer-by spots it and asks you to check your wallet to see if it's yours, or offers to share it with you. The story ends either with your own money disappearing by sleight of hand or with you being accused of theft. Ignore anything dropped at your feet and walk away as quickly as possible.
- Someone asks you to carry a package or letter to their friend or relative in another town or country – they may be smugglers and the

contents could well be drugs. With this in mind, don't carry packages for other people.

- Some street moneychangers are adept at ripping you off by sleight of hand while counting notes, or of passing you forged notes; some even have specially rigged calculators. If you can, change money or travellers' cheques at a bank or *casa de cambio* – rates aren't much different these days anyway.

Hazards of nature

Latin America is home to pretty much the full range of dangerous natural phenomena, including lava-spewing volcanoes, catastrophic floods, landslides and earthquakes, not to mention deadly venomous snakes. However scary these might all sound, the chance of you experiencing any of them is remote.

If you're the sort of person who likes to prepare for any eventuality, *The Worst Case Scenario Survival Handbook*, by Joshua Piven and David Borgenicht, has detailed tips on everything from surviving a shark attack to wrestling an alligator.

Earthquakes and volcanoes

The western edge of Central and South America runs along the Pacific Rim, at the meeting point of two of the earth's major tectonic plates, which means it experiences an unusually high level of volcanic and seismic activity. El Salvador, Colombia, Mexico and Peru have all experienced major earthquakes in recent decades, while the capitals of both Mexico and Ecuador, as well as many smaller cities and towns in the region, live in the shadow of highly active volcanoes. The Pacific coast of Latin America is also vulnerable to tsunamis. Seismologists are notoriously poor at predicting when earthquakes will strike, and while major volcanic eruptions are usually detectable some time in advance – and you should check the state of alert before travelling near active volcanoes – they can also strike with frightening suddenness. Realistically, however, the chances of you being caught up in a major natural disaster are very small.

If you are unlucky enough to be caught in a major earthquake, it's best to stay inside unless you're close to a large open space, as falling debris from buildings is a major cause of fatalities. Stay away from windows to avoid splintering glass, and shelter under a doorway or strong table if the building looks like it might collapse. Although phone lines are usually damaged by major quakes, try to contact friends or relatives at home as soon as possible to let them know you're safe.

Hurricanes and floods

The hurricane season in Mexico and Central America runs from roughly October to November and affects both the Atlantic and (to a lesser extent) Pacific coasts. Hurricanes are usually predicted well in advance (you can check the latest forecasts in the local media or on the US National Hurricane Center website at ⓦwww.nhc .noaa.gov), but they can change course fairly quickly. If you're in the path of a hurricane, get out of the area if you can. If you can't, stay indoors away from windows, preferably on high ground to avoid the risk of flooding, taking plenty of food and water with you. As well as loss of life, hurricanes can cause massive damage to transport and other infrastructure, and drinking water may become contaminated: if a region you're planning to visit is hit by a major hurricane, think seriously about revising your itinerary.

Hurricanes often cause substantial flooding, which can also occur following heavy rain anywhere throughout tropical Latin America. Flooding in mountainous regions often wipes out bridges and causes landslides which block roads. Never camp in creeks or dry riverbeds in mountainous areas, as sudden rain can bring devastating flash floods. In addition, don't camp on small islands in rivers in rainforest regions such as the Amazon, and be wary of camping on river beaches, as water levels can rise very quickly, even if it isn't raining where you are.

Snakes and other potentially dangerous creatures

The chances of encountering venomous snakes – such as the lethal and aggressive bushmaster, which uses infrared vision to track its prey – is obviously greater in, say, the Amazonian rainforest than in most places back home (the same goes for other dangerous creatures like spiders and scorpions). But though the thought of a snake in your sleeping bag or a tarantula in your trousers might make you wish you never thought of visiting Latin America, in reality you're highly unlikely to suffer anything worse than a few mosquito bites, especially if you listen to local advice and take sensible precautions.

- Trek with local guides who know the terrain and potential hazards.
- Give snakes a wide berth, and don't ever antagonize them. Most snakes are usually as scared of you as you are of them, and they tend to avoid humans as far as possible, although they will strike if they feel threatened. Wearing thick boots and long trousers, watching where you step and making plenty of noise all reduce the chances of getting bitten.
- If a snake bites you, chances are it won't have injected enough venom to be dangerous, so try to remain calm. Clean the wound, immobilize the limb and avoid all movement to slow the progress of any venom through your bloodstream, and seek medical help immediately. If possible, kill the snake for identification.
- Shake your shoes or boots out every morning: spiders and, especially, scorpions sometimes sleep inside. It's also a good idea to look before you place your hand on the ground or a branch in outdoor areas – arachnids won't look to attack you, but if you disturb or threaten them they will bite or sting, and some species are extremely dangerous.
- Though fairly rare, rabies does exist in Latin America and does kill people, so give dogs a wide berth. Even if not rabid, dogs are often aggressive and can be dangerous, though you can usually dissuade them from matching their bark with a bite by waving a stick or throwing a few stones in their general direction (for more on rabies see p.312).

Hazardous activities

Activities like whitewater rafting, kayaking, mountain climbing, and skiing are not known as dangerous sports for nothing, and though the degree of risk is minimal, safety standards in Latin America are not generally as high as they are back home. Many of the companies that offer such activities may not even be licensed or insured, their "expert" guides may not be properly trained, and their equipment may be shoddy or even dangerous. Don't suspend your usual criteria for judging danger just because you're travelling, check your insurance covers you for specific activities before you undertake them, and always go with a recommended and reputable company, even if it means paying more – dangerous sports are one area where it's really not a good idea to go for the cheapest option.

Swimming

Swimming in the sea can be hazardous due to sharks, poisonous creatures such as sea snakes and jellyfish, heavy surf that can batter you unconscious, and dangerous currents that can drag you out to sea (riptides) or drag you under the water (undertows). Only the most popular resort beaches have lifeguards, so it's best to exercise caution before going for a swim – if you do get into difficulties in the water you can't count on getting rescued. The best guide is to ask locals whether it's safe to swim before getting in the water: if no one else is swimming, you should definitely ask why before doing so yourself. Riptides are formed when two currents running parallel to the shore meet, forcing one current out to sea in a powerful stream. They are usually found on beaches with heavy surf or near river estuaries. Some are permanent, while others "migrate" up and down the beach. If you get caught in one and find yourself being dragged out to sea, don't panic or exhaust yourself by trying to fight it and swim back to shore. Instead, try to attract the attention of people on land, and when the current slackens after taking you away from the shore, swim back in at a 45-degree angle so as to avoid being caught in the current again. Undertows, which drag you beneath the surface of the water, are more difficult to escape: the best thing is to avoid getting in the water in the first place, so always check if the beach is safe before swimming. The same goes for dangerous sea creatures such as sharks and jellyfish: ask local people if it is safe to swim before getting in the water, and get out quick if you see a shark or other hazard.

Swimming in fresh water can also be hazardous. River and lake currents can be deceptive, while buoyancy in fresh water is less than in salt water – a dangerous combination that increases the risk of drowning. Piranha fish, found in tropical South American rivers, are far less dangerous than books and films would have you believe (most eat fruit rather than humans), but they pack a painful bite and do sometimes attack in shoals, especially when concentrated in small pools at the end of the dry season, or if their victim is already bleeding. Cayman crocodiles rarely attack humans, but you should still avoid swimming in waters where they are present. Other fresh-water hazards include electric eels, which pack a powerful shock equivalent to 500 volts, and the infamous candiru, a small, parasitic eel-like fish with a penchant for swimming up the urethra to feed on blood and lodging there using its sharp barbs, an extremely painful – and even fatal – condition which can only be cured by surgery; always wear swimming trunks or a costume and don't urinate in the water while swimming. Always check with locals before swimming in tropical rivers and lakes. Freshwater stingrays also pose a risk, so wear shoes or boots and probe sandy riverbeds with a stick before wading across them. Finally, though many of the volcanic hot springs scattered around Latin America are safe to bathe in, it's always a good idea to check the temperature before plunging in, as this can vary from day to day, and some unfortunate travellers have been badly scalded by springs which were generally considered perfectly safe.

Guerrillas, bandits and civil unrest

Until the early 1990s, many countries in Latin America were riven by bloody civil wars and other armed conflicts, usually between Marxist guerrillas and oppressive military regimes. Fortunately,

△ Police checkpoint, Chile

most of these have now been resolved, and democracy (albeit often of a limited kind) is now the rule across the region. A notable exception to all this is Colombia, large areas of which remain off-limits to travellers because of fighting – the risk of being kidnapped or caught in the crossfire between left-wing rebels, right-wing paramilitaries and the security forces is very real. Research the current situation carefully before visiting Colombia, and take local advice on which areas are safe when there. This conflict sometimes spills over into the border areas of neighbouring countries, and the Darién Gap between Colombia and Panama in particular should be avoided. Some remote parts of Peru are still off-limits because of the presence of remnant bands of the Shining Path (*Sendero Luminoso*) rebel group, and parts of the southern Mexican state of Chiapas, where the stand-off between the Zapatista rebels and the Mexican army continues, should also be avoided.

The end of the region's armed conflicts has left many countries awash with arms and with former combatants who have few prospects and little to lose; some of these have turned to banditry (itself a long-standing Latin American tradition), holding up cars and buses on isolated roads. However, this is usually confined to very localized areas and the risk of encountering bandits is small, and can be further reduced by taking local advice on which regions or roads are dangerous and avoiding travelling by night where possible.

Though the era of armed conflicts and brutal dictatorships has largely passed, many Latin American countries – including in recent years Argentina, Peru, Bolivia, Ecuador, Venezuela, Nicaragua and Guatemala – are still subject to periods of serious political and economic upheaval. This very much goes with the territory in Latin America, and will usually have little effect on your travel plans, though strikes, roadblocks or protests can sometimes paralyse cities or entire countries, so it's worth keeping an eye on local and international news sources (check ⓦwww.bbc.co.uk or ⓦwww.cnn .com). It's best to steer clear of political demonstrations: these can spiral out of control very quickly and police responses are often extreme. Elections, too, sometimes involve considerable tension, and even when they don't, extra security measures and travel restrictions may prove a problem. If you get caught up in any major political upheaval it's best to sit tight in your hotel and wait until things blow over – everything's likely to be shut anyway.

You should also be wary of discussing politics in public and with strangers, as tempers can get very heated, and be cautious about getting directly involved in local politics – a recent vogue for so-called "guerrilla tourism" in the southern Mexican state of Chiapas has seen many young travellers expelled from the country.

Sexual harassment

Though it varies in degree between countries and regions (it's generally weaker in areas where indigenous culture is strong) machismo – the cultural stereotype that characterizes women as weak and submissive, and men as strong and dominant – is alive and well in Latin America, and attitudes to gender equality and the rights of women are a long way behind those you're probably used to at home. Under traditional machismo stereotypes, women are viewed either as virgins or whores – foreign women in particular are widely considered to fall into the latter camp, an attitude reinforced by films and magazines. The local perception of female travellers is often one of sexual availability and promiscuity (the very fact that you have the freedom to travel the world is seen as confirming this), so as a female traveller you're likely to face some degree of verbal or physical harassment, something many Latin American women suffer from as well. Having said that, most female travellers to Latin America don't experience any serious problems, even when travelling alone, and if you rely on the instincts you use to avoid sexual harassment at home, you should be able to prevent it from spoiling your trip. The following tips may help:

- Exercise at least the same degree of caution as you do at home: don't walk alone down dark streets at night; avoid hiking or camping alone or in small groups; avoid taking taxis alone at night and, if you do, try to call a radio taxi rather than flag one down on the street.
- Always carry enough cash on you in case you need to take a taxi back to your hotel.
- Make sure your hotel room is secure, taking care to check door and window locks. You may want to use your own padlock.
- Harassment usually takes the form of whistling or cat-calling: the best way to deal with it is to ignore it.
- Be aware of the different interpretations that may be placed on your behaviour in Latin America: what may pass for simple flirtation or even just friendly conversation back home may be seen as a direct come-on by Latin American men.
- Be assertive: if you find yourself the subject of unwanted male attention don't be afraid to politely but firmly tell them where to go. Men who grope or harass you can be shamed into leaving you alone if you draw public attention to their actions.
- Observe how local women dress. While skimpy bikinis and figure-hugging lycra may be all the rage in some coastal resorts, in remote areas they can cause deep offence and may even get you chased out of town.
- Many Latin American bars are pretty much men-only and should be avoided: if you want to go out for a drink, choose more upmarket places or those frequented by other travellers.
- If you're not married, invent a mythical husband: some unmarried women travellers wear a wedding ring to ward off potential pests.
- Don't automatically trust male travellers just because of cultural familiarity or shared language.
- Remember that sexual harassment can work both ways: many men can feel extremely uncomfortable with the direct approach of Latin American prostitutes in some areas. Latin American attitudes to homosexuality are also generally conservative. Though some countries (especially Brazil) and cities have thriving gay communities, in much of the region homosexuality is frowned upon and kept under wraps. Gay travellers are unlikely to suffer any direct abuse, but it's best to be discreet and avoid public displays of affection.

Drugs

The production and trafficking of illegal drugs – particularly cocaine, but also marijuana and heroin – is a major industry in many countries in Latin America, and despite what governments in the region would have you believe, local consumption is also on the increase. However, though drugs are widely available in many areas, penalties for possession – never mind trafficking – are very severe. Under heavy pressure from the US to stamp out the drug trade, local authorities are particularly happy to throw the book at foreign offenders, and being caught with even small amounts of an illegal substance can get you a long sentence in a Latin American jail, as many travellers have found to their cost.

If this doesn't put you off, be warned that in tourist areas, set-ups by dealers and the police are commonly used as a way of extorting money from unwary travellers. Areas where drugs are produced – particularly the coca-growing regions of Bolivia, Colombia and Peru – should be given a wide berth, as you're likely to be taken either for a trafficker or a foreign drug-enforcement agent. Coca leaf itself – the raw material from which cocaine is produced – is legal in Peru and Bolivia, where it has been used for thousands of years by local indigenous people as a mild stimulant and a key ingredient in traditional rituals and medicine (it's also used to make a herbal tea which is useful in combating altitude sickness). It's illegal in other Latin American countries and the rest of the world, however, so if you buy some be sure to get rid of it before you cross any borders or get on a plane home.

Corruption and the police

In general, the police rarely trouble tourists, and with any luck, your contact with them will be limited to frontiers and road checkpoints. Even so, it's important to be polite in any dealings you have with them, as they can easily make problems for you if you're not. Bear in mind that police officers are invariably armed, and may well shoot you if you run away from them. Anyone claiming to be an undercover policeman is probably a thief or confidence trickster (see p.341); don't get in a car with them or show them your documents or valuables, and insist on the presence of a uniformed officer. If you do need to contact the police, it's best to go to the tourist police, where they exist; they'll probably have a better understanding of your problem, and are more likely to speak English.

Latin American police are generally very poorly paid, and in many countries graft has become an accepted part of the job. It's not unusual to be offered an opportunity to bribe a policeman even if you've done nothing wrong. Often they're just trying it on, and there's no need to pay if you're innocent of any misdemeanour: refusing politely or acting like you don't understand is usually enough. In some circumstances, however, it can work to the advantage of both parties – if you've committed an offence, paying a small bribe is certainly preferable to going to jail. Beware of initiating a bribe unless you're very sure of your footing and speak the language reasonably well, however, as doing so can sometimes cause offence and make the situation worse; in Chile, for instance, the police have a scrupulous reputation for honesty and won't take kindly to being offered a bribe.

Corruption is by no means limited to the police: throughout much of Latin America it's very much a normal part of everyday life that involves

Official encounters

We drove slowly to the gate marking the border of Mexico, and stopped at the fumigation office. While I fended off the moneychangers, a man sprayed the car inside and out. When the fumes subsided, the border gate was lifted, and we entered Guatemala. We pulled over and went into the immigration office. The border officials were amazingly friendly. They took our information, stamped our passports, and we handed over 30 pesos (just over US$3), laughing as we recalled horror stories we'd read about having to bribe border officials with exorbitant amounts of cash. The customs officials were even friendlier. They looked in the car, fingered a few things, asked us what they were, and filled out a form or two.

An hour after we'd arrived at the border, we were on our way, still laughing about how nervous we had been. But we weren't in the clear yet. We began snaking our way along a valley set below incredible mountains, and not thirty minutes into Guatemala, we found ourselves driving behind a police vehicle. I saw someone in the back seat turn around and look at us, and seconds later the lights went on. "Oh please, not already," I thought. Sure enough, I saw a hand poke out of the passenger side window and motion for us to pull over. We did, and out of the vehicle came three policemen with enormous machine guns. I smiled my best "oh my god, look at those guns" smile, and said "Buenas tardes." "Buenos dias," they responded. Thinking that perhaps we'd entered a new time zone when we crossed the border, I asked them what time it was. They told me it was midday, and smiling, they said "Si, buenas tardes." Then they asked where we were from and where we were going, took a glance around the car, smiled again, and wished us a good trip. Even before they'd walked away, we began to laugh in disbelief – yet again. It seemed they just wanted to say hello!

Julie Feiner

everyone from presidents down to minor officials – there may be times when you're invited to pay a bribe or a "tip" to ensure you get a seat on that plane or get through border formalities without hassle or delays. Once again, there's no need to pay if you don't want to – asking for a receipt is a good way of avoiding irregular payments to officials – but there may be occasions when it's easier just to hand over a small sum and be on your way. If you choose to do so, however, bear in mind that you're oiling the wheels of a system that many Latin Americans feel is one of the main causes of the region's poverty and under-development (even as they themselves pay up).

If disaster strikes

If disaster strikes and you're robbed or find yourself in trouble with the authorities, your embassy or consulate abroad can:

- Issue emergency passports – having a photocopy of the original will speed this up immediately.
- Contact friends and family and ask them for help with money or tickets.
- Put you in touch with local doctors and lawyers.
- Contact or visit you in prison.
- Inform next-of-kin in case of serious illness.

- Evacuate you from the country in the event of major political upheaval or civil war.

However, your embassy or consulate cannot:

- Give you money (though they may give an emergency loan under very strict criteria).
- Pay to fly you home, other than in very exceptional circumstances.
- Get you out of prison. You won't get much sympathy or help if you're on a drugs charge.

You may also need to:

- Contact the police if you have been the victim of a crime, and to get a written report for insurance purposes if you've been robbed.
- Contact your insurance company. You should carry your policy number and emergency contact details with you and leave a copy at home. Be aware of the procedures you need to follow in the event of robbery or illness, as failure to do so could invalidate your claim. In the case of theft or loss of possessions, you can usually wait until you get home, but in the event of serious medical emergencies you'll need to contact your insurer promptly, especially if you need them to cover hospital or air-evacuation costs.
- Cancel your credit cards if they're stolen – make sure you have an international 24-hour hotline number for doing this. If your travellers' cheques are lost or stolen you'll need to contact the issuer with full details to order replacements.

15

Coming home

Everyone expects to experience culture shock when they travel to Latin America, but culture shock works both ways, and after a long period away you may find returning home a surprisingly difficult transition to make. Even though it's initially exciting to be surrounded once again by familiar things and people, normal life back home may soon seem tedious and banal compared to the excitement of travel, and friends and relatives may not be able to relate to experiences of life on the road. You may find that your outlook on life has been transformed by your travels, even while those closest to you hope you've "got it out of your system" and are now ready to settle down. At worst, exchanging the freedom of travel and the joy of experiencing new things every day for the sometimes-humdrum realities of work and life back home can be very depressing. Short of immediately setting off on further travels, there's no real antidote for the homecoming blues. However, the following tips should make it easier to cope with:

● Before you go away, try to set aside some money as your coming-home fund – returning home is bad enough, never mind doing so without a penny to your name.
● While you're still on the road make some plans – however basic – for the immediate future after you get home. Returning home with nothing to look forward to is the worst possible scenario; having

a job, university place or some other project lined up makes the transition much easier to deal with.

- Make sure you keep in touch with people back home who are important to you, so they're aware of your experiences and thoughts. That way, they won't be too surprised by how you may have changed while you've been away.

- Don't expect everyone at home to be enthralled by your traveller's tales and photographs. Some people may find your experiences boring or difficult to relate to, while others may simply feel envious that you've been off having an adventurous time while they've been stuck in the same old routine.

- Get in touch with other travellers you've met on the road, and with friends and relatives who've been travelling themselves: they will probably understand what you're going through and will be much more interested in hearing about your trip.

- Keep in touch with locals you've met during your travels, and send out those photos you promised them.

- If you live in a large city with a Latin American community, seek out their bars, restaurants and cultural events where you can relive some of your favourite experiences. Taking salsa classes, learning to cook some classic Latin American dishes, reading books and watching films about Latin America are also all good ways of keeping the experience alive.

- If the worse comes to the worst, start planning and saving money for your next trip. If that's not possible, remember Latin America will always be there, so you will be able to go back one day.

Getting involved

However much you enjoy travelling in Latin America, the chances are you will have found some aspects of life there depressing and shocking, such as the extreme poverty faced by most of the population, the corruption and political oppression, the dearth of basic public services and lack of opportunities. You may also have been dismayed by the rate at which many of the beautiful natural environments you've experienced are being destroyed in the name of economic development. If so, getting involved with some of these issues when you return is a good way of maintaining your interest in Latin America; it's also a positive way of using your experiences and of making sense of all that you saw and did while you were there. The following are some of the major organizations that campaign about issues in Latin America and make a contribution towards tackling some of the problems you may feel strongly about.

- **Amnesty International** (⊕www.amnesty.org) Leading international human rights organization which publishes reports on political oppression in countries around the world, including many in Latin America. Their website has a huge amount of information (including much which governments would prefer you didn't see) as well as excellent links to other human rights-related sites.

- **Brazil Network** (⊕www.brazilnetwork.org) A London-based campaign group that provides information on social, environmental and cultural issues in Brazil that rarely make it into the mainstream media. They stage frequent cultural events and have a good website with a wide range of information on Brazil.

- **Greenpeace** (⊕www.greenpeace.org) An international environmental group best known for its dramatic direct-action protests, Greenpeace campaigns on many issues relevant to Latin America, including climate change, genetically modified crops, tropical rainforest conservation and biodiversity protection.

- **Latin America Bureau** (⊕www.lab.org.uk) London-based independent research and publishing organization working to

△ Trekking, Peru

broaden public understanding of issues of human rights and social and economic justice in Latin America and the Caribbean. Publishes a huge range of non-specialist books and is the main point of reference in the UK for people interested in Latin America, with a website full of information and a list of organizations sending voluntary workers to Latin America.

- **One World** (Ⓦwww.oneworld.net) A network of more than a thousand human rights, anti-poverty and environmental organisations, with masses of information on Latin America, as well as lists of job vacancies and volunteering opportunities.
- **Rainforest Action Network** (Ⓦwww.ran.org) International campaign network working to prevent rainforest destruction and protect the human rights of forest peoples, with a website full of information on Latin America's dwindling forests and links to other relevant sites.
- **Survival International** (Ⓦwww.survival-international.org) Campaigns for the rights of tribal people all over the world and against governments, armies, corporations, banks, missionaries and anyone else who threatens their future.

Making your trip work for you

After your travels you may be looking for work, either at home or overseas. Your prospects with future employers will be better if you can not only describe your trip as an enjoyable adventure but also show that you developed useful abilities or experiences while travelling. Doing some kind of voluntary work during part of your trip always looks good on a CV or resume. Speaking Spanish or Portuguese is a valuable skill, so you might want to polish what you picked up while travelling by taking further language tuition.

In the longer term, your experiences in Latin America can help prepare you for work in the travel industry, either working for a travel agency at home or as a guide back in Latin America. To get work as a tour guide you'll need to speak pretty good Spanish and/or Portuguese and convince the tour operator that you have the necessary background knowledge, social skills and ability to take responsibility before they entrust a group of paying clients to your care. Look out for job adverts in the travel press and don't be afraid to approach tour operators if you think you've got what they need. When you are travelling you may well run into people working in the industry who you can ask about what the work is like, and what potential employers are looking for. Back home, travel fairs are a good place to find out more.

If you've taken good photographs or written about your travels you may be able to make some money out of it when you return, or even turn it into a career. If you want to sell photos or travel stories, it's worth having a good look at the kind of material different newspapers and magazines favour before you go. Unless you have good contacts or previously published work you're unlikely to elicit much interest before you set off on your trip, and you'll have to submit articles and photos to publications on spec when you get back. Obviously, travel magazines with small circulations or which are distributed free are much more likely to look at your work than national newspapers and major magazine titles. They don't pay much, but the first step is to get something into print, which you can then use to approach other publishers. In several Latin American countries there are small English-language newspapers, which can be a good place to get your picture or stories published. Most national newspapers and travel magazines run annual travel-writing competitions for young people, which are an excellent way of getting into the industry – even if you don't win, a good entry can get you noticed and bring future commissions. Photographers are better off approaching picture agencies and libraries rather than magazines – remember, if you're hoping to sell your photos, you'll really need to take slides or high-resolution digital images rather than colour prints. Both travel writing and photography are difficult areas to break into, and even if you succeed you still may well struggle to make a living, but it's a big industry that always has room for new talent. Have a look at Guy Marks' very useful *Travel Writing and Photography, All You Need to Know to Make it Pay* or Louise Purwin Zobel's *The Travel Writers Handbook, How to Write and Sell Your Own Travel Experiences* for further advice.

First-Time Latin America

Directory

1   Discount travel and online booking agents   361

2   Specialist tour operators   364

3   Volunteer organizations   367

4   Health   369

5   Official advice on international trouble spots   371

6   Responsible tourism   372

7   Travel book and map stores   373

8   Online travel resources   374

9   Specialist Latin American resource centres   376

10   Travel equipment suppliers   377

11   Final checklist   379

Discount travel and online booking agents

UK

Apex Travel Ireland ☎01/241 8000, ⓦwww.apextravel.ie. Specialists in flights to the US and Latin America.

Aran Travel International Ireland ☎091/562595, ⓦwww.iol.ie/~arantv /aranmain. Good value flights to all parts of the world.

Bridge the World UK ☎0870/443 2399, ⓦwww.bridgetheworld.com. Specializing in round-the-world tickets with good deals aimed at the backpacker market.

Co-op Travel Care UK ☎0870/112 0085, ⓦwww.travelcare.co.uk. Cheap flights and holidays to Brazil.

ebookers UK ☎020/7757 2444, ⓦwww.ebookers.com, Ireland ☎01/241 5689, ⓦwww.ebookers .com/ie. Low fares on an extensive selection of scheduled flights.

Flights 4 Less UK 0871/222 3423, ⓦwww.flights4less.com. Good discount airfares to most countries in the region.

Joe Walsh Tours Ireland ☎01/872 2555 or 676 3053, ⓦwww .joewalshtours.ie. General budget fares agent.

Lee Travel Ireland ☎021/277111, ⓦwww.leetravel.ie. Flights and holidays worldwide.

London Flight Centre UK ☎020/7244 6411, ⓦwww .topdecktravel.co.uk. Long-established discount flight agent.

Maxwell's Travel Ireland ☎01/679 5700, ⓔsales@worldwideadventure .ie. Veteran Latin American operator.

McCarthy's Travel Ireland ☎021/427 0127, ⓦwww .mccarthystravel.ie. General flight agent.

North South Travel UK ☎01245/608291, ⓦwww .northsouthtravel.co.uk. Friendly and competitive travel agency offering discounted fares worldwide – profits are used to support projects in the developing world, especially the promotion of sustainable tourism.

Premier Travel Northern Ireland ☎028/7126 3333, ⓦwww .premiertravel.uk.com. Discount flight specialists.

Rosetta Travel Northern Ireland ☎028/9064 4996, ⓦwww .rosettatravel.com. Flight and holiday agent.

STA Travel UK ☎08701/600599, ⓦwww.statravel.co.uk. Worldwide specialists in low-cost flights and tours for students and under-26s, though other customers are welcome.

Trailfinders UK ☎020/7628 7628, ⓦwww.trailfinders.co.uk, Ireland ☎01/677 7888, ⓦwww.trailfinders .ie. One of the best-informed and most efficient agents for independent travellers; they also produce a very useful quarterly magazine worth scrutinizing for RTW routes.

Travel Cuts UK ☎020/7255 2082, ⓦwww.travelcuts.co.uk. Canadian company specializing in budget, student and youth travel and RTW tickets.

USIT Now Northern Ireland ☎028/ 9032 7111, Republic of Ireland

⊕01/602 1600, ⓦwww.usitnow.ie.
Student and youth specialists for
flights and trains.

US and Canada

Air Brokers International
⊕1-800/883-3273 or 415/397-1383,
ⓦwww.airbrokers.com. Consolidator
and specialists in RTW and Circle
Pacific tickets.

Airtech ⊕212/219-7000, ⓦwww
.airtech.com. Standby seat broker;
also deals in consolidator fares and
courier flights.

Airtreks ⊕1-877-AIRTREKS or
415/912 5600, ⓦwww.airtreks.com.
Specialist in RTW and Circle Pacific
tickets; their website features an
interactive database that lets you
build and price your own round the
world itinerary.

Educational Travel Center
⊕1-800/747-5551 or 608/256-5551,
ⓦwww.edtrav.com. Student/youth
discount agent.

STA Travel US ⊕1-800/781-4040,
ⓦwww.statravel.com, Canada
⊕1-888/427-5639, ⓦwww.sta-travel
.ca. Worldwide specialists in independent travel; also sell student ID,
travel insurance, car rental and rail
passes.

Travac ⊕1-800/TRAV-800,
ⓦwww.thetravelsite.com.
Consolidator and charter broker
with offices in New York City and
Orlando.

Travel Avenue ⊕1-800/333-3335,
ⓦwww.travelavenue.com. Full
service travel agent that offers
discounts in the form of rebates.

Travel Cuts Canada ⊕1-800/667-
2887, US ⊕1-866/246-9762,

ⓦwww.travelcuts.com. Canadian
student travel organization.

Travelers Advantage ⊕1-877/259-
2691, ⓦwww.travelersadvantage
.com. Discount travel club; annual
membership fee required (three
months' trial membership costs
US$1).

Worldtrek Travel ⊕1-800/243-1723,
ⓦwww.worldtrek.com. Discount
travel agency for worldwide travel.

Australia and New Zealand

Anywhere Travel Australia
⊕02/9663 0411, ⓦwww
.anywheretravel.com.au. Discount
flight and travel agent.

Backpackers Travel Centre
Australia ⊕02/9215 2400, ⓦwww
.backpackerstravel.com.au

Budget Travel New Zealand
⊕09/366 0061 or 0800/808040,
ⓦwww.budgettravel.co.nz.
Discounted flights and packages.

Destinations Unlimited New
Zealand ⊕09/373 4033, ⓦwww
.destinations-unlimited.co.nz.
Discount fares and tours.

Flight Centres Australia ⊕02/9235
3522 (for your nearest branch call
⊕13/1600), ⓦwww.flightcentre
.com.au, New Zealand ⊕09/358
4310, ⓦwww.flightcentre.co.nz.
Competitive discounts on airfares
and holidays.

Holiday Shoppe New Zealand
⊕0800/808 480, ⓦwww
.holidayshoppe.co.nz

Northern Gateway Australia
⊕1800/174800, ⓦwww
.northerngateway.com.au. Discount
fares and holidays.

STA Travel Australia ☎1300/733035, ⓦwww.statravel.com.au, New Zealand ☎0508/782872, ⓦwww.statravel.com.nz. Discount fares for students and under-26s, student cards and travel insurance.

Student Uni Travel Australia ☎02/9232 8444, ⓦwww.sut.com.au, New Zealand ☎09/379 4224, ⓦwww.sut.co.nz. Student/youth discounts and travel advice.

Thomas Cook Australia ☎02/9231 2877, ⓦwww.thomascook.com.au, New Zealand ☎09/379 3920, ⓦwww.thomascook.co.nz. Global travel agent with discounts on fares and travellers' cheques.

Trailfinders Australia ☎1300/780 212, ⓦwww.trailfinders.com.au. Independent travel advice and specializes in cheap flights.

Online booking agents

ⓦwww.cheapflights.co.uk (in UK & Ireland), ⓦwww.cheapflights.com (in US), ⓦwww.cheapflights.ca (in Canada), ⓦwww.cheapflights.com.au (in Australia). Flight deals, travel agents, plus links to other travel sites.

ⓦwww.cheaptickets.com Discount flight specialists (US only). Also at ☎1-888/922-8849.

ⓦwww.ebookers.com Efficient, easy to use flight finder, with competitive fares.

ⓦwww.expedia.co.uk (in UK), ⓦwww.expedia.com (in US), ⓦwww.expedia.ca (in Canada). Discount airfares, all-airline search engine and daily deals.

ⓦwww.flyaow.com "Airlines of the Web" – online air travel info and reservations.

ⓦwww.hotwire.com Last-minute savings of up to forty percent on regular published fares. Travellers must be at least 18 and there are no refunds, transfers or changes allowed.

ⓦwww.kelkoo.co.uk Useful UK-only price-comparison site, checking several sources of low-cost flights (and other goods & services) according to specific criteria.

ⓦwww.lastminute.com (in UK), ⓦwww.lastminute.com.au (in Australia), ⓦwww.lastminute.co.nz (in New Zealand), ⓦwww.site59.com (in US). Good last-minute holiday package and flight-only deals.

ⓦwww.opodo.co.uk Popular and reliable source of low UK airfares. Owned by, and run in conjunction with, nine major European airlines.

ⓦwww.orbitz.com Comprehensive web travel source, with the usual flight, car rental and hotel deals but also great follow-up customer service.

ⓦwww.priceline.co.uk (in UK), ⓦwww.priceline.com (in US). Name-your-own-price website that has deals at around forty percent off standard fares.

ⓦwww.skyauction.com Bookings from the US only. Auctions tickets and travel packages to destinations worldwide.

ⓦwww.travelocity.co.uk (in UK), ⓦwww.travelocity.com (in US), ⓦwww.travelocity.ca (in Canada),

ⓦwww.travelshop.com.au Australian site offering discounted flights, packages, insurance and online bookings; can also be reached at ☎1800/108 108.

www.travelzoo.com Great resource for news on the latest airline sales, cruise discounts and hotel deals. Links bring you directly to the carrier's site.

travel.yahoo.com Incorporates some Rough Guides material in its coverage of destination countries and cities across the world, with information about places to eat and sleep.

www.zuji.com.au (in Australia). Destination guides, hot fares and great deals for car rental, accommodation and lodging.

Specialist tour operators

UK and Ireland

Andean Trails ☏0131 467 7086, www.andeantrails.co.uk. Specialist tour operator offering challenging small group hiking and adventure travel in the southern Andes and Amazon.

Birdfinders ☏01258/839066, www.birdfinders.co.uk. Two-week specialist birdwatching tours in Costa Rica.

Blue Green Adventures (No phone in the UK; book online or through Journey Latin America), www.bluegreenadventures.com. The leading specialist in horse-riding expeditions in Patagonia and the Chilean and Argentine Lake Districts.

Condor Journeys and Adventures ☏01700/841 318, www.condorjourneys-adventures.com. Imaginative ecotourism company with dozens of different themed tours.

Dragoman ☏01728/861 133, www.dragoman.co.uk. Eight-week overland camping expeditions through Mexico to Panama in specially built trucks.

Jagged Globe ☏0845 345 8848, www.jagged-globe.co.uk. Well-established company offering 24-day Aconcagua expeditions.

Journey Latin America ☏020/8747 3108, www.journeylatinamerica.co.uk. Long-established specialists in flights, packages and interesting tailor-made trips to Latin America. Also organize Spanish-language course holidays.

Last Frontiers ☏01296 653000, www.lastfrontiers.com. Environmentally sensitive, specialist tour operator offering tailor-made itineraries for independent travellers in Latin America and Antarctica: riding, hiking and multi-activity including scheduled departures.

Pura Aventura ☏0845/22 55 058, www.pura-aventura.com. Challenging small-group adventure holidays in Chile, Costa Rica, Mexico, Nicaragua and Peru.

Reef and Rainforest Tours ☏01803/866965, www.reefandrainforest.co.uk. Individual itineraries from a very experienced company focusing on nature reserves, research projects and diving.

South American Experience

☎020/7976 5511, ⓦwww
.southamericanexperience.co.uk.
Escorted tours with experienced
specialists.

South American Safaris

☎020/8767 9136, ⓦwww
.southamericansafaris.com. Budget
camping trips (3–14 weeks) in
purpose-built trucks.

Tucan Travel ☎020/8742 8612,
ⓦwww.tucantravel.com. Latin
American specialists offering three-
week adventure tours and overland
camping expeditions.

US and Canada

Active South America ☎1-800/500-
3398, ⓦwww.activesouthamerica
.com. Outdoor and adventure sports
specialists with hiking and biking
tours to Peru, Ecuador and the
Galápagos Islands.

Adventure Life ☎1-800/344-6118,
ⓦwww.adventure-life.com. Small
personal organization with a
community focus.

Andean Treks ☎1-800/683-8148,
ⓦwww.andeantreks.com. Camping
and trekking tours in the mountains.

Far Horizons ☎1-800/552-4575,
ⓦwww.farhorizon.com. Superb
archeological trips to remote Maya,
Inca and Easter Island sites led by
renowned experts in the field.

Go South Adventures ☎1-888/305-
4544, ⓦwww.go-south-adventures
.com. Small group offering culturally
sensitive adventure travel in South
America. Hiking and multi-activity.

Green Tortoise Adventure Travel
☎1-800/867-8647, ⓦwww
.greentortoise.com. Tours through

Mexico and Central America from
November through April on converted
buses with sleeping space.

Guatemala Unlimited ☎1-800/733-
3350, ⓦwww.guatemalaunlimited
.com. Eight-day comprehensive
tours or shorter one to three tours
of Maya ruins both obscure and well
known.

Latin Trails ☎1-800/747-0567,
ⓦwww.latintrails.com. Expert travel
agency with 20 years experience in
Galápagos tours and Amazon
travel.

Myths and Mountains ☎1-800/670-
6984, ⓦwww.mythsandmountains
.com. Socially responsible cultural
tours, including exploration of the
medicinal heritage of the Andes and
rainforest, and visits to community
projects.

Southern Explorations

☎1-877/784-5400, ⓦwww
.southernexplorations.com.
Specialists in private and small
group tours (max 8) to South and
Central America with a focus on
sustainable tourism and personalized adventure travel.

Australia and New Zealand

Adventure Associates Australia
☎02/9389 7466, ⓦwww
.adventureassociates.com.
Comprehensive tour company with
cultural trips, city stopovers and
activity holidays including mountain
biking and sports fishing.

Austral Tours Australia ☎03/9600
1733, ⓦwww.australtours.com.
Central and South American
specialists.

Australian Andean Adventures Australia ☎02/9235 1889, ⓦwww .andeanadventures.com.au. Trekking specialist with mountain-climbing courses in Bolivia and Peru.

Latin Link Adventure New Zealand ☎03/525 9945, ⓦwww.latinlink .co.nz. Small organized tours to many regions within Latin America.

Peregrine Adventures Australia ☎03/9663 8611, ⓦwww .peregrineadventures.com. Extended overland and sea adventures from southern Mexico through Central and South America.

South American Adventure Travel Australia ☎07/3845 1022. Independent and group travel specialists.

South American Travel Centre ☎1800/655051, ⓦwww.satc.com .au. Specialists in luxury, tailor-made tours to South and Central America and Cuba.

Volunteer organizations

There are hundreds of volunteer projects based in Latin America – the websites and books listed in Chapter 2 are a great place to start your research. Also check your guidebook for schemes running in individual countries. Listed below are some of the largest global voluntary organizations – most accept volunteers from all over the world as well as national citizens.

UK organizations

British Council ☎020/7930 8466, ⓦwww.britishcouncil.org. Publishes a book, *Year Between*, aimed principally at gap-year students detailing volunteer programmes.

British Trust for Conservation Volunteers (BTCV) ☎01302/572 244, ⓦwww.btcv.org. One of the largest environmental charities in Britain with a programme of international working holidays (as a paying volunteer) in many parts of Latin America.

Concordia ☎01273/422293, ⓦwww .concordia-iye.org.uk. Environmental, archeological and arts projects in Argentina, Brazil, Ecuador, Mexico and Peru are among some of the wide range offered for young people.

I-I International Projects ☎0870 333 2332, ⓦwww.i-to-i.com. Award-winning company offering pricey voluntary placements in teaching, conservation, business and medical schemes in Bolivia, Costa Rica, Guatemala, Ecuador, El Salvador and Honduras.

Peace Brigades International ☎0207/561 9141, ⓦwww .peacebridgades.org. NGO dedicated to protecting human rights with placements accompanying human-rights workers in trouble spots.

US organizations

Amerispan ☎800/879-6640, ⓦwww
.amerispan.com. Highly rated
educational travel company that
specializes in language courses but
also runs volunteer programmes all
over Latin America.

Amigos de las Americas
☎1-800/231-7796, ⓦwww
.amigoslink.org. Veteran non-profit
organization placing young people
in child health and other community
schemes in Costa Rica, Honduras,
Nicaragua and Panama.

**Council on International
Educational Exchange (CIEE)**
☎888-COUNCIL, ⓦwww.ciee.org.
Runs volunteer projects for students
and recent graduates in 25 countries
worldwide including parts of Latin
America. Publishes *Work, Study,
Travel Abroad* and *Volunteer! The
Comprehensive Guide to Voluntary
Service in the US and Abroad*.

Earthwatch Institute ☎1-800/776-
0188, ⓦwww.earthwatch.org.
International non-profit organization
with offices in the US, England,
Australia and Japan. Volunteers work
in the field with trained professionals
on conservation and archeological
projects.

Experiment in International Living
☎1-800/345-2929, ⓦwww
.usexperiment.org. Month-long
community, environmental placements in half a dozen Latin American
countries including Belize and Brazil.

Global Volunteers ☎1-800-398-
8787, ⓦwww.globalvolunteers.org.
Projects include working with
children in Ecuador or on conservation in the Monteverde cloudforest
in Costa Rica as well as others in
Mexico and Peru.

Habitat for Humanity ☎229/924-
6935, ⓦwww.habitat.org.
Non-profit, non-denominational
Christian organization that builds
simple homes in impoverished areas
in over 80 countries worldwide. One-
to three-week building trips.

Volunteers for Peace ☎802/259-
2759, ⓦwww.vfp.org. Non-profit
organization with links to a huge
international network of "work
camps", two- to four-week
community-based projects.

Australian organizations

Australian Volunteers International
☎61/39279 1788, ⓦwww.ozvol.org
.au. Postings for up to two years in
Costa Rica, Guatemala, El Salvador
and Nicaragua with shorter-term
projects for younger volunteers.

Global Volunteer Network ☎04/569
9080, ⓦwww.volunteer.org.nz.
Voluntary placements on community
projects worldwide.

International Exchange Programs
☎0800/443 769, ⓦwww.iepnz
.co.nz. A variety of work, teach and
study abroad programmes for New
Zealanders wishing to go to Costa
Rica.

Health

UK

British Airways Travel Clinics
There are 28 regional clinics (call
℡0845/600 2236 for the nearest or
consult Ⓦwww.britishairways
.com); in London: 156 Regent St,
W1 (no appointment necessary), or
101 Cheapside, EC2 (appointment
required). All clinics provide vaccinations, anti-malarial drugs, tailored
up-to-the-minute advice and a
complete range of travel healthcare
products.

Communicable Diseases Unit
Brownlee Centre, Glasgow G12
0YN,℡0141/211 1074. Travel
vaccinations including yellow fever.

Edinburgh Travel Health Clinic
14 East Preston St, Edinburgh EH8
9QA, ℡0131/667 1030, Ⓦwww
.healthytrip.co.uk. Friendly, expert
medical advice and very competitive
rates on all major vaccinations.

**Hospital for Tropical Diseases
Travel Clinic** 2nd floor, Mortimer
Market Centre, off Capper St,
London WC1E 6AU, ℡020/7388
9600, Ⓦwww.thehtd.org. The
clinic is open Mon–Fri 9am–5pm by
appointment. A consultation costs
£15 that is waived if you have your
injections here. A recorded health
line (℡0906/133 7733; 50p per min)
gives advice on disease prevention
and appropriate immunizations.

**Liverpool School of Tropical
Medicine** Pembroke Place, Liverpool
L3 5QA ℡0151/708 9393, Ⓦwww
.liv.ac.uk/lstm/lstm. Walk-in clinic
Mon–Fri 1–4pm. An appointment is
only required for yellow fever jabs.

Malaria Helpline ℡0891/600 350;
24-hour recorded message for 60p
a minute.

**MASTA (Medical Advice Service
for Travellers' Abroad)** Ⓦwww
.masta.org. Forty regional clinics
(call ℡0870/606 2782 for nearest).
Also operates a pre-recorded 24-hour
Travellers' Helpline (℡0906/822 4100
in the UK, 60p a minute; ℡01560/147
000 in Ireland, 75p a minute), giving
written information tailored to your
journey by return of post.

Nomad Pharmacy 40 Bernard St,
London WC1 and 3–4 Wellington
Terrace, Turnpike Lane, London
N8. Immunizations and free travel
advice at clinics, open Mon–Fri
9.30am–6pm (℡020/7833 4114;
appointments necessary). Telephone
helpline (℡09068/836 3414) costs
60p a minute.

Ireland

Dun Laoghaire Medical Centre 5
Northumberland Ave, Dun Laoghaire,
Co Dublin ℡01/280 4996, Ⓦwww
.iol.ie/-tmb. Advice on travel
medicine.

**Travel Health Centre, Department
of International Health and
Tropical Medicine** Royal College
of Surgeons in Ireland, Mercers
Medical Centre, Lower Stephen's St,
Dublin ℡01/402 2337. Expert pre-
trip advice and inoculations.

Travel Medicine Services PO Box
254, 16 College St, Belfast BT1 6BT,
℡028/9031 5220. Operates a travel
clinic (Mon 9–11am and Wed 2–4pm)
that can give inoculations after a GP

referral, but primarily administers yellow fever vaccine.

Tropical Medical Bureau Grafton Buildings, 34 Grafton St, Dublin 2, ☎1850/487 674, ⓦwww.tmb.ie. Branches throughout Dublin and rest of Ireland, offering all-in consultations covering everything from DVT to malaria prophylaxis.

US and Canada

American Society of Tropical Medicine and Hygiene 60 Revere Drive, Suite 500, Northbrook, IL 60062, T847/480-9282. Society of tropical medical specialists with a comprehensive online directory of travel clinics.

Canadian Society for International Health 1 Nicholas St, Suite 1105, Ottawa, ON K1N 7B7, ☎613/241-5785, ⓦwww.csaih.org. Distributes a free pamphlet, *Health Information for Canadian Travellers*, containing an extensive list of travel health centres in Canada.

Centers for Disease Control 1600 Clifton Rd NE, Atlanta, GA 30333 ☎1-800/311-3435, ⓦwww.cdc.gov. Publishes outbreak warnings, suggested inoculations, precautions and other background information for travellers. Excellent website and International Travellers Hotline on ☎1-877/FYI-TRIP.

International Association for Medical Assistance to Travellers (IAMAT) 417 Center St, Lewiston, NY 14092 ☎716/754-4883 and 1287 St Clair Ave W, Suite #1, Toronto, ON M6E 1B8, ☎416/652-0137, ⓦwww.iamat.org. A non-profit organization that provides details of English-speaking doctors in the country you're going to, climate charts and leaflets on various diseases and inoculations.

International SOS Assistance Eight Neshaminy Interplex Suite 207, Trevose, US 19053-6956 ☎1-800/523-8930, ⓦwww.intsos .com. Members receive pre-trip medical referral info as well as overseas emergency services designed to complement travel insurance coverage.

Travel Medicine 369 Pleasant St, Suite 312, Northampton, MA 01060 ☎1-800/872-8633, ⓦwww.travmed .com. Sells travel-related health products.

Travelers Medical Center 31 Washington Square West, New York NY 10011 ☎212/982-1600. Consultation service on immunizations and treatment of disease for travellers to developing countries.

Australia and New Zealand

Travel-Bug Medical and Vaccination Centre 161 Ward St, North Adelaide ☎08/8267 3544.

Travellers' Medical and Vaccination Centres Branches include: in Australia, 7/428 George St, Sydney ☎02/9221 7133; 27–29 Gilbert Place, Adelaide ☎08/8212 7522; in New Zealand, 1/170 Queen St, Auckland ☎09/373 3531; Shop 15, Grand Arcade, Willis St, Wellington ☎04/473 0991, ⓦwww.tmvc.com .au. Has vaccination centres throughout Australia and New Zealand and provides general information on travel health. Excellent website.

Travellers' Immunization Service
303 Pacific Hwy, Sydney ☎02/9416
1348

Travel health websites

**Centers for Disease Control and
Prevention** Ⓦwww.cdc.gov. The US
government's official site for travel
health.

Fit For Travel Ⓦwww.fitfortravel
.scot.nhs.uk. British National Health
Service website carrying information
about travel-related diseases and
how to avoid them.

**The International Society of
Medicine** Ⓦwww.istm.org. The
website of the International Society
of Travel Medicine, with a full list of
clinics specializing in international
travel health.

Travel Health Online Ⓦwww
.tripprep.com. Travel Health Online
provides an online-only comprehensive database of necessary vaccinations for most countries, as well
as destination and medical service
provider information.

Travel Medicine Program Ⓦwww
.TravelHealth.gc.ca. Canadian
government website with comprehensive lists of travel clinics throughout the country.

Travel-Vax Ⓦwww.travelvax.net.
Website detailing everything you
could ever want to know about
diseases and travel vaccines.

World Health Organization Ⓦwww
.who.int. World Health Organization's
website provides useful data on
disease prevalence, prevention and
current outbreak trends.

Official advice on international trouble spots

**Australian Department of Foreign
Affairs** ☎1300 555 135, Ⓦwww.dfat
.gov.au

**British Foreign and
Commonwealth Office** ☎0845 850
2829, Ⓦwww.fco.gov.uk

**Canadian Department of Foreign
Affairs** ☎1-800/267-8370, Ⓦwww
.dfait-maeci.gc.ca

**New Zealand Department of
Foreign Affairs** ☎04/439 8000,
Ⓦwww.mft.govt.nz

**US State Department Travel
Advisory Service** ☎202/512 1800,
Ⓦwww.travel.state.gov

Responsible tourism

UK

International Centre for Responsible Tourism University of Greenwich, ⓦwww.icrtourism.org. Post-graduate training centre with courses in responsible tourism and a website with excellent links to all matters concerning ethical and responsible tourism.

Tourism Concern Stapleton House, 277–281 Holloway Rd, London N7 8HN ⓣ020/7133 3330, ⓦwww.tourismconcern.org.uk. Campaigns for the rights of local people to be consulted in tourism developments affecting their lives. Also produces a quarterly magazine of news and articles.

US

EarthWise Journeys ⓦwww.teleport.com/~earthwyz. American organization that researches and promotes the travel programmes of non-profit organizations, responsible ecotour providers, learning institutes and travel enterprises.

Global Exchange ⓣ415/255-7296, ⓦwww.globalexchange.org. Not-for-profit organization that leads "reality tours" to developing countries that give participants the chance to learn about the country while seeing it.

Partners in Reponsible Tourism PO Box 237, San Francisco, CA 94104-0237, ⓦwww.pirt.org. An organization of individuals and travel companies promoting responsible tourism to minimize harm to the environment and local cultures. Their website features a "Traveler's Code for Traveling Responsibly".

Online resources

ⓦ**www.ecotourism.org** Website produced by the US-based International Ecotourism Society with online fact sheets and reviews of eco-lodges and ecotour operators.

ⓦ**www.green-travel.com** Hundreds of links to green companies around the world.

ⓦ**www.planeta.com** Award-winning clearinghouse with hundreds of articles including official reports on ecotourism in Latin America and thousands of links to more general travel websites.

W www.responsibletravel.com
Website created by Body Shop
founder Anita Roddick, which
reviews hundreds of ecotours and
accommodation around the world.

Travel book and map stores

UK and Ireland

Blackwell's Map and Travel Shop
50 Broad St, Oxford OX1 3BQ
℡01865/793 550, W maps.blackwell
.co.uk, W books.blackwell.co.uk

Daunt Books 83 Marylebone High
St, London W1M 3DE ℡020/7224
2295; 193 Haverstock Hill, London
NW3 4QL ℡020/7794 4006.

Easons Bookshop 40 O'Connell St,
Dublin 1 ℡01/873 3811, W www
.eason.ie

The Map Shop 15 High St, Upton
upon Severn, Worcs WR8 OHJ
℡01684/593146, W www
.themapshop.co.uk

National Map Centre 22–24 Caxton
St, London SW1H 0QU ℡020/7222
2466, W www.mapsnmc.co.uk; 34
Aungier St, Dublin ℡01/476 0471,
W www.mapcentre.ie

Stanfords 12–14 Long Acre,
London WC2E 9LP ℡020/7836
1321, W www.stanfords.co.uk. Other
branches within British Airways
offices at 156 Regent St, London
W1R 5TA ℡020/7434 4744, and 29
Corn St, Bristol BS1 1HT
℡0117/929 9966.

The Travel Bookshop 13–15
Blenheim Crescent, London W11
2EE ℡020/7229 5260, W www
.thetravelbookshop.co.uk.

Traveller 55 Grey St, Newcastle-
upon-Tyne NE1 6EF, ℡0191/261
5622, W www.newtraveller.com

US and Canada

Book Passage 51 Tamal Vista Blvd,
Corte Madera, CA 94925 ℡1-800/
999-7909, W www.bookpassage.com

California Map and Travel Center
3312 Pico Blvd, Santa Monica Ca
90405 ℡310/396-6277

Distant Lands 56 S. Raymond Ave,
Pasadena, CA 91105 ℡1- 800/310-
3220, W www.distantlands.com

Get Lost 1825 Market Street San
Francisco, CA 94103 ℡415/437-
0529, W www.getlostbooks.com

**International Travel Maps and
Books** 530 W Broadway, Vancouver,
BC V5Z 1ED, T604/879-3621,
W www.itmb.com

Longitude Books 115 W 30th St,
#1206, New York, NY 10001,
℡1-800/342-2164, W www
.longitudebooks.com

Open Air Books and Maps 25
Toronto St, Toronto, ON M5R 2C1
℡416/363-0719

Rand McNally ℡1-800/333-0136,
W www.randmcnally.com. Around
thirty stores across the US; dial ext
2111 or check the website for the
nearest location.

The Travel Bug Bookstore 2667 W Broadway, Vancouver V6K 2G2 ☎604/737-1122, ⒲www.travelbugbooks.ca

Ulysses Travel Bookshop 4176 St-Denis, Montréal ☎514/843-9447, ⒲www.ulyssesguides.com

Wide World Books and Maps 4411A Wallingford Ave, N Seattle, WA 98103 ☎206/634-3453, ⒲www.wideworldtravels.com

World of Maps 1235 Wellington St, Ottawa, ON K1Y 3A3 ☎1-800/214-8524, ⒲www.worldofmaps.com

Australia and New Zealand

Map Centre ⒲www.mapcentre.co.nz

The Map Shop 6–10 Peel St, Adelaide, SA 5000 ☎08/8231 2033, ⒲www.mapshop.net.au

Mapland 372 Little Bourke St, Melbourne, Victoria 3000, ☎03/9670 4383, ⒲www.mapland.com.au

Map World 371 Pitt St, Sydney ☎02/9261 3601, ⒲www.mapworld.net.au

MapWorld 173 Gloucester St, Christchurch ☎0800/627 967, ⒲www.mapworld.co.nz

Perth Map Centre 1/884 Hay St, Perth, WA 6000 ☎08/9322 5733, ⒲www.perthmap.com.au

Specialty Maps 46 Albert St, Auckland 1001 ☎09/307 2217, ⒲www.wiseformaps.co.nz

Travel Bookshop Shop 3, 175 Liverpool St, Sydney ☎02/9261 8200

Online travel resources

For country-specific websites, see the individual country profiles on pp.19–123. Websites for travel and online booking agents start on p.361, while travel health websites are listed on p.369.

General travel websites

⒲**www.about.com/travel** Huge information resource with some of the best destination guides on the web and well-organized links.

⒲**www.bootsnall.com** Travel for backpackers with good links, articles and message board.

⒲**www.budgetravel.com** Thousands of links from around the world on all matter of subjects of interest to budget travellers.

⒲**www.gapyear.com** Comprehensive information on taking a year out with articles on fund raising, working and studying abroad as well as practical information on planning a trip.

⒲**www.itisnet.com** A useful source of current info for budget travellers that is regularly updated by travellers and researchers.

⒲**www.journeywoman.com** Recommended site aimed at women travellers with features such as

"What Should I Wear, Where", travelogues and advice on health and travelling solo.

Ⓦ **www.travel-library.com** Travel writers' website with collection of articles from well-established writers on dozens of countries and themes.

Ⓦ **www.worldtravelguide.net** Destination guides with useful background and tourist information.

Latin American websites

Ⓦ **www.lanic.utexas.edu/la** The Latin American Network Information Centre, based at the University of Texas, is easily the best online resource on Latin America. Thousands of efficiently catalogued links to cultural, political and recreation issues among others.

Ⓦ **www.lata.org** The Latin American Travel Association, based in London, is a non-profit organization that provides information on all aspects of travel to Latin America.

Ⓦ **www.latinamericalinks.com** Comprehensive site aimed at travellers and featuring links on art, music, archeology, business etc as well as travel and tourism.

Ⓦ **www.latinnews.com** Good selection of current news reports from all parts of Latin America.

Ⓦ **www.latinworld.com** Large search engine with links to hundreds of Latin American websites.

Ⓦ **www.planeta.com** Award-winning Latin American ecotourism clearinghouse with links to other, lighter subjects as well as articles and official reports on the environment.

Ⓦ **www.travellatinamerica.com** A selection of news and features about travelling in the region as well as a currency converter, consulate details and web links for each country.

Ⓦ **www.zonalatina.com** Articles from the US press on Latin American issues and links to the homepages of all Latin America's newspapers, magazines and other media.

Travellers' forums, newsgroups and bulletin boards

rec.travel.latin-america and **soc .travel.latin-america** Newsgroups (go to Ⓦwww.groups.google.com, or use a dedicated newsreader) with thousands of messages posted.

Ⓦ **www.roughguides.com** Interactive site for independent travellers, with forums, bulletin boards, travel tips and features plus online travel guides.

Ⓦ **www.samexplo.org** Website of the South American Explorers' Club, based in Lima, Peru, which has general information on South America and a message board.

Specialist Latin American resource centres

The following places (most connected to academic institutions) run courses and lectures on Latin American themes. They also have specialist book collections and organize film showings and exhibitions – check their websites to find out about events.

UK

Canning House 2 Belgrave Square, London SW1X 8PJ, ⓦwww .canninghouse.com

Centre of Latin American Studies University of Cambridge, West Road, Cambridge CB3 9EF, ⓦwww .latin-american.cam.ac.uk

Institute of Latin American Studies 31 Tavistock Square, London WC1H 9HA, ⓦwww.sas.ac.uk/ilas

Latin America Bureau 1 Amwell St, London EC1R 1UL, ⓦwww.lab .org.uk

US

There are hundreds of Latin American resource centres in the US – these are some of the best.
Center for Latin American and Caribbean Studies 53 Washington Square South, Floor 4w, New York, NY 10012, ⓦwww.nyu.edu/gsas /program/latin

Center for Latin American Studies University of California, 2334 Bowditch St, Berkeley, CA 94720, ⓦwww.clas.berkeley.edu/clas/

Center for Latin American Studies 3520 Prospect St, Washington DC 20057-0885, ⓦwww.georgetown .edu/sfs/programs/clas/

Latin American Network Information Center (LANIC) Sid W Richardson Hall 1.310, Austin, TX 8712-1284, ⓦwww.lanic.utexas .edu

Canada

Center for Research on Latin America and the Caribbean York University, 4700 Keele St, North York, ON, M3J1P3, ⓦwww.yorku .ca/cerlac

Latin American Research Centre Social Sciences Bldg 714, 2500 University Drive NW, Calgary, Alberta T2N 1N4, ⓦwww.ucalgary.ca

Australia

Institute of Latin American Studies La Trobe University, Bundorra, Victoria 3083, ⓦwww.latrobe.edu.au

Travel equipment suppliers

UK

Cotswold Outdoor Ltd 42–46 Uxbridge Rd, London W12 8ND ⊤020/8743 2976, ⓦwww .cotswold-outdoor.co.uk; branches countrywide. ⊤01285/643434 for mail order catalogue.

Field and Trek 42 Maiden Lane, Covent Garden, London WC2E 7JL ⊤020/7379 3793, ⓦwww.field -trek.co.uk; branches countrywide. ⊤01268/494444 for mail order catalogue.

Nomad Pharmacy and Travellers' Store 3 Wellington Terrace, Turnpike Lane, London N8 OPX ⊤020/8889 7014; STA, 40 Bernard St, London WC1N ILJ ⊤020/7833 4114; 4 Potters Rd, New Barnet, Herts EN5 5HW ⊤020/8441 7208; ⓦwww .nomad-travstore.co.uk. Specialist in travellers' medical supplies and first-aid equipment; also stocks general-purpose travel accessories.

YHA Adventure Shops Branches countrywide; ⓦwww.yhaadventure .co.uk.

US and Canada

Campmor PO Box 700, Saddle River, NJ 07458-0700 ⊤1-800/226-7667, ⓦwww.campmor.com. Clothing plus outdoor and camping gear.

Moosejaw ⊤1-877/666-7352, ⓦwww.moosejaw.com. Several stores in Michigan and Illinois, plus offbeat mail-order catalogue. Sells a good selection of outdoor apparel.

Mountain Equipment Co-op ⓦwww.mec.ca. Eleven stores across

Canada selling a wide range of outdoor gear and clothing. For the store nearest you, call ⊤1-888/847-0770.

Mountain Gear 2002 N Division Spokane, WA 99207 ⊤1-888/829-2009, ⓦwww.mgear.com. Sells an extensive collection of outdoor clothing, camping equipment, and hiking and climbing gear.

Recreational Equipment Inc PO Box 1700, Sumner, WA 98352-0001 ⊤1-800/426-4840, ⓦwww.rei.com. Sixty stores selling outdoor gear and clothing.

Sierra Trading Post 5025 Campstool Rd, Cheyenne, WY 82007-1802 ⊤1-800/713-4534, ⓦwww.sierratradingpost.com. Clothes, shoes and small equipment.

Travel Medicine 369 Pleasant St, Northampton, MA 01060 ⊤1-800/872-8633, ⓦwww .travelmed.com. Sells first-aid kits, mosquito netting, water filters and other health-related travel products.

Travel Smith 60 Leveroni Court #1, Novato, CA 94949 ⊤1-800/950-1600, ⓦwww.travelsmith.com

Australia and New Zealand

A-Roving 112 Toorak Rd, Toorak, vic 3142 ⊤03/9824 1714. Suppliers of travel luggage and accessories, maps and travel guides.

Bivouac 5 Fort St, Auckland 1 ⊤09/366 1966. Several stores in New Zealand stocking a full range of backpacking and camping gear.

Katmandu PO Box 1191, Collingwood, VIC 3066 ☏03/9417 2480. A mail-order company with outlets in all major Australian and New Zealand cities, offering an extensive range of quality outdoor and climbing gear.

Mountain Designs 105 Albert St, Brisbane, QLD 4000 ☏07/3221 6756; branches in major Australian and New Zealand cities. Australian-designed, lightweight mountaineering and adventure equipment, specializing in sleeping bags, Gore-Tex and fleeces.

Mtn Equipment Pty Ltd 491 Kent St, Sydney, NSW 2000 ☏02/9264 5888; branches in Chatswood and Hornsby. Comprehensive range of lightweight, functional gear for outdoor and sporting activities.

Final checklist

Documents

- Airline tickets
- Credit and debit cards
- Guidebooks
- Insurance policy
- International drivers' licence
- Maps
- Passport
- Phrasebook
- Phonecard
- Photocopies of vital documents
- Travellers' cheques

The bare essentials

- Backpack
- Clothes
- Daypack
- Fleece jacket
- Money belt
- Sarong
- Shoes
- Sun hat

Basic odds and ends

- Alarm clock
- Batteries
- Camera equipment and film
- Contact lens stuff/glasses
- Contraceptives
- First-aid kit
- Flashlight

- Mosquito repellent
- Padlock and chain
- Penknife
- Sunglasses
- Tampons
- Toiletries
- Towel
- Wallet

Other items worth considering

- Books
- Cigarette lighter
- Compass
- Earplugs
- Games
- Mosquito net
- Notebook or journal and pens
- Personal stereo and CDs
- Photos/postcards of home
- Rain gear/umbrella
- Sewing kit
- Sheet sleeping bag
- Shortwave radio
- Sink plug
- String
- Water bottle, water purifier or purification tablets
- Waterproof money-holder

Travel store

UK & Ireland

Britain
Devon & Cornwall
Dublin DIRECTIONS
Edinburgh DIRECTIONS
England
Ireland
The Lake District
London
London DIRECTIONS
London Mini Guide
Scotland
Scottish Highlands & Islands
Wales

Europe

Algarve DIRECTIONS
Amsterdam
Amsterdam DIRECTIONS
Andalucía
Athens DIRECTIONS
Austria
Baltic States
Barcelona
Barcelona DIRECTIONS
Belgium & Luxembourg
Berlin
Brittany & Normandy
Bruges DIRECTIONS
Brussels
Budapest
Bulgaria
Copenhagen
Corfu
Corsica
Costa Brava DIRECTIONS
Crete
Croatia
Cyprus
Czech & Slovak Republics
Dodecanese & East Aegean
Dordogne & The Lot
Europe
Florence & Siena
Florence DIRECTIONS
France
French Hotels & Restaurants

Germany
Greece
Greek Islands
Hungary
Ibiza & Formentera DIRECTIONS
Iceland
Ionian Islands
Italy
The Italian Lakes
Languedoc & Roussillon
Lisbon
Lisbon DIRECTIONS
The Loire
Madeira DIRECTIONS
Madrid DIRECTIONS
Mallorca DIRECTIONS
Mallorca & Menorca
Malta & Gozo DIRECTIONS
Menorca
Moscow
The Netherlands
Norway
Paris
Paris DIRECTIONS
Paris Mini Guide
Poland
Portugal
Prague
Prague DIRECTIONS
Provence & the Côte d'Azur
Pyrenees
Romania
Rome
Rome DIRECTIONS
Sardinia
Scandinavia
Sicily
Slovenia
Spain
St Petersburg
Sweden
Switzerland
Tenerife & La Gomera DIRECTIONS
Turkey
Tuscany & Umbria
Venice & The Veneto
Venice DIRECTIONS
Vienna

Asia

Bali & Lombok
Bangkok
Beijing
Cambodia
China
Goa
Hong Kong & Macau
India
Indonesia
Japan
Laos
Malaysia, Singapore & Brunei
Nepal
The Philippines
Singapore
South India
Southeast Asia
Sri Lanka
Taiwan
Thailand
Thailand's Beaches & Islands
Tokyo
Vietnam

Australasia

Australia
Melbourne
New Zealand
Sydney

North America

Alaska
Boston
California
Canada
Chicago
Florida
The Grand Canyon
Hawaii
Honolulu
Las Vegas DIRECTIONS
Los Angeles
Maui DIRECTIONS
Miami & South Florida
Montréal
New England
New Orleans DIRECTIONS
New York City

New York City DIRECTIONS
New York City Mini Guide
Orlando & Walt Disney World DIRECTIONS
Pacific Northwest
The Rocky Mountains
San Francisco
San Francisco DIRECTIONS
Seattle
Southwest USA
Toronto
USA
Vancouver
Washington DC
Washington DC DIRECTIONS
Yosemite

Caribbean & Latin America

Antigua & Barbuda DIRECTIONS
Argentina
Bahamas
Barbados DIRECTIONS
Belize
Bolivia
Brazil
Cancùn & Cozumel DIRECTIONS
Caribbean
Central America
Chile
Costa Rica
Cuba
Dominican Republic
Dominican Republic DIRECTIONS
Ecuador
Guatemala
Jamaica
Mexico
Peru
St Lucia
South America
Trinidad & Tobago
Yúcatan

TRAVEL

Africa & Middle East
Cape Town & the Garden Route
Egypt
The Gambia
Jordan
Kenya
Marrakesh DIRECTIONS
Morocco
South Africa, Lesotho & Swaziland
Syria
Tanzania
Tunisia
West Africa
Zanzibar

Travel Theme guides
First-Time Around the World
First-Time Asia
First-Time Europe
First-Time Latin America
Travel Online
Travel Health
Travel Survival
Walks in London & SE England
Women Travel

Maps
Algarve
Amsterdam
Andalucia & Costa del Sol
Argentina
Athens
Australia
Baja California
Barcelona
Berlin
Boston
Brittany
Brussels
California
Chicago
Corsica
Costa Rica & Panama

Crete
Croatia
Cuba
Cyprus
Czech Republic
Dominican Republic
Dubai & UAE
Dublin
Egypt
Florence & Siena
Florida
France
Frankfurt
Germany
Greece
Guatemala & Belize
Hong Kong
Iceland
Ireland
Kenya
Lisbon
London
Los Angeles
Madrid
Mallorca
Marrakesh
Mexico
Miami & Key West
Morocco
New England
New York City
New Zealand
Northern Spain
Paris
Peru
Portugal
Prague
Rome
San Francisco
Sicily
South Africa
South India
Spain & Portugal
Sri Lanka
Tenerife
Thailand
Toronto
Trinidad & Tobago
Tuscany
Venice
Washington DC
Yucatán Peninsula

Dictionary Phrasebooks
Croatian
Czech
Dutch
Egyptian Arabic
French
German
Greek
Hindi & Urdu
Italian
Japanese
Latin American Spanish
Mandarin Chinese
Mexican Spanish
Polish
Portuguese
Russian
Spanish
Swahili
Thai
Turkish
Vietnamese

Computers
Blogging
iPods, iTunes & Music Online
The Internet
Macs & OS X
Music Playlists
PCs and Windows
Website Directory

Film & TV
Comedy Movies
Cult Movies
Cult TV
Gangster Movies
Horror Movies
James Bond
Kids' Movies
Sci–Fi Movies

Lifestyle
Ethical Shopping
Babies
Pregnancy & Birth

Music Guides
The Beatles
Bob Dylan
Cult Pop
Classical Music
Elvis
Frank Sinatra
Heavy Metal
Hip-Hop
Jazz
Opera
Reggae
Rock
World Music (2 vols)

Popular Culture
Books for Teenagers
Children's Books, 0-5
Children's Books, 5-11
Conspiracy Theories
Cult Fiction
The Da Vinci Code
Lord of the Rings
Shakespeare
Superheroes
Unexplained Phenomena

Sport
Arsenal 11s
Celtic 11s
Chelsea 11s
Liverpool 11s
Man United 11s
Newcastle 11s
Rangers 11s
Tottenham 11s
Cult Football
Muhammad Ali
Poker

Science
The Universe
Weather

& MORE

Visit us online

www.roughguides.com

Information on over 25,000 destinations around the world

- **Read** Rough Guides' trusted travel info

- **Share** journals, photos and travel advice with other readers

- Get exclusive Rough Guide **discounts** and travel deals

- Earn membership points every time you contribute to the

  Rough Guide community and get free books, flights and trips

- Browse thousands of **CD reviews** and artists in our music area

ONLINE

Rough Guide Maps, printed on waterproof and rip-proof
Polyart™ paper, offer an unbeatable combination of practicality,
clarity of design and amazing value.

CITY MAPS

Amsterdam ·Athens · Barcelona · Berlin · Boston · Brussels · Chicago · Dublin
Florence & Siena · Frankfurt · Hong Kong · Lisbon · London · Los Angeles Madrid
· Marrakesh · Miami · New York · Paris · Prague · Rome · San Francisco Toronto ·
Venice · Washington DC and more...

US$8.99   Can$13.99   £4.99

COUNTRY & REGIONAL MAPS

Algarve · Andalucía · Argentina · Australia · Baja California · Brittany · Crete Croatia
· Cuba · Cyprus · Czech Republic · Dominican Republic · Dubai · Egypt · Greece ·
Guatemala & Belize · Iceland · Ireland · Kenya · Mexico · Morocco · New Zealand
· Northern Spain · Peru · Portugal · Sicily · South Africa · South India · Sri Lanka ·
Tenerife · Thailand · Trinidad & Tobago · Tuscany · Yucatán Peninsula · and more...

US$9.99   Can$13.99   £5.99

MAPS

NOTES

Small print and
Index

A Rough Guide to Rough Guides

Published in 1982, the first Rough Guide – to Greece – was a student scheme that became a publishing phenomenon. Mark Ellingham, a recent graduate of English from Bristol University, had been traveling in Greece the previous summer and couldn't find the right guidebook. With a small group of friends he wrote his own guide, combining a highly contemporary, journalistic style with a thoroughly practical approach to travelers' needs.

The immediate success of the book spawned a series that rapidly covered dozens of destinations. And, in addition to impecunious backpackers, Rough Guides soon acquired a much broader and older readership that relished the guides' wit and inquisitiveness as much as their enthusiastic, critical approach and value-for-money ethos.

These days, Rough Guides include recommendations from shoestring to luxury and cover more than 200 destinations around the globe, including almost every country in the Americas and Europe, more than half of Africa and most of Asia and Australasia. Our ever-growing team of authors and photographers is spread all over the world, particularly in Europe, the USA, and Australia.

In the early 1990s, Rough Guides branched out of travel, with the publication of Rough Guides to World Music, Classical Music, and the Internet. All three have become benchmark titles in their fields, spearheading the publication of a wide range of books under the Rough Guide name.

Including the travel series, Rough Guides now number more than 350 titles, covering: phrasebooks, waterproof maps, music guides from Opera to Heavy Metal, reference works as diverse as Conspiracy Theories and Shakespeare, and popular culture books from iPods to Poker. Rough Guides also produce a series of more than 120 World Music CDs in partnership with World Music Network.

Visit www.roughguides.com to see our latest publications.

Many Rough Guide travel images are available for commercial licensing at www.roughguidespictures.com

Rough Guide credits

Text editor: Steven Horak
Layout: Jessica Subramanian
Cartography: Ed Wright
Picture editor: Sarah Smithies
Production: Katherine Owers
Proofreader: Amanda Jones
Cover design: Chlöe Roberts and Diana Jarvis
Editorial: **London** Kate Berens, Claire Saunders, Geoff Howard, Ruth Blackmore, Polly Thomas, Richard Lim, Clifton Wilkinson, Alison Murchie, Karoline Densley, Andy Turner, Ella O'Donnell, Keith Drew, Edward Aves, Nikki Birrell, Helen Marsden, Alice Park, Sarah Eno, Joe Staines, Duncan Clark, Peter Buckley, Matthew Milton, Tracy Hopkins; **New York** Andrew Rosenberg, Richard Koss, AnneLise Sorensen, Amy Hegarty, Hunter Slaton, April Isaacs
Design & Pictures: **London** Simon Bracken, Dan May, Mark Thomas, Jj Luck, Harriet Mills; **Delhi** Madhulita Mohapatra, Umesh Aggarwal, Ajay Verma, Amit Verma, Ankur Guha
Production: Julia Bovis, Sophie Hewat

Cartography: **London** Maxine Repath, Katie Lloyd-Jones; **Delhi** Manish Chandra, Rajesh Chhibber, Jai Prakash Mishra, Rajesh Mishra, Ashutosh Bharti, Animesh Pathak, Jasbir Sandhu, Karobi Gogoi
Online: **New York** Jennifer Gold, Kristin Mingrone; **Delhi** Manik Chauhan, Narender Kumar, Shekhar Jha, Rakesh Kumar, Lalit K. Sharma, Chhandita Chakravarty
Marketing and publicity: **London** Richard Trillo, Niki Hanmer, David Wearn, Demelza Dallow, Louise Maher; **New York** Geoff Colquitt, Megan Kennedy, Katy Ball; **Delhi** Reem Khokhar
Custom publishing and foreign rights: Philippa Hopkins
Manager India: Punita Singh
Series editor: Mark Ellingham
Reference director: Andrew Lockett
PA to Managing and Publishing directors: Megan McIntyre
Publishing director: Martin Dunford
Managing director: Kevin Fitzgerald

Publishing information

This second edition published March 2006 by
Rough Guides Ltd,
80 Strand, London WC2R 0RL
345 Hudson St, 4th Floor,
New York, NY 10014, USA
14 Local Shopping Centre, Panchsheel Park,
New Delhi 110017, India
Distributed by the Penguin Group
Penguin Books Ltd,
80 Strand, London WC2R 0RL
Penguin Putnam, Inc.
375 Hudson Street, NY 10014, USA
Penguin Group (Australia)
250 Camberwell Road, Camberwell
Victoria 3124, Australia
Penguin Books Canada Ltd,
10 Alcorn Avenue, Toronto, Ontario,
Canada M4V 1E4
Penguin Group (New Zealand)
Cnr Rosedale and Airborne Roads
Albany, Auckland, New Zealand

Typeset in Bembo and Helvetica to an original design by Henry Iles.
Printed and bound in China
© Polly Rodger Brown and James Read, 2006

400pp includes index
A catalogue record for this book is available from the British Library
ISBN 1-84353-585-8

1 3 5 7 9 8 6 4 2

Help us update

We've gone to a lot of effort to ensure that the second edition of **The Rough Guide to First-Time Latin America** is accurate and up to date. However, things change – places get "discovered", opening hours are notoriously fickle, restaurants and rooms raise prices or lower standards. If you feel we've got it wrong or left something out, we'd like to know, and if you can remember the address, the price, the time, the phone number, so much the better.

We'll credit all contributions, and send a copy of the next edition (or any other Rough Guide if you prefer) for the best letters. Everyone who writes to us and isn't already a subscriber will receive a copy of our full-colour thrice-yearly newsletter. Please mark letters: **"Rough Guide First-Time Latin America Update"** and send to: Rough Guides, 80 Strand, London WC2R 0RL, or Rough Guides, 4th Floor, 345 Hudson St, New York, NY 10014. Or send an email to **mail@roughguides.com**

Have your questions answered and tell others about your trip at **www.roughguides.atinfopop.com**

Acknowledgments

The authors would like to thank Kate Berens for getting this project started and Andrew Rosenberg for guiding it this time around; Steven Horak for his patience, good humour and expert editing; Gavin Thomas, our first editor and the book's "third man", and the excellent editorial team at Rough Guides. Thanks also to the Rough Guides authors, correspondents and readers who contributed information, advice, and anecdotes (keep them coming), including Harry Ades, Danny Aeberhard, Brendan Birkett, Gary Bowerman, Bernard Brierley, Faye Cook, Mihai Cucos, Staffan Gnosspelius, Melissa Graham, Dilwyn Jenkins, Jean McNeil, Ross Monaghan, Rosalba O'Brien, Zora O'Neil, Iain Stewart and Paul Whitfield; all the production team at Rough Guides, including Ed Wright for cartography; Jessica Subramanian for typesetting; Sarah Smithies for tracking down the photos; Amanda Jones for proofreading; to Julie Feiner, Mary Green and Claire Southern; and to Rafe Stone, Tim Murray-Walker and Miguel Vega at Journey Latin America.

James: Thanks to everyone who's helped me on the road in Latin America, and to all the amigos and compadres who've made it so much fun. With much love to Emma, Freya and Iris; I hope we'll visit all these wonderful places together one day.

Polly would also thank her friends and family for their faith, encouragement and support, and especially Eileen Gaughan whose idea it was to go to Latin America in the first place.

Photo credits

The big adventure

p.131 Utilay Bay, Utila Island, Honduras © Yann Arthus-Bertrand/Corbis

p.148 Kuna women, San Blas Archipelago, Panama © Around the World in a Viewfinder/Alamy

p.165 Studying at the University of Buenos Aires, Argentina © Owen Franken/Corbis

p.175 Peru passport stamp © Sean Hunter

p.190 The Pacific coastline, Costa Rica © Chris Caldicott/Axiom

p.206 Casa de cambio, Mexico © Michael Stravato/Corbis

p.217 Booksellers, Mexico City © Robert Fried/Alamy

p.227 Backpackers in Patagonia, Argentina © Andre Jenny/Alamy

p.247 Bolivian hostel © Zak Waters/Alamy

p.254 São Paulo, Brazil © ImageState/Alamy

p.275 Panamanian bus © Humberto Olarte Cupas/Alamy

p.290 Mountain biking in Bolivia © Mark A. Johnson/Corbis

p.300 Kapawi Lodge, Kapawi Lagoon, Ecuador © Alison Wright

p.316 Canoeing in the Amazon © Carl & Ann Purcell/Corbis

p.331 Toucan phone, Bolivia © Tony Morrison/South American Picture Library

p.346 Police checkpoint, Atacama Desert, Chile © Joel Sartore/Getty

p.356 Trekkers approaching Nevado de Ausangate, Peru © John Cleare/Worldwide Picture Library/Alamy

Index

Map entries are in colour.

Country abbreviations		
Argentina..........................A	Ecuador ....Ec	Nicaragua ....N
Belize ....Bel	El Salvador ....ES	Panama ....Pan
Bolivia ....Bol	French Guiana..............FG	Paraguay ....Par
Brazil .... Br	Guatemala .... Gua	Peru ....Per
Chile..............................Ch	Guyana .... Guy	Suriname ....S
Colombia.................... Col	Honduras........................ H	Uruguay ....U
Costa Rica ....CR	Mexico............................M	Venezuela V

A

accommodation... 294–307
adventure sports 136
AIDS 325
airports
  arrival 243–245
  check-in 241
  security 241
altitude sickness........... 319
Amazon 8, 40, 109, 132
Andes 133
Angel Falls (V)................ 120
Antigua (Gua).................. 73
archeology.................... 143
Arequipa (Per).............. 110
Argentina 19–24
Argentina........................ 20
  attractions 21–23
  best time to go........... 19, 187
  costs 19
  itineraries............................ 23
  online................................. 24
  routes in and out................ 23
Asunción (Par) 105
Atacama Desert (Ch) 47
Ayacucho (Per) 111
Aztecs............................ 145

B

backpacks 226–229
Bahia (Bra)...................... 40
Baja California (M).......... 91
Baños (Ec) 64
bargaining..................... 204
Bay Islands (H) 84
behaviour, appropriate
  .... 253–256, 267–269
Belize 25–29

Belize 26
  attractions 27
  best time to go......... 25, 187
  costs 25
  itineraries............................ 28
  online................................. 29
  routes in and out................ 28
bicycles 289–291
birdwatching................ 140
boats 282
Bocas del Toro (Pan) 101
Bolivia 30–35
Bolivia 31
  attractions 32–34
  best time to go........... 30, 187
  costs 30
  itineraries............................ 34
  online................................. 35
  routes in and out................ 34
books on Latin America
  215–221
bookstores.................... 373
boots and shoes 233
border crossings 154
Brazil 36–43
Brazil 38–39
  attractions 40–42
  best time to go........... 36, 187
  costs 36
  itineraries............................ 42
  online................................. 43
  routes in and out................ 42
  visas requirements........... 173
budgeting 199–205
Buenos Aires (A)............ 21
bungee-jumping 137
buses............ 274–280, 284

C

Cajamarca (Per)............. 111
Cali (Col) 53

cameras........................ 236
camping........................ 303
car rental 287
Caracas (V) 122
Caribbean coast, itinerary
  130
Carnaval see carnival
carnival 34, 40, 79, 196
Cartagena (Col) 51
cash.............................. 206
Caye Caulker (Bel).......... 27
Central America, itinerary
  129
Central America................ 4
ceviche 111
Chachapoyas (Per) 111
changing money........... 209
Chiapas (M) 91
Chichén Itzá (M) 89, 128
children, travelling with
  157
Chile........................ 44–49
Chile 45
  attractions 46–48
  best time to go........... 44, 187
  costs 44
  itineraries............................ 48
  online................................. 49
  routes in and out................ 48
Chiloé (Ch)...................... 47
Chiriqui Highlands (Pan)
  101
Chocó (Col) 53
cholera.......................... 311
climate 187–194
climbing........................ 136
clothes.......... 231–233, 256
coffee.............................. 54
Colombia 50–55
Colombia........................ 51
  attractions 51–54
  best time to go........... 50, 187
  costs 50

itineraries............................. 54
online................................... 55
routes in and out............... 54
visa requirements............. 173
communications ... 327–335
contraception 235, 325
Copán (H) 84, 128
Copper Canyon (M)........ 91
Corn Islands (N)............. 95
corruption 350
Costa Rica............... 56–60
Costa Rica 57
attractions 57–59
best time to go............ 56, 187
costs 56
itineraries............................ 60
online.................................. 60
routes in and out............... 59
Costa Verde (Bra) 41
credit cards 208
crime..................... 336–342
Cuenca (Ec) 63
Cusco (Per)................... 109
customs....................... 244
Cuyabeno Reserve (Ec) ... 63
cycling 289–291

D

Darién Gap (Pan, Col),
   crossing 153
Day of the Dead (M)
   ....91, 197
daypacks 229
debit cards 208
diarrhoea 321
diving.........27, 84, 91, 137
documents 231, 338
dress codes.................. 256
drugs, illegal 350

E

earthquakes................. 342
Easter Island (Ch) 48
eco-lodges 297
Ecuador 61–66
Ecuador.......................... 62
attractions 63–65
best time to go........... 61, 187
costs 61
itineraries............................ 65
online.................................. 65
routes in and out............... 64
El Niño 189

El Salvador 67–71
El Salvador...................... 68
attractions 69
best time to go...... 67, 187
costs 67
itineraries............................ 70
online.................................. 71
routes in and out............... 70
email 327
entry cards 173
exchanging currency 209

F

Fernando de Noronha
   (Bra) 41
fiestas 194–197
films about Latin America
   222–224
first-aid kits.................. 310
Fitz Roy Massif (A) 22
flights 151, 176–182
airpasses........................... 179
buying a ticket 180-182
charter............................... 179
courier 179
discount agents 361
internal 272
long-haul 240
online booking 363
floods............................ 343
food...................... 263–265
safety 321
vegetarian 264
football.......................... 10
French Guiana 77–81
see also The Guianas
French Guiana 79

G

Galápagos Islands (E) ... 63,
   141
Garifuna (H) 85
gauchos................. 22, 115
gay and lesbian travellers
   253
Glaciar Perito Moreno
   (A) 22
government travel advice
   371
Gran Chaco (Par).......... 105
Gran Sabana (V) 121
Granada (N) 94
Guanajuato (M)............... 89

Guatemala............... 72–76
Guatemala...................... 74
attractions 73–75
best time to go.......... 72, 187
costs 72
itineraries............................ 76
online.................................. 76
routes in and out............... 75
guerrillas, bandits and
   civil unrest 346
Guiana Space Station
   (FG) 79
The Guianas 77–81
The Guianas................... 79
attractions 78
best time to go.......... 77, 187
costs 77
itineraries............................ 80
online.................................. 81
routes in and out............... 80
guidebooks................. 212
Guyana................... 77–81
see also The Guianas
Guyana 79

H

hammocks.................... 303
hang gliding................. 137
health.................. 308–326
health websites 371
heat, coping with.......... 317
hepatitis....................... 312
hiking 141
hitchhiking 291
home stays................... 302
Honduras................ 82–86
Honduras 83
attractions 84
best time to go........... 82, 187
costs 82
itineraries............................ 85
online.................................. 86
routes in and out............... 85
hotels 294–307
Huaraz (Per)................. 109
hurricanes.................... 343
hypothermia 318

I

Iguaçu/Iguazú Falls
   (A, Bra)................... 21, 41
Inca........................ 109, 144
Inca trails 32, 109

indigenous culture........ 147
insurance.............. 182–185
Internet 327
Inti Raymi (Per) 197

J

jet lag............................248

K

Kaieteur Falls (Guy) 78
Kuna Yala (Pan) 99

L

La Paz (Bol) 32
Lago de Atitlán (Gua) 73
Lago Titicaca (Bol/Per)
............................32, 111
Laguna San Rafael
   (Ch) 47
language, learning
  160–163
Leticia (Col)......................54
Liberia (CR).....................59
Lima (Per) 111
lorries............................280
Los Llanos (Ven) 140

M

machismo......................348
Machu Picchu (Per)......109
magazines 214
mail..............................333
malaria..........................314
maps....................213, 373
Maya.................91, 74, 143
media............................334
Mérida (V) 121
Mexico 87–93
Mexico 90
   attractions 89–92
   best time to go........... 87, 187
   costs 87
   itineraries.......................... 92
   online................................. 93
   routes in and out............... 92
money 205–210
   ATMs 208

credit and debit cards...... 208
currency exchange 209
travellers' cheques............ 207
wiring................................. 210
moneybelts...................230
Montevideo (U) 114
mosquitoes...................314
motorbikes 287, 289
mountain biking............137
mountaineering............136
movies about Latin
   America 222–224

N

Nazca lines (Per)...........109
Nicaragua 94–97
Nicaragua......................95
   attractions 94–97
   best time to go........... 94, 187
   costs 94
   itineraries.......................... 97
   online................................. 97
   routes in and out............... 97

O

Oaxaca (Mex) 89
Osa Peninsula (CR) 58

P

Panama 98–102
Panama 100
   attractions 99–102
   best time to go........... 98, 187
   costs 98
   itineraries.......................... 102
   online................................. 102
   routes in and out............... 101
   visa requirements............. 173
Panama Canal (Pan).......99
Panama City (Pan)..........99
Pantanal (Bra).........41, 140
Paraguay 102–106
Paraguay......................104
   attractions 105
   best time to go........ 103, 187
   costs 103
   itineraries.......................... 106
   online................................. 106
   routes in and out............. 106
   visa requirements............. 173
Paramaribo (Sur) 78
parasites.......................323

Patagonia (A, Ch) ...21, 135
Península Valdés (Arg)
  141
Peru..................... 107–113
Peru..............................108
   attractions 109–112
   best time to go......... 107, 187
   costs 107
   itineraries.......................... 112
   online................................. 113
   routes in and out.............. 112
Petén (Gua)...................140
photography 236, 266
police............................350
Portobelo (Pan).............101
post 333
Potosí (Bol) 33
poverty 256
Puerto Viejo (CR) 58
Punta del Este (U) 114

Q

Quito (Ec)........................63

R

rabies............................312
radio 335
Rapa Nui (Ch).................48
resource centres.......... 376
responsible tourism......267
Rio de Janeiro (Bra)........40
routes
   overland from the US....... 152
   by sea 154
Ruta Maya 128

S

safety 280, 336–353
Salar de Uyuni (Bol)........32
salsa dancing 53
Salta (A) 23
Salvador da Bahia (Bra)
  40
San Agustín (Col)............53
San Blas archipelago
   (Pan) 99
scams 341
security 228
Semana Santa..............195
sexual harassment 348

shoes and boots 233
skiing 47, 137
snakes 343
snorkelling 137
Sololá (Gua) 74
South America 5
studying in Latin America
...........................161–165
Suchitoto (ES) 69
Sucre (Bol) 33
surfing 139
Suriname 77–81
see also The Guianas
Suriname 79
swimming 345

T

taxis 245–247, 285
teaching English 170
telephones 330
television 335
theft, avoiding 338–341
Tierra del Fuego (A, Ch)
...........................23, 135
Tikal (Gua) 74, 128
toilets 306
tour operators 364–367
tourism, responsible 267,
372
tours 157, 292
trains 281

transport 270–293
travel bookshops 373
travel clinics 369
travel equipment
suppliers 377
travel writing 358
travellers' cheques 207
trekking 141
trucks 280
Trujillo (Per) 111

U

Uruguay 114–117
Uruguay 115
attractions 114–116
best time to go 114, 187
costs 114
itineraries 117
online 117
routes in and out 116
Uxmal (M) 89, 128

V

vaccinations 309, 369
Valparaíso (Ch) 47
Venezuela 118–123
Venezuela 120
attractions 120
best time to go 118, 187
costs 118

itineraries 122
online 123
routes in and out 122
visa requirements 173
visas 172–176
extending 174
overstaying 175
Volcán Arenal (CR) 58
volcanoes 58, 63, 75
volunteering 165–169
volunteer organizations
....................................367

W

water, drinking 320
weather 187–189
websites, travel 374
(see also entries under
individual countries)
whitewater rafting 137
wildlife 139
working in Latin America
...........................169–171

Y

yellow fever 313
youth hostels 301
Yucatán Peninsula (M) 91